the PROCESS of PSYCHOTHERAPY

Modern Applications of Psychology
under the editorship of
Joseph D. Matarazzo
University of Oregon Medical School

the PROCESS of PSYCHOTHERAPY

empirical foundations and systems of analysis

Donald J. Kiesler
Emory University

Foreword by
Hans H. Strupp
Vanderbilt University

Aldine
Publishing
Company
Chicago

ABOUT THE AUTHOR

Donald J. Kiesler received his A.B. from Bellarmine College in Louisville, Kentucky, and his Ph.D. from the University of Illinois. He has taught at the University of Illinois and University of Iowa,and is presently Associate Professor of Psychology at Emory University in Atlanta, Georgia. He has served as Advisory Editor for the *Journal of Consulting and Clinical Psychology*, *Psychological Bulletin*, and the *Journal of Abnormal Psychology*. His other publications include *The Therapeutic Relationship and Its Impact* (with C.R. Rogers, E.T. Gendlin, and C.B. Truax); *The Experiencing Scale* (with M.H. Klein, P.L. Mathieu, and E.T. Gendlin); and articles in the major psychology journals.

First published 1973 by
Aldine Publishing Company
529 South Wabash Avenue
Chicago, Illinois 60605

ISBN 0-202-26059-3
Library of Congress Catalog Number 78-182912

Printed in the United States of America

Acknowledgments

For material from E.S. Bordin, P.L. Cutler, A.T. Dittmann, N.I. Harway, H.L. Raush, & D. Rigler:
Copyright 1954 by the American Psychological Association, and reproduced by permission. From *Journal of Consulting Psychology,* Vol. 18.
For material from S. Fisher:
Copyright 1956 by the American Psychological Association, and reproduced by permission. Form *Journal of Consulting Psychology,* Vol. 20.
For material from N.I. Harway, A.T. Dittmann, H.L. Raush, E.S. Bordin, & D. Rigler:
Copyright 1955 by the American Psychological Association, and reproduced by permission. From *Journal of Consulting Psychology,* Vol. 19.
For material from E.S. Howe & B. Pope:
Copyright 1961 by the American Psychological Association, and reproduced by permission. From *Journal of Consulting Psychology,* Vol. 25.
For material from L.N. Rice:
Copyright 1965 by the American Psychological Association, and reproduced by permission. From *Journal of Consulting Psychology,* Vol. 29.
For material from L.N. Rice & Wagstaff, A.K.:
Copyright 1967 by the American Psychological Association, and reproduced by permission. From *Journal of Consulting Psychology,* Vol. 31.
For material from C.S. Hall & P.L. Van de Castle:
From: *The Content Analysis of Dreams,* by Calvin S. Hall and Robert L. Van de Castle. Copyright © 1966. Reprinted by permission of the publishers, Appleton-Century-Crofts Educational Division, Meredith Corporation.
For material from H.L. Lennard & A. Bernstein:
From H.L. Lennard & A. Bernstein, *The Anatomy of Psychotherapy: Systems of Communication and Expectation* (New York: Columbia University Press, 1960).
For material from H.H. Strupp:
From H.H. Strupp, *Psychotherapists in Action* (New York: Grune & Stratton, Inc., 1960). Reprinted by permission.
For material from L. Festinger & D. Katz:
From *Research Methods in the Behavioral Sciences* edited by Leon Festinger and Daniel Katz. Copyright © 1953 by Holt, Pinehart and Winston, Inc. Reprinted by permission of Holt, Pinehart and Winston, Inc.
For material from A.N. Wiens, D.A. Molde, D.C. Holman & J.D. Matarazzo:
Copyright 1966 by The Journal Press, and reproduced by permission. From *Journal of Psychology,* Vol. 63.

For material from W.U. Snyder:
Copyright 1945 by The Journal Press, and reproduced by permission. From *Journal of General Psychology,* Vol. 33.
From W.U. Snyder, *Dependency in Psychotherapy: A Casebook* (New York: The Macmillan Company, 1963). Copyright 1963, by the Macmillan Company.
For material from W.U. Snyder & B.J. Snyder:
From W.U. Snyder & B.J. Snyder, *The Psychotherapy Relationship* (New York: The Macmillan Company, 1961). Copyright 1961, by the Macmillan Company.
For material from A.W. Siegman & B. Pope:
Reprinted with permission of author and publisher: A.W. Siegman, & B. Pope. An empirical scale for the measurement of therapist specificity in the initial psychiatric interview. *Psychological Reports,* 1962, 11.
For material from C.B. Truax and Robert R. Carkhuff:
Reprinted From Charles B. Truax and Robert R. Carkhuff, *Toward Effective Counseling and Psychotherapy* (Chicago: Aldine Publishing Company, 1967); copyright © 1967 by Charles B. Truax and Robert R. Carkhuff.
For material from E.S. Bordin; from T. Leary & M. Gill; from G. Saslow & J.D. Matarazzo:
Copyright 1959 by the American Psychological Association, and reproduced by permission. From E.A. Rubinstein & M.B. Parloff, Eds., *Research in Psychotherapy: Volume one:*
For material from J.M. Butler, L.N. Rice & A.K. Wagstaff; from H.H. Strupp:
Copyright 1962 by the American Psychological Association, and reproduced by permission. From H.H. Strupp & L. Lubershy, Eds., *Research in Psychotherapy: Volume Two.*
For material from J.D. Matarazzo, A.N. Wiens, R.G. Matarazzo & G. Saslow:
Copyright 1968 by the American Psychological Association, and reproduced by permission. From J.M. Schlien et al., Eds., *Research in Psychotherapy: Volume Three.*
For material from G. Marsden:
Copyright 1965 by the American Psychological Association, and reproduced by permission. From *Psychological Bulletin,* Vol. 63.
For material from E.J. Murray:
Copyright 1956 by the American Psychological Association, and reproduced by permission. From *Psychological Monographs,* Vol. 70, No. 113.
For material from L.A. Gottschalk & G.C. Gleser (1969):
Originally published by the University of California Press; reprinted by permission of The Regents of the University of California.
For material from L.A. Gottschalk, C.N. Winget & G.C. Gleser (1969):
Originally published by the University of California Press; reprinted by permission of The Regents of the University of California.
For material From H.L. Lennard & A. Bernstein (1969):
From *Patterns in Human Interaction* (San Francisco: Josey-Boss, Inc., 1969).
For material from B. Pope & A.W. Siegman (1965):
From *Journal of Verbal Learning and Verbal Behavior,* Vol. 4, 1965.
For material from G. Gerbner, O.R. Holsti, K. Krippendorf, W.J. Paisley, & P.J. Stone (Eds.):
From *The Analysis of Communication Content: Developments in Scientific Theories and Computer Techniques* (New York: John Wiley & Sons, 1969).
For material from J. Dollard & F. Auld Jr. (1959):
From *Scoring Human Motives: A Manual* (New Haven: Yale University Press, 1959).
For material from M.H. Klein, P.L. Mathieu, E.T. Gendlin & D.J. Kleisler (1970):
From *The Experiencing Scale: A Research and Training Manual* (Two volumes) (Madison: Wisconsin Psychiatric Institute (Bureau of Audio Visual Instruction), 1970).
For material from C.R. Rogers, E.T. Gendlin, D.J. Kiesler & C.B. Truax (1967):
From *The Therapeutic Relationship and Its Impact: A Study of Psychotherapy with Schizophrenics* (Madison: University of Wisconsin Press, 1967).

To a cool kid named Barry

Contents

Foreword

With the advent of modern psychotherapy toward the end of the last century, it became apparent that psychological and behavior change occurred in a fair percentage of patients undergoing the experience. Successes were sufficiently encouraging to convince therapists and patients that something useful was transpiring. The observation that change could be produced by psychological techniques was of course not new, but Freud was the first empirical scientist to develop a complex theory to account for change by linking it to psychodynamic considerations and the therapist's operations. Freud conceived of psychotherapy (subsuming psychoanalysis), particularly in his early work, as a set of treatment techniques analogous to a surgical procedure performed by a physician on a patient. Psychoptherapists following Freud gradually became convinced that psychotherapy must be understood in terms of the interactions or transactions between patient and therapist. This conceptual change had far-reaching implications, leading eventually to the view that the communications between the two participants are critical. Stated in another way, if one is interested in understanding the process of psychotherapeutic change, one must look at the psychotherapeutic process. The crucial information is somehow embedded in the verbal and nonverbal communications, and it is the job of the researcher to impose order on the process in such a way that meaningful answers emerge.

Psychotherapy, in these terms, involves the exchange of communications between two (or more) participants. As a result of this exchange, modifications in the personality and behavior of patients and therapists are expected to occur. The changes in the patient usually receive the major attention, and they are the raison d'etre for the enterprise; the changes occurring in the therapist are manifestly "fringe benefits," part of the gratifications of his work. What is the nature of therapeutic messages? How do they produce changes in the patient? What aspects of the message are important for therapeutic change? Which components are inert? How can we document and evaluate the changes that occur? These are some of the important issues to which process research in psychotherapy has been addressed.

From a technical standpoint, if the therapeutic force is somehow encoded in the messages, where shall we look for it? In the sentence structure? In the emotional overtones? In the gestures, facial expressions, fine body movements that accompany the verbal message? How can we partition the ongoing communication process so as to extract the "pure" elements of the psychological influence? Shall we count words, sentences, time spans, silences, positive or negative feelings, or construct any one of many possible indexes? These are but a few of the difficult problems the content analyst faces.

Thus, systems of content analysis are techniques for capturing the essential aspects of the diffuse process of psychotherapy—"essential" hinging to a significant degree upon the analyst's theoretical notions of what it is critical to assess. Like a fisherman's net, a system of content analysis is a tool designed for a specific purpose. Depending on the analyst's purpose, the net is constructed in a particular way; it will capture certain kinds of phenomena and disregard many others. Since there is no general agreement in psychotherapy about the nature of the process or its essential ingredients, systems of content analysis tend to be more or less idiosyncratic to the content analyst's predilections. This is one reason why a given system tends to be preferred by researchers within one school and is virtually ignored by the adherents of another. Ultimately, of course, the value of a system lies in its heuristic value, but that too is dependent upon the prevailing *Zeitgeist* and its peculiarities. Any system must be thoroughly anchored to a theory, and the developer of a system, in addition to his methodological concerns, must have in mind certain objectives for his research in psychotherapy. There is no atheoretical system of content analysis.

Developments in the area of content analysis have been supported by the convictions that appropriate techniques will aid in unraveling the mysteries of the psychotherapeutic process and that content analysis represents the royal road to its understanding.

Content analysis as a tool for process research in psychotherapy came into being about a quarter of a century ago; when research in this area became a serious occupation. Indeed, content analysis has occupied an important place in psychotherapy research since that time. However, content analysis has been more germane to the "traditional" insight psychotherapies, exemplified by psychoanalysis and client-centered therapy. Concomitant with the decline of these therapies, content analysis seems to have lost some of its luster. Few new systems seem to be developing. Nor are the old ones being used very vigorously.

Content analysis in psychotherapy has always impressed me as an area in which short-lived efforts abound. The pattern seems to be as follows. An investigator becomes intrigued by the possibilities of measuring one or several aspects of the communication content. He seems to say, "If we could only measure, X, Y, or Z, we would really make significant inroads on the psychotherapeutic process." The answer seems to lie in the propositions of a particular theory that become the framework for a system then being developed. Almost immediately the system is applied to a substantive issue in the area, usually to the analysis of recorded interviews. Not infrequently, a system is developed for the specific purpose of dealing with a substantive issue that the investigator wishes to explore. Soon thereafter, the investigator loses interest in the problem, and turns to other pursuits. Few colleagues find his system sufficiently congenial to put it to use in their own research, and the initial flurry of activity subsides. I realize there are exceptions to these observations, but the foregoing description seems to delineate a trend, from which implications may be formulated. (1) Content analysis in psychotherapy is an exceedingly difficult undertaking. (2) It demands an unusual amount of patience, persistence, and dedication because the payoffs are typically not spectacular or rewarding. (3) Content analysis is not terribly "exciting" to review committees of granting agencies. (4) Perhaps most important, there are gnawing doubts whether available or foreseeable technical skills will enable us to mine a significant amount of gold from a systematic analysis of patient-therapist interactions. Obviously, this is not to say that efforts along these lines are not promising, but it is predictable that progress will be slow and tedious—too slow for many young investigators in a hurry.

Professor Donald Kiesler, happily, is not one of these men. He has shouldered the ardous task of assembling the available tools of process research in psychotherapy between the covers of one book, something which has not been done before. While critical reviews of the pertinent literature have appeared from time to time, no one previously had taken the trouble to collect the scattered references and present the instruments in a way that is useful to the graduate student or seasoned investigator. Professor Kiesler's contribution, however, goes far beyond a mere compilation. Drawing on his thorough knowledge in the area of psychotherapy research, to which he has made numerous significant contributions, he has classified the various systems and presented each—systematically, fairly, and succinctly. The end product bespeaks a high level of sustained effort, fine scholarship, and genuine dedication. Professor Kiesler's book should prove of distinct value to students and researchers in the area, and his penetrating discussions of basic issues are bound to open new perspectives.

Hans H. Strupp
Vanderbilt University

Preface

For the past seven years I've been involved in psychotherapy research as an investigator, teacher, and supervisor of graduate student research. One of the continuing frustrations of these years has been a sporadic uneasiness, while preparing a lecture or publication, that I'm ignoring a relevant piece of research, yet continuing to do so since locating that particular research could take weeks of literature search. Another frustration has involved advising graduate students away from psychotherapy process for graduate research topics since, with the studies scattered as they are, it would involve too much time even to begin to get on top of the relevant literature. Without mastering this literature they would be sitting ducks, and rightfully so, for their departmental research committees.

The basic fact underlying these frustrations is that psychotherapy process research has to rank near the forefront of research disciplines characterized as chaotic, prolific, unconnected, and disjointed, with researchers unaware of much of the work that has preceded and the individual investigator tending to start anew completely ignorant of closely related previous work.

Probably the central factor leading to this chaos is that psychotherapy process research has been and continues to be a bastard child, an interdisciplinary activity including clinical psychologists, psychiatrists, social workers, counseling psychologists, pastoral counselors, anthropologists, sociologists, psychobiologists, psycholinguists, and very likely others. This factor, in turn, explains publication of psychotherapy research in innumerable journals, books, discussion papers—the journals, for example, ranging from something like the Dubuque High School *Social Science Review* all the way to

Psychology Today or perhaps even the *Reader's Digest*! What has been direly missing in the area has been a single source to which one could refer novices in order to allow them quickly and easily to get on top of the area. The major purpose of this volume is to provide this single source.

As an initial integrating attempt for so complex an area of research, this volume undoubtedly will contain omissions, errors, and other deficiencies. These perhaps could be avoided if I pursued this task for another year or so. Instead, I have decided to go with what I have, confident that this volume incorporates at least 95 percent of the process systems extant in the literature.

The first decision required in putting this manuscript together was how to select the "major" process systems. What criteria could be applied in selecting systems for relatively intensive analysis in this volume? The following criteria were decided on, yielding the seventeen major systems presented in Part II.

First, a measure should be more than a one-shot attempt. The more an author has invested methodologic and validity study into his process instrument and the more other investigators have utilized the measure, the more heuristic promise the system offers for the field of psychotherapy. It was by this criterion primarily that the distinction is made in this volume between "major" and "minor" process systems. The minor systems summarized in Chapter 6 were each judged to have not yet met this criterion.

Second, the more a particular instrument is derived from a specific theoretical network, the more likely the system will prove heuristic for the science of behavior modification. Interestingly, the large majority of the seventeen major systems presented in Part II are theoretically derived.

Third, the more a particular instrument has been refined methodologically (methodological issues are described in detail in Chapter 2), the more powerful the measure, and the more likely replicable findings will accumulate. Most of the systems presented in this volume show deficiencies in regard to this last criterion, although there are some shining exceptions.

My biases and inadequacies were undoubtedly operative in applying these criteria. If the volume errs, it is likely it does so in omitting systems that are more developed than I could determine from my literature search. For these omissions I ask tolerance from the authors who may be involved.

I recommend to the reader that he first read Part I, particularly Chapter 2, before going to Parts II and III. Part I presents a theoretical and methodologic perspective for psychotherapy process research. Chapter 1 considers psychotherapy process from the viewpoint of communication theory and linguistics. Chapter 2 presents basic methodologic issues vital to sophisticated process research and the critical stance by which process systems presented in Part II are evaluated. Tables in Chapter 2 also summarize the major systems according to various methodologic similarities and differences.

Part II is devoted to "direct" measures of psychotherapy process. These instruments were developed to code or rate live therapy interviews, or some direct representation of the contents of these interviews (typescripts, tape, or video recordings). Chapters 3, 4, and 5 present the seventeen major direct process systems that have been developed to date. Chapter 3 describes the omnibus systems attempting to measure comprehensively both therapist and patient interview behaviors. Chapter 4 analyzes the systems designed to measure one or more aspects of therapist behavior in psychotherapy. Chapter 5 is devoted to systems that assess patient interview behaviors. Chapter 6 presents a summary of all other (minor) process systems I could locate that are not included among the seventeen in Chapters 3, 4, and 5.

Part III is concerned with various questionnaire measures of psychotherapy process, designed to tap "indirectly" either therapist, patient, or both participants' behaviors in particular interviews. These measures tend to focus on relationship aspects of the psychotherapy transaction, and are filled out by therapist and/or patient contiguously with particular therapy interviews. They tend to tap "state" variables of both participants, rather than more enduring "trait" characteristics.

For each of the major systems presented in Part II, a corresponding table presents an abbreviated version of the process instrument developed. This will assist the reader in grasping the nature of the variables involved. Likewise, in Chapters 2 and 6, both major and minor systems are presented in summary tabular form to help the reader to determine what constructs have already been grappled with in the literature. It remains essential, however, for the reader interested in a particular system to consult the original sources for authoritative detail. Study of this volume, then, is a first but insufficient condition for becoming an authority on a particular system; the original sources are indispensible.

A few words now about what the volume does not include. Its focus is insight-oriented individual psychotherapy of late adolescents or adults who come to various outpatient clinics or agencies. Hence, instruments designed for analyzing group, family, or child psychotherapy or behavior therapy interactions are not included in this volume, and unfortunately are not summarized elsewhere to date. Likewise, measures designed primarily for nonpsychoneurotic or nonborderline adult outpatients (such as hospitalized schizophrenics, affective psychotics, brain damaged, etc.) are not included. By arbitrary fiat, physiological measures used in psychotherapy process investigations are omitted. After reading authorities in the field of psychophysiological measurement, it seemed brash for a layman such as myself to attempt to deal with the real issues involved in this assessment.*

Finally, the reader will notice that I have not attempted an explicit evaluation or critical integration of the systems reviewed other than to develop a theoretic and methodologic perspective for psychotherapy process investigation. This evaluational attempt is omitted since it would involve considerably more work and another volume this size. Besides, it strikes me that an attempt at integration would be a premature and empty gesture in light of the rudimentary stage of methodological development demonstrated by this volume. Regardless, the less creative and more limited intent of this volume is to spotlight important issues of process research and simultaneously to review, in one place and according to a standard format, the process systems available to date.

Instrumentation is important in any science, and is no less crucial for the science of behavior modification. The intent of this volume is to summarize where we are instrumentally in the area of insight-oriented psychotherapy process investigation. The hope is that the volume will service investigators in search of a measure for naturalistic or experimental psychotherapy investigation, provide a concise and comprehensive overview regarding the extent to which meaningful operationalization of constructs has been accomplished to date, and suggest studies which may not have occurred to some readers had they not inspected the concrete measures that are included. If any one of these purposes is accomplished, the volume will have served its purpose.

*To obtain an idea of some of the problems involved as well as an overview of some psychophysiological applications to psychotherapy process research, the reader is referred to Averill, J. R., and Opton, E. M., Psychophysiological assessment rationale and problems. In P. McReynolds (Ed.), *Advances in psychological assessment.* Palo Alto, Cal.: Science and Behavior Books, 1968, pp. 265-88. See also Lacey, J. I., Psychophysiological approaches to the evaluation of psychotherapeutic process and outcome. In E. A. Rubinstein and M. B. Parloff (Eds.), *Research in psychotherapy*, Vol. 1. Washington, D.C.: American Psychological Association, 1959, pp. 160-208.

the PROCESS of PSYCHOTHERAPY

I

Method and Theory in Psychotherapy Process Analysis

1

A Communication Model for Psychotherapy Process Analysis

Psychotherapy process studies generally deal with the therapist–patient interaction, that is, with the interchange between therapist and patient. Outcome studies focus on the changes that take place in the patient as the result of therapy. Psychotherapy process has been studied by various content analysis procedures, by scales or questionnaires developed to measure therapist, patient, or interactional dimensions; outcome investigations have focused on patient changes in test or other extratherapy behavior from the beginning to the termination of therapy.

I have argued elsewhere that this process-outcome distinction has led to some confusion in psychotherapy research. "Two unfortunate effects seem to have followed from this somewhat ambiguous distinction: 'outcome' researchers have tended to focus exclusively on pre-post patient differentiations; and patient process changes have not been considered legitimate outcome" (Kiesler, 1966, p. 126). Three criticisms are pertinent here:

(1) The traditional process-outcome distinction has perpetuated the relatively exclusive use of pre-post designs in outcome studies, with the unfortunate effect that information about the form of the function that represents the improvement between the two end points, as well as for follow-up periods, has not been clarified; repeated measures designs would offer this essential type of information.

(2) The use of only two measurement points entails the likelihood that any differences observed may be only chance fluctuations due to unreliability of measures.

(3) Patient in-therapy improvement, manifested in his interview behavior, is just as legitimate an outcome as extratherapy change.

> Certainly not all process investigation is equivalent to outcome—for example, if the investigator is focusing exclusively on the therapist, or on one point only of the therapy sequence. But to the extent that one is investigating in-therapy patient changes, he is concerned directly with outcome; and to the extent that one is interested in outcome, he needs to be cognizant of in-therapy patient changes. . . . To say this differently, there seem to be two important arenas of patient change: that change manifest in the therapy hours themselves, and concomitant changes observed outside the therapy interaction (in situ). Process research begins with the in-the-interview behavior of the patient (or therapist); outcome investigation begins with his outside-the-interview improvement. The crucial implication is that for either to be maximally useful, it must consider the other focus or perspective. It is necessary for both investigators to formulate some clear paradigm of the dependent variables of psychotherapy, both in- and extra-therapy, and their theoretical interrelationships. (ibid. p. 127)

Although the term "process" contains some ambiguities and has led to some research confusion, it will be retained here, primarily since most of its operational referents are clear-cut and popularly known. In this volume, process refers to any research investigation that, totally or in part, contains as its data some direct or indirect measurement of patient, therapist, or dyadic (patient-therapist interaction) behavior in the therapy interview. Process studies, then, are those assessing therapy interview behaviors in some fashion. If there is no measurement of interview behaviors, the study is not of process.

This volume focuses on and presents the major measurement systems developed for assessing patient, therapist, or interactional behaviors occurring within the psychotherapy interview. It thereby excludes any measurement procedures developed or adapted to measure patient or therapist behaviors, trait or state, outside of the therapy interview (in situ). Among those procedures excluded would be any questionnaires measuring trait conditions of either patient or therapist. Hence patient measures such as the MMPI or Taylor MAS do not belong in a process volume, nor do therapist trait measures such as the Whitehorn and Betz A-B Scale (Betz, 1967; Carson, 1967). Likewise, peer or other ratings of patient (or therapist) behaviors in the home, at work, or in other social situations—for hospitalized patients, ward behavior ratings—do not belong in the process domain. Finally, performance tests of various sorts, designed to assess patient or therapist behaviors in experimental or standardized-naturalistic situations, would be excluded from process analysis.

What *is* included in the process domain is the following: (1) category or dimensional systems for coding therapist, patient, or interactional behaviors directly from representations of psychotherapy interviews, that is by live observations, or by means of movie, video tape, audio tape, or typescript transcriptions of live interview data; and (2) questionnaire or physiological[1] measures designed to tap momentary patient, therapist, or interactional behaviors (for example, patient state anxiety in a particular interview, or a therapist's liking or understanding of his patient in a particular interview). The content of this volume is, therefore, restricted to the above two assessment domains.

Another characteristic of process research is implicit. Process research has been primarily naturalistic research, it has focused on the live, untampered-with, naturally occurring patient and therapist behaviors in therapy interviews. This is not, however, a necessary characteristic of process research. More recently, process instruments have been applied to experimental interviews that are intended to simulate some aspect of naturalistic psychotherapy. As a result, the generalist-naturalistic or experimental-correlational contrasts (Kiesler, 1971) do not precisely identify and distinguish the process domain, although to date the major part of process research has been naturalistic-correlational.

There is an overlap between "process research" and "content analysis" studies of psychotherapy. Moreover, in discussing content analysis, one must consider the scientific disciplines of communication, linguistics, and psycholinguistics; the remainder of this chapter will describe, contrast, and interrelate these various disciplines with process research. The theme of the rest of the chapter is that psychotherapy process research gains considerably from defining itself within the broader perspective of communication analysis. Psychotherapy, and its process investigation, then become restricted instances of human dyadic communication, and the focus becomes the analysis of patient-therapist behaviors as limited examples of human dyadic communication in an interpersonal framework.

Psychotherapy: A Communication System

Since Harry Stack Sullivan, many psychotherapists have begun to conceptualize psychotherapy within an interpersonal communication framework (Alexander, 1957; Buck and Cuddy, 1966; Buehler and Richmond, 1965; Greenhill, 1958; Hoch and Zubin, 1958; Riess,

1. Physiological process measures of patient or therapist are not included in this volume, as explained in the Preface.

1957; Rioch, 1964; Rioch and Weinstein, 1964; Ruesch, 1961; Ruesch and Bateson, 1951; Scheflin, 1965; Scheflin, English, Hampe, and Auerbach, 1966; Sebeok, Hayes, and Bateson, 1964; Watzlawick, Beavin, and Jackson, 1967; Williamson, 1959). Ruesch and Bateson (1951) state:

> Psychiatric therapy aims at improving the communication system of the patient . . . the psychotherapist aims at restoring a broken-down system of interpersonal communication on a semantic or interaction level. . . . Regardless of the school of thought adhered to, or the technical terms used, the therapist's operations always occur in a social context. Implicitly, therefore, all therapists use communication as a method of influencing the patient. (p. 12)

Alexander (1957) outlines and criticizes

> A tendency which I can historically analyze but cannot understand [which is] to disregard the basic natural faculty to understand another human being, and rather to introduce into psychology other methods which are really somewhat alien to it since they are borrowed from other sciences. . . . What is this natural faculty? The ability to communicate with each other. Everyone possesses it. Without it social life would not be possible. If they speak the same language, one person can communicate to another what is going on in his mind. . . . It is by this process that the psychoanalyst obtains information about a patient's motivation. From this motivation he can draw inferences. (p. 344)

Pittenger and Smith (1957) observe that "differences in communication patterns are the bases of much of the medical classifications of patients. . . . Psychiatric inferences, hypotheses, and theories about the internal as well as the interactional aspects of the person are based largely upon observations of communications. . . . Linguistic analysis offers an opportunity to re-examine, describe, and clarify some of the differentiating features" (p. 76).

In this same vein, Ruesch (1961) states:

> Only when we learn to diagnose the difficulties of our patients in terms of the same scientific universe in which we explain our therapeutic methods will we be able to evaluate therapy in a meaningful way. As long as the diagnosis is made in terms of one system and therapy is explained in terms of another system we cannot match therapy to pathology. Therefore, it seems feasible

> that patients be diagnosed in terms of their ability to communicate and the disturbances that interfere with it. The therapeutic diagnosis thus is principally based upon the evaluation of the communicative behavior of the patient, and therapeutic communication is designed to overcome the difficulties. (1961, p. 74)

Greenhill (1958) argues:

> Communication is the rubric of the psychotherapeutic method. The psychotherapist is the expert in one-to-one communication and relies upon its devices to achieve his goals. Communication is so fundamental to the action of psychotherapy that I am herewith advancing the theory that movement and results in psychotherapy are largely dependent upon it more than any other factor. (p. 31)

Finally, Frank (1961) makes a similar point within a more general framework:

> Psychotherapy . . . deals with interpersonal relationships, either as formulated by Freud, or more literally conceived by Rank or Sullivan. In that regard, all research that deals with the dynamics of any one-to-one interpersonal relationship, such as with hypnosis, non-clinical studies of attitude change, etc., are relevant for an understanding of psychotherapy. One can reason that all these are but special instances of the dyadic relationship, therefore, the phenomena pertinent to one should be pertinent to the others. In addition, within the context of social psychology, psychotherapy may be viewed in terms of the communication process and communication theory. (pp. 89-90)

The upshot is that there is ample theoretical precedent for the view that psychotherapy is a specific situation of one-to-one interpersonal communication. To the extent that this notion is correct, therapy theory and research can gain considerably by placing psychotherapy in the more general communication framework, which includes the disciplines of linguistics and psycholinguistics. I drew a similar analogy previously in discussing psychotherapy paradigms:

> In summary, then, the basic skeleton of a paradigm for psychotherapy seems to be something like the following: The patient communicates something; the therapist communicates something in response; the patient communicates and/or experiences something different; and the therapist, patient, and others like the change (although they may like it to different degress, or for

> divergent reasons). What the therapist communicates (the independent variables) is very likely multidemensional (and the patterning of this multidimensionality needs to be specified), and may be different at different phases of the interaction for different kinds of patients. Similarly, what the patient communicates and/or experiences differently (the dependent variables) is likely multidimensional (and the patterning of this multidimensionality needs to be clarified) and may be different at distinct phases of the interaction. The enormous task of psychotherapy theory and research is that of filling in the variables of this paradigm. (Kiesler, 1966, p. 130)

Communication: Linguistics and Psycholinguistics

It seems appropriate and useful to look in some detail at the scientific domains of linguistics and psycholinguistics to determine more clearly how the communicative process of psychotherapy fits into these perspectives.

Communication is the most general term of the three (Schramm and Pool, 1969; Thayer, 1966). It refers to the process of transmitting information from sender (encoder) to receiver (decoder). Morris (1946) proposes a tripartite division of communication which has become popular. As Laffall explains it, according to Morris:

> There are three aspects of the science of language: the syntactic, the semantic, and the pragmatic. The syntactic area has to do with the formal relations of signs to each other. The semantic area has to do with the relations between signs and the objects to which the signs are applicable. The pragmatic area has to do with the relations between signs and users of signs. Linguistics would be classified under syntactics, since it devotes itself to the descriptive study of formal characteristics of language, excluding to a large extent any concern with matters relating to meaning and the user of the language. . . . Some linguists must, of course, by the very nature of their work, deal with content and reference in language. Such, for example, are the lexicologists, and their work is accordingly in the semantic area. Many anthropological studies would be classified under the semantic aspect of language forms. . . . Psychologists clearly group near the pragmatic side of this tripartite division, since the individual users of language are of critical interest to them. (Laffall, 1965, p. 22)

As an alternative to Morris' classification, Jacobsen (1959) recognizes as factors of the speech situation: the sender, the receiver, the topic or reference, the code, and the message. All are involved in every communication, but one or another factor may dominate. Markel (1969), modifying Jacobsen's scheme somewhat, presents a communication model which, I think, is clearest and most useful. In Markel's model, communication encompasses the "encoder," the "message," and the "decoder." The encoder is the originator of the message; the decoder is the recipient of the message; and the message is a response of an encoder which may be the stimulus for a decoder. Communication results when a response of an encoder is received as a stimulus for a decoder. Markel then presents a model of "channels of communication" which has considerable value for defining the roles of linguistics and psycholinguistics. "Individuals interact via channels of communication. . . . All studies of human interaction must specify the channel or channels of communication under investigation by indicating the source and the destination of each channel" (p. 5). The six major channels of human "face to face" communication, defined in terms of their source and destination, are: speech (source: vocal tract; destination: ear), kinesics (body movement; eye), odor (chemical processes; nose), touch (body surface; skin), observation (body surface; eye), and proxemics (body placement; eye). It is clear that psychotherapy communication can involve all six channels, and it will become evident that psychotherapy process investigators have been concerned primarily with the speech channel although more recently they have begun to study the channels of kinesics, observation, and proxemics.

The scientific disciplines of linguistics and psycholinguistics focus primarily on the speech channel of communication. Linguistics, or philology, is the scientific study of human language or speech.

> It is the study of messages once they are "on the air." The material of language can itself be looked at, or examined, or structured in a threefold way. It can be examined as sounds, or as the shapes (forms) constituted by sequences of sounds, or as the meaningful arrangements, the sense, from which the symbolizing functions arise. . . . The structural analysis makes possible the science of linguistics. The sounds are studied in phonology, the shapes in morphology, the sense in semology (or syntax). (Trager, 1966, p. 73)

Linguists assume that languages are "codes that can be described without reference to meaning, and that the spoken language has primacy over the written language. Beyond descriptive linguistics is generative or transformation grammar, which tries to explain why the native speaker is able to understand and produce an infinity of novel sentences" (DeCecco, 1967, p. vii). Basic linguistic texts are: Bloomfield (1933), Chomsky (1965), Chomsky and Halle (1968), Dixon and Horton (1968), Gleason (1961), Lenneberg (1967), and Miller and Smith (1966).

Psycholinguistics, a much more recent development, is the "discipline concerned with the study of the relation between messages on the speech channel and the cognitive or emotional states of human encoders and decoders who send and receive the messages" (Markel, 1969, p. 5). For a review of theory and research in the area of psycholinguistics, the reader can consult the following volumes: DeCecco (1967), Deese (1970), Jakobovits and Miron (1967), Markel (1969), Rosenberg (1965), Saporta (1961), and Sebeok (1960). According to Markel (1969), there are two subfields of psycholinguistics: Verbal learning and verbal behavior (experimental linguistics), and speech and personality. Verbal learning and verbal behavior is "concerned with the relation between messages on the speech channel and the *cognitive* states of the encoders and decoders" (p. 5). According to Rosenberg (1965), this first subfield includes, among other things, "studies of (1) the influence of verbal and nonverbal antecedent conditions upon verbal behavior and verbal learning, (2) the influence of verbal stimuli upon nonverbal behavior and learning, (3) the role of verbal mediators in behavior, (4) interrelationships among various dimensions of verbal response, (5) relationships between verbal and nonverbal response dimensions, (6) language acquisition and language development, and (7) strictly normative studies of language behavior" (p. 4). For Markel (1969), the second subfield of psycholinguistics, speech and personality, "is concerned with the relation between messages on the speech channel and the *emotional* (attitudinal, motivational) states of encoders and decoders" (p. 5). This definition puts the second subfield of psycholinguistics very close to the area of content analysis, as we shall see.

Stylistics (Sapir, 1958; Miller, 1969) falls under the speech and personality subdivision of psycholinguistics. Many of the measures originally developed for stylistics were among the first content analysis procedures applied in psychotherapy process studies. Stylistics is the study of individual differences in the selection of words in various contexts. Study of stylistics, since its major concern is words, uses linguistic techniques from the subarea of morphology. This will be clarified further below. It qualifies as a psycholinguistic procedure since it is concerned with relations between messages on the speech channel (words) and the emotional-attitudinal (personality) states of encoders and decoders. It has been traditionally involved with the analysis of written words, and its applications in psychotherapy research have been to typescripts of interview interaction. Miller

(1966) summarizes the indexes used to assess stylistic variables in human communication. His summary includes statistical indexes of vocabulary size, verbal diversity (for example, Carroll's "index of diversification" and Johnson's "type-token ratio"), sentence length, styles in punctuation, diverse use of different parts of speech (for example, Busemann's "verb-adjective ratio"), readability, and the like. These indexes are primarily designed for written communications, although several of them (such as type-token and verb-adjective ratios) have been applied directly to typescripts of therapy interviews. Stylistics assumes that people differ in their verbal styles and that these differences are fairly constant. As Sapir (1958) observes:

> There are certain words which some of us never use. There are other favorite words which we are always using. Personality is largely reflected in the choice of words. . . . We all have our individual styles in conversation and considered address, and they are never the arbitrary and casual things we think them to be. There is always an individual method, however poorly developed, of arranging words into groups and of working these up into large units. (p. 54)

This brief, and probably oversimplified, run through the areas of communication, linguistics, and psycholinguistics is necessary as a perspective for psychotherapy process research. We shall see in the next section that process analysis and content-analysis studies are very close conceptually to the psycholinguistic division of linguistics. However, I will first present a schema for linguistic analysis which has direct relevance for psychotherapy process measurement in that it provides an outline of the aspects of speech-channel communication that linguists have differentiated. If psychotherapy process researchers keep these distinctions in mind, their choice of measures for study will be facilitated and they can define more precisely the aspects of communication on which their particular measures focus.

The basic distinction is that the "speech channel of communication" consists of sounds which are either language or nonlanguage.

> [Language sounds] are those that are essential for the production of words of a language. For example, if I want to say the word "tin" it is absolutely essential that I produce a "t" sound. . . . [Nonlanguage sounds are] all sounds not essential to word formation. . . . A particular sound may be a language sound for the speaker of one language and the same sound may be a nonlanguage sound for the speaker of another language. . . . Language is always accompanied by nonlanguage. That is, whenever a

speaker is producing sounds to form words he is also producing sounds which are not essential to form words. For example, if I want to say the word "tin" I must say it with a particular loudness which may range from a very soft whisper to a very loud shout. (Markel, 1969, pp. 5-6)

Markel further observes:

The language versus nonlanguage distinction has an aspect that is of special interest for those concerned with personality. An individual has very little option in either producing the specific sounds of language, or in determining their distribution. To produce words the individual is obligated to produce highly stereotyped, specific sounds the quality of which cannot vary significantly when he intends to form words. . . . On the other hand, the individual usually has a number of options in producing nonlanguage sounds. (p. 6)

The units used in the analysis of *language* sounds are rather well known. For phonology they are phoneme, phone, and syllable; for morphology, morpheme, morph, and word; and for grammar or syntactics, part of speech, constituent, and sentence—in each case going from the simplest to the more complex unit. Much less well known are the recent attempts to distinguish the basic units of *nonlanguage* sounds. Several systems of classifying nonlanguage or extralinguistic phenomena have been proposed by Newman (1939), Sanford (1942a), Sapir (1958), Sebeok, Walker, and Greenberg (1954), Pittenger and Smith (1957), Pittenger (1958), and Trager (1958). These nonlanguage units have been called "paralanguage" by Trager (1958). Many of them have been implicitly and explicitly incorporated into previous psychotherapy process systems.

The outline presented here is derived primarily from Trager (1958). For Trager, besides language proper, there are three basic components of speech: voice set, voice qualities, and vocalizations.

(1) *Voice set* is defined as "the physiological and physical peculiarities resulting in the patterned identification of individuals as members of a societal group and as persons of a certain sex, age, state of health, etc." This distinction reflects that language takes place in the setting of the act of speech, which results from activities that create a background of voice set. This background includes the idiosyncratic—the speaker's physiological function, the total physical setting, and the influence of past events. The next two categories define the units of paralanguage.

(2) *Voice qualities* (also referred to as voice dynamics) "are

continuous features of the voice that establish a background in which sentences are spoken. They are 'background' in the sense that their variation has no effect on the grammatical function of either the sentence as a whole or the individual morphs within a sentence. The voice qualities affect the connotative meaning of sentences but not their denotative meaning" (Markel, 1969, p. 8). These phenomena include, in the various systems, the speaker's control of articulation, tempo, intensity, quantity, pitch height, pitch range, articulation control, continuity, rhythm, tessitura, and register. Voice quality, then, "refers to those characteristics which are present more or less all the time that a person is talking: it is a quasi-permanent quality running through all the sound that issues from his mouth" (Abercrombie, 1969, p. 112).

(3) *Vocalizations* "are discrete sounds which are not used to produce morphs in a particular language. An example . . . for speakers of English is the clicking sound [tsk-tsk] that is used to indicate 'too bad.' This [vocalization] does have meaning, but it is not a morph nor is it a sound that is used to construct morphs in English. . . . They are segmental sounds, but are not analyzed as being part of the phonemic structure of the language" (Markel, 1969, pp. 8, 78). Trager differentiates three subcategories of vocalizations: vocal characterizers (laughing, crying, yelling, whispering, blocking, yawning, mooing), vocal qualifiers (intensity, pitch, height, extent), and vocal segregates (uh-hmm, hm?, shh, pauses, coughs, snorts, sniffs, imitations of animal cries).

This ends the brief synopsis of the science of human communication. Psychotherapy process research belongs to this science since psychotherapy is a limited instance of human communication, that is, it is communication occurring in the dyadic interpersonal relationship between patient and therapist.

More recently, process investigators have chosen various aspects of *paralanguage* as communication units for analysis. Some of these investigators are Brodsky (1967), Deutsch (1966), Dittmann and Wynne (1961, 1966), Duncan (1964, 1965), Eldred et al. (1954), Eldred and Price (1958), Feldstein (1964), Gottschalk (1961), Hargreaves and Starkweather (1964), Kramer (1963), Mahl and Schulze (1964), McQuown (1957), Nathan, Schneller, and Lindsley (1964), Osgood and Sebeok (1965), Pittenger, Hockett, and Danehy (1960), Rennecker (1960), Scheflin et al. (1966), Sebeok et al. (1964), and Starkweather (1961)

Researchers who have focused on the study of *stylistic* communication variables in psychotherapy include Berg (1958), Goldman-Eisler (1954), Grummon (1950), Mahl and Schulze (1964), Mann (1944), Markel et al. (1964), Mitchell (1951), Page (1953), Rioch and Weinstein (1964), Sanford (1942a), Sebeok et al. (1964), Tomkins and Izard (1965), and Weintraub and Aronson (1962).

Still others have focused on the study of body movements, postures, and gestures in psychotherapy, that is, on *kinesic* variables. Such researchers include Birdwhistell (1952, 1963), Boomer and Dittman (1964), Deutsch (1966), Dittmann (1962), Ekman (1964, 1965), Ekman and Friesen (1968, 1970), Fretz (1966a, 1966b), Haggard and Isaacs (1966), Mahl (1968), McQuown (1957), and Scheflin (1964). Examples of the kinds of behaviors scored in kinesic investigation of psychotherapy interviews are "clasps hands," "moves head forward," "right hand to mouth," "right foot moves upward," "nods," and the like. Ekman and Friesen (1968) indicate that the rationale for studying nonverbal behavior in research on psychotherapy rests on five assumptions:

> (1) Nonverbal language can be considered a relationship language, sensitive to, and the primary means of, signalling changes in the quality of an ongoing relationship. . . .(2) It is the primary means of expressing or communicating emotion. . . . (3) Nonverbal behavior has special symbolic value, expressing in body language basic, perhaps unconscious, attitudes about the self or body-image. . . . (4) [It serves] the metacommunicative function of providing qualifiers as to how verbal discourse should be interpreted. . . . (5) Nonverbal behavior is less affected than verbal behavior by attempts to censure communication. (pp. 180-81)

By far the majority of psychotherapy process investigators have focused on communication units involving *language proper* although many of these systems have implicitly incorporated aspects of paralanguage phenomena. For reviews of these studies see Auld and Murray (1955), Cartwright (1957), Dittes (1959), Gottschalk and Auerbach (1966), Marsden (1965, 1971), Rubinstein and Parloff (1959), Shlien et al. (1968), Strupp (1962), Strupp and Luborsky (1962), and Part II of this volume. This predominant emphasis is probably justified. As Trager (1966) himself emphasizes:

> The basic, all pervading and ever-present and primary human communication modality is language. It is always accompanied by paralanguage and kinesics, and often enough by tactile and olfactory activities. But the primacy of language becomes evident from an examination of the intricacy, extensiveness, and independence of its structure. Paralanguage, as its name implies, occurs only with language; it has a structure simpler and less extensive, and is dependent. Kinesics can take place without language, but its

> availability for communication is limited to lighted places, and its structure is analagous to that of paralanguage. Tactile communication is limited by distance, as is olfactory communication. The latter is very little developed and apparently is very simply structured. . . . In all human interaction it is what people say that is of first importance. It is heard, reacted to, interpreted, responded to. All other communication serves as background or commentary on what is said. (pp. 70-71)

We can sharpen considerably our process measurement systems if we keep in mind the perspectives outlined above for the sciences of linguistics and psycholinguistics. As these disciplines continue to develop and mature, they can only be more helpful to psychotherapy process analysis. Duncan (1964) has characterized the developing situation quite well.

> Recently (roughly since 1955) there has been, simultaneously from several sources, a limited but increasing interest in using the technical tools of linguistics to describe or isolate important speech behaviors occurring in either interpersonal communication or problem-solving situations. The promise of linguistic tools in psychotherapy research lies in their more differentiated specification of communication behaviors. Their heightened precision and acuity open the way for more incisive analysis of therapy interaction. (pp. 3-4)

It is important to keep in mind that human communication and psychotherapy process research involve not only the speech channel, but also Markel's five other channels as well.

> As filming and video taping of interviews are increased and as technical problems in this filming are solved, kinesics promises to be a useful suppliment to knowledge gained through content and linguistic analysis. There seems a real possibility that the information provided by kinesics will suggest answers to problems and fill in important areas of variance not available to researchers limited to the study of speech alone. (Duncan, 1964, p. 7)
>
> Duncan concludes:
>
> While the entire field of interview analysis is still at a relatively primitive stage of development, it seems clear that the analytic descriptive methods presently being developed by linguists and their colleagues, especially in the area of paralinguistics, have a

> great deal to offer the psychologist or psychiatrist in his study of psychotherapy. . . . Despite their promise, however, clear-cut difficulties accompany the use of these linguistic techniques. Beyond the work involved in acquiring a working knowledge of the techniques and their applications, the researcher faces the necessity of making major innovations and integrations in the area of methodology. He must devise adequate, practical, and useful ways of applying linguistic techniques to specific research interests. (Duncan, 1964, pp. 13-14)

The Discipline of Content Analysis

"Content analysis was born (or reborn) in this century in the field of journalism research. It has now attained some maturity in fields ranging from cultural anthropology to psychiatry" (Paisley, 1969, p. 283). It is clearly a multidisciplinary activity.

> Perhaps more than any other research method available to social scientists and humanists, content analysis has been marked by a diversity of purpose, subject matter, and technique. It has been used for purposes as different as inferring enemy intention from wartime propaganda and settling questions of disputed authorship. Its subject matter has included not only the familiar products of the mass media but also ancient pottery fragments and psychoanalytic interviews. Content analysts have been armed with instruments of measurement as simple as the wooden ruler and as complex as multimillion-dollar computers. And finally, they have dealt with measurement problems ranging from counting column inches on the first page of the local newspaper to assessing the degree of "need achievement" in the literary products of various cultures. (Holsti, 1969a, p 355)

Other uses involve analysis of newspaper editorials, international exchanges of an official governmental character, personal documents (letters and diaries), interview transcripts, and social group interactions, as well as analysis of poetic and musical compositions.

Historically, content analysis seems to have been, first and foremost, an attempt to make quantitative, objective, and publically replicable what had previously been qualitative, intuitive, and privately judgmental. Berelson (1952) defined content analysis as "a method for studying the content of communication in an objective, systematic, and quantitative way" (p. 18). Hall and Van De Castle (1966) emphasize: "Nearly all writers on the subject agree that [content analysis] is done in order to quantify that which is qualitative. Content analysis converts verbal or other symbolic material into numbers in order that statistical operations may be performed on such material. This purpose is accomplished by formulating classes, tabulating frequencies, and figuring rates" (p. 1). It also seems to have focused primarily on written communication, in contrast to speech, or on written forms (typescripts) of spoken communications.

Definitions of content analysis have changed somewhat since Berelson, but most recent examples seem to show relatively good agreement as to what it encompasses (Gerbner, et al., 1969). Perhaps most representative is the definition provided by Goldhammer (1969): Content analysis refers to "the approaches that seek to make specific inferences from a text to some characteristics of its source that are not directly observable" (p. 343). For Deese (1969), it is simply "a collection of techniques for providing interpretations of texts and similar products. . . . The purpose of the analysis is to determine some underlying themes in the message intended by the author of some work, or at least one that, perhaps in an unconscious way, reflects the personalities and motives of the producer" (pp. 39-40).

These definitions reveal a striking similarity between the disciplines of content analysis and psycholinguistics that Markel (1969) defined as "the discipline concerned with the study of the relation between messages on the speech channel and the cognitive or emotional states of human encoders and decoders who send and receive these messages" (p. 5). The only clearly divergent aspect of the definitions of psycholinguistics and of content analysis presented above has to do with Deese's focus on "texts or similar products," while Markel lists "messages on the speech channel." In other words, traditional content analysis has focused on *written* forms of communication, while traditional psycholinguistics (incorporating the linguistic assumption that spoken language has priority) has emphasized *spoken* forms of human communication. Obviously there could be clear instances of overlap for the two disciplines, when, for example, transcripts of speech interactions are to be analyzed. Evidently, the two disciplines are identical in purpose—to make specific inferences (in one case, from "text," in the other, from "messages on the speech channel") to some characteristics of the source or encoder of the communication. Content analysis, then, clearly belongs to the science of linguistics and specifically to its subarea of psycholinguistics, including stylistics. "The early formulations of content analysis were direct extensions of these methods of statistical linguistics to the semantic level" (Rapaport, 1969, p. 25).

For extensive surveys of the content-analysis literature, the reader can consult Barcus (1959), Berelson (1952), Gerbner et al. (1969), Holsti (1968, 1969c), Pool (1959), and Stone et al. (1966). Two recent conferences summarize the literature as well as the emerging trends in the area. The first was the Allerton House conference (Pool, 1959), the second was the Annenberg conference (Gerbner et al., (1969). The Allerton House conference focused on three topics: (1) the what and how of measurement (units, the qualitative-quantitative debate, utility and limitations of frequency, categorizing, and intensity measures); (2) questions of theories and models of communication applicable to content analysis; and (3) the problem of structured categories for content analysis. The recent Annenberg conference covered four major areas: (1) theories and analytical constructs for content analysis; (2) the problem of inference from content data; (3) ways of recording and notation of "text" in different modes—nonverbal as well as verbal; and (4) recent computer techniques for content analysis.

Some of the trends summarized during the 1969 Annenberg conference are particularly interesting, especially in regard to psychotherapy process or content-analysis research. For example:

> One of the questions frequently discussed among content analysts is that of *standard* categories to facilitate comparative and cumulative research findings. There are few areas of content analysis in which such categories have emerged, however, and Pool's assessment of a decade ago is still reasonably accurate: "It is questionable, however, how ready we are to establish standard measures . . . in content analysis. Such a measure is convenient when a considerable number of researchers are working on the same variable, and when someone succeeds in working out good categories for that variable. It is doubtful that either of these criteria can be met in most areas of content analysis" (Pool, 1959, p. 213). (Holsti, 1969a, p. 114)

Another citation reminds one of the lively discussions of the APA-sponsored psychotherapy research conferences:

> Discussions of measurement during the 1950s tended to focus on several issues, one of which was the relative merits, with respect to the quality of inferences, of qualitative and quantitative content analysis. At times the controversy would be reduced to two viewpoints: "If you can't count it, it doesn't count," versus "If you can count it, that ain't it." This issue has almost disappeared from the recent literature. . . The viewpoint that the analyst should use a combination of all methods that aid the process of

inference seems to dominate the field today. (Holsti, 1969a, p. 112)

The next trend cited from the Annenberg conference takes us directly into the topic of the next section, content analysis in psychotherapy:

> There are several reasons for the limited progress [of content analysis]. Many areas of social inquiry have not achieved sufficient consensus on theory to inform the selection and operational definition of categories. But this is not the sole explanation. The premium on "originality" in research and the concomitant reluctance of analysts to adopt the categories of others—tendencies clearly not limited to content-analytic research—is a factor of no little importance. Perhaps this observation can best be illustrated in studies of psychotherapeutic interviews. The volume of investigations, as well as the quality and ingenuity of many studies, is impressive. But even allowing for diversity stemming from theoretical differences, the proliferation of research has not been matched by efforts to replicate and integrate methods and findings. (Holsti, 1969a, p. 114)

Content Analysis of Psychotherapy

Content-analysis studies of psychotherapy have been reviewed in several places (Auld and Murray, 1955; Cartwright, 1957; Dittes, 1959; Gottschalk and Auerbach, 1966; Marsden, 1965, 1971; Rubinstein and Parloff, 1959; Shlien et al., 1968; Strupp, 1962; Strupp and Luborsky, 1962; and, of course, in the present volume. The need for the compilation and critical analysis provided by the present book is evident from the cries and moans present in previous reviews, and is engraved on the author's psyche as the result of the tedious and frustrating search required for the present volume.

> Since about 1940 many attempts have been made to devise conceptual schemes as well as categories, dimensions, and rating devices to capture "relevant" aspects of the content of psychotherapy. Such schemes are typically attempts at content analysis, but they vary greatly in their focus, level of abstraction, and the content they include as well as exclude. . . . It is noteworthy that no single system has received sustained interest from many investigators other than the originator; instead, investigators have typically preferred to develop systems of their own. (Strupp, 1962, p. 363)

Typically, each investigator develops his own system for content analysis (if he does not borrow the Bales system, which is not highly appropriate for the therapy situation). Typically the new system is applied in a single study or, occasionally, in several studies. Because of their complexity, content-analysis studies are rarely based on more than a handful of cases. Thus, results are not cross-validated and their generalizability is severely limited. (Lorr and McNair, 1966, p. 583)

And Truax and Carkhuff (1967) observe:

A large part of the lack of impact of past research arises from the fundamental characteristics of the whole field of psychotherapy and counseling research. The subject matter or substance of the majority of research is highly idiosyncratic. The chaos of labels and concepts that are used even in only one or two studies is striking. . . . [With some exceptions] the outcome and even process studies of the therapeutic encounter are seldom, if ever, replicated. Each investigator has his own favorite variable which is studied in one or a few contexts and then dropped. Beyond this, the same label may be used with radically different meanings in studies of operationally different concepts. . . . The result is that there is very little real accumulation of systematic knowledge. (p. 375)

Marsden (1965) concludes his review of content-analysis studies in therapeutic interviews in a similar vein:

Despite the burgeoning of content-analysis studies of therapeutic interviews in the past two decades. . . . one is struck by the relative infrequency with which any of these systems has resulted in more than an initial thrust at a given research problem. System after system has been developed and presented in one or two demonstration studies, only to lie buried in the literature, unused even by its author. Moreover, few variables or notions about therapeutic interviews have received anything approaching programmatic or extensive content-analysis investigation. This has resulted in redundancy; systems were developed with apparent unawareness that other approaches to the same problem, or efforts to apply the same approach to other problems, had already been reported. (p. 315)

The need for the present volume is clear from these quotations. The content analysis literature is enormous and relatively inaccessible—one need simply note the different books, discussion reports, and journals from scattered disciplines present in the references of this volume. Psychotherapy process research is redundant, as defined by Marsden above. Topics studied are highly idiosyncratic and their number is prolific. Systems are developed, applied as demonstrations, and then dropped by the originator; others rarely use someone else's system. Investigators develop new systems with no knowledge, citation, or integration of previous systems. The upshot is that the area is chaotic.

The major purpose of this book is to eliminate this choas. By bringing under one cover and systematizing the literature of psychotherapy process and/or content analysis research, it is hoped that the scientific study of psychotherapy process will proceed more orderly, less redundantly, with future work building systematically on that which has preceded it.

To obtain closure on the perspective presented in this chapter, it is necessary now to consider further the phrase "content analysis of psychotherapy." As stated above, content analysis belongs to the science of linguistics, and particularly to the subdiscipline of psycholinguistics. Psychotherapy content analysis clearly bridges the gap between the "text" of content analysis and the "speech channel" of psycholinguistics in that the raw data of psychotherapy content analysis studies are transcriptions of the live *speech* of therapy interview participants. As a result, psychotherapy content analysis more clearly belongs to linguistics and psycholinguistics than do other applications of content analysis in journalism and literature.

We have thus come full circle from psychotherapy process research, through communication, linguistic, and psycholinguistic research, through the general area of content analysis, to the specific application of content analysis in psychotherapy research. We find that they are all in the same ballpark, and need to acknowledge and nurture each other's existence. After the original confusion of the various terminologies one finds that order is nevertheless present. This discovery can only make one optimistic about the future of psychotherapy process research, since convergence from diverse directions offers the attainable promise of greater conceptual and methodological precision, of theoretical integration, and of considerable validity and generality of future findings.

It should be added that both psychotherapy and, more generally, content analysis have focused on measuring communications with a particular emphasis on *categorizing* or using *nominal* scales. Dollard and Auld (1959), for example, state that "in its general social-science definition, [content analysis] means the classification of what is said according to some *set of categories*" (p. 27). Dittes (1959) refers to its primary purpose as "the sorting of units of communication into various categories" (p. 339). If one examines the psychotherapy content analysis literature or studies the present volume, it is evident that nominal scaling (or category systems) has predominated to date, although ordinal scaling has also been attempted, particularly more recently. Although content analysis has emphasized nominal measurement, as the science develops there is room for more refined measurement involving ordinal, interval, and ratio scaling. As Marsden (1965) observes, content analysis "typically involves procedures for division of content into units, for assignment of each unit to a category *or to a position on a metric*" (p. 298).

Summary: A Communications Definition of Psychotherapy Process Research

Therapist-patient interaction in psychotherapy interviews are but restricted instances of more general human dyadic communication and interpersonal interaction. It is useful for psychotherapy researchers to conceptualize their efforts in communication terminology, since the communication model is the most general available that is still isomorphic with the events of psychotherapy. By adopting the communication model, psychotherapy process researchers can thereby use the concepts and methodology of the science of linguistics and psycholinguistics to achieve greater precision and replicability of their efforts. The traditional areas of psychotherapy process research and content analysis of psychotherapy are virtually identical, and both define a subarea of the science of psycholinguistics.

Psychotherapy process research, and psychotherapy content analysis, can be redefined as the scientific study of human dyadic communication, in the specific cultural institution of the psychotherapy interview, using as its raw data the live communication behavior (or some transcription of it) between the patient and therapist participants. Psychotherapy process research includes, but encompasses more than, the science of linguistics. This is the case since communication channels other than speech (the speech channel includes both language and nonlanguage phenomena) can be utilized for useful and relevant study (for example, kinesics). As a scientific endeavor, process research requires measurement, or as Marsden (1965) puts it, an "assignment of each unit to a category or to a position on a metric, and for summarizing coded units and arriving at inferences concerning the significance of the summation" (p. 298). In conclusion, psychotherapy process study refers to any research investigation that, totally or in part, contains as its data some direct or indirect representation of patient, therapist, or interactional communication behavior occurring in the psychotherapy interview.

The remainder of the book follows this definition. Chapter 2 discusses in detail some essential methodological considerations for psychotherapy process research and draws a critical stance for evaluating current systems of psychotherapy process analysis. Then, the systems themselves will be presented. They will be divided first into direct (the measure utilizes some transcription of interview behavior) and indirect (various questionnaire and other methods geared toward assessing momentary interview perceptions and behaviors) psychotherapy process systems. The "major" direct systems are subdivided into those designed to measure both patient and therapist (or interactional) interview behaviors (Chapter 3); therapist interview behaviors (Chapter 4); and patient interview behaviors (Chapter 5). The many "minor" direct systems will be summarized in Chapter 6.

References

Abercrombie, D. Voice qualities. In N. N. Markel (Ed.), *Psycholinguistics: an introduction to the study of speech and personality*. Homewood, Ill.: Dorsey Press, 1969.

Alexander, F. In H. D. Kruce (Ed.), *Integrating the approaches to mental disease*. New York: Hoeher-Harper, 1957.

Auld, F., Jr., and Murray, E. J. Content-analysis studies of psychotherapy. *Psychological Bulletin*, 1955, 52, 377-95.

Barcus, F. E. Communications content: analysis of the research, 1900-1958. Doctoral dissertation, University of Illinois. Ann Arbor, Mich: University Microfilms, Inc., 1959.

Berelson, B. *Content analysis in communications research*. Glencoe, Ill.: Free Press, 1952.

Berg, I. A. Word choice in the interview and personal adjustment. *Journal of Counseling Psychology*, 1958, 5, 130-35.

Betz, B. J. Studies of the therapist's role in the treatment of the schizophrenic patient. *American Journal of Psychiatry*, 1967, 123, 963-71.

Birdwhistell, R. L. *Introduction to Kinesics*. Louisville, Ky.: University of Louisville Press, 1952.

———. The Kinesic level in the investigation of the emotions. In P. Knapp (Ed.), *Expression of the emotions in man*. New York: International Universities Press, 1963, Pp. 123-39.

Bloomfield, L. *Language*. New York: Holt, Rinehart & Winston, 1933.

Boomer, D. S., and Dittman, A. T. Speech rate, filled pause, and body movement in interviews. *Journal of Nervous and Mental Diseases*, 1964, 7, 139-324.

Brodsky, G. The relation between verbal and non-verbal behavior change. *Behavior Research and Therapy*, 1967, 5, 183-91.

Buck L. A., and Cuddy, J. M. A theory of communication in psychotherapy. *Psychotherapy: Theory Research & Practice*, 1966, 3, 7-13.

Buehler, R. E., and Richmond, J. F. Interpersonal communication therapy. *Corrective Psychiatry Journal of Social Therapy*, 1965, 11, 204-216.

Carson, R. C. A and B therapist "types": A possible critical variable in psychotherapy. *Journal of Nervous and Mental Disease*, 1967, 144, 47-54.

Cartwright, D. S. Annotated bibliography of research and theory construction in client-centered therapy. *Journal of Counseling Psychology*, 1957, 4, 82-100.

Chomsky, N. *Aspects of the theory of syntax*. Cambridge, Mass.: MIT Press, 1965.

Chomsky, N., and Halle, M. *The sound patterns of English*. New York: Harper and Row, 1968.

DeCecco, J. P. (Ed.) *The psychology of language, thought, and instruction*. New York: Holt, Rinehart & Winston, 1967.

Deese, J. Conceptual categories in the study of content. In G. Gerbner et al. (Eds.), *The analysis of communication content*. New York: Wiley, 1969. Pp. 39-56.

_______. *Psycholinguistics* Boston: Allyn & Bacon, 1970.

Deutsch, F. Some principles of correlating verbal and nonverbal communication. In L. A. Gottschalk and A. H. Auerbach (Eds.), *Methods of research in psychotherapy*. New York: Appleton-Century-Crofts, 1966. Pp. 166-84.

Dittes, J. E. Previous studies bearing on content analysis of psychotherapy. In J. F. Dollard and F. J. Auld Jr. (Eds.), *Scoring human motives*. New Haven, Conn.: Yale University Press, 1959. Pp. 325-51.

Dittmann, A. T. The relationship between body movements and mood in interviews. *Journal of Consulting Psychology*, 1962, 26, 480.

Dittman, A. T., and Wynne, L. C. Linguistic techniques and the analysis of emotionality in interviews. *Journal of Abnormal and Social Psychology*, 1961, 63, 201-204.

_______. Linguistic techniques and the analysis of emotionality in interviews. In L. A. Gottschalk and A. H. Auerbach (Eds.), *Methods of research in psychotherapy*. New York: Appleton-Century-Crofts, 1966. Pp. 25-33.

Dixon, T. R., and Horton, D. L. (Eds.) *Verbal behavior and general behavior theory*. Englewood Cliffs, N.J.: Prentice-Hall, 1968.

Dollard, J. F. and Auld, F. J. *Scoring human motives*. New Haven, Conn.: Yale University Press, 1959.

Duncan, S., Jr. Paralinguistic methods in therapy research. *Counseling Center Discussion Paper*, University of Chicago, 1964, 10, 1-17.

_______. Paralinguistic analysis of psychotherapy interviews. *Revista de Psiconalisis*, 1965, 22, 263-78.

Duncan, S., Jr., Rice, L. N., and Butler, J. M. Therapists paralanguage in peak and poor psychotherapy hours. *Journal of Abnormal Psychology*, 1968, 73, 566-70.

Ekman, P. Body position, facial expression, and verbal behavior during interviews. *Journal of Abnormal and Social Psychology*, 1964, 68, 295-301.

_______. Communication through non-verbal behavior: a source of information about an interpersonal relationship. In S. S. Tomkins and C. E. Izard (Eds.), *Affect, cognition and personality*. New York: Springer Press, 1965. Pp. 390-442.

Ekman, P., and Friesen, W. V. Non-verbal behavior in psychotherapy research. In J. M. Shlien (Ed.), *Research in psychotherapy*. Volume 3. Washington, D.C.: American Psychological Association, 1968. Pp. 179-216.

_______. *Studies in nonverbal behavior*. Elmsford, N.Y.: Pergamon Press, 1970.

Eldred, S. H., Hamburg, D. A., Inwood, E. R., Salzman, L., Meyersburg, H. A., and Goodrich, G. A procedure for the systematic analysis of psychotherapeutic interviews. *Psychiatry*, 1954, 17, 337-45.

Eldred, S. H., and Price, D. B. The linguistic evaluation of feeling states in psychotherapy. *Psychiatry*, 1958, 21, 115-21.

Feldstein, S. Vocal patterning of emotional expression. In T. H. Masserman (Ed.), *Science and psychoanalysis*. New York: Grune & Stratton, 1964, 7, 193-208.

Frank, G. H. On the history of the objective investigation of the process of psychotherapy. *Journal of Psychology*, 1961, 15, 89-95.

Fretz, B. R. Postural movements in a counseling dyad. *Journal of Counseling Psychology*, 1966, 13, 335-43. (a)

———. Personality correlates of postural movements. *Journal of Counseling Psychology*, 1966, 13, 344-47. (b)

Gerbner, G., Holsti, O. R., Krippendorf, K., Paisley, W. J., and Stone, P. J. (Eds.) *The analysis of communication content: developments in scientific theories and computer techniques*. New York: Wiley, 1969.

Gleason, H. A. *An introduction to descriptive linguistics*. New York: Holt, Rinehart & Winston, 1961.

Goldhammer, D. H. Toward a more general inquirer: convergence of structure and context of meaning. In G. Gerbner, O. R. Holsti, K. Krippendorf, W. J. Paisley, and P. J. Stone (Eds.), *The analysis of communication content*. New York: Wiley, 1969. Pp. 343-53.

Goldman-Eisler, F. A study of individual differences and of interaction in the behavior of some aspects of language in interviews. *Journal of Mental Science*, 1954, 100, 177-97.

Gottschalk, L. A. (Ed.) *Comparative psycholinguistic analysis of two psychotherapeutic interviews*. New York: International Universities Press, 1961.

Gottschalk, L. A. and Auerbach, A. H. *Methods of research in psychotherapy*, New York: Appleton-Century-Crofts, 1966.

Greenhill, M. H. The focal communication concept. *American Journal of Psychotherapy*, 1958, 12, 30-41.

Grummon, D. L. An investigation into the use of grammatical and psychogrammatical categories of language for the study of personality and psychotherapy. Unpublished doctoral dissertation, University of Chicago, 1950.

Haggard, E. A., and Isaacs, K. S. Micromomentary facial expressions as indicators of ego mechanisms in psychotherapy. In L. A. Gottschalk and A. H. Auerbach (Eds.), *Methods of research in psychotherapy*. New York: Appleton-Century-Crofts, 1966, Pp. 154-65.

Hall, C. S., and Van De Castle, R. L. *The content analysis of dreams*. New York: Appleton-Century-Crofts, 1966.

Hargreaves, W. A., and Starkweather, J. A. Voice quality changes in depression. *Language and Speech*, 1964, 7, 84-88.

Hoch, P. A. and Zubin, J. (Eds.) *Psychopathology of communication*. New York: Grune & Stratton, 1958.

Holsti, O. R. (with the collaboration of Loomba, J. K., and North, R. C.) Content Analysis. In G. Lindzey and E. Aronson (Eds.), *The handbook of social psychology* Reading, Mass.: Addison-Wesley, 1968.

———. Introduction of Part II. In G. Gerbner, O. R. Holsti, K. Krippendorf, W. J. Paisley, and P. J. Stone, *The analysis of communication content*. New York: Wiley, 1969. Pp. 109-21. (a)

———. A computer content-analysis program for analyzing attitudes. In G. Gerbner, O. R. Holsti, K. Krippendorf, W. J. Paisley, and P. J. Stone, *The analysis of communication content*. New York: Wiley, 1969. Pp. 355-80. (b)

———. *Content analysis for the social sciences and humanities*. Reading, Mass.: Addison-Wesley, 1969. (c)

Jacobsen, R. Boas' views of grammatical meaning. In W. Goldschmidt (Ed.), The anthropology of Franz Boas. *The American Anthropologist*, Memoir No. 89, 1959, 139-45.

Jakobovits, L. A., and Miron, M. S. (Eds.) *Readings in the psychology of language*. Englewood Cliffs, N. J.: Prentice-Hall, 1967.

Kiesler, D. J. Some myths of psychotherapy research and the search for a paradigm. *Psychological Bulletin*, 1966, 65, 110-36.

________. Experimental designs in psychotherapy research. In A. E. Bergin and S. L. Garfield (Eds.), *Handbook of psychotherapy and behavior change*. New York: Wiley, 1971. Pp. 36-74.

Kramer, E. Judgment of personal characteristics and emotions from nonverbal properties of speech. *Psychological Bulletin*, 1963, 60, 408-20.

Krippendorf, K. Introduction to Part I. In G. Gerbner, O. R. Holsti, K. Krippendorf, W. J. Paisley and P. J. Stone (Eds.), *The analysis of communication content*. New York: Wiley, 1969, Pp. 3-16.

Laffal, J. *Pathological and normal language*. New York: Atherton Press, 1965.

Lenneberg, E. H. *The biological foundations of language*. New York: Wiley, 1967.

Lorr, M., and McNair, D. M. Methods relating to the evaluation of therapeutic outcome. In L. A. Gottschalk and A. H. Auerbach (Eds.), *Methods of research in psychotherapy*. New York: Appleton-Century-Crofts, 1966. Pp. 573-94.

Mahl, G. F. Exploring emotional states by content analysis. In I. Pool (Ed.), *Trends in content analysis*. Urbana: University of Illinois Press, 1959. Pp. 89-130.

________. Gestures and body movements in interviews. In J. M. Shlien (Ed.), *Research in psychotherapy*. Washington, D.C.: American Psychological Association, 1968, 3, 295-346.

Mahl, G. F. and Schulze, G. Psychological research. In T. A. Sebeok, A. S. Hayes, and M. C. Bateson (Eds.), *Approaches to semiotics*. The Hague: Mouton & Co., 1964. Pp. 51-143.

Mann, M. B. Studies in language behavior: III. Quantatative differentiation of samples of written language. *Psychological Monographs*, 1944, 56, 41-74.

Markel, N. N. *Psycholinguistics: an introduction to the study of speech and personality*. Homewood, Ill.: Dorsey Press, 1969.

Markel, N. N., Meisels, M., and Houchk, J. E. Judging personality from voice quality. *Journal of Abnormal & Social Psychology*, 1964, 60, 458-63.

Marsden, G. Content-analysis studies of therapeutic interviews: 1954 to 1964. *Psychological Bulletin*, 1965, 63, 298-321.

________. Content analysis studies of psychotherapy: 1954 through 1968. In A. E. Bergin and S. L. Garfield (Eds.), *Handbook of psychotherapy and behavior change*. New York: Wiley, 1971. Pp. 345-407.

McQuown, N. A. Linguistic transcription and specification of psychiatric interview materials. *Psychiatry*, 1957, 20, 79-86.

Miller, G. A., and Smith, F. (Eds.) *The genesis of language*. Cambridge, Mass.: MIT Press, 1966.

Mitchell, F. H. A test of certain semantic hypotheses by application to client-centered counseling cases: intensionality-extensionality of clients in therapy. Unpublished doctoral dissertation, University of Chicago, 1951.

Morris, C. *Signs, language, and behavior*. Englewood Cliffs, N.J.: Prentice-Hall, 1946.

Nathan, P. E., Schneller, P., and Lindsley, O. R. Direct measurement of communication during psychiatric admission interviews. *Behavior Research and Therapy*, 1964, 2, 49-57.

Newman, S. Personal Symbolism in language patterns. *Psychiatry*, 1939, 2, 177-84.

Osgood, C. E., and Sebeok, T. A. (Eds.), *A survey of psycholinguistic research: 1954-1964.* Bloomington: Indiana University Press, 1965.

Page, H. A. An assessment of the predictive value of certain language measures in psychotherapeutic counseling. In W. U. Snyder (Ed.), *Group report of a program of research in psychotherapy.* Psychotherapy Research Group, Pennsylvania State University, 1953. Pp. 88-93.

Paisley, W. J. Introduction of Part III. In G. Gerbner, O. R. Holsti, K. Krippendorf, W. J. Paisley, and P. J. Stone, *The analysis of communication content.* New York: Wiley, 1969. Pp. 133-46.

Pittenger, R. E. Linguistic analysis of tone of voice in communication of affect. *Psychiatric Research Reports,* 1958, 8, 41-54.

Pittenger, R. E., Hocket, C. F., and Danehy, J. J. *The first five minutes.* Ithaca, N.Y.: Paul Martineau, 1960.

Pittenger, R. E. and Smith H. L. Jr. A basis for some contributions of linguistics to psychiatry. *Psychiatry*, 1957, 20, 61-78.

Pool, I. (Ed.) *Trends in content analysis*. Urbana: University of Illinois Press, 1959.

Rapaport, A. A system-theoretic view of content analysis. In G. Gerbner, O. R. Holsti, K. Krippendorf, W. J. Paisley, and P. J. Stone (Eds.), *The analysis of communication content.* New York: Wiley, 1969. Pp. 17-38.

Rennecker, R. E. Microscopic analysis of sound tape: a method of studying preconscious communication in the therapeutic process. *Psychiatry*, 1960, 23, 347-56.

Riess, B. F. Communication in psychotherapy. *American Journal of Psychotherapy*, 1957, 11, 774-89.

Rioch, D. McK. (Ed.), *Disorders of communication.* Proceedings of ARNMD. Baltimore: Williams & Wilkins, 1964.

Rioch, D. McK., and Weinstein, E. A. (Eds.) *Disorders of communication.* Baltimore: Williams & Wilkin, 1964.

Rosenberg, S. (Ed.) *Directions in psycholinguistics.* New York: Macmillan, 1965.

Rubinstein, E. A., and Parloff, M. B. (Eds.) *Research in Psychotherapy.* Vol. 1 Washington, D.C.: American Psychological Association, 1959.

Ruesch, J. *Therapeutic communication.* New York: Norton, 1961.

Ruesch, J., and Bateson, G. *Communication: the social matrix of psychiatry.* New York: Norton, 1951.

Sanford, F. H. Speech and personality. *Psychological Bulletin*, 1942, 39, 811-45. (a)

________. Speech and personality: a comparative case study. *Character and Personality*, 1942, 10, 169-98. (b)

Sapir, E. Speech as a personality trait. In D. G. Mandelbaum (Ed.), *Language, culture and personality*. Berkeley: University of California Press, 1958. Pp. 533-43.

Saporta, S. *Psycholinguistics: a book of readings.* New York: Holt, Rinehart & Winston, 1961.

Scheflin, A. E. The significance of posture in communication systems. *Psychiatry*, 1964, 27, 316-31.

________. Communication systems such as psychotherapy. In J. H. Masserman (Ed.), *Current psychiatric therapies.* New York: Grune & Stratton, 1965. Pp. 33-41.

Scheflin, A. E., English, O. S., Hampe, W. N., and Auerbach, A. H. *Research in psychotherapy: a study of the Whitaker-Malone method,* 1966.

Schramm, W., and Pool, I. (Eds.) *The handbook of communication.* Chicago: Rand McNally, 1969.

Sebeok, T. A. *Style in language.* Cambridge, Mass.: MIT Press, 1960.

Sebeok, T. A., Hayes, A. S., and Bateson, M. C. (Eds.) *Approaches to semiotics.* The Hague: Mouton & Co., 1964.

Sebeok, T. A., Walker, D. C., and Greenberg, J. H. Nonlinguistic organization. In C. E. Osgood and T. A. Sebeok (Eds.), *Psycholinguistics: a survey of theory and research problems.* Baltimore: Williams & Wilkins, 1954.

Shlien, J. M., Hunt, H. F., Matarazzo, J. O., and Savage, C. (Eds.). *Research in psychotherapy.* Vol. 3. Washington, D.C.: American Psychological Association, 1968.

Starkweather, J. A. Vocal communication of personality and human feelings. *Journal of Communication,* 1961, 11, 63-72.

Stephenson, W. Critique of content analysis. *Psychological Records,* 1963, 13, 155-62.

Stone, P. J., Dunphy, D. C., Smith, M. S., and Ogilvie, D. M. *The General Inquirer: computer approach to content analysis.* Cambridge, Mass.: MIT Press, 1966.

Strupp, H. H. Patient-doctor relationships: The psychotherapist in the therapeutic process. In A. J. Bachrach (Ed.), *Experimental foundations of clinical psychology.* New York: Basic Books, 1962. Pp. 576-615.

Strupp, H. H., Chassan, J. B., and Ewing, J. A. Toward the longitudinal study of the psychotherapeutic process. In L. A. Gottschalk and A. H. Auerbach (Eds.), *Methods of research in psychotherapy* New York: Appleton-Century-Crofts, 1966.

Strupp, H. H., and Luborsky, L. (Eds.). *Research in Psychotherapy* Vol. 2. Washington, D.C.: American Psychological Association, 1962.

Thayer, L. (Ed.) *Communication: theory and research.* Springfield, Ill: Charles C Thomas, 1966.

Tomkins, S. S., and Izard, C. E. (Eds.) *Affect, cognition and personality.* New York: Springer Press, 1965.

Trager, G. L. Paralanguage: a first approximation. *Studies in Linguistics,* 1958, 13, 1-12.

———. Language and psychotherapy. In L. A. Gottschalk and A. H. Auerbach (Eds.), *Methods of research in psychotherapy* New York: Appleton-Century-Crofts, 1966. Pp. 70-84.

Traux, C. B., and Carkhuff, R. R. *Toward effective counseling and psychotherapy: training and practice.* Chicago: Aldine, 1967.

Watzlawick, P., Beavin, J. H., and Jackson, D. D. *Pragmatics of human communication: a study of interactional patterns, pathologies, and paradoxes.* New York: Norton, 1967.

Weintraub, W., and Aronson, H. The application of verbal behavior analysis to the study of psychological defense mechanisms: methodology and preliminary report. *Journal of Nervous and Mental Disease,* 1962, 134, 169-81.

Williamson, E. G. The meaning of communication in counseling. *Personnel and Guidance Journal,* 1959, 88, 6-14.

2

Basic Methodological Issues in Psychotherapy Process Research

The serious investigator of psychotherapy process must be simultaneously concerned with both methodological and substance issues in his research investigations. Heuristic psychotherapy process study does not take the form of one-shot research attempts, but is manifested by long-range programs of investigation confronting both theoretical and methodological problems. Psychotherapy process research moves forward on a firm scientific base only by painstaking consideration of these issues (Bordin et al., 1954; Kiesler, 1966, 1971a).

Psychotherapy process research was defined in the preceding chapter as the scientific study of hyman dyadic communication, in the specific cultural institution of the psychotherapy interview, using as its raw data the live communication behavior (or some transcription of it) between the patient and therapist participants. Important methodological issues jump to the fore when one seriously confronts the mass of this "raw data" for purposes of scientific analysis. At the end of data collection for the Wisconsin schizophrenia study (Rogers, Gendlin, Kiesler, and Truax, 1967), for example, the researchers possessed 1,204 hours of tape-recorded therapeutic interaction with twenty-eight patients. How does one go about applying a psychotherapy process system to such a formidable collection of recorded psychotherapy data? It is practicably impossible, and probably irrelevant, to score every minute of each of the 1,204 therapy hours. Obviously, then, process research involves methodological decisions at the very inception of data analysis, decisions which are vitally relevant to the particular results obtained.

A Brief History and Problems of Recording Psychotherapy Interviews

Controlled research in psychotherapy is a relatively recent event. According to Strupp, "its starting date may be fixed around 1940, with an emerging interest, particularly by Carl Rogers and his students, in applying the methods of psychological research to the process of psychotherapy" (1962, p. 579). The major technical development which made this research feasible was the refinement of electronic audial recording. Dittes gives an intimate and detailed account of early applications of this technology, presented here in abbreviated form. It is difficult at this date to realize either the excitement or the controversy that accompanied these early efforts.

> Content analysis of psychotherapy has become feasible only in the last quarter century, as technical developments have enabled us to capture an accurate, word-for-word record of the therapeutic transaction. . . . The world's pioneer in the recording of the psychoanalytic transaction was Earl F. Zinn . . . who began his work in 1925 and pursued his purpose inflexibly for twenty years. With the help of the Dictaphone Corporation, a system for recording analytic interviews on wax cylinders was developed. . . . Zinn had begun experimentation on the recording of interviews in 1929; he began his analytic training in Berlin in the fall of 1931, and upon his return from Berlin in 1932 he began recording analytic interviews (in New York City). . . . Harold D. Lasswell (1928) set up a recording laboratory (at the University of Chicago in the Social Science Research Building) and, using special Dictaphone equipment, began—apparently in 1930—to make sound recordings of analytic interviews. He also recorded skin resistance, heart rate, breathing, and bodily movements of the patient. . . . Percival M. Symons was one of the first to make recordings of counseling interviews (somewhere around 1938). . . . Carl R. Rogers is deservedly famous for his pioneering work in recording counseling interviews. . . . The recording procedures of Rogers and his colleagues were first described by Bernard J. Covner (1942). (The recording by Covner began in 1940, when Rogers first came to Ohio State University.) The desirability of recording was stressed by Rogers (1942). Prior to coming to Ohio state he had tried the conventional mandrel-type Dictaphone without success, and gave it up. (Covner's thesis, which compared phonograph typescripts with interviewers' reports, showed that the discrepancies were great enough to show the superiority of the phonograph typescripts for research purposes.) . . . At Yale University the first

> recordings were those made by Earl F. Zinn. . . . With the development of magnetic recording . . John Dollard began making magnetic recordings of his own psychotherapy interviews and Richard Newman began to use a wire recorder for the same purpose. Also F. C. Redlich, chairman of the Department of Psychiatry, began to tape-record his own interviews for use in teaching. . . . It became apparent that better facilities for recording were needed, and with the aid of grants . . . interviewing rooms were constructed and high-fidelity equipment was obtained. These facilities have been described in two papers, by Redlich et al. (1950; see also Brody et al., 1951) and by Mahl et al. (1954).
>
> This quick review of some of the origins of sound-recording of psychotherapy brings out that those who pioneered recording had to overcome not only equipment problems, not only prejudices against recording of interviews, but also their own doubts about the feasibility of capturing the therapeutic transaction on disk, cylinder, wire, or tape. Would the patient be disturbed? Would the therapy be so changed that no scientific value could accrue from a study of the records? Could the patient be told that the recording was being made? These scientists did not know what the answers would be, but they went ahead and recorded. Now we know—thanks to the courage of these researchers—that the patient is seldom disturbed by the recording (and if he is, it is a problem to be dealt with like any other problem arising in the therapy), that the essential features of the therapy are not changed, and that one can risk telling the patient that one would like to record his sessions. (Dittes, 1959, pp. 344-50)

Generally the research evidence supports the notion that electrical recording of interviews offers fewer psychological obstacles than many formerly assumed, and that patients or clients have far less objection to it than anxious practitioners often expected. Findings suggest that recording devices of various sorts have an observable but not deleterious effect upon the therapeutic interview. Therapists are sometimes bothered by the recording procedure, but it is unlikely that these uneasy or bothered feelings actually influence the process proper (Berman, 1955; Covner, 1942; Greenblatt et al., 1954; Haggard, Hiken, and Isaacs, 1965; Harper and Hudson, 1952; Kogan, 1950; Kubie, 1952; Lamb and Mahl, 1956; Park, Slaughter, Covi, and Kniffin, 1966; Parloff, Iflund, and Goldstein, 1960; Shakow, 1949, 1960; Sternberg, Chapman, and Shakow, 1958; Watson and Kanter, 1956). As Carmichael (1966) observes, "patients usually do not show resistance to being sound-recorded on tape or sound-film, whereas therapists almost all show great resistance and reluctance to having their methods and techniques of psychotherapy made available for others to hear and observe. The danger of damage to their self-esteem seems to give them considerable anxiety" (p. 57).

A more recent study, however, does indicate that potential research biases can result from the introduction of observational techniques. Roberts and Renzaglia (1965) found that although the quantity and the ratio of talking by counselor and client did not change as various recording procedures were introduced, the introduction of recording led patients to make more favorable self-reference statements and led Rogerian counselors to behave in less client-centered ways.

Although the Roberts and Renzaglia study would suggest that the recording of therapy interviews be approached with caution, the procedures are now solidly entrenched and provide such vast opportunities that their discontinuance would represent a huge step backwards in psychotherapy analysis. It is helpful to keep in mind Shakow's (1960) comments about the problems of having the therapist himself report the therapy events.

> Mainly, these inadequacies stem from the fact that the data are reported by a participant-observer, the therapist. . . . Like any reported observations, the data are bound by the capacity of the human observer as a reporting instrument. No matter how good human beings may be as conceptualizers, they are markedly handicapped sensorially, mnemonically, and expressively as observers and reporters. Put simply, they are limited in how much they can grasp, in how much they can remember of what they do grasp, and in how much and how well they can report even the slight amount they have grasped and remembered. The situation of the psychoanalytic interview places an even greater stricture upon the data because we are dependent upon a participant-observer whose participation is very special and intensive. Distortions, both of omission and commission, arising from the situation and the personality of the therapist, undoubtedly enter. (pp. 83-84)

In contrast, the advantages of sound or other recordings of the events in therapy are clearcut: The records are permanent, they can be reviewed at any time, and they are not dependent upon the original investigator or therapist for reliability of interpretation; they are unbiased, veridical representations of the original events. Some form of recorded transcription of the events of psychotherapy provides the data of choice for therapy process investigations.

Choice of Process Variables for Study

Guetzkow (1950) argues that two methodological problems are basic to the content analysis of verbal or other quantatative material. The first is the formulation of a system of classification; the second, the selection of a unit of analysis. Selection of a *theoretical* variable for study is the essential first step in psychotherapy process study. This selection is intimately related to the resolution of other methodological problems. Much methodological confusion has resulted from not giving priority to theoretical considerations. Marsden (1965) argues the same point:

> Discussions of content-analysis methodology tend to treat the problem of unit and category selection as relatively unrelated issues. This tendency is manifest in most of the studies considered in this paper. While specific category systems were developed, presumably because of their relation to the research problem, choice of units has often reflected only the need to divide communication material into segments in a systematic fashion. Infrequently have investigators argued for their choice of a unit in terms of its logical or psychological relation to either the category structure or the question under investigation. (p. 315)

Strupp (1962) voices similar concerns:

> Since communication between patient and therapist is mediated primarily by linguistic symbols, a first requirement for objective research is to devise *conceptual* tools which permit the investigator to abstract and quantify relevant aspects of the verbal interchange. Obviously there are innumerable ways of accomplishing this end, and the measures upon which the investigator decides are as noteworthy for what they include as for what they leave out. The selection is dictated by theoretical as well as practical considerations, and in a sense it represents a prejudgment of what is important to measure. A content-analysis system is therefore not a neutral yardstick. (p. 585)
>
> If we are to proceed with the all-important task of studying psychological phenomena by techniques uniquely suited to their study, it is indispensable to take that study seriously. If we are to study the phenomena of psychotherapy and of doctor-patient relationships intelligently and productively, it is essential to have a thoroughgoing knowledge of the clinical findings, insights, and principles which clinical psychoanalysis and psychotherapy have distilled over the years. (p. 610)

In discussing content analysis in the social sciences more generally, Cartwright (1966) states:

> One of the most serious criticisms that can be made of the research employing content analysis is that the "findings" have no clear significance for either theory or practice. In reviewing the work in this field, one is struck by the number of studies which apparently have been guided by a sheer fascination with counting. Unfortunately, it is possible for a content analysis to meet all the requirements of objectivity and quantification . . . without making any appreciable contribution to theory or practice. It is an all too common error to equate "scientific" with "reliable and quantatative." Unless the findings of a content analysis have implications for some theory, however vaguely formulated, the study can merit serious attention only on the highly tenuous claim that some day the significance of the findings will become apparent. . . . It should be apparent that the value of a content analysis will depend upon the quality of the a priori conceptualization. It will depend, also, upon the adequacy with which this conceptualization gets translated into the variables of the analysis. Finally it will depend upon having data to analyze which are appropriate to the variables of the system. (pp. 447-48)

Unless a process investigator has a clear conceptualization of the construct or constructs he is attempting to measure, he may inadvertently make methodological decisions along the way that conflict with his theoretical framework, and hence make the obtaining of valid answers to the questions unlikely. Hopefully this point will become crystal clear as subsequent methodological issues are discussed. "Experience has shown that the most fruitful scientific investigations are those that bear some relation to a general theory or, at least, to a well-thought-out hypothesis" (Wilson, 1952; Auld and Murray, 1955, p. 390).

Marsden (1965, 1971) makes a distinction that is quite relevant to an investigator's choice of constructs and measures in psychotherapy process research. He defines three models of content analysis, the primary distinctions having to do with the inferential level of constructs in a particular system. The *classical* model is defined by Berelson's definition of content analysis, which emphasizes the quantification of the manifest content of communication. By using the word "manifest" Berelson "intended to limit content analysis to the semantic and syntactic aspects of communication, and to prevent its extension to the pragmatic aspect—to the relationship between the communication symbol and its user" (Marsden, 1965, p. 299). The *pragmatic* model challenges Berelson's restriction.

> While in the classical model units are coded to categories descriptive of the content itself, in the pragmatic model units are coded to categories descriptive of some condition of the communicator, or of the relationship between him and his communication. In the classical model, once the units are coded, the analyst may make further inferences about the internal state of the communicator. . . . In the pragmatic model, this kind of inference is made initially, at the time of coding, and is the basis of the coding . . . . The pragmatic model attempts to realize psychological meaningfulness by working directly with complex clinical constructs. (Marsden, 1965, p. 299)

Marsden cites Dollard and Auld's system (see Chapter 3) as the most thoroughgoing example of the pragmatic model, since its essential focus is on the dynamic motive states of the patient, which could be either conscious or unconscious.

> Heyns and Zander (1966) make the identical distinction. Some category systems require that the observers coding the behavior proceed from the actual behavior which they noted to a deduction about this behavior [for example, shows hostility, demands submission, desires support, resents dependence]. At the other extreme are procedures which require the observers to place the behavior they saw or heard into categories with no requirement of inference [for example, shoves other children, calls other children names, asks for help] . . . .The essential difference between the two category systems is who makes the inference. In either case, some theoretical system is required on the basis of which inferences are made, either by the experimenter when he confronts the data presented to him by observers, or by the observers when they observe the behavior. . . . In the first case the observer notes the incidence of behavior in categories and the investigator makes the inferences during the analysis of the data; in the second case, the experimenter asks the observer to make inferences after he has instructed him as to the kinds of inferences that can be made. (p. 390)

The major process systems presented in Part II of this volume could be ranked along an inferential continuum between the end points represented by Marsden's classical and pragmatic models. Table 2.1* presents a summary of the patient and therapist constructs measured in the seventeen major process systems presented in Part II. This summary table should make it considerably easier for a process investigator to determine at a glance whether a variable he is considering for investigation has already been operationalized in some form by previous researchers. If so, he can then turn to Part II for more

*All tables are in the appendix, starting p. 375.

detailed definitions of the respective variables and measures. It is apparent from the table that widely different levels of inference are involved in the measures of the various constructs. Table 6.1 in Chapter 6 summarizes all the other "minor" systems of measurement the author could locate. Anyone interested in psychotherapy process investigation can profit considerably from study of both tables.

In the long run, psychotherapy research will progress more if based on the classical model of Berelson. This model is more likely to lead an observer reliability, widespread use, and replicability of findings than is the pragmatic model. The pragmatic models developed for psychotherapy have been creative and challenging, but they do not seem to progress beyond initial empirical demonstrations of the method. This lack of systematic progress seems to result from the complexity of the definitions of the inferential constructs involved, the necessity for highly trained and quite sophisticated scorers, and the general problems of observer reliability and heuristic impact of extremely complicated systems. On the other hand, if pragmatic models are developed which limit their focus to one or only a few constructs, instead of the prevalent omnibus systems, some of these problems may be sidetracked. Auld and Murray (1955) draw a similar conclusion:

> Content systems are inevitably criticized for what they leave out. The practicing clinician often feels that the measured part of the therapeutic transaction is pitifully small alongside the complex of stimuli that he senses as a participant observer. Yet it seems unfair to expect any single content-analysis system to describe all of this complex situation. We would probably make a fairer appraisal of content systems if we expected each system to deal with only a part of this complexity. An adequate descriptive and causal analysis of psychotherapy will most likely require a large number of measures, each of them shown to be reliable and valid for its limited purpose. . . . By the combination of a variety of measures, each useful in its own domain, we may in time construct an adequate science of psychotherapy. (p. 391)

The final model Marsden (1965) differentiates is the *nonquantitive* model.

> The studies representing it share the purpose of attempting to develop alternatives to the frequency approach of measuring intensity in communication materials. . . . [In the classical model and in many pragmatic systems] the assumption is made that frequency of occurrence of units in a category is highly correlated with the intensity of that category in the communication. This assumption

> has been a major target of criticism directed at classical content analysis. Advocates and antagonists alike have asked how much of the variance this correlation could be expected to explain. They have wanted to know what factors other than frequency of occurrence are significant carriers of intensity and in what situations they become important. Above all they have asked how might they be measured. . . Some investigators have attempted to measure both frequency and nonfrequency aspects of intensity by using rating scales within categories, or weighted units.(p. 299)

Marsden lists George's (1959) "nonfrequency analysis" and Osgood's (1959) work on evaluative assertions as "more rigorously formulated nonquantitive approaches, though not yet applied to analysis of therapeutic interviews" (Marsden, 1965, p. 300).

At this point, a few words about measurement are necessary. Measurement usually means the assigning of numbers to observations; analysis of data consists in manipulating these numbers. Numbers assigned to observations fall on a scale, which can be nominal, ordinal, interval, or ratio in nature (Stevens, 1951). Nominal and ordinal scaling clearly predominate in psychotherapy process research, and will likely continue to do so for some time. In nominal scaling, observed behaviors are assigned to separate categories. A category is a statement describing a given class of phenomena into which observed behavior may be coded; a category system consists of two or more categories. Ordinal scaling involves the use of various rating scales which subsume a set of points that describe varying degrees of the dimension being observed. The majority of the systems presented in this volume are category systems, although more recently rating scales focusing on observable patient or therapist behaviors are becoming more prevalent.

The Unit Problem

After formulating the variables in which he is interested, and after developing a measurement system (nominal or ordinal) for assessing these variables, the investigator must decide what to do with the slices of the psychotherapy transaction to which his system is to be applied. In other words, he has to determine the unit of behavior to be rated or categorized. It is surprising how often in the past unit issues have been ignored or obscured. "That unitizing and categorizing are distinct acts, even when performed simultaneously by the same person, has been recognized by most content analysts who have studied psychotherapy. But the importance of care in unitizing and of evaluating reliability of unitizing has not been widely recognized.

Clear definitions of units and full reports on reliability of unitizing are rare" (Dittes, 1959, p. 339). Failure to state clearly to observers the precise limits of the unit to be scored is a frequent source of unreliability. Reliability of coding depends in part on the reliability of deciding what constitutes a unit of behavior. As Heyns and Zander state (1966), the issue is "the extent of agreement among observers with respect to the number of units coded... [or] the extent to which the observers agree as to the boundaries of the unit which is to be categorized... Unreliability in this area is an important factor affecting the reliability of categorization itself. It seems clear that until there is rater agreement as to the boundaries of units to be categorized, there is little purpose in assessing rater agreement on categorizing" (p. 411).

The choice of unit is an equally perplexing problem for process investigators focusing on paralinguistic and/or kinesic aspects of psychotherapy communication. Ekman and Friesen (1968), for example, describe the "nonverbal act" as their basic unit of kinesic analysis: "A movement within any single body area (head, face, shoulders, hands or feet) or across multiple body areas, which has visual integrity and is virtually distinct from another act... An act begins when a movement is first detectable, and ends when a movement is no longer apparent or when another visually distinctive type of movement commences" (pp. 193-94). They emphasize that

> the choice of unit depends upon assumptions about the origin and functions of nonverbal (kinesic) behavior, the level at which meaning might conceivably be coded in nonverbal activity. The choice of unit may also result from compromises dictated by limitations in data recording equipment, or attempts to accelerate data processing. But, these are crucial decisions which radically influence the results obtained. One can get no more out of a judge of nonverbal behavior than what he is shown; if the judge is limited to seeing only one body area (most often the face) or arbitrary time slices (usually the still photograph or the 5-second or 2-minute movie burst), his inferences are limited and in part determined by how badly such selective processes mutilate the natural flow of nonverbal activity... Thus, the test of the validity of the unit of measurement is the result obtained. Unfortunately, too often negative or only modest results are interpreted as raising doubt only about the communication value of nonverbal behavior, and not about the possibility that the definition of the behavoral unit was not appropriate. (p. 192)

A variety of units have been proposed for or used in process analysis of psychotherapy. These include single words, phrases, sentences, the utterance (everything one participant says between two successive productions of the other participant), problem-area units (all the contiguous statements dealing with the same problem topic), discussion topic units (all the conversation of both patient and therapist about the same topic or subject), the typescript page, various length of time samples (for example, two- or four-minute random segments), the "initial period" of therapy (for example, the first ten interviews), etc.

The question raised, then, is which of these many possible units should process investigators use as data-blocks to be observed and scored by judges on the variables of interest? The answer seems clearly to vary, depending on the particular construct or constructs of interest, and on the questions being asked by a particular study. To say this differently, in process research there are as many different units as there are distinct constructs requiring separate measurement.

> What kind of division one should make depends, of course, on the researcher's aims. If one wishes to get an overall view of a whole case without paying attention to details, one may use a whole series of interviews as the unit ("the first period," "the second, fruitful period," "the third period"). One may want a medium close-up view of the therapy, for which a whole hour of the case will serve as the unit. One may wish to study the psychotherapy in even greater detail, choosing a topic or theme within an hour, an utterance . . . or the sentence as the unit. (Dollard and Auld, 1959, pp. 9-10)

Bordin et al. (1954) argue that "the sheer extensivity and extreme complexity of the data of psychotherapeutic interaction force upon the research worker the decision as to what aspects of the data to present to the judge. Here again, one's conception of the variable and the theory behind it will determine what one presents to the judge" (p. 80).

If, for example, one is measuring "empathic understanding" of the therapist, it would seem to make little sense to choose only the therapist's utterances as one's unit (that is, only the Ts in the P-T-P communication sequence). One could assess from the isolated therapist's utterances the degree of effort he is expending to understand the patient, or his expressive ability in communicating whatever he has decoded. But it seems contradictory to the construct of empathic understanding not to assess both the patient's and the therapist's utterance, since the judgment regarding the therapist's level of understanding depends on the isomorphism between the patient's statement and the therapist's subsequent response. To the extent that this is correct, individual P-T-P units (the patient's utterance, the therapist's response utterance, the patient's subsequent response utterance) would be more appropriate for analyzing the therapist's empathic understanding. On the other hand, if one is interested in assessing therapist "warmth," individual therapist utterances alone might well be appropriate units. Bordin et al. (1954) provide similar illustrations:

> It seems clear—again on the face of it—that transference comes in larger packages than does reflection of feeling; and that to ask someone to judge transference on the basis of a small unit would be destroying what you want to look at before you get a chance to look at it. But while the direction of choice of unit seems clear in the case of this variable, the issue is not as simple in other cases, as, for example, when we are investigating therapist's level of participation, where momentary fluctuations are the rule rather than the exception. In large units these fluctuations would be wiped out, while in very small units the variable might not be comprehensible to the judge. (p. 80)

It is quite important, further, to distinguish among several different uses of the term "unit." Berelson (1952) and Dollard and Auld (1959) make a formal distinction between recording or "scoring" units and "contextual" units. Dollard and Auld also define a third unit, the "summarizing" unit. As Marsden (1965) states, "these distinctions . . . are necessary and important; the failure of content analysts working with therapeutic interview material to make them has, at times, led to conceptual confusion and ambiguous results" (p. 301).

The *scoring* (recording) unit is the entity that is actually coded and counted. It is the specific segment of the content that is characterized by placing it in a given category. An example might be the sentence that the judge rates or classifies, or each emotionally loaded patient word. The *contextual* unit consists of that portion of the interview that is considered when one assigns a score to the scoring unit, or the largest body of content that may be examined in characterizing a scoring unit, or the communication material surrounding the scoring unit that is considered before the latter is assigned to a category. A coder might, for example, count each emotionally loaded word (the scoring unit) but refer to an entire paragraph (the contextual unit) to be sure that he records its correct meaning.

"Whenever the scoring unit is scored in isolation, without the scorer's having knowledge of any other material, the scoring unit is the same as the contextual unit" (Dollard and Auld, 1959, p. 10). An example where the two units are identical is in the case of Experiencing Scale ratings (Klein, Mathieu, Gendlin, and Kiesler, 1970). In this case, five-minute segments are randomly extracted from tape-recordings of psychotherapy interviews. The audial contents of particular five-minute segments represent the scoring unit, but also represent the contextual unit, since the judges consider only the five-minute segment in making a particular Experiencing rating.

> A contextual unit could consist of only slightly more than the scoring unit or of considerably more than that. How large the contextual unit is depends on the arrangement of the scoring task, for instance on whether the scorer takes the material consecutively. If the scorer has scored consecutively all of the case up to the scoring unit, he is influenced to some degree by everything that comes earlier. The researcher cannot eradicate such influence by sternly advising the scorer to consider only the preceding page. It seems to us, therefore, that the wisest course for the researcher is to describe the whole set of arrangements and instructions for scoring, so that any scientist examining the study can estimate for himself what kind of context the scorer had. (Dollard and Auld, 1959, p. 11)

The *summarizing* unit is the group of scoring units about which some statement is made, or the unit in terms of which quantification is performed. "The summarizing unit, including usually a number of scoring units, consists of that part of the material about which the researcher makes a summary statement. For example, the summarizing unit can be an hour of a case, which the researcher characterizes as having only a few, or a moderate number, or a great number of sentences that are resistant. Again, the summarizing unit may be the successive ten-minute periods during an interview" (Dollard and Auld, 1959, p. 11).

In contrasting the three types of units, Marsden (1965) gives the following example: "The number of nouns in two-minute segments of an interview are counted, and judgments made as to whether a word is a noun based on its use in the sentence in which it occurs. The two-minute segments represent summarizing units. The nouns themselves are the scoring units, and the sentences in which the nouns appear are the contextual units" (p.301). It should be evident, furthermore, that there can be more than one summarizing unit in a particular study. For example, one could sample 3 two-minute segments (in Marsden's example) from each interview; the entire interview could then become the summarizing unit, with the number of nouns averaged for the 3 two-minute segments. Likewise, we could sample 3 two-minute segments from every interview in an entire therapy case. The number of nouns could then be averaged across all the interviews, yielding on overall value for the entire case (now the summarizing unit).

Surprisingly, few process investigators have tested how different sizes or choices of units might affect the scores obtained for their particular measures (Bordin et al., 1954; Kiesler, Mathieu and Klein, 1967; Muthard, 1953). Kiesler et al. (1967), for example, studied the comparative effects of different segment lengths on experiencing (EXP) ratings. EXP ratings were compared for two, four, eight, and sixteen-minute segments drawn from each of two therapy hours with eight normal, eight schizophrenic, and eight neurotic subjects. Only the absolute level of EXP ratings was influenced by segment length, with longer segments receiving higher ratings. The reliabilities, the range, and the discriminatory power of the ratings were independent of the length of the segment. Thus, while it would obviously be unwise to mix segment lengths in a given study, EXP ratings from short or from long segments are likely to differentiate among patients equally reliably.

PARTICIPANT CONTEXT

Another aspect of context not considered by Dollard and Auld might be called "participant context." It has to do with the presence or absence in the scoring and/or contextual units of the interview participant who is not being scored on a particular variable. One must be concerned about the likelihood of confounding when either specific therapist or specific patient behaviors are rated from scoring and/or contextual units where both participants' verbalizations are present. In some cases, particularly when therapist behaviors are measured, the construct of concern may necessitate a scoring unit containing the utterances of both participants (for example, accurate empathy). In these cases, the investigator has an artifactual confounding built into his measure (an unavoidable one), and consequently must be very careful about interpreting the results of his scale.

Let us assume one finds a high positive correlation between therapists' accurate empathy behavior in therapy interviews and eventual successful outcome of patients. One would be tempted to conclude that therapists' high empathy leads to successful outcomes. But, it is equally plausible that some *patient* factor is being used implicitly by the empathy raters as their cue of level of therapist empathy (since the patients' verbalizations are also present in the scoring and/or contextual unit), and that this patient variable is itself related to eventual successful outcome. If this potential confounding is not considered carefully in the construction of the measure and in data analysis, the investigator can easily draw erroneous conclusions.

Similarly, let us consider the case where an investigator applies one therapist measure and one patient measure to the same therapy interviews, and uses as samples scoring and/or contextual units that contain *both* therapist and patient verbaliziations. Let us assume that separate groups of judges rate the "accurate empathy" of the therapist and the "experiencing" of the patient (Rogers et al., 1967), and that one finds a high positive correlation between these therapist empathy and patient experiencing ratings. Since both participants are present on the samples for both sets of judges, one may ask whether both sets of judges actually based their separate rating judgments on the same thing, on, for instance, the patient's behavior? Is it possible to rate the therapist's level of empathic understanding without considering the patient's verbalizations, which are at some level of experiencing? Again the possibility of confounding is present.

In the measuring of patient behaviors, confounding from the participant context is usually less of a problem since with patient variables the scoring and/or contextual units can more legitimately exclude the therapist's verbalizations. It remains an issue, however, when both participants' verbalizations are included in the units. This issue must be addressed both conceptually and empirically. For example, Schoeninger, Klein, and Mathieu (1967) examined the participant-context issue for the Experiencing Scale. Four judges rated the same therapy segments under two conditions: First they rated each segment with all the therapist's speech removed; later each segment was rated again with the therapist's speech present. The findings indicated that, in terms of reliability, means, variances, and intercorrelation of the two sets of ratings, there were virtually no differences between ratings made under the two conditions. This finding suggests that Experiencing can be rated reliably from the patient's speech alone, but that similar ratings result when the therapist's speech is present, which eliminates the need to edit.

The participant-context issue was also investigated by Bordin et al. (1954) in regard to a variable representing the degree to which the therapist stays within the patient's frame of reference. Ratings based on the total typescript were compared with ratings where only the therapist responses were available (and these responses either in correct sequence or in random order). Bordin et al. concluded from their findings: "We feel that the necessity for testing the effect of context is underlined by the (theoretically) embarrassing results that the different contexts for the ratings in this study were a negligible source of variance in the agreement among raters" (p. 81). In other words, theoretically, the authors expected the absence of participant context to make a difference—their variable, the degree to which the therapist stays within the patient's frame of reference, seemed of necessity to require not only the therapist's statements but also those of the patient. The fact that these expected results did not show caused the authors to reconsider the validity of their measurement operation. This illustrates very nicely how resolution of a particular methodological issue for a process variable often provides important information regarding construct validity. Another interesting example of this same strategy is provided by Chinsky and Rappaport (1970), who challenge Traux and Carkhuff's (1967) conclusion regarding the effects of participant-context removal on accurate empathy ratings (see Chapter 4).

It is important in constructing and reporting on process systems to keep the three separate meanings of "unit" (scoring, contextual, and summarizing), as well as the participant-context issue, sharply distinguished. The distinctions will be incorporated in the subsequent analyses of major systems presented in Part II. The conclusion here is that, in choosing appropriate scoring, contextual, and summarizing units, the process investigator is assisted considerably by an intensive theoretical analysis of the construct; he also stands to gain substantatively by submitting his choice as well as alternatives to empirical test. Bordin et al. (1954) have repeatedly emphasized "that empirical tests of the questions should be made for each variable under consideration before the variable is used for theory testing" (p. 80).

Table 2.2 presents a summary of the "scoring" and "contextual" units employed by the authors of the seventeen major process systems analyzed in Part II of this volume. The following scoring units have been used:

1. The clause: whether independent or dependent; instances where either the subject or predicate is omitted but understood are considered as scorable clauses (Gottschalk and Gleser).
2. The sentence (also called "proposition" or "statement or meaning phrase"): the smallest portion of speech that can be fully understood by itself; a minimum free utterance, or the single free utterance (Dollard and Auld; Lennard and Bernstein; Murray).
3. The statement (also called "communication," "response," or "utterance"): an uninterrupted sequence of sentences uttered by either the patient or therapist; everything said between two therapist responses (for patient), and everything said between two patient responses (for therapist) (Butler, Rice, and Wagstaff; Rice; Lennard and Bernstein; Matarazzo and Saslow; Harway et al.; Siegman and Pope; Strupp).
4. The idea: a clearly indicated change in the subject matter or attitude of the patient's or therapist's thinking (Snyder).
5. The interaction exchange (also called "sequential dependency"): a therapist's statement followed by a patient's statement, or vice versa (Dollard and Auld; Lennard and Bernstein).

6. The time segment: primarily four- or five-minute segments extracted from tape-recordings of particular therapy sessions (Klein et al; Truax).

The most popular scoring unit used to date in psychotherapy process research is the statement. It is clear from Table 2.2 that investigators have been frequently imprecise in their use of the "contextual unit" for their respective systems.

Sampling Issues in Psychotherapy Process Research

The issues dealt with in this section are conceptually close to the unit problems discussed above. The unit problem has to do with the slice of psychotherapy communication necessary to assess validly a particular construct operationalized as a process variable. The issue in this section is representativeness: How representative are units of patient or therapist behaviors occurring in the larger context, that is, of an entire interview or of the entire therapy case? Unit choice determines the measurement of specific instances of patient or therapist behaviors being assessed. Sampling issues are concerned with whether and to what extent the particular instances are representative of behaviors occurring in entire therapy interviews as well as in entire therapy cases.

Much of the process research to date has been intensive analyses of one or several interview interactions. The number of interviews analyzed is relatively small. In these studies, sampling is not a significant issue, since an entire interaction is analyzed, and the amount of data from each interaction is small enough to be manageable. The researchers have not been primarily interested in generalizing their results.

The sampling issue becomes important when one is interested in describing the events of the entire psychotherapy (using a particular process variable of interest) for groups of cases. It is very possible that an investigator may possess tape recordings of a thousand or more individual sessions. How does one go about applying his particular process system to such a formidable collection of recorded therapy data? It is practically impossible and probably irrelevant to score each minute of the more than one thousand therapy tapes. Sampling obviously becomes crucial when one is confronted with this mass of data. Given the practical fact that one cannot analyze the total recorded data of the therapy interaction, how does one decide how much of the therapy continuum, and which stages of that continuum, to analyze?

The first and most important point to be made here (as with choice of unit) is that the sampling problem has to be considered within the particular theoretical framework, and for the particular constructs, one is studying. The answer to the sampling question depends on the questions one is asking of the data. For example, Rogers' (1957) "necessary and sufficient" therapist conditions are explicitly formulated to operate pervasively over the entire therapy encounter, to function independently of any particular problem being discussed, and to have their effect in a cumulative way over the therapy encounter. The sampling issue is resolved rather simply, consequently, by sampling at random–e.g. every third interview–the therapy interview continuum. This sampling is representative of the entire therapy interaction continuum, and no previous content editing is required.

Working with different variables within a different theoretical framework, one could very easily arrive at different sampling decisions. When dealing with Freudian constructs, one would likely have to start by editing each psychotherapy case into different problem or topic areas, as well as into different interactive conditions of patient and therapist. Analysis of patient resistance regarding sex, for example, might be scored from a fifteen-minute excerpt identified in the third session, a five-minute interchange in the seventh interview, and so on. The test of Freudian hypotheses regarding resistance to sex would be limited to these specified and identified interactive areas. Clearly the sampling problem is more complex for a test of Freudian variables than for Rogerian variables.

Sampling issues come down to two problems: (1) the problem of sample location for a particular therapy hour: Should it be extracted at random from the fifty minutes, or at some standard point (for example, late in the hour)? and (2) the problem of sample location for the entire series of therapy interviews: Which interviews (early, middle, late) in the case interaction should be sampled in order to tap the variables of theoretical interest? Most process investigators (with the exceptions of Kiesler et al., 1965, and Mintz, 1969) have neither considered nor empirically addressed these issues. Kiesler, Klein, and Mathieu (1965) considered the differential effects of sampling from various locations within a particular interview on Experiencing Scale ratings and from random and systematic sampling within individual sessions, for samples of neurotic, schizophrenic, and normal patients. Twenty-four therapy hours, chosen from both early and late interviews, were each divided into five successive eight-minute segments. Experiencing scores obtained for the three diagnositc groups were significantly different. The neurotic patients showed a consistently upward linear trend of experiencing–they were talking most meaningfully about themselves near the end of the hour. The schizophrenics showed a saw-toothed pattern and the normals an inverted U-shaped trend of experiencing. Next, two random samples were drawn from the same data and the results were compared with those obtained for the five systematically obtained time blocks. Different profiles of significance were obtained. One random sample and the later time blocks reflected differences between groups; the other random sample and the earlier time blocks did not. Klein et al. concluded:

> Random sampling may be superior in providing data more representative of the range of process in a given group and may afford more equitable coverage to several groups, provided that the number of observations is sufficiently large that the bias from unequal representation of certain interview points is minimized. Sampling of standard time periods may have more precision and offer better control of the time factor in small samples, but it may not always yield representative data or data that can be readily interpreted without supporting information regarding the specific nature of interview process trends. Thus, it is important to bear in mind that the precision of any systematic sampling is strictly contingent upon the amount of reliable information available to the researcher regarding trends in the population as a whole. (p. 33)

For the second sampling issue there are only two available studies, both dealing with the Experiencing variable. Rogers et al. (1967) and Kiesler (1971b) have demonstrated that the function of Experiencing over the first thirty therapy sessions takes a nonmonotonic function —it is U-shaped until approximately the twentieth interview, after which it again drops. The conclusion drawn for the Experiencing variable is that one can misrepresent the trend of Experiencing occurring from initiation to termination of therapy if he analyzes only a few points of the therapy sequence. Trends derived from samples from the second and second-from-last interviews, for example, would distort the trend of Experiencing that actually occurred in therapy; obviously it would be easy to draw erroneous conclusions from data based on very limited sampling. For the Experiencing variable, then, it is quite important to obtain many repeated measures across the interview sequence in order to obtain results representative of the behavior trends actually occurring for a particular case.

The important point for psychotherapy process research is that it is extremely important to consider these sampling issues for a particular variable of interest. One decides the issues on an a priori basis in line with the definition of the construct, but ultimately he must submit his sampling decisions to empirical test.

Data Form Issues

Which data medium best provides reliable and valid measures of a particular psychotherapy process variable? What is the differential information loss, in terms of the particular variable being measured, when one is scoring typewritten transcripts of the therapy interaction in contrast to audio tape recordings or silent or sound movies of the same interaction?

From the communication and linguistic framework developed in the previous chapter, one would expect different results from the various forms of raw data. The audio dimension adds the extralinguistic or paralinguistic variables of voice pitch, tempo, volume change, and so on that are lost in the typescripts. Movies add additional communication channels, supplying the kinesic, postural, and movement cues that are lost in audio recording.

The serious investigator will first consider the most appropriate data form for his particular process variable by submitting his construct to this kind of communicational-linguistic analysis. Yet one cannot decide the issue on an a priori basis alone. The researcher must submit the question to empirical test. Bordin et al. (1954) emphasized the same point.

> If one believes that a judge can get everything he needs for the judgment from the typescript, then there is no question as to how to present the material to him. Some researchers, however, might think that some variables depend also on nonlanguage factors such as tone of voice, emphasis on different words, and the like. An example is the variable of "warmth" in which it seems true on the face of it that a judge deprived of tone of voice would be judging something else besides warmth. On the face of it, however, is never the best basis for decisions, and one should test empirically before going on to relate judgments on one variable with judgments on another. (p. 80)

Several of the authors of the major systems presented later in this volume have considered the data form issue (Matarazzo and Saslow; Harway et al.; Traux; Gottschalk and Gleser). The reader can consult Part II for descriptions of these studies. Apparently, the only other study on this issue available in the literature is that of Giedt (1955), who focused primarily on clinicians' ability to make accurate judgments of a patient's personality and to predict his verbal behavior. Interviews with four patients were presented as silent films, written transcripts, sound recordings, or complete sound films to 48 psychiatrists, social workers, and psychologists who made ratings of the personality characteristics and predicted the responses to incomplete sentences of the patients who were interviewed. Giedt found that clinicians' assessment abilities interacted with the data media involved. (1) There was a markedly greater accuracy of personality ratings when content cues were included, as compared to the silent film. (2) Markedly better predictions were made from written transcripts, sound recordings, and complete sound films, than from silent films which actually led to predictions that were worse than could be expected on a chance basis. (3) In the case of the predictions, the level of accuracy varied for different patients, but the pattern for each over the four modes of presentation remained quite similar. But with the personality ratings, some patients were more accurately rated in one condition and less in another, which suggests considerable interaction between the effects of the patient being rated and the type of observation. Giedt's findings, at the least, suggest that similar interactions with data forms might be present in assessing psychotherapy process variables.

Table 2.3 presents a summary of the data forms used by authors of the seventeen major process systems presented in Part II of this volume. Inspection of the table reveals that of the systems, ten use typescripts only; three typically employ tape recordings only; one uses typescripts and tape recordings concurrently; one uses all the media, including typescripts, tape recordings, movies, and video tapes, and one initially used live observations but subsequently has switched to tape recordings. Typescripts, then, predominate, at least to date, as the preferred mode of presentation of interview data to judges for process assessment.

In the case of typescripts, there can be intertypist reliability problems. Bordin et al. (1954) caution that

> attention should be called to the problems associated with clear recordings and consequently the reliability of transcriptions. On the surface, these seem to be of little importance, since this aspect of engineering is much simpler than human interaction. Consequently, a belief has developed that electrical recording guarantees objectivity in research on interview material. Unfortunately, we have not always found this guarantee to hold. Informal studies of intertypist agreement in transcribing interviews indicate that objectivity is highly dependent on the quality of the original tapes. Even good tapes are to some extent projective techniques for typists, raising problems which may be interesting in themselves, but not helpful to research in psychotherapy. In some cases we found complete reversals of meaning in therapist or patient statements from one typist to another. Hence, selectivity must be exercised in choosing those recordings which will be used as data.

> Another method of insuring greater objectivity in transcriptions includes the development of standard instructions to typists for indicating pauses, voice inflection, laughter, weeping, and the sequence and numbering of responses. (p. 81)

An excellent example of this standardization can be found in Gottschalk, Winget, and Gleser's (1969) manual for their process variables. These authors present extensive rules for preparing typescript verbal samples for coding (see Gottschalk, Winget, and Gleser, 1969, p. 10ff).

Dimensionality Considerations

Process workers at some point should be concerned whether their particular variable is measuring a single (unitary) dimension rather than several confounded and intermeshed factors. This dimensional unraveling is crucial before accurate and precise interpretation of variable correlations is possible.

When one is working with multiple process variables, such as several rating scales or omnibus-like category systems, the techniques of factor analysis can be utilized for this dimensional analysis. However, the issue is equally important when dealing with single process instruments. As Bordin et al. (1954) point out:

> In applying currently used measurement devices to any data, one must first be aware of the extent to which the device itself predetermines the form in which the data are studied. As Coombs has pointed out, one may impose unidimensionality upon an attribute when, in fact, it does not exist. Such an imposition is possible by forcing raters to rate every stimulus along some arbitrarily defined unidimensional continuum, even though the raters may not agree that every stimulus belongs on that continuum. Such is the case with the typical "Q sort" situation. In fact, in "Q sorting," the measurement device imposes not only unidimensionality, but also the shape of the distribution and the characteristics of an interval scale. Rating scales, which are the most frequently used measurement devices for psychotherapy variables, force data into unidimensional continua. (p. 79)

Bordin and his associates and Howe and Pope (see Chapter 5) have considered this issue in detail for their Depth of Interpretation scale and Therapist Activity Level scale, respectively. Bordin's group has applied Coombs' scaling technique, while Howe and Pope have used Osgood's semantic differential as devices for extracting and describing the dimensions operative in their respective therapist scales.

Osburn (1952) analyzed a variable defined as ambiguity of a therapist's behavior in defining himself and the therapeutic task. This variable was subjected to a test of the assumption of unidimensionality, and support was found for the assumption.

As Bordin et al. (1954) state, "There are . . . many variables in psychotherapy research whose unidimensionality [have] not yet been demonstrated" (p. 79). At the very least, this suggests that process investigators must be cautious about interpreting the relationships found for their particular variables since some other intermeshed dimensions, or different ones entirely, may actually be operative. Also, in some cases when low interjudge reliabilities are obtained for a particular variable, this occurrence can reflect that the assumed dimension of study is multiple rather than unitary.

Clinical Sophistication of Judges

The process researcher must consider the level of clinical experience and/or theoretical sophistication necessary for judges who do the codings or make the ratings for his particular process variable. This issue is intimately tied to the degree of inference required of the judging task, and hence is tied to Marsden's (1965) distinction between classical and contextual models of content analysis. To the extent that one's variable of interest falls near the classical model end of the continuum, he can ignore the necessity for sophisticated judges; to the extent that his system falls near the contextual model end-point, the necessity for sophisticated judges becomes crucial. Another way of saying this, of course, is that to the extent the judging task itself requires inference regarding complex and higher-level theoretical constructs, sophisticated judges become a necessity.

Bordin et al. (1954) have something to say about this issue also.

> One theory, namely the psychoanalytic, stresses freedom from personal conflict in training for therapists. Presumably, this theory would also state that those raters who are the most free of personal conflict would be the most sensitive to emotionally toned aspects and significances of therapeutic interactions. Requiring all raters to be free of conflict would cut down on the amount of research completed, but requiring training or experience in psychotherapy leads to problems which are just as hard to deal with. . . . It is necessary that judges have acquired the observational attitudes which will make for sensitivity to the phenomena they are asked to judge. (p. 81)

Again, few process investigators have empirically addressed this issue. Kiesler (1970) compared Experiencing ratings of two groups of four judges each, one group composed of naive undergraduate judges, the other of clinically sophisticated and experienced therapist judges. The findings showed that the reliabilities obtained for the two groups were equivalent and high (in the 90s). Ratings from the two groups correlated very highly, and the means and variances were almost identical. The author concluded that when groups of clinically experienced and naive judges rate the same tape-recorded samples of individual psychotherapy the resulting Experiencing ratings are equivalent in all respects. Shapiro (1968a, 1968b) and Shapiro, Foster, and Powell (1968) found that, if asked to rate along a seven-point semantic differential scale, neophyte raters (college undergraduates) can do about as well as highly trained raters, both in reliability and validity. There are only slight advantages discernible for the experts. They found further that a therapist's facial cues are more important for warmth and empathy ratings than are his bodily cues (judged from still pictures), especially for the neophyte rater.

Table 2.4 presents a summary of the levels of clinical sophistication and experience required for judges using the seventeen major systems presented in Part II of this volume. Of the systems, six require considerable experience and sophistication (professional psychotherapists), two demand only minimal experience and sophistication (usually graduate students in clinical training), five employ primarily clinically naive and unsophisticated judges (usually undergraduates), and four demand a level of experience that is either unspecified or unclear. Table 2.4 also indicates whether the respective investigators have published or otherwise made available training manuals for their systems. A training manual typically provides theoretical and methodological discussions, reviews of studies using the system, detailed definitions of the categories or scale stages, examples of these categories or scale stages, rules for scoring, and standard procedures for training judges in the use of the system. To date, only five of the systems are available in training manual form (Dollard and Auld; Gottschalk and Gleser; Hall and Van De Castle; Klein et al.; and Matarazzo and Wiens). Nevertheless, the emergence of these five manuals should considerably increase the applications of the systems, as well as spur other investigators to emulate these laudable examples.

It is necessary for a process investigator to consider the required level of clinical sophistication of the judges who will be assessing his process variable. Valuable information about his variable can be gained, furthermore, if he empirically assesses the differential effects of using judges varying in level of sophistication. The economics of the situation are, of course, that considerable financial savings result if one can legitimately use naive judges as raters; in addition, naive judges are much more readily available for psychotherapy process analysis.

Training of Judges

The level of training required of judges varies directly with the clarity of the definition of the variable being assessed, as well as with the degree of inference required in the judgmental task. The degree of training necessary, then, is also related to Marsden's continuum of classical and contextual content-analysis models.

Experience in psychotherapy process research seems to indicate that high interjudge reliability can be more easily obtained when the variables being measured are tied rather closely to observable patient and therapist behaviors; the inferential judgments required of the raters are then kept at a minimum (the classical model). High interjudge reliability is also obtained when judges have undergone standardized and relatively intensive training. It seems that future process investigations might profit from this experience. Bordin et al. (1954) suggest that

> as different theories of psychotherapy stress different aspects of training for therapists, so might they stress different aspects of training for raters of therapy variables. . . . In some cases, not to specify prerequisite training may be equivalent to asking an observer to describe a microscopic organism without benefit of a microscope. On the other hand, we want to be sure that training contributes only sensitivity to phenomena and not sensitivity to [irrelevant] catch phrases. . . . If two experts agree, we want to be sure that they are not simply involved in a theoretical *folie a deux*. . . . In developing effective communication to judges one must first evolve a clear and concrete definition of the variable under consideration. Next, instructions must be written in terminology which is maximally communicative to the judges. . . . No matter how self-evident the issue of training may be, here again we have something which can and should be subjected to empirical test. (pp. 80-81)

Interjudge and Intrajudge Scoring Reliability

There are several important distinctions to keep in mind when discussing reliability for psychotherapy process research. First, it is crucial to differentiate the reliability of the behavior being scored from the reliability of the scoring process itself. "In assessing the reliability of a system of . . . observation, it is necessary to differentiate the reliability of the behavior being observed from the reliability of the categorization or rating which is made of that behavior. . . . The consistency of behavior is a substantive problem, whereas the consistency of an observer is a methodological problem. Once the consistency of an observer has been established, it becomes possible to tackle the problem of the consistency of the behavior" (Heyns and Zander, 1966, p. 410). The remainder of this section is concerned only with scorer reliability.

It is also important to distinguish between the reliability of the unitization process and of the scoring process. This distinction becomes relevant when determination of the "scoring unit" is not an automatic or standardized process (such as taking five-minute samples, or using "words" as scoring units), but requires some level of inference. If one is using "ideas" as his unit (for example, Snyder, 1945) one cannot automatically assume that his unitization represents a reliable event; unless clear definitions of what constitutes an idea are presented, the process is likely to be unreliable. In this case, separate assessment of reliability of the unitization process is required. It might be helpful to remember that Dollard and Auld (1959; see also Auld and White, 1956) went to considerable trouble to dictate the criteria for unitizing "the sentence." Hence, in those cases where high interjudge reliability is not obviously apparent for the unitization process, it is necessary for the investigator to present reliability figures for both his unitization and his scoring processes. As Dittes (1959) observes: "In view of the scant attention previously given to unitizing, it is clear that Murray (1955, 1956) poineered in drawing attention to its importance, in making the unitizing task distinct from categorizing, in formulating definitions of the unit, and in making an adequate appraisal of reliability of unitizing" (p. 340).

The investigator should present reliability figures for the particular "summarizing units" he is using in his data analyses. As Heyns and Zander (1966) emphasize, "the investigator ought to be concerned with the reliability of the measure actually used in the analysis of the data. For example, it is a matter of relative unimportance whether observers agree with respect to the number of units of behavior assigned to a specific individual, if the score with which the investigator is concerned is the number of units in each category made by the group as a whole" (p. 412).

The next distinction, between intrajudge and interjudge reliability, is etymologically obvious. But, interestingly, few process researchers present figures concerning the consistency and equivalency with which the same judge scores the same units at two different times, that is, a stability coefficient. The more crucial coefficient is, admittedly, that of interjudge consistency since the scores used in data analyses are typically averages of two or more judges' ratings of the same units.

Finally, it is helpful to keep in mind that different problems and different statistics are involved in assessing reliability for nominal (category systems) in contrast to ordinal (dimensional rating) scales. For the ordinal scales, if only two judges are involved, various correlation coefficients can be used to assess interjudge reliability; if more than two judges are involved, the investigator can choose among Ebel's (1951), Horst's (1949), and Cronbach, Rajaratnam, and Gleser's (1963) assessment formulas.

The case for assessing interjudge reliability for category or classification systems is actually more complex than for ordinal scales. Dollard and Auld (1959) and Dittes (1959) take some pains to discuss the choices involved. They reject the percentage of agreement index since it yields biased estimates of interjudge reliability. This index is obtained by calculating the percentage of the total number of items which are classified in the same way by two or more observers. Dollard and Auld (1959) conclude:

> In view of the tendency of the percentage-of-agreement index to rise with fewer categories and whenever some few categories get a lion's share of the classified units, one cannot use percentage-of-agreement to compare the reliabilities of content-analysis systems having different numbers of categories, or differing in the degree to which units are concentrated in a few of the categories. . . . The index has still another flaw: In a system having more than two categories, it tells us only the over-all level of agreement, failing to give any indication of which categories are well discriminated and which are poorly discriminated. (pp. 305-306)

In regard to the use of chi-square (which can be computed by comparing the frequency of assignment of units to various categories by the scorers), Dittes (1959) concludes that the index "is a risky one to use in deciding how well the scorers agree; for the smaller the sample, the more likely one would be to suppose that they were agreeing well—but one's trust in the result would most likely be shattered if one had a larger sample" (p. 344).

Both Dollard and Auld (1959) and Dittes (1959) conclude that the fewest problems are involved if one uses Kendall's 1938 *tau* as his assessment of interjudge reliability for category systems. "Like the percentage-of-agreement index, *tau* counts as 'agreement' only the concordance of scorers on individual items. . . . But *tau*, unlike the percentage-of-agreement measure, is not inflated by the possibility of hitting on similar categorizations by chance. With *tau* this chance level of agreement has, so to speak, been subtracted out" (Dittes, 1959, p. 343). Dollard and Auld (1959) argue:

> This coefficient, as we use it, is based on a set of 2 x 2 tables, one table for each category; and so we avoid the bais of increased index when there are fewer categories in the whole system. *Tau* corrects for concentration of the units, because the computation of *tau* in effect subtracts the chance agreement from the total agreements, thereby preventing high concentration, which raises chance agreement, from raising the coefficient. Finally, *tau* is computed for each category separately, so that deficiencies of individual categories are not masked by the excellences of other categories within a summary index for the system as a whole. (p. 306)

Dollard and Auld presented both tau and tetrachoric correlation coefficients for the various categories of their content analysis system (see Chapter 3), which seems to represent a useful compromise between what is statistically and what is traditionally indicated. It appears the area of reliability analysis for nominal systems might be worth exploring further. Until that occurs, process researchers using category systems can profit considerably from Dollard and Auld as well as from Dittes.

Computerization of Psychotherapy Process Analysis

Computers have been applied for some time to the areas of automated education, medical administration and diagnosis, and more recently to psychological diagnosis. In the 1960s computers were applied in content analysis generally, and more specifically in the content analysis of psychotherapy interviews. Just as the tape recorder gave a tremendous boost to scientific analysis of psychotherapy, so it is hoped that computer analysis will permit a new era of analytic progress.

The basic aspect of the computer that makes its use in content analysis a possibility is the fact that "although a computer, with its programs, usually uses numbers . . . the input and output equipment associated with a computer can take care of translating letters (and words) into numbers and vice versa. Thus, a computer has the potentiality for processing huge quantities of written or alphabetic data as well as numbers" (Meany, 1962, p. 4). Holsti (1969) lists the advantages of this technology for content analysis:

> Probably the most important development in content analysis . . . has been the development of a wide variety of computer-based techniques. . . . We can consider the role of the computer in improving the quality of inference in several ways. (*a*) Perhaps the most obvious of these is that because computers

> improve the reliability of coding they enhance the quality of inference. . . . (*b*) One of the limitations of computers—that their tolerance for ambiguity is zero—can also contribute to the quality of inference by forcing greater clarity in the explication of theory. . . . (*c*) The ability of computers to process reliably enormous quantities of documentary data is also an obvious point that requires little elaboration. . . . Finally, (*d*) there are indications that recent developments in computer-based content analysis may facilitate development of standard categories. (pp. 118-20)

In psychotherapy research, computers have been used in two ways: as high-speed content coding systems, and as simulators of human interaction in the interview.

> For many investigators the computer has been a substitute for a great army of clerks in accomplishing the large-scale task of counting many thousands of words or phrases. More recently, the computer has been used to simulate one or both sides of interview situations, and thus has required the development of more complex methods for the computer to deal with language content. As computers have become capable of interacting with human users in a conversational fashion, it has been necessary to develop recognition methods for the immediate handling of human responses. (Starkweather, 1969, p. 339)

One of the important functions of the Annenberg conference on content analysis (see Chapter I) was that for the first time investigators concerned with different approaches to computer-aided content anlysis assembled and discussed their work. The publication resulting from that conference (Gerbner et al., 1969) and Taylor (1970) are the best sources for obtaining an overview and comparison of the available computer-aided content-analysis approaches. The assembled investigators' "purposes in being involved in computer-aided content analysis were as varied as the fields they represented: political science, psychiatry, sociology, English, and social psychology. Each had a complicated data-analysis problem. Each was trying to solve his problem in a way that seemed most reasonable. Yet, together, their approaches were very different" (Stone, 1969a, p. 335).

Computer Approaches

The remainder of this section will present very briefly descriptions of the computer approaches developed for content analysis and interactional simulation of psychotherapy interviews. It will draw heavily on Gerbner et al. (1959). The reader is referred to that volume and to Taylor (1970) as well as to the original sources cited for further information and detail.

THE GENERAL INQUIRER

If, in content analysis of interview material, one tries for

> prearranged structure and automated procedures which can be done entirely by computer, we must build a general purpose dictionary into a computer program in sufficient detail that it can handle the coding of verbal material from a variety of patients. We take on a task which is at least as complex as the problem of automatic translation of language, and we do not have as firm a criterion against which to work. This approach undoubtedly requires construction of an extremely large dictionary and this, in turn, demands a time consuming search for each word and each phrase in the text we are analyzing. One of the most complete attempts in this direction has been the development . . . of the *General Inquirer* (Stone et al., 1962, 1966). (Starkweather and Decker, 1964, p. 875)

> This program expects incoming textual data to be arranged as sentences. It examines the text by making references to a dictionary of word stems, using a dictionary that is variable and that may be developed with specific relevance and classifications useful for a particular area of investigation. Dictionaries for the General Inquirer, for example, have been developed to analyze political documents (by Holsti) and psychiatric interviews (by Stone). More general dictionaries are also used, and rules have been developed to code words which have multiple meanings. The sentence is used as a unit of measurement (thus becoming the "scoring unit"), and the incoming text is sometimes coded and preedited for the syntax position of words within sentences. (Starkweather, 1969, p. 340)

With this procedure, patients' interviews must still be typed from tapes and categorized. But once this is done, answers to statistical questions can be gained extremely rapidly.

HARWAY - IKER AND STARKWEATHER - DECKER APPROACH

Another set of approaches are those of Harway and Iker (1964) and Starkweather and Decker (1964), who independently developed almost identical procedures.

> Quantatative method developed for the study of verbatim transcripts of spoken material has tended to focus on word usage. The

> computer has been used as a clerical assistance to develop a form of specialized dictionary which applies only to the word usage of an individual person, or to specific documents under study. Examples of this may be observed in the work of Harway and Iker (1964) and Starkweather and Decker (1964). Both of these approaches have resulted in a statistical definition of word groups which were associated with each other in an individual speaker's usage. Such methods have been applied in a number of psychiatric case studies. (Starkweather, 1969, p. 340)

The total text to be analyzed is reduced by the computer's grouping words of different grammatical form, apparent synonyms, and the like. Then the computer divides the text into small (summarizing) units, one minute for Harway and Iker, and 200 words for Starkweather and Decker. It subsequently intercorrelates the frequency of words across units, and factor analyzes the resulting matrix. In therapy research, one can trace the trends of the factors across the interview segments and search for relationships. The methodology has so far been used primarily in single case studies for exploratory purposes.

Compared to the General Inquirer,

> This approach tends to center on the word as a unit for measurement, rather than the sentence. This avoids some problems encountered in handling unrehearsed spoken language rather than written language, but limits the linguistic complexity of the analysis. The method tends to use statistical procedures such as factor analysis or cluster analysis to develop a description of structure in the obtained data. Investigations have been interested in the change shown in such factors across time and for a change in speaking situation, as well as differences in such structure for different people. (Starkweather, l969, pp. 340-41)

SIMULATED COMPUTER INTERACTION

Simulated computer interaction methods basically involve use of programmed branching sequences.

> The computer's instructions can . . . be written to provide for "branching" from the fixed sequence to various alternative sequences. For example, in a psychotherapy interview the therapist could vary (or branch) his questions depending on the previous responses of the patient: that is, he could ask about either the patient's father or work situation, depending on the patient's previous responses. . . . Thus, branching would allow for flexibility in a psychotherapy program. (Meany, 1962, p.5)

When we become involved in the use of a computer for interaction between man and machine, it becomes necessary to find methods for immediate content analysis which can be specified and programmed as an entirely automatic process. The machine must have a means to recognize language responses by a subject and rapidly develop appropriate replies in return. We may look upon such activities as attempts to simulate human information processing, and we may build machine methods to imitate human activity in as many respects as possible. On the other hand, we may simply use whatever machine methods seem practical and appropriate in view of current machine capability and our present state of knowledge about conversational language. The results may or may not model what humans do.

Kennneth Colby's (1966, 1967) program attempts to build up assocations, or a belief structure, characteristic of a respondent dealing with an interactive system. Bellman, Friend, and Kurland (1966) describe the scoring of responses as having convergent versus divergent attributes with reference to the goals of an interview. Their program models the interview as a multi-stage decision process having a branching structure of potential questions and replies. Joseph Weizenbaum (1966, 1967) has been particularly interested in the creditability of machine response to a subject who is interacting with it in a conversational fashion. . . . Starkweather has developed similar concerns through attempts to use the computer conversationally (Starkweather, 1965, 1967). (Starkweather, 1969, pp. 341-42)

COMPUTER PROCESSING OF INTERACTION DATA

Several psychotherapy researchers have been interested in formal interactional variables such as duration of talk and silence by patient and therapist in psychotherapy interviews (see Lennard and Bernstein; Matarazzo, Chapter 3 below; and Siegman and Pope, Chapter 4 below). Recently computer technology has been developed for automatic analysis of these promising interaction variables. Wiens, Matarazzo, and Saslow (1965) developed the Interaction Recorder, an electronic punched-paper tape unit, leading directly to computer analysis, for recording their speech and silence duration variables during interviews. Jaffe and Feldstein (1970) outlined the final development of a completely automated technique which measures the same variables and feeds directly into a computer system. The Automatic Vocal Transaction Analyzer (AVTA) is based on audio pickup of interview interaction directly from a two-channel tape recorder.

It is apparent that computer applications in psychotherapy process research offer exciting possibilities for advancing knowledge in the area. Some of the approaches have already demonstrated their utility, while the promise of others is less clear cut. Nevertheless, it seems clear the process investigator of the future will need to keep close tabs on developments in computer applications to psychotherapy. If he doesn't, he may be ignorant of technology that could make his scientific efforts markedly simpler and considerably more fruitful. On the other hand, it seems appropriate to keep in mind Ford and Urban's (1969) caution: "Computers can handle more data, but they can't select the important variables nor can they provide the conceptual framework for understanding results" (p. 356).

Some Miscellaneous Considerations

The process investigator might gain considerably by having a check on the validity of the viewpoint arrived at by judges using his system or scale, by assessing both the patient's and therapist's viewpoints of what is occurring in psychotherapy sessions. Interesting and marked discrepancies between these viewpoints have appeared in the literature (Feifel and Eells, 1963; Kamin and Caughlan, 1963; Keith-Spiegel and Spiegel, 1967; Muench, 1965; Robertson, 1957; Rogers et al., 1967), and these discrepancies must be dealt with.

Second, the researcher can obtain much in terms of construct validity evidence by attempting to show that his scale results cannot be explained more parsimoniously. Is it possible, for example, that formal content variables such as duration of talk or silence, or other paralinguistic of kinesic variables, can account for much of the variance present in the results he obtains with his scale measure? To evaluate whether experiencing ratings are confounded by speech patterns of the therapist or patient, Kiesler, Mathieu, and Klein (1967) compared EXP ratings with Interaction Chronograph measures taken from the same eight-minute segments of therapy in twenty-four cases. There was no evidence that the EXP ratings were systematically influenced by the amount or tempo of the patient's speech, by the amount or tempo of the therapist's speech, or by any other interaction characteristics measured. Further, when the covariance for IC variables was partialled out, previously obtained differences in EXP for neurotics, schizophrenics, and normals were not altered significantly. The authors concluded that "these findings were consistent with our intention that EXP ratings assess the quality of the patient's verbal expression, independent of the rate of speech or other interactional characteristics of the therapy interaction."

Finally, psychotherapy process researchers must become more cognizant of each other's work and measuring instruments. As emphasized in Chapter 1, process scales have multiplied with much overlap, divergent results, and little integration of closely related predecessors. It is hoped that this volume will henceforth make it inexcusable for this kind of ignorance of the work of others to occur.

Summary: A Critical Framework for Evaluating Process Systems

One needs to concern himself with a long-range program of both methodological and substantative research when he introduces a new process instrument for investigating psychotherapy interviews. The many one-shot attempts pervasive in the literature can only be frustrating to the serious investigator. It is only by painstaking confrontation with these basic issues, however, that psychotherapy process research will move forward on a solid methodological foundation.

References

Auerbach, A. H. and Luborsky, L. Accuracy of judgments of psychotherapy and the nature of the "good hour." In J. M. Shlien et al. (Eds.), *Research in Psychotherapy*, Vol. 3. Washington, D.C.: American Psychological Association, 1968. Pp. 155-68.

Auld, F., Jr., and Murray, E. J. Content-analysis studies of psychotherapy. *Psychological Bulletin*, 1955, 52, 377-95.

Auld, F., Jr., and White, A. Rules for dividing interviews into sentences. *Journal of Psychology*, 1956, 42, 273-81.

Bellman, R., Friend, M. B., and Kurland, L. *A simulation of the initial psychiatric interview*. Santa Monica, Cal.: The Rand Corporation, 1966.

Berelson, B. *Content analysis in communication research*. Glencoe, Ill.: Free Press, 1952.

Berman, L. Some problems in the evaluation of psychoanalysis as a therapeutic procedure. *Psychiatry*, 1955, 18, 387-90.

Bordin, E. S., Cutler, R. L., Dittmann, A. T., Harway, N. I., Raush, H. L., and Rigler, D. Measurement problems in process research on psychotherapy. *Journal of Consulting Psychology*, 1954, 18, 79-82.

Brody, E. B., Newman, R., and Redlich, F. C. Sound recording: the problem of evidence in psychiatry. *Science*, 1951, 113, 379-80.

Carmichael, H. T. Sound–film recording of psychoanalytic therapy: a therapist's experience and reactions. In L. A. Gottchalk and A. H. Auerbach (Eds.), *Methods of research in psychotherapy*. New York: Appleton-Century-Crofts, 1966. Pp. 50-59.

Cartwright, D. S. A rapid nonparametric estimate of multi-judge reliability. *Psychometrika*, 1956, 21, 17-29.

________. Annotated bibliography of research and theory construction in client-centered therapy. *Journal of Counseling Psychology*, 1957, 4, 82-100.

________. Analysis of qualitative material. In L. Festinger and D. Katz (Eds.), *Research methods in the behavioral sciences*. New York: Holt, Rinehart, and Winston, 1966. Pp. 421-70.

Cassota, L., Feldstein, S., and Jaffe, J. AVTA: a device for automatic vocal transaction analysis. *Journal of the Experimental Analysis of Behavior*, 1964, 7, 99-104.

Chinsky, J. M., and Rappaport, J. Brief critique of the meaning and reliability of "Accurate Empathy" ratings. *Psychological Bulletin*, 1970, 73, 379-82.

Cohen, R. A., and Cohen, M. B. Research in psychotherapy: a preliminary report. *Psychiatry*, 1961, 24, 46ff.

Colby, K. M. Experimental treatment of neurotic computer program. *Archives of General Psychiatry*, 1964, 10, 220-27.

Colby, K. M., Watt, J., and Gilbert, J. P. A computer model psychotherapy. *Journal of Nervous and Mental Disease*, 1966, 142, 148-52.

Colby, K. M. Computer simulation of change in personal belief systems. *Behavioral Science*, 1967, 12, 248-53.

Covner, B. J. Studies in phonographic recordings of verbal material: I. The use of phonographic recordings in counseling practice and research. *Journal of Consulting Psychology*, 1942, 6, 105-13.

———. Studies in phonographic recordings of verbal material: III. The completeness and accuracy of counseling interview reports. *Journal of General Psychology*, 1944 30, 181-203. (a)

———. Studies in phonographic recordings of verbal material: IV. Written reports of interviews. *Journal of Applied Psychology*, 1944, 28, 89-98. (b)

Cronbach, L. J., Rajaratnam, N., and Gleser, G. C. Theory of generalizability: a liberalization of reliability theory. *British Journal of Statistical Psychology*, 1963, 16, 137-63.

Cutler, R. L., Bordin, E. S., Williams, J., and Rigler, D. Psychoanalysts as expert observers of the therapy process. *Journal of Consulting Psychology*, 1958, 22, 335-40.

Dipboye, W. J. Analysis of counselor style by discussing units. *Journal of Counseling Psychology*, 1954, 1, 21-26.

Dittes, J. E. Previous studies bearing on content analysis of psychotherapy. In J. Dollard and F. Auld, Jr. *Scoring human motives: a manual*. New Haven, Conn.: Yale University Press, 1959. Pp. 325-51.

Dollard, J., and Auld, F., Jr. *Scoring human motives: a manual*. New Haven, Conn.: Yale University Press, 1959.

Ebel, R. L. Estimation of reliability of ratings. *Psychometrika*, 1951, 16, 407-24.

Ekman, P., and Friesen, W. V. Nonverbal behavior in psychotherapy research. In J. M. Shlien et al. (Eds.), *Research in psychotherapy*. Vol. 3. Washington, D.C.: American Psychological Association, 1968, Pp. 179-216.

Feifel, H., and Eells, J. Patients and therapists assess the same psychotherapy. *Journal of Consulting Psychology*, 1963, 27, 310-18.

Ford, D. H., and Urban, H. B. Psychotherapy. *Annual Review of Psychology*, 1967, 18, 333-72.

Ford, J. D., Jr. Automatic detection of psychological dimensions in psychotherapy transcripts by means of content words. *SP Series: SP-1220*. Santa Monica, Cal.: System Development Corporation, 1963.

George, A. L., Quantitative and qualitative approaches to content analysis. In I. de Sola Pool (Ed.), *Trends in content analysis*. Urbana: University of Illinois Press, 1959. Pp. 7-32.

Gerbner, G., Holsti, O. R., Krippendorf, K., Paisley, W. J., and Stone, P. J. (Eds.). *The analysis of communication content*. New York: Wiley, 1969.

Giedt, F. H. Comparison of visual, content, and auditory cues in interviewing. *Journal of Consulting Psychology*, 1955, 19, 407-16.

Goldhammer, D. H. Toward a more general inquirer: convergence of structure and context of meaning. In G. Gerbner, P. R. Holsti, K. Krippendorf, W. J. Paisley, and P. J. Stone (Eds.), *The analysis of communication content.* New York: Wiley, 1969. Pp. 343-54.

Gottschalk, L. A. (Ed.) *Comparative psycholinguistic analysis of two psychotherapeutic interviews.* New York: International Universities Press, 1961.

Gottschalk, L. A., Winget, C. N., and Gleser, G. C. *Manual of instructions for using the Gottschalk-Gleser content analysis scales.* Berkeley: University of California Press, 1969.

Greenblatt, M., Dimascio, A., Sutter, E., Watson, P. D., and Kanter, S. S. The polygraph approach to research on psychotherapy. *Journal of Nervous and Mental Disease*, 1954, 120, 413-15.

Guetzkow, A. Unitizing and categorizing problems in coding qualitative data. *Journal of Clinical Psychology*, 1950, 6, 47-58.

Haggard, E. A., Hiken, J. R., and Isaacs, K. S. Some effects of recording and filming on the psychotherapeutic process. *Psychiatry*, 1965, 28, 169-91.

Hall, C. S., and Van De Castle, R. L. *The content analysis of dreams.* New York: Appleton-Century-Crofts, 1966.

Hargreaves, W. A. A model for speech unit duration. *Language and Speech*, 1960, 3, 164-73.

Harper, R. A., and Hudson, J. W. The use of recordings in marriage counseling: a preliminary empirical investigation. *Marriage and Family Living*, 1952, 14, 332-34.

Harway, N. I., and Iker, H. P. Computer analysis of content in psychotherapy. *Psychological Reports*, 1964, 14, 720-22.

Heynes, R. W., and Zander, A. F. Observation of group behavior. In L. Festinger and D. Katz (Eds.), *Research methods in the behavioral sciences.* New York: Holt, Rinehart, and Winston, 1966. Pp. 381-417.

Holsti, O. R. A computer content-analysis program for analyzing attitudes: the measurement of qualities and performance. In G. Gerbner, O. R. Holsti, K. Krippendorf, W. J. Paisley, and P. J. Stone (Eds.), *The analysis of communication content.* New York: Wiley, 1969. Pp. 355-80.

Horst, P. A generalized expression for the reliability of measures. *Psychometrika*, 1949, 14, 21-31.

Iker, H. P., and Harway, N. I. A computer systems approach toward the recognition and analysis of content. In G. Gerbner, O. R. Holsti, K. Krippendorf, W. J. Paisley, and P. J. Stone (Eds.), *The analysis of communication content.* New York: Wiley, 1969. Pp. 381-406.

Jaffe, J. Electronic computer in psychoanalytic research. In J. H. Masserman, (Ed.), *Science and Psychoanalysis.* Vol. 6 New York: Grune & Stratton, 1963. Pp. 160-70.

Jaffe, J., and Feldstein, S. *Rhythms of dialogue.* New York: Academic Press, 1970.

Janis, I. The psychoanalytic interview as an observational method. In G. Kindsey (Ed.), *Assessment of human motives.* New York: Holt, Rinehart, and Winston, 1958. Pp. 149-82.

Kamin, I., and Caughlan, J. Patients report the subjective experience of outpatient psychotherapy: a follow-up study. *American Journal of Psychotherapy*, 1963, 17, 660-68.

Keith-Spiegel, P., and Spiegel, D. Perceived helpfulness of others as a function of compatible intelligence levels. *Journal of Counseling Psychology*, 1967, 14, 61-62.

Kendall, M. G. A new measure of rank correlation. *Biometrika*, 1938, 30, 81-93.

Kiesler, D. J. Basic methodological issues implicit in psychotherapy process research. *American Journal of Psychotherapy*, 1966, 20, 135-55.

———.Comparison of Experiencing Scale ratings of naive vs. clinically sophisticated judges. *Journal of Consulting and Clinical Psychology*, 1970, 35, 134.

——— Experimental designs in psychotherapy research. In A. E. Bergin and S. L. Garfield (Eds.), *Handbook of psychotherapy and behavior change*. New York: Wiley, 1971. Pp. 36-74. (a)

———. Patient experiencing and successful outcome in individual psychotherapy of schizophrenics and psychoneurotics. *Journal of Consulting and Clinical Psychology*, 1971,37,370-85. (b)

Kiesler, D. J., Klein, M. H., and Mathieu, P. L. Sampling from the recorder therapy interview: the problem of segment location. *Journal of Consulting Psychology*, 1965, 29, 337-44.

Kiesler, D. J., Mathieu, P. L. and Klein, M. H. Sampling from the recorded therapy interview: a comparative study of different segment lengths. *Journal of Consulting Psychology*, 1964, 28, 349-57.

———. Patient experiencing level and interaction chronograph variables in therapy interview segments. *Journal of Consulting Psychology*, 1967, 31, 224.

Klein, M. H., Mathieu, P. L., Gendlin, E. T., and Kiesler, D. J. *The experiencing scale: a research and training manual*. Madison: Bureau of Audio-Visual Instruction, University of Wisconsin, 1970.

Kogan, L. S. The electrical recording of social casework interviews. *Social Casework*, 1950, 31, 371-78.

Kubie, L. S. Problems and techniques of psychoanalytic validation and progress. In E. Pumpian-Mindlin (Ed.), *Psychoanalysis as science*. Stanford, Cal.: Stanford University Press, 1952. Pp. 46-124.

Lamb, R., and Mahl, G. F. Manifest reactions of patients and interviewers to the use of sound recording in the psychiatric interview. *American Journal of Psychiatry*, 1956, 112, 731-37.

Lasswell, H. D. The problem of adequate personality records: a proposal. *American Journal of Psychiatry*, 1928, 85, 1057-66.

———.Verbal references and physiological changes during the psychoanalytic interview: a preliminary communication. *Psychoanalytic Review*, 1935, 22, 10-24.

Mahl, G. F., Dollard, J., and Redlich, F. Facilities for the sound recording and observation of interviews. *Science*, 1954, 120, 235-39.

Marsden, G. Content-analysis studies of therapeutic interviews: 1954 to 1964. *Psychological Bulletin*, 1965, 63, 298-321.

———.Content-analysis studies of psychotherapy: 1954 through 1968. In A. E. Bergin and S. L. Garfield (Eds.), *Handbook of psychotherapy and behavior change*. New York: Wiley, 1971. Pp. 345-407.

Meany, J. The automation of psychotherapy. *SP Series: SP-1050*. Santa Monica, Cal.: System Development Corporation, 1962.

Mintz, J. Dimensions of psychotherapy and their relation to outcome. Unpublished doctoral dissertation, New York University, 1969.

Morris, R. L., Johnston, G. I., Bailey, D. D., and Wiens, A. N. A twenty-four channel temporal-event digital recording system. *Medical Research Engineering*, 1968, 7, 32-37.

Mosier, C. I. On the reliability of a weighted composite. *Psychometrika*, 1943, 8, 161-68.

Muench, G. A. An investigation of the efficacy of time limited psychotherapy. *Journal of Counseling Psychology*, 1965, 12, 294-98.

Muthard, J. E. The relative effectiveness of large units used in interview analysis. *Journal of Consulting Psychology*, 1953, 17, 184-88.

Osburn, H. G. An investigation of the ambiguity dimension of counselor behavior. Unpublished doctoral dissertation, University of Michigan, 1952.

Osgood, C. E. The representation model and relevant research methods. In I. de Sola Pool (Ed.), *Trends in content analysis*. Urbana: University of Illinois Press, 1959. Pp. 33-88.

Park, L., Slaughter, R., Covi, L., and Kniffin, H. The subjective experience of the research patient: an investigation of psychiatric outpatients' reactions to the research treatment situation. *Journal of Nervous and Mental Disease*. 1966, 143, 199-206.

Parloff, M. B., Iflund, B., and Goldstein, N. Communication of "therapy values" between therapist and schizophrenic patients. *Journal of Nervous and Mental Disease*, 1960, 130, 193-99.

Pittenger, R. E., Hockett, C. F., and Danehy, J. J. *The first five minutes: a sample microscopic interview analysis*. Ithaca, N. Y.: Paul Martineau, 1960.

Psathas, G. Analyzing dyadic interaction. In G. Gerbner, O. R. Holsti, K. Krippendorf, W. J. Paisley, and P. J. Stone (Eds.), *The analysis of communication content*. New York: Wiley, 1969. Pp. 437-58.

Psathas, G., Cleeland, C., and Heller, K. Application of a computer system of content analysis of therapy analogue interviews. In G. E. Stollak, B. G. Guerney, and M. Rothberg (Eds.), *Psychotherapy research: selected readings*. Chicago: Rand McNally, 1966. Pp. 681-96.

Redlich, F. C., Dollard, J., and Newman, R. High fidelity recording of psychotherapeutic interviews. *American Journal of Psychiatry*, 1950, 107, 42-48.

Roberts, R. R., and Renzaglia, G. A. The influence of tape recording on counseling. *Journal of Counseling Psychology*, 1965, 12, 10-16.

Robertson, M. H. A comparison of client and therapist ratings on two psychotherapeutic variables. *Journal of Consulting Psychology*, 1957, 21, 110.

Robinson, F. P. The unit in interview analysis. *Educational and Psychological Measurement*, 1949, 9, 709-16.

Rogers, C. R. Electrically recorded interviews in improving psychotherapeutic techniques. *American Journal of Orthopsychiatry*. 1942, 12, 429-35.

Rogers, C. R., Gendlin, E. T., Kiesler, D. J., and Truax, C. B. *The therapeutic relationship and its impact: a study of psychotherapy with schizophrenics*. Madison: University of Wisconsin Press, 1967.

Schoeninger, D. W., Klein, M. H., and Mathieu, P. L. Sampling from the recorded therapy interview: patient experiencing ratings made with and without therapist speech cues. *Psychological Reports*, 1967, 20, 250.

Shakow, D. The evaluation of the procedure. In A. F. Bronner (Ed.), The objective evalutation of psychotherapy. *Psychiatry*, 1949, 19, 463-91.

_______. The recorded psychoanalytic interview as an objective approach to research in psychoanalysis. *The Psychoanalytic Quarterly*, 1960, 29, 82-97.

Shapiro, J.G. Relationship between expert and neophyte ratings of therapeutic conditions. *Journal of Consulting and Clinical Psychology*, 1968,32,87-89. (a)

_______. Relationships between visual and auditory cues of therapeutic effectiveness. *Journal of Clinical Psychology*, 1968, 24, 236-38. (b)

Shapiro, J. G., Foster, C. P., and Powell, T. Facial and bodily cues of genuineness, empathy, and warmth. *Journal of Clinical Psychology*, 1968, 24, 236-38.

Snyder, W. U. An investigation of the nature of nondirective psychotherapy. *Journal of Genetic Psychology*, 1945, 33, 193-223.

Starkweather, J. A. Computest: a computer language for individual testing, instruction, and interviewing. *Psychological Reports*, 1965, 17, 227-37.

_______. Psychiatric interview simulation by computer. *Methods of Information in Psychiatry*, 1967, 6, 15-23.

________. Overview: computer-aided approaches to content recognition. In G. Gerbner, O. R. Holsti, K. Krippendorf, W. J. Paisley, and P. J. Stone (Eds.), *The analysis of communication content.* New York: Wiley, 1969. Pp. 339-42.

Starkweather, J. A., and Decker, J. B. Computer analysis of interview content. *Psychological Reports*, 1964, 15, 875-82.

Stephenson, W. Critique of content analysis. *Psychological Records*, 1963, 13, 155-62.

Sternberg, R. S., Chapman, J., and Shakow, D. Psychotherapy research and the problem of intrusions on privacy. *Psychiatry*, 1958, 21, 195-203.

Stevens, S. S. Mathematics, measurement, and psychophysics. In S. S. Stevens (Ed.), *Handbook of experimental psychology*. New York: Wiley, 1951. Pp. 1-49.

Stone, P. J. and Cambridge Computer Associates, Inc. *User's manual for the General Inquirer*. Cambridge, Mass.: MIT Press. 1968. (a)

Stone, P. J. Introduction: Part IV. In G. Gerbner, O. R. Holsti, K. Krippendorf, W. J. Paisley, and P. J. Stone, *The analysis of communication content.* New York: Wiley, 1969. Pp. 335-38.

Stone, P. J. Confrontation of issues: excerpts from the discussion section at the conference. In G. Gerbner, O. R. Holsti, K. Krippendorf, W. J. Paisley, and P. J. Stone (Eds.), *The analysis of communication content*. New York: Wiley, 1969. Pp. 523-38. (b)

Stone, P. J., Bales, R. F., Namenwirth, J. Z., and Ogilvie, D. M. The General Inquirer: a computer system for content analysis, and retrieval based on the sentence as a unit of information. *Behavorial Science*, 1962, 7, 484-98.

Stone, P. J., Dunphy, D. C., Smith, M. S., and Ogilvie, D. M. *The General Enquirer: a computer approach to content analysis.*. Cambridge, Mass.: MIT Press, 1966.

Strupp, H. H. Patient-doctor relationships in the therapeutic process. In A. J. Bachrach (Ed.), *Experimental foundations of clinical psychology*. New York: Basic Books, 1962. Pp. 576-615.

Taylor, K. (Ed.) *Computer applications in psychotherapy: bibliography and abstract.* U.S. Public Health Service Publication No. 1981. Washington, D.C.: N.I.M.H. National Clearinghouse for Mental Health Information, 1970.

Traux, C. B., and Carkhuff, R. R. *Toward effective counseling and psychotherapy*. Chicago: Aldine, 1967.

Watson, P. D., and Kanter, S. S. Some influences of an experimental situation on the psychotherapeutic process: a report based on 44 treatment interviews, of the reaction of a patient and therapy to observation, recording, and physiological measurement. *Psychosomatic Medicine*, 1956, 18, 457-70.

Weizenbaum, J. Eliza. A computer program for the study of natural language communication between man and machine. *Communication of the ACM*, 1966, 9, 36-45.

________. Contextual understanding by computers. *Communications of the ACM*, 1967, 10, 474-80.

Wiens, A. N., Matarazzo, J. D., and Saslow, G. The interaction recorder: an electronic punched paper tape unit for recording speech behavior during interviews. *Journal of Clinical Psychology*, 1965, 21, 142-45.

Wilson, E. B., Jr. *An introduction to scientific research*. New York: McGraw-Hill, 1952.

II

Systems of Direct Psychotherapy Process Analysis

3

Major Process Systems for Analyzing Interview Behaviors of Therapist and Patient

The seven systems presented in this chapter tend to be "omnibus" ventures; the authors attempt to capture comprehensively, through the multiple variables included in their systems, the major relevant psychotherapy behaviors of both therapist and patient. Since the systems were designed as multifactor systems, they are more complex in structure than those presented in Chapters 4 and 5.

The seven systems are presented alphabetically by author. The oldest of the systems is Snyder's, which first appeared in 1945. Murray's system was published in 1956. Dollard and Auld, Leary and Gill, and Matarazzo all followed in 1959. The most recent systems are those of Lennard and Bernstein, 1960, and Butler, Rice, and Wagstaff, 1962. Rice's modifications of the latter system came several years later.

All seven systems had theoretical origins. Two of the systems (Butler, Rice, and Wagstaff—and Rice's modification—and Snyder) come directly from Rogerian client-centered theory, three from psychoanalytic theory (Dollard and Auld, Leary and Gill, and Murray), and two from theories in anthropology and sociology (Lennard and Bernstein, Matarazzo).

Bales' Interaction Recorder, an influential process system which first appeared in 1947 and then in book form in 1950, antedated all but one of the seven systems presented here. Research with his system has more recently been brought up to date in his 1969 volume. Bales' system was the model that many early therapy investigators either emulated or started from. It was modified several times for direct applications to psychotherapy interviews.

Bales' Interaction Process Analysis focused on formal interactional aspects of group participants' behavior. It was based on a theory of small group behavior which conceived of interaction as problem-solving activity distributed across members over time. Its twelve categories represented dimensions of instrumental-adaptive and social-emotional behavior. The categories included: (l) shows solidarity (raises other's status, gives help, reward), (2) shows tension release (jokes, laughs, shows satisfaction), (3) agrees (shows passive acceptance, understands, concurs, complies), (4) gives suggestion (direction, implying autonomy for other), (5) gives opinion (evaluation, analysis, expresses feeling, wish), (6) gives orientation (information, repeats, clarifies, confirms), (7) asks for orientation (information, repetition, confirmation), (8) asks for opinion (evaluation, analysis, expression of feeling), (9) asks for suggestion (direction, possible ways of action), (10) disagrees (shows passive rejection, formality, withholds help), (11) shows tension (asks for help, withdraws from field), and (12) shows antagonism (deflates other's status, defends or asserts self).

Measures are scored independently by observers viewing through a one-way vision mirror a group of people engaged in a problem-solving task. As applied to psychotherapy, assumed in this context to be largely a rational problem-solving process, the Bales system is used to score both the remarks of the therapist and those of the patient. Bales used the categories to test hypotheses such as the following: In problem-solving groups, discussion tends to proceed through various stages, from orientation in the earliest period, through evaluation, suggestions, agreements, and disagreements, to tension release, and finally to indications of group cohesiveness.

It soon became apparent that the Bales' system was inappropriate for precise analysis of psychotherapy interviews. As new systems designed for therapy appeared, the Bales procedure and its modifications were gradually abandoned. However, it was not until about 1960 that alternative instruments were more generally available in the literature. Until that time, many investigators initiated their process efforts with serious consideration of Bales' Interaction Recorder.

References

Bales, R. F. Interaction content analysis. In *Preliminary Report of the First National Training Laboratory on Group Development*. National Education Association and Research Center for Group Dynamics, M.I.T., 1947. (Obtainable from National Education Association, Washington, D.C.)

———. *Interaction process analysis: a method for the study of small groups*. Reading, Mass.: Addison-Wesley, 1950.

———. *Personality and interpersonal behavior*. New York: Holt, Rinehart & Winston, 1969.

A Client and Therapist Classification System

John M. Butler, Laura N. Rice, and Alice K. Wagstaff*

1. Rationale for Development of the System

The original authors have presented in detail (1962, 1963) the philosophy of science and theory of psychotherapy perspectives that guided the development of their classification system for coding the events of psychotherapy. They present a theoretical rationale and a corresponding mathematical analogue for naturalistic observation, which they argue is the basic empirical stance for psychological science.

> When one considers the philosophy and teaching of science, it is significant that little, if any, formal attention is paid to naturalistic observation and research, although it is quite clear that they are the foundation of all science. In modern science, discussion is usually concentrated upon questions of verification and the nature of scientific knowledge. . . . [Yet, it is quite clear that] when a scientist enters into an inquiry in a new domain, his ideas, however precise as ideas, are hazy with respect to the domain simply because it is a new domain. When the phenomena under consideration are not well described, when relationships at the phenomenal level are not known, the person who insists on starting out with precise experiments lacks the imagination required to observe, to look around and see, at the first level, what seems to be going on. Experiments which precede rather than succeed observation amount to being precise about vagueness and suggest a disproportionate concern for the opinions of other scientists with a disproportionate lack of concern for truth which, above all, should characterize the scientist. It seems to the writers that the scientist who wishes to bring a new domain under the sway of science should seek to observe, to arrive at preliminary hypotheses or systems of hypotheses on the basis of his observations. His ultimate aim, of course, should be the ultimate aim of any scientist, that of generating sets of propositions which, at crucial points, are verifiable in the sense of scientific method. His immediate aim then should be to arrive at fruitful hypotheses. . . . [Hence,] the aim here will be to describe an approach to the data of naturalistic

*The material discussed in this section is also presented in a revised version by Laura N. Rice.

> observation which, it is hoped, will encourage the development of fruitful hypotheses with respect to the domain of inquiry [psychotherapy]. (Butler, Rice and Wagstaff, pp. 178-79)

The authors then offer a general definition for any classification system, and list criteria to be observed in developing a given specific system.

> As conceived here, the naturalistic observer approaches his domain of inquiry . . . with several sets of convictions, beliefs, frames of reference, biases, prejudices—call them what you will—which will hereafter be called a classification system. To a first approximation, at least, the observer knows what behavior is. That is, he has a definition, explicit or implicit, of what behavior is and he knows in a preliminary way what behavior he is interested in observing. (Butler et al., 1962, p. 179)

Requisite criteria to be met by any classification system are: (1) The classification should be objective (specifiable and reliable) "in the sense that two observers would to a very high degree classify behavior the same way" (p. 181). (2) "The classification system should have mutually exclusive sub-categories. . . . When the classes are not mutually exclusive, cross-classifications may be dependent; some of the possible cross-classification will be mere artifacts" (p. 181). (3) "Since the number of classified behaviors or data may be very large, it seems that an additional criterion of a minimally satisfactory classification system would be that it be susceptible of objective analysis, preferably analysis of a type which treats the classification system and the data as a unit" (p. 182). (4) The more a system is fine-grained, that is, with relatively many subclasses in contrast to relatively few categories, and the more exhaustive, or the more responses are classified into the explicit categories and not placed into the unclassifiable and remainder classes, the more productive it is likely to be. The authors conclude:

> A naturalistic investigation is concluded when analysis of the data results in a demonstration that the system is unproductive or productive as the case may be. If the system is productive, the end result should be a sharpened and refined set of hypotheses leading to a better classification system with which to approach the domain. Or it may result in a set of hypotheses so refined as to indicate what is to be controlled and varied in an experimental attack upon the domain of inquiry. (Butler et al., 1962, p. 184)

Butler, Rice, and Wagstaff (1962) next define the "theoretical" structure which guided the development of their naturalistic quantification system.

> We have said that observation should precede experimentation, and yet we recommend that the naturalistic observer should bring to the construction of his classification system all the creativity and experience he can muster. It is precisely here, in our opinion, that the function of theorizing enters in. We conceive of theorizing—more accurately, perhaps, construction building—at this stage, not as a source of testable propositions, but as a systematization of experience, one's own and that of others, which can stimulate and enhance our individual creativity. It should serve to guide us in deciding which of literally hundreds of aspects of the behavior might be interesting to observe. (pp. 186-87)

Having presented the function of theory more generally, the authors then present their own theory (Butler and Rice, 1960; Rice and Butler, 1963) of "Self-actualization, New Experience, and Psychotherapy." The basic postulate of their system is a human drive of self-actualization, similar to Rogers' notions, but extended in its definition.

> We arrived at the conviction that self-actualizing processes have a primitive base, that this primitive base has many of the characteristics of the so-called physiological drives; that it is as independent of the physiological drives as the physiological drives are of each other; and that as a derivative or result, self-actualization depends primarily upon the satisfaction of this drive. We consider that this drive, which we have called "stimulus hunger," is the basis for much of what is constructive, creative, and self-actualizing in human life, and on the negative side for much, though far from all, of what is negative, destructive, and self-limiting. This drive, stimulus hunger, shows in behavior as an ever-present tendency for the organism to get new experience, either in the form of new stimulus objects or in the form of change in the level and mode of stimulation. . . . Stimulus hunger has to do with a wide variety of thinking and as a process the range and variety of thinking or conceptualizing provides new experience for the organism in much the same sense as the presence of new stimulus configurations. (Butler et al., 1962, pp. 187-88)

The authors apply this motivational system to psychotherapy, and subsequently to their classification system, in the following manner.

> We see therapy as a continuing search [on the client and thera-

pist's part] for new elements, and the forming of creative recombinations of new and old elements. At its best there is a tremendous amount of new experience, proving painful certainly, but also intensely satisfying. The effect of a stimulating therapist style is to arouse or re-arouse within the individual more associations, images, trains of thought, etc. It enables the client to generate new experiences for himself. It seems obvious that the stimulus (therapist communication and behavior) with the greatest connotative range, with the most far-reaching reverberations within the organism, results in a maximum of satisfying experience (p. 188.)

From these basic theoretical assumptions, Butler, Rice and Wagstaff (1962) derive two specific propositions that form the context for their empirical investigation. The first defines more clearly what is meant by therapist style. "Given semantically equivalent statements [by the therapist], the one possessing the greatest range of connotation is that which is the most stimulating" (p. 188). The second modified Roger's "necessary and sufficient conditions" hypothesis to include stimulating therapist style. "Under the three conditions of prizing, understanding, and stimulating, we hypothesize that the self-actualizing tendencies of clients will function" (p. 188).

Finally, the authors pull out of this conceptualization more specific postulates regarding the "stylistic" behavior of both client and therapist in psychotherapy.

In client-centered therapy the therapist controls the content of his responses in the sense that he chooses to stay within the frame of reference of the client. . . . Even though the impact of the therapist may be lessened . . . by his staying within the client's frame of reference, this still leaves the therapist with, at least potentially, a very high stimulus value simply in his style of participation. It is just here, however, that the therapist tends to become client controlled, though not usually as a conscious or deliberate choice. . . . The implications of this thinking for the conduct of therapy might be as follows: (1) While the content of his responses is controlled by the conscious choice of the therapist, his style of participation is not usually a matter of choice and tends to become similar to that of the client. (2) The client is in turn influenced by the style of the therapist, tending to move toward his style, though probably at a slower rate. (3) In addition to their impact on the therapist, certain dimensions of the client style of participation are in themselves vehicles of therapeutic change, and can be shown to be related to measures of therapy outcome. (4) If the therapist could establish stylistic independence of the client on a fairly expressive level, the client would be stimulated toward

> more expressive participation. (5) This change in style of participation of the client would in turn be accompanied by a more favorable outcome than would be predicted under usual still further circumstances. (1962, pp. 189-90)

2. *Description of the Original (1962) System*

Butler, Rice and Wagstaff present their initial classification system concerning stylistic behaviors of patient and therapist in psychotherapy. Rice (1965) defines "stylistic" by stating that "although content is involved in the lexical aspects of [patient and therapist's] message, the concern . . . is with the *way* in which a theme is expressed, rather than with specific content" (p. 156). Client statements or responses fall into three major groupings: Level of Expression, the analysis of action, analysis of feeling, and responsiveness; Voice Qualities and Manner of Speaking, that is emotional, focused, externalized, limited; and Quality of Participation, participating and/or observing. Likewise, therapist statements are coded into three major categories: Freshness of Words and Combinations, with five subcategories; Voice Quality, with eight subcategories; and Functional Level of Response, with seven subcategories.

> The Client classification system and therapist classification system are both based on a combination of the empirical and the theoretical. In the case of the client system, classes of behavior were chosen which seemed to differentiate between interviews which were considered "good," "mediocre," or "bad" by the client and/or therapist. From listening to these we tried to identify styles of participation that varied in a meaningful way in relation to the seeming value of the interview. Then each of the preliminary classes was considered from the standpoint of our theorizing about therapy. Does each subclass of each class make clinical sense, or are they perhaps just concomitants of some more significant stylistic variable?
>
> In the case of the therapist classification system, the situation was somewhat reversed. We first thought of aspects which seemed likely to be crucial in the impact of the therapist on the client, and then listened to selected tapes to see if therapists did indeed seem to vary significantly along these dimensions. In both classification systems, however, the relationship between the observed behavior and the theory is the same. The subclasses of each class are specified by the behaviors to be included and not by the supposed clinical meaning. It is the discrimination between kinds of behavior which is central, not the verbalized description or definition of

the categories. Clinical hypotheses were not being tested but were to be generated by the analysis. (Butler et al. 1962, p. 190)

The authors make the final point that the subclasses within their various categories represent nominal rather than ordinal subsystems. "The subclasses with each aspect are not intended to be scales. Some behaviors are, of course, thought to be more therapeutic than others, but the subclasses contain *qualitatively* different kinds of behavior which may prove to be important in their own right"(p. 190).

EVALUATION OF THE INITIAL (1962) SYSTEM

The strategy of the authors was first to try out their original classification system on a sample of successful and unsuccessful therapy cases and, from analysis of the coding data, to sharpen their hypotheses and revise their empirical category system. Partial results of this analysis are presented in their 1962 paper. These results will be summarized briefly here; the remainder of the discussion will focus on Rice's (1965; Rice and Wagstaff, 1967) modifications of both the client and therapist classification systems as a result of the 1962 analyses.

Butler, Rice, and Wagstaff (1962) applied the original system to twenty-four completed therapy cases selected from a larger block of research cases. "All cases were treated by therapists with a Rogerian orientation and were selected so as to provide an equal number of tape-recorded interviews from cases rated as success and failure cases by their therapists. A group of cases rated at the mean of the nine-point scale used in rating [success] were also included in the study. Length of treatment was balanced among the cases" (p. 194). The interviews selected for analysis were the second and next-to-last interviews, which were then divided into thirds by time. "Then ten successive responses of client and therapists were taken from each third of the interview and classified. All classifications were based on listening to tapes; transcripts were not used" (p. 194).

After the interviews were coded by judges, scores for the patient and therapist statements were put into separate matrices and respectively factor analyzed[1] by a procedure developed by Butler (1955;

1. In a personal communication (1971) Butler states that "it is somewhat misleading to call our method factor analysis. It is more like a latent class analysis where there are more than two categories of response than it is like factor analysis. We never named our method but, I suppose, 'multiple category analysis' or 'multiple class analysis' is more appropriate than factor analysis. Also, it would be better to call the 'factors' that we, and later Rice and Wagstaff, extracted 'behavior factors' rather than just factors, for the matrices analyzed were matrices showing similarity of behavior rather than similarity of scores. The distinction is important because we were basing our analysis on direct observations of behavior rather than upon scores in which information is lost." In the subsequent discussion, however, the term factor analysis will be retained for sake of convenience.

Butler, Rice and Wagstaff, 1963) and Wagstaff (1959). The procedure is described (Rice, 1955) as a method of "vector analysis designed to test for structural relations underlying classes of behavioral events. The quantitative relationship between classes, the metric of the system, emerges from the analysis rather than being built into the classification system" (p. 156). The factor structure that results apparently is based on similarity between interviews, which in the case on the 1962 study was based on a sequence of thirds of interviews.

The factorial results of that study were limited to the client category data. The factor analysis revealed three major factors operating among the category scores. Butler et al. (1962) summarize the analysis:

> Factor I behavior was more optimal for therapy than the other types. The client's energy, openness of expression, and ability to directly communicate experience seem to point toward the likelihood of favorable personal reorganization. Factor II behavior seems more questionable. On the one hand the client communicates relevant material in a somewhat expressive way, but some of the important ingredients of expressiveness seem to be missing. Factor III behavior by contrast seems more unequivocal. The self-avoidant, nonparticipating, describing, verbal behavior with its externalizing quality, seems unlikely to be associated with favorable outcomes in therapy. (pp. 198-99)

The authors then checked the "external productivity" of their system by correlating the above extracted factors with various external therapy indexes such as success ratings by therapist and client, therapist experience, and the Taylor MAS and Barron ES questionnaires. These findings generally indicated that Factor I clients were rated as more successful, tended to have more experienced therapists, showed more favorable change in self-description (Q-sort), showed decrease in anxiety over therapy, and higher ego strength. They contrasted with Factor III patients who showed failure patterns on these indexes, and Factor II patients who showed a mixed pattern. In other words, "in comparing the factors each with the other, it seems that the factors represent classes of behavior which can be arranged on a continuum of expressiveness of linguistic behavior in the Order I, II, III, and that the placement of clients on the continuum is related to outcome of therapy from the vantage point of the therapist, the client, and of test instruments which are essentially diagnostic in nature" (Butler et. al. 1962, p. 202).

The authors concluded from the study that "the results of the analysis of client and therapist responses, as viewed through the perspectives of the classification system employed, suggest that there are casual relationships between client expressiveness, therapist expressiveness, the process of psychotherapy, and the outcomes of psychotherapy" (p. 203).

RICE'S 1965 AND 1967 REVISIONS OF THE ORIGINAL CLASSIFICATION SYSTEM

Rice subsequently restructured and redefined the original classification system in line with the empirical results reported above, and submitted the new system to similar kinds of analyses.

In regard to the new Therapist Classification System, Rice (1965) focused on the characteristics of the therapist's *style* of participation, that is, "with the way in which a theme is expressed, rather than with specific content" (p. 156). The assumption underlying her system is as follows: "The more expressive the verbal and vocal behavior of the therapist, the more the client is stimulated to generate new experience. The more constricted the therapist's behavior, the more the client tends to be confined within the grooves of his own repetitive thinking processes" (p. 156). Therapist statements are scored in three major categories: Aspect A, Freshness of Words and Combinations–fresh connative language and ordinary language; Aspect B, Voice Quality–expressive, usual, and distorted; and Aspect C, Functional Level–inner exploring, observing, outside focus, and unscorable. The Therapist Classification System is presented in Table 3.1. It is important to point out that the categories were defined empirically to the judges who used them, so that they were not provided the descriptions in the table. "The definition of each class lay in the series of tape examples that were used in training the raters. The raters themselves were given only letters and numbers to designate classes" (p. 156).

Rice's new Client Classification System (Rice and Wagstaff, 1967) is also presented in Table 3.1. The new system was designed to meet the following criteria.

> (1) It was designed to focus on stylistic aspects of the client's participation rather than on specific content. (2) It was intended to distinguish the moment-to-moment behavior of the client rather than being used to characterize a total hour. (3) The distinctions were to be made as much as possible on the behavioral level with a *minimum of inferences about meaning.* Client responses classed together were to be similar as behavior, rather than judged to be similar on conceptual grounds. In other words, the system was intended to be descriptive rather than containing built-in explanations. (4) The system focused on aspects of behavior that gave promise of being important components of the client's attempts to

> express himself, picking up the vehicles of self-exploration rather than its comcomitants. Also, an attempt was made to select aspects likely to have impact on the therapist apart from the content of the communication. (5) Finally, of course, the coded behaviors were to be quantifiable in such a way as to permit scrutiny of relationships among behaviors and between behaviors and independent measures of therapy outcome. (p. 558)

The revised Client Classification System "addresses itself to two levels of communication. The first concerns voice quality, that which is vocal but nonverbal. The second is lexical, having to do with meanings conveyed through words, but focusing on the manner of expressing experience rather than specific content" (p. 558). The scoring system (see Table 3.1) correspondingly consists of two major categories: Aspect A, *Voice Quality*—emotional, focused, externalizing, and limited; and Aspect B, *Expressive Stance*—objective analysis and description, subjective reaction, static feeling description, and differentiated exploration. In developing the first major category, Voice Quality, Rice and Wagstaff (1967) stated:

> The strategy used was to locate a limited number of voice patterns that varied among clients, showed variation over sessions, and seemed to differentiate meaningfully among sessions that had previously been characterized by therapists as good or poor hours. The patterns thus located were then described in terms of energy, pitch range, tempo, stress patterns, etc. These descriptions, together with representative taped samples, were used by the judges in making their distinctions. It seems probable that these voice patterns have to do with the degree and nature of the client's involvement in the therapy process. (p. 558)

This first category, then, focuses on paralinguistic indexes of communication behavior.

Finally, Rice and Wagstaff (1967) caution that some modification of the revised client system might be necessary for other than client-centered clients.

> This classification system has been developed within the client-centered framework, in which the primary task of the therapist is to help the client to engage in a process of self-exploration with as much freshness and immediacy as possible. Some adaptations would be necessary before using this system to characterize therapy process in another orientation. It seems probable that the vocal dimension would be relevant in any situation involving self-exploration in an interpersonal context. The lexical dimension, expressive

stance, is probably more specific to a therapy in which both therapist and client stay primarily in the client's internal frame of reference. (p. 558)

The sections that follow will focus entirely on Rice's new versions of the Client and Therapist Classification System (Rice, 1965; Rice and Wagstaff, 1967), unless explicitly stated otherwise.

3. *Data Collection Context*

Rice's system to date has been applied exclusively to tape-recorded psychotherapy sessions drawn from the tape library of the University of Chicago Counseling Center. The samples of therapists and clients involved have operated within a predominant client-centered framework. The basic research strategy has been to investigate the intercorrelation of her measures of therapist and patient within-the-interview behaviors with various measures of more- and less-successful psychotherapy outcome.

4. *Data Form*

As with the original form of the system (1962) both of Rice's later studies (1965; Rice and Wagstaff, 1967) have used only tape-recorded transcriptions of psychotherapy as the data presented to coders for their judgments. "All classifications were based on listening to tapes. No transcripts were used" (1965, p. 157, 1967, p. 559). Rice has not yet considered the differential effects on her category scores of judges scoring typescript compared with audio and audio-visual transcriptions of the same therapy samples. Such a study would provide interesting validity data regarding her system since, inasmuch as the scoring emphasizes stylistic and paralinguistic features of verbalizations, the audio dimension at least would be necessary for valid ratings; and to the extent that this is correct, codings of typescripts alone should provide dramatically different findings than scoring of tape recordings.

5. *Choice of Units*

The basic scoring unit for classification used by Rice is identical to that used in the 1962 study. The particular unit the judges score is also the same for both client and therapist classifications. For the client, the unit is the P in the T-P-T communication sequence; for the therapist, it is the T in the P-T-P sequence. The scoring unit is referred to as the "total response," "which was defined for the therapist as everything said between two client responses" (Rice, 1965, p. 157); and the client responses "were classified separately on each of the two aspects, with each response being placed in one and only one subclass of each aspect" (Rice and Wagstaff, 1967, p. 559).

6. Participant-Context Restrictions

From Rice's descriptions, most of the classification decisions are apparently made out of context, without observation of the other participant's responses. In classifying therapist responses, the "raters listened to preceding client responses only when necessary to understand antecedents to pronouns, etc. They did not listen to the client's response to the therapist's statement" (Rice, 1965, p. 157). When classifying the client's statements, "judges were instructed not to listen to the following therapist response, and to listen to the preceding therapist response only when necessary to understand antecedents to pronouns, etc." (Rice and Wagstaff, 1967, p. 559).

7. Type of Sampling Indicated

Rice has not explicitly considered the choice between random and systematic sampling of psychotherapy sessions. The sampling choices she made suggest that she combines both procedures. She attempts to attain representativeness by first sampling somewhat systematically along the time dimension (both within the hour and across interviews), and then selects a standard number of response units to be taken successively from the time unit sampled. The exact procedure will be described in the succeeding two sections.

8. Sample Location Within the Interview

The procedure for extracting samples from particular therapy sessions has also been standard since the 1962 study. "Each interview was divided into thirds on the basis of elapsed time, and from each of these thirds ten consecutive [client or therapist] responses were taken. Thus, there were 30 [client or therapist] responses from each interview, ten each from the beginning, middle, and end of each interview" (Rice, 1965, p. 157; Rice and Wagstaff, 1967, p. 559).

The method, therefore, is systematic sampling along the time dimension. Rice has not contrasted this procedure with random sampling from particular sessions in terms of differential effects on her category scores. The ten consecutive client or therapist responses represent the basic "summary unit" in Rice's system. The "contextual unit" is, for the most part, identical with this "summary unit," except that raters listen to the other participant's preceding comments when necessary to understand antecedents to pronouns, etc.

9. Sample Location Over Therapy Interviews

Rice has somewhat systematically sampled along the time dimension in extracting interviews representative of the entire therapy interaction. In her 1965 study she sampled primarily the second and next-to-last interviews for each case, although she added for each case an interview drawn from near the middle of the case. The Rice and Wagstaff (1967) study focused on clients all of whom had twenty therapy sessions as participants in a study of time-limited therapy. For this study, "three interviews from each client were studied, the first, second, and eleventh" (p. 559).

Rice has not explicitly discussed the issue of sampling nor has she considered alternatives. Her attempt, as reflected in the procedures above, seems to be to sample more than one interview from a case, extracting samples from at least very early and very late in therapy, and sometimes near the middle. It seems that both random and other systematic procedures should be empirically contrasted with those mentioned above, particularly since it seems probable that very early and very late interviews may be atypical of the majority of therapy interviews since the early sessions are atypically one-sided (patient focuses on a description of his problem) and the last few interviews tend to focus on termination issues and some reinstatement of defensive structures.

10. Clinical Sophistication of Judges

Judges who apply Rice's classification system have been minimally experienced graduate students in, presumably, clinical and/or counseling psychology. Classification of therapists' responses in the 1965 study "was done by five advanced graduate students, all of whom had received training in client-centered therapy and were currently seeing clients. Each tape was independently rated by two judges, with a third judge invoked to break ties" (Rice, 1965, p. 157). The 1967 coding of clients' statements "was done by graduate students with some knowledge of client-centered therapy" (Rice and Wagstaff, 1967, p. 559).

Rice has not explicitly discussed or empirically assessed the differential effects on category scores of judges of various levels of clinical sophistication, for example, naive undergraduates and/or experienced clinicians in contrast to the usual graduate students.

11. Training Required of Judges

Rice does not outline the specifics procedures used in training judges.[2] She does indicate that training tapes are used, and specifies (Rice and Wagstaff, 1967) the criterion by which she decides that training has been successfully completed.

> Earlier work with this kind of material has shown that interjudge agreement can be raised by means of additional training even after a level had been reached that clearly exceeded chance beyond the 0.05 level of significance. Therefore, for each of the main classes a standard was set which had as a lower bound, a 0.05 level of significance using Cohen's kappa (Cohen, 1960) and which had as an upper bound the degree of agreement reached by the two most reliable judges. A judge was considered trained when he reached this degree of agreement with the standard judges on three successive training tapes. In practice this involved an interjudge agreement of 75 percent or above on each of the [various] aspects. (p. 559)

Apparently, then, some level of relatively standardized training is used for judges which involves use of some number of training tapes. Unfortunately the procedure is not spelled out in detail. Evidently, also, the judges are not given the category definitions to study before they tackle the training of experimental tapes, [3] at least insofar as the therapist category system is concerned. Rice (1965) states that for the therapist categories "the definition of each class lay in the series of taped examples that were used in training the raters. The raters themselves were given only letters and numbers to designate classes" (p. 156). It would seem safe to assume that a similar procedure was followed for scoring client categories, although Rice does not specify whether this is the case in the 1967 article.

12. Training Manual

There is not yet a training manual available. As mentioned above, Rice offers little detailed material regarding the exact judge training procedure.

2. In a personal communication (1971) Rice states that "a series of training tapes was used for all judges, who went through them in a standard order. These tapes were regular interviews, of which 30 responses had been rated by two expert judges. Tapes were selected to present a variety of rating problems. The judges rated each tape and then compared their ratings with the standard. Periodically they met with the trainer and discussed rating problems.

3. In a personal communication (1971) Rice states that "this was true in the early study. In the 1965 and 1967 studies I did use definitions and about half a page of description for each class, as well as some examples."

13. Interrater and Intrarater Reliabilities Reported

Rice reports no reliability coefficients or percentages of agreement for judges using either the client or therapist classification system. This is a deliberate omission. Rice states that reliability of classification is controlled by the training procedure. In other words, judges were given taped samples of responses with their classification. The judges were trained until they reached a standard of reliability set by the investigator. Upon attaining that standard, the judges were considered reliable judges, and their subsequent scorings were considered to be in agreement.

In their early work, the authors introduced, and Rice continued, a very interesting quality control feature. After the judges were trained and had begun their experimental ratings, they would be asked at intervals to rerate standard tapes as a check that the level of reliability of their ratings had not slipped over time.

14. Dimensionality Considerations

In all three major studies using the original and modified classification systems, the authors have been very concerned with the factor structure of their system. They have not focused, as is more usual, on the intercorrelation of categories at a given moment. Rather, their approach has been to look at factor structure across interviews in order to assess interview similarity regarding the factors.

> The method of analysis used was one analogous to factor analysis and was developed by Butler, Rice, and Wagstaff (1962). In contrast to the more usual analysis which starts with a matrix of intercorrelations of scores, the present analysis involves a matrix, the entries of which represent on a scale between zero and unity the degree to which pairs of interviews share the same behaviors. After communality estimates have been added, each matrix is factored by the principal-axis method in the usual way. . . . For each point in time the loadings of each interview [are obtained on each of the factors extracted]. Each factor represents an interview type which could be described in terms of the [client or therapist] behaviors characterizing it. That is, an interview type is defined by the most frequently appearing behavior classes in interviews with high loadings on the factor in question and low loadings on the other factors. (Rice and Wagstaff, 1967, pp. 559-60)

15. Validity Studies

The strategy of data analysis has been identical in the Butler, Rice, and Wagstaff (1962), Rice (1965), and Rice and Wagstaff (1967) studies. The first part of each study presents factor analytic data on the classification system involved. The remainder of each report explores the relationship between the client or therapist factors extracted and various independent measures of outcome for a sample of therapy cases. The 1962 study dealt primarily with the original client classification system, although it presented some data regarding the original therapist categories. Rice used the findings of that study to revise the entire system, and presented the revised client classification system in 1965 and the revised therapist system in 1967.

In the 1965 study of the therapist classification system, three major factors were extracted by this procedure. Type I interviews subsumed "therapist responses expressed in language that is commonplace rather than fresh and connotative. The voice quality tends to be even and relatively uninfected, seldom expressive and never distorted" (Rice, 1965, p. 158). In Type II interviews "in more than half of the [therapist] responses there is a distorted voice quality. Only a few of the responses are expressed in fresh, connotative language" (p. 158). Finally, in Type III interviews, "the therapist uses somewhat more fresh, connotative language. Over two-thirds of the responses are characterized by an expressive voice quality" (p. 158). Rice then related these three factors to more and less successful dichotomies constructed by using various rating and questionnaire criteria.

> The presence of Type II therapist behavior either early or late in therapy is characteristic of therapies that are seen as unsuccessful by both therapist and client. The appearance of Type III behavior early in therapy seems to be relatively unrelated to outcome as viewed by both therapist and client. In other words, Type III behavior seems to be a correlate but not a predictor of therapeutic success. There is some suggestion that Type I behavior early in therapy may be predictive of successful outcome. If it continues or appears late in therapy, however, there seems to be no relationship with favorableness of outcome. (Rice, 1965, p. 159)

In the 1967 study, Rice applied the same factor analytic procedures, this time to the revised client classification system. In this case, four factors were extracted. Type I interviews were "characterized by the client's use of an externalizing voice quality and an expressive stance of objective analysis and description. That is, the client seemed to be turning his energy outward, talking at the therapist, and viewing himself and his world as objects to be objectively analyzed or described." Type II interviews were "also characterized by the expressive stance of objective analysis and description, but in this case the client was using a limited voice quality." Type III interviews were "characterized by a focused voice quality and an expressive stance about equally divided between objective analysis and subjective reaction. . . . About half of the time was devoted to the client's exploration of his own subjective reactions to things impinging upon him, with the other half spent in a more analytic or descriptive approach" (p. 560). The last interview type, Type IV, "involved an externalizing voice quality and an expressive stance of subjective reaction" (p. 561). The fifty-three counseling-center clients included in the analysis were separated into five outcome groups by various criteria. Group S was the "unequivocal success" group; Group M, the "pure minimal change" group; Group TH, in which therapist rated success high, client low; Group CH, in which client rated high, therapist low; and Group At, consisting of the twelve clients who completed fewer than ten interviews.

> The above analyses have shown that Group At could be differentiated from three of the other groups as early as the first interview. The two pure groups, Groups S and M, were clearly differentiated from each other by the second interview. . . . Although Group S was not significantly different from TH until the eleventh interview, it did show somewhat more favorable process in both the first and second interviews than did TH. . . . Mixed Group CH, however, fell not in the middle, but below Group M in favorable process at each point in time. (p. 562)

Rice concludes that "the evidence seems clear that the two aspects embodied in the present classification system do provide a satisfactory description of some of the crucial features of the client's ongoing behavior" (Rice and Wagstaff, 1967, p. 563).

References

Butler, J. M. The analysis of successive sets of behavior data. *Counseling Center Discussion Papers*. University of Chicago Library, Vol. 1, 1955.

Butler, J. M., and Rice, L. N. Self-actualization, new experience, and psychotherapy. *Counseling Center Discussion Papers*. University of Chicago Library, Vol. 6, 1960, 12.

Butler, J. M., Rice, L. N. and Wagstaff, A. K. On the definition of variables: an analogue of clinical analysis. In H. H. Strupp and L. Luborsky (Eds.), *Research in psychotherapy*. Vol. 2. Washington, D.C.: American Psychological Association, 1961, Pp. 178-205.

———. *Quantitative naturalistic research.* Englewood Cliffs, N. J.: Prentice-Hall, 1963.

Rice, L. N. Therapist's style of participation and case outcome. *Journal of Consulting Psychology* 1965. 29, 155-60.

Rice, L. N., and Butler, J. M. Adience, self-actualization, and drive theory. In J. Wepman and R. Heine (Eds.), *Concepts of personality*. Chicago: Aldine, 1963.

Rice, L. N., and Wagstaff, A. K. Client voice quality and expressive style as indexes of productive psychotherapy. *Journal of Consulting Psychology*, 1967, 31, 557-63.

Wagstaff, A. K. Sucessive set analysis of verbal styles in psychotherapy. Unpublished doctoral dissertation, University of Chicago, 1959.

A Motivational System for Scoring Patient and Therapist Behavior

John Dollard and Frank Auld, Jr.

1. Rationale for Development of the System

Dollard and Auld developed their system as an attempt to operationalize constructs from psychoanalytic and learning theories (Dollard and Miller, 1950).

> No theory of human personality which does not take [Freudian] factors into account . . . can be realistic. Every personal act and, no less, the chained actions of man's history become more intelligible if one supposes man to be the kind of creature that Freud depicted. (Dollard and Auld, 1959, p. 6)
>
> Learning theory, like Freudian theory, is part of the frame of reference in which we work. All professional students of culture believe that social behavior is somehow learned . . . that cultural traits and habits are learned, lawfully learned, and, if changed, lawfully changed. The work of a generation of behavior scientists has created a body of principles which we may view as laws of learning. . . . These principles indicate that the crucial element in selecting and preserving culture traits and individual habits is drive reduction. . . . As in the case of Freudian theory, it seems to us that learning theory can act as a great organizing force in the understanding of human events. (p. 7)

Within this framework, Dollard and Auld attempted to assess both obvious and subtle motivational aspects of human interaction in psychotherapy, encompassing both conscious and unconscious forces.

> Many will find our attempt dishearteningly prosaic and will feel that the beauty of unconscious emotional interaction has been lost or destroyed by the gritty work of scientific analysis. The therapist, in particular, who knows the splendor of unconscious interaction, who can feel the answer generating the question, may be appalled at our too-simple-seeming categories. Perhaps his will prove to be the intelligent response to our effort: "too soon, too simple." But another voice arises within us to ask: If not this, what are you going to use for data? Surely not what a man thinks he said, or thinks another man said, some hours or days before. Data, in the case at hand, must be more than memories. It must be the living stuff of the [psychotherapy] conversation with all relevant emotional signs attached. This conversation, electronically recorded, is available to the cultivated senses of a second or third observer. Transcribed, it can be provisionally divided into units and the units assigned to categories. These categories can be tested, and accepted or rejected. Such a transaction is "public" in the sense that science uses the word. It is our belief that no other method will suffice. No units, no science; no categories, no science; no numbers, no science. (pp. 1-2)

The major goal of Dollard and Auld's (1959) system was to capture the feeling and/or motivational concurrents of patients' statements in psychotherapy.

> If the human whole is to be hacked to pieces, the pieces should be at least natural and unitary parts of the whole. Sentences divested of their proper emotional accompaniments would be unnatural units. For us, the sentence and the emotion belong together. The lawfulness which is obscurely but powerfully evident in human interaction can never be discerned unless this fact is understood: Sentences always have defining emotional and other reactions attached to them. Our purpose, then is to describe such sentence units, summarize them, render them comparable, and eventually predict what may co-occur when they appear. . . . The system is built to show growth, progression, and change within the patient —if there is any—and the evolution of the relationship between patient and therapist. (pp. 2-3)
>
> [It] might seem that the ability to discern emotion attached to a written sentence would be rare. We think, however, that this is not the case. . . . Emotional response to the written word is . . . we

> believe, a common and not a rare skill. If it were not so, the empathic reading of novels or dramas would be impossible. Just as sentence and emotion are tightly linked in daily life so they are still linked when the sentence appears in written form. It is this widely shared ability to respond emotionally to the written sentence which makes content scoring possible. (p. 3)

The approach of Dollard and Auld to scale development involved the arduous task of naturalistic observation—in their case, careful auditing and relistening to tape-recorded psychotherapy sessions.

> In developing our system we deliberately adopted a naive viewpoint. We came, as it were, fresh to the material and tried to see what kind of system of analysis it called for. . . . Many variables were suggested by theory and by the work of other investigators. We resisted inventing a sign to meet any theoretical system or adopting one merely because someone else had used it. (p. 4)
>
> A sign was invented only when it seemed to deal with a problem which posed itself repeatedly in the clinical data. We use no imaginary examples [for our scoring system]; every example given occurred in an actual case. . . . With analytic or behavior theory as a guide, many other signs could have been invented; unless our material forced us to add a new sign, we did not do so. (p. 30)
>
> This is of course a merit, but there is an attached demerit: Our repertory of signs [that is, categories] is limited by the nature of material available to us. During the development of our system we scored 68 interviews by 6 different therapists with 8 patients and one normal person. . . . The cases were mainly carried on by student apprentices who, of course, use psychotherapeutic methods least well. The interviews are mainly beginnings of cases, the early hours of what, if carried to conclusion, would have been a long therapeutic process. Thus we do not have the terminal hours of protracted—successful—therapy cases. It may well be that some of the "best" material was thus denied us, material which, if analyzed, would have made our system look different and better than it does. (p. 4).
>
> [Finally,] others faced with new problems in material might elaborate or abridge our system for special purposes. . . . Certainly our system will have to be elaborated before it can catch the full scope of the transaction in psychoanalysis between patient and analyst. So be it; we have forced the matter as far as we are able at this time and have made what we consider a suitable first try. (p. 30)

The empirical base of departure for developing their system was the previous work of E. J. Murray (see below, this chapter).

> Our concern with content analysis did not begin with the present work. One of us (Dollard and Mowrer, 1947) had worked with an earlier form called the DRQ. This was an interesting measure but too rough in its nature for refined work. It seemed to have no chance of capturing the detailed events of the psychotherapeutic transaction. We had therefore somewhat lost interest in the problem of content analysis. Our interest in the problem was reawakened by the vigorous work of E. J. Murray, who took content analysis of psychotherapy as a thesis problem. He devised a more elaborate content system and showed that it could be reliable, that is, that a more complex system than that of the DRQ could be made to work. . . . Excited by Murray's original work and stimulated by the advances he had made, we took up again the problem of content analysis. At first we began fiddling with Murray's categories to check on their reliability. Then we became interested in the categories themselves and, as we warmed to our task, in various new problems, that is, the desirability of signs to represent unconscious processes, the elaboration of the sign system to give more adequate coverage, the problem of teaching scorers, and the reliability with which scorers could sort individual sentences. The path that Murray had opened turned out to be a high road of new problems and challenges. (Dollard and Auld, 1959, p. 8)

2. *Description of the Scoring System*

Judges using the system are urged to score the content of what the patient (and therapist) states. They are to avoid theoretically-hinged inferences, although they are admonished to use their empathic abilities.

> So far as he can, the scorer stays close to what the patient has said. The scorer resists guessing about motives that are unknown to him. He does not "reach" for scores. . . . The scorer doesn't assume motives that according to theory *should* be present; he scores what is, not what ought to be. (Dollard and Auld, 1959, pp. 22-23)

> [But] the scorer tends to be influenced in his scoring by his sense of what he himself would feel in the situation described by the patient. Such empathic response is, of course, necessary to sensible scoring of the emotional transaction that is presented in psychotherapy protocols. Empathy is the instrument of under-

> standing. . . . One is tempted, in order to avoid . . . problems of the scorer as he identifies with the patient and tries to understand what is going on, to try to make the scoring a quite routine matter, in which empathy would play no part. . . . We chose rather to suffer with the difficulties of allowing the scorer to react freely to the material, in order to let him make use of the incomparable empathic instrument of understanding. (pp. 25-26)

> We have demonstrated the feasibility of getting reliable measures not from simple, objective features of the therapy situation, but through a procedure that makes use of the empathic understanding of the observer. (Auld and Dollard, 1966, p. 92)

The category system encompasses twenty "signs" or classes for patient statements and six classes for therapist statements. Some of the patient categories can be scored as combinations, which permit subclassifications. The therapist groupings, in contrast, cannot be combined in scoring, they are mutually exclusive. Some of the patient categories can be scored either as conscious (capital letters) or as unconscious (lower-case letters).

The patient and therapist scoring categories are presented in Table 3.2.

> The therapist categories derive largely from the psychoanalytic theory of the action of analytic psychotherapy, which tells us that the aim of therapy is to make the unconscious conscious, creating ego where id was; that the therapist must overcome resistance; that he does this by means of interpretations; that he utilizes the positive transference to bind the patient to the therapeutic task; that he, at times, directs the patient's attention to fruitful areas for exploration; and that he can err by allowing countertransference to distort his actions, by failing to make use of appropriate technical maneuvers, by making premature or wrong interpretations, by failing to interpret when he should, or by giving a wrong structure to the therapeutic situation. Our categories of the therapist allow us to code some of his actions which are relevant to these variables. (Auld and Dollard, 1966, p. 88)

Therapist statements are scored in one of six categories.

> For the moment we are trying to get along with as few signs as possible. . . . Our [six] signs are, we think, few but crucial. . . . In the sign system . . . the three vital variables are represented: the case where the therapist motivates patient (drive or demand); the case where the therapist rewards patient (tension reduction or

> reward); and the case where therapist labels—that is, names, connects, or discriminates (interpretation). From our standpoint, for this moment, these are the vital principles. (Dollard and Auld, 1959, p. 186)

The additional three therapist categories score mm-hmms, serious therapist errors, and residual-unscorable statements.

For patients, motivations (anxiety, dependency, hostility, self-hatred, love, reduction in drive, social mobility, sex), momentary emotional states (laughter, sighs, weeping), symptoms (obessional, psychosomatic), reactions to therapist statements (confirmation, dream, negation, reasoning or insight, resistance, affirmation), and an unscorable category are included.

The authors make no attempt to score individual sentences for strength or intensity of motive. "There is no differential weighting of the sentence units. A strong expression of hostility counts for no more than a mild expression. . . [Instead] we expect that strength of motive will be shown by an increase in the number of sentences of a particular kind—the stronger the motive, the more sentences expressing it" (p. 24).

Dollard and Auld take some pains to make explicit the assumptions guiding their work, as well as the criteria for descriminating unconscious motives. They list three assumptions underlying their scoring of patient motives.

> [1] No matter how complex or bizarre an item of behavior may seem . . . each such unit is motivated. . . . [2] . . . behavior is never nonsensical but is always lawful. If a behavior sequence does not make ordinary sense, it makes some kind of extraordinary sense. We assume that behavior proceeds from motive to response to reward (or lack of it); each behavior sequence must be studied from this standpoint. . . . [3] For us "conscious" means the named or nameable; "unconscious" means the unnameable. . . . Any or all units in a behavior chain can be unconscious: motive, response, cues to which subject reacts, or rewards which occur. (pp. 30-33)

As stated previously, Dollard and Auld intend to measure unconscious motivation as well as conscious. They state that "there is no problem in evaluating a conscious motive. The subject names his emotion. He is 'sexy'; he is angry; he is guilty; he is afraid. We do not score a motive as unconscious if the subject merely *neglects* to name it; a motive is deemed unconscious only when the reporter is *unable* to name it" (p. 38). The authors then list four criteria judges should follow in detecting and scoring unconscious motives.

> [1] We will not be wrong many times out of a hundred if we impute to a participant that motive which the environing situation should evoke. . . . If having been in such a situation, a person denies having experienced the appropriate emotion, we will often conclude that the suspected motive is active but unconscious. . . . [2] A person exposed to a provocative situation may react with signs of [bodily, physiological] mobilization for action which he himself does not recognize—that is, does not label correctly. A slamming heart or quickened breathing or fearful perspiration may testify to an active but unconscious motive. . . . [3] If a person in a provocative situation reports an avoidant response while denying the motive appropriate to the situation, we tend to credit him with an unconscious motive. . . . Very often the avoidant reaction will be one of actual physical escape from the situation; at another time it will be one of anxious alarm. . . . [4] If in a situation which arouses fear, a patient is able to name the motive which would ordinarily evoke fear, we are inclined to credit him with said motive even though he denies feeling anything. We argue that if a person can name a motive, some inward representation of that motive will exist even though it is not strong enough to deserve labeling. (pp. 38-41)

3. Data Collection Context

The authors derived their system by naturalistic observation of tape-recorded psychotherapy sessions. All applications of their system to date similarly have focused on recordings of live therapy sessions. Studies include analyses of both groups of psychotherapy patients as well as more intensive assessment of single cases.

4. Data Form

Patient and therapist statements are scored directly from typewritten transcriptions of recorded psychotherapy interviews. The typist, besides recording the transcript, times all pauses with a stopwatch, and notes all weeping, laughing, and sighing. These latter three categories are the only ones which require auditory cues for scoring; all others are scored from the typescript only. In some cases the scorer may refer to the sound recording in addition to the typescript. "In order to sort by motivational category the scorer must feel the emotion 'attached' to the sentence as best the transcript permits him to feel it. In crucial bases of doubt the scorer can recur to the sound recording from which the transcript was made. . . . In most cases the transcript alone will suffice" (Dollard and Auld, 1959, p. 3).

The authors have not to date considered differential effects on their category scores of judging sound or movie versions (in contrast to their typescript) of psychotherapy sessions.

5. Choice of Units

The basic typescript "scoring unit" for the Dollard and Auld patient and therapist categories is the sentence.

> For our research we wished a unit that is very small, so that we would be able to study the detail of the interaction between therapist and patient. By definition, the sentence is the smallest portion of speech that can be fully understood by itself; it is, linguists say, a "minimum free utterance." Thus the sentence seemed appropriate to our aims, and we chose it as our unit. (Dollard and Auld, 1959, pp. 9-10)

> Having decided to use the sentence as our unit to be scored, we faced the task of identifying sentences. In developing instructions for dividing interviews into sentences, we built on the work of grammarians and linguists, especially the work of Leonard Bloomfield (1933) and of Charles Carpenter Fries (1952). Fries defined a sentence as a single free utterance—free in the sense that it is not included in any larger structure by means of any grammatical device. Starting from this definition, he sought to identify the cues in a person's speech that signal to the listener, "This is a sentence." In framing our rules for unitizing we invented instructions for finding and responding to the cues that Fries has shown perform this signalling. (p. 12)

The authors present these unitizing rules on pages 13 to 18 of their volume (see also Auld and White, 1956). In addition, extensive examples that clarify the application of these rules are presented in Appendix B (Dollard and Auld, 1959, pp. 353-67).

To summarize, the basic "scoring unit" is the sentence, which is defined as a single free utterance.

> The single free utterance may be a minimum free utterance having only the barely necessary structures for a communication that could stand alone; or it may be an expanded free utterance. A sentence may be a greeting for farewell, a call, a question, a request, or a statement. Speeches of the patient and therapist are to be separately unitized. (Dollard and Auld, 1959, pp. 12-13)

In regard to the "contextual-unit," it is clear that for Dollard and Auld sentences cannot be scored in isolation. Instead the coder needs to consider the context, the preceding and subsequent verbalizations.

> Though each sentence is scored separately, and is scored for itself, context must be considered. Many sentences could not be scored at all in isolation; their meaning depends on the surrounding sentences. We believe, furthermore, that the scorer should not so fix his attention on the single sentence that he loses his sense of what is going on in the case. (p. 24)

The principle the authors adopt regarding the contextual unit is that the coder

> . . . should know whatever the therapist knows up to the time of the hour being scored, but [he] should know nothing more than this. . . . He should make sure he knows what has happened in the case up to the point where he begins scoring, whether or not he scored each hour of the case. For example, if he scored only the odd-numbered hours, he should be sure to read all the even-numbered hours also. (p. 20-21)

In preparing to score, the coder reads the entire page, then scores the sentences as he reads the same page a second time.

> [Furthermore,] we have found that it is sometimes necessary to read ahead a bit to understand the point of a certain utterance. . . . We settled on letting the scorer go to the end of the page as a usual thing, and a little further than that if necessary to complete the topic the patient is discussing. We want to allow the scorer at least as much freedom as the therapist has, *not* to have to respond immediately, to be able to delay making a formulation. (p. 21)

Finally, as mentioned previously, in cases of doubt the scorer may refer to the sound recording in addition to the typescript.

To date the authors have not empirically assessed their conviction that context is crucial for scoring by comparing category scores resulting from coding sentences with and without context present.

6. Participant-Context Restrictions

Dollard and Auld urge that both patient and therapist sentences be scored concurrently as the coder progresses down the transcript page. "If one doesn't score the therapist's sentences at the same time as one is scoring the patient's, one tends to neglect and pass over the therapist's role in the interaction. Therefore, one needs to know how to score the therapist's sentences in order to score the patient's sentences adequately" (1959, p. 28). On the other hand, of course, this scoring procedure, not being independent, builds in hidden and unknown relationships between patient and therapist categories which may reflect relationships existing only in the mind of the scorer. Because of this biasing difficulty, it seems it would be quite beneficial to test whether in fact equivalent scoring would result from separate judges independently scoring patient and therapist categories respectively, in contrast to having the same judge score both concurrently. The interpretive gains from independent scoring, if feasible, would be considerable.

7. Type of Sampling Indicated

In their 1959 manual, Dollard and Auld do not explicitly discuss whether random or some systematic sampling procedure is indicated for their particular scoring system. The studies reported in that volume sampled, in an unspecified way, early interviews from the cases studied. However, particular sessions were scored in their entirety; thus, no sampling was involved.

8. Sample Location Within the Interview

The 1959 manual and subsequent studies all involved categorizing the entire sessions studied. In other words, Dollard and Auld typically have not sampled from a particular therapy hour, but instead have scored each in its entirety. To date they have not considered whether different sized "summary units" (number of sentences included) or summary units selected from various stages of particular interview hours yield category scores differentially representative of behaviors for the entire therapy sessions.

9. Sample Location Over Therapy Interviews

As mentioned in the introductory section, the tapes the authors used to develop their system were of interviews from the beginning of therapy cases—"the earlier hours." Some subsequent studies focused on initial interviews only. Others divided cases into quarters, for example, an "introductory quarter" (first three sessions), and an "active period" (the remaining ten sessions). Apparently, the typical procedure again is not to sample, but to score exhaustively the sessions involved. To date they have not explicitly discussed or empirically assessed differential effects on their category scores of sampling from various stages of the treatment series.

10. Clinical Sophistication of Judges

Dollard and Auld (1959) explicitly indicate that judges must have considerable clinical sophistication in order to produce valid scoring.

> The scorer has to understand what is going on in the case. In doing this, he will in our opinion be greatly helped by a knowledge of psychoanalysis. He will do well to be familiar with Freud's distinction between manifest and latent content . . , since some of the more important currents of the therapy run below the surface. (pp. 21-22)

> Our best judgment—out of our experience in scoring therapy interviews—is that the scorer must have freedom from severe neurotic conflicts in himself, and that it is likely that especially talented persons do not need a personal analysis or special training in psychoanalysis, though these would certainly be advantageous. We believe that these questions can be answered adequately only by having different kinds of persons . . . try their hands at the scoring. We have not done this as yet—all of the scoring on which this book is based was done by the two authors—and so it remains to be determined who can score. (p. 26)

It seems it would be extremely advantageous to settle this issue empirically. For if relatively naive judges can learn the system as it now stands, or could be trained relatively quickly to do so, economic savings and wider and easier applicability of the system would be assured.

11. Training Required of Judges

The authors state that some training of judges is a necessity, and they outline the training procedure to be followed by prospective coders. "If one hopes to score psychotherapy interviews intelligently, one cannot plunge right into the task without preparation" (Dollard and Auld, 1959, p. 20). They outline the steps that have to be gone through as necessary preparation (cf. pp. 21-27).

Clearly, then, training is required for valid application of the Dollard and Auld system. Although the rules of procedure and scoring are spelled out in some detail in the 1959 manual, the authors have yet to determine whether the manual alone is sufficient for producing judges who can reliably apply the system with results equivalent to those of the scale authors.

12. Training Manual

There is a training manual available. The authors' 1959 volume provides definitions and examples of each of the patient and therapist scoring categories; procedures to be followed in learning to apply the system; rules to be followed for scoring the various categories; rules for unitizing transcripts into sentences; and extensive examples of both the unitizing and scoring procedures.

13. Interrater and Intrarater Reliabilities Reported

The authors discuss both interjudge agreement of the unitizing process (dividing the transcript protocol into sentence units) as well as of the scoring categories themselves.

In their unitizing study, they taught "two intelligent persons" to unitize

> using as instructional material the rules just presented and the examples given in Appendix B. No oral instruction of any kind was given. . . . The material used in this test consisted of excerpts from five psychotherapy cases. An excerpt contained ten pages of completely unpunctuated, uncapitalized transcription taken from a randomly selected place in each of the cases. Altogether the material included about 900 sentences. . . . [For all five cases] the two workers agreed on the placement of 86 percent of the unit marks. Agreement ranges from 83 percent on the poorest case to 91 percent on the best. . . . We consider this amount of agreement in unitizing to be satisfactory, especially in view of the rigorous conditions of the test. (Dollard and Auld, 1959, pp. 18-19)

The authors present an interesting and penetrating discussion in regard to assessing reliability of scoring categories (nominal classification systems) more generally, and for their particular system. They discuss and present data demonstrating the reliability of their system in producing a category profile for a whole case, and in producing category distributions over a series of interviews. The reader can consult pages 298 to 304 of their manual for more detail regarding these analyses. The interjudge agreement to be discussed here is restricted to the reliability of classification of single sentences, the basic scoring units of the system.

Dollard and Auld reject the use of percentage-of-agreement indexes of reliability since these percentages are a function of the number of categories in a particular system (the indexes tend to be inflated with fewer categories) and of the extent to which scores are concentrated in a few of the categories. However, in several of their subsequent investigations (White, Fichtenbaum, and Dollard, 1966a, 1966b) they do report percentage-of-agreement figures as their primary reliability assessment procedure. For these studies, the percentage-of-agreement between two judges as to category assigned (only selected categories from the total system were used) fell in the seventh decile for patient and therapist category scores.

The 1959 manual presents only Kendall *tau* coefficients (with tetrachoric rs included for comparison only). "This coefficient, as we use it, is based on a set of 2x2 tables, one table for each category; and so we avoid the bias of an increased index when there are fewer categories in the whole system" (p. 306). The *tau* coefficient indicates approximately how much better the scorers agree than they would be expected to do if only chance contributed to their agreements.

For the scorings in the 1959 volume, the authors obtained the following *tau* values: for patient categories, the *tau*'s ranged from 0.08 to 0.89, with a median coefficient of 0.44—the corresponding tetrachoric rs ranged from 0.56 to 0.99, with a median of 0.78; for therapist categories, *tau*'s ranged from 0.42 to 0.93, with a median of 0.69—the corresponding tetrachoric rs ranging from 0.78 to 0.99, with a median of 0.91. These figures generally indicate that inter-judge reliability in scoring individual sentences is good, with some categories showing very high and others very low agreement. The authors conclude:

> We have reported the reliability of scoring for our content analysis system. We have shown that there is very high agreement between scorers in their evaluation of an entire case; that there is fairly good agreement between scorers in the number of sentences they assigned to a category in each hour of a series of hours . . . and that there is fairly good agreement between scorers in the assignment of single sentences to categories. The reliability of some categories is much better than that of others; therefore, it might be possible to study some hypotheses, but not others, with the system as it now stands. (Dollard and Auld, 1959, p. 314)

They further report (Auld and Dollard, 1966) that others who have subsequently used the category system or parts of it (Goldenberg & Auld, 1964; Snyder, 1965; Hampton, 1963; and Klein, 1965) have obtained similar levels of agreement, all achieving scoring reliability "good enough to make the system useful for their purposes" (p. 89).

14. Dimensionality Considerations

The authors have not to date examined the dimensional structure present among the patient and therapist categories by submitting scores to an empirical factor analysis of one or another sort. Invariably, interpretative clarity is enhanced by this or some similar dimensional unraveling.

15. Validity Studies

Dollard and Auld's 1959 volume provides little data bearing on the validity of their scoring system. "Since the development of reliable measures was our primary aim, we concentrated our energies on that task and gave relatively little attention to application of our content-analysis method" (p. 315). They do extrapolate from the data presented, however, some evidence for the validity of their system. For example, in studying one therapy case, they predicted that "sexual material and anxious statements would tend not to occur in the same hour, since anxiety would have to be extinguished before sexual thoughts could appear. We found a correlation of -0.42 between A and S" (p. 317). For another case, one prediction was that hostility would be negatively correlated with resistance. "We expected that in hours when he was resistant the patient would not express his hostile feelings; in hours when he expressed his hostile feelings he would not be resistant. The prediction is derived from psychoanalytic hypotheses about the function of resistance . . . . [We] found a very slight negative correlation between H and Res. (r=-0.12)" (pp. 318-19). They also summarize a previous report (Auld and White, 1959) studying "what follows what" (sequences of categories during interviews) in psychotherapy. One finding of this investigation was that "silence does indeed occur more often after resistant talk than after nonresistant talk. The probability is 0.24 that a silence of at least five seconds will occur after a sentence scored as resistant; it's only 0.04 that a silence will occur after a nonresistant sentence. Furthermore, 'silences' are likely to be followed by resistant talk" (Dollard and Auld, 1959, p. 322).

Another finding was that categories do indeed persist.

> . . . for instance, the likelihood of a sentence scored S is greater after S sentences than after other sentences. . . . A typical finding is that for the H category. The chances are 71 out of 100 that sentence $n + 1$ was scored H if sentence n was scored H. However, if sentence n was not scored H, chances are only 3 out of 100 that sentence $n + 1$ was scored H. (pp. 321-22)

Dollard and Auld summarize the 1959 evidence as follows:

> Our ability to apply our method of scoring to a variety of cases treated by a number of therapists, the striking difference between neurotic and psychotic cases, the demonstration that some predicted correlations between variables could be found, and the successful testing of four hypotheses about sequences of categories in psychotherapy all give evidence for the validity of the method. (p. 324)

Since 1959, studies by White, Fichtenbaum, and Dollard (1964a, 1964b, 1966a, 1966b) have extended the evidential base for the validity of the Dollard and Auld scoring system. These studies focused on both an intensive analysis of single therapy cases, as well as an analysis of initial interviews of patients who later were designated "remainers" and "dropouts." One study (1966), for example, found that

> . . . the therapist focused more than the patient did during [an earlier] period of therapy on the areas of sex and evaluation of self. Therefore, these were considered goal areas. [Next] the scored content of the patient's talk during the first quarter and the last quarter of treatment was compared. In the areas of sex and evaluation of self there were significant changes in the amount of units classified as adaptive. . . . These measures established that the therapist had to some degree achieved his goals. (p. 47)

Another study of the patient silence in initial interviews (1964b) tested silence in relation to other variables for a sample of 70 recorded (initial) interviews with patients, conducted by nine resident psychiatrists. Results showed that the mean percentage of silence in initial interviews was greater for patients who dropped out than for those who continued for at least three more appointments; that dropping out of therapy increased as the social status of individuals decreased; that the percentage of silence units in initial interviews increased as the social status of individuals decreased; and that there was a significant interaction effect between silence, social class, and dropping out of therapy.

Goldenberg and Auld (1964) repeated the portion of the Auld and White study that dealt with the correlation between silence and resistant sentences, and confirmed the original findings. Snyder (1965) found the coding system for patient's sentences useful for the description of therapeutic process in the intensive study of a single case. Hampton (1963) adopted the coding system for scoring sentence-completion responses. Klein (1965) used the coding system for identifying resistant segments in psychotherapy interviews. Using GSR recordings, he found that patients are relatively comfortable when resistance is strong and stable, that they are quite anxious and aroused in periods of unstable resistance, and they are somewhat labile but not extremely anxious during periods of low resistance. Tourney et al. (1966) have added other categories to the 1959 system, and have developed rating scales for all of them. Their work has focused on studying therapist "errors," both of omission (for example, failure to ask appropriate motivating questions, failure to interpret, lack of empathic response) or of commission (for example, unnecessary advice, wrong or ill-timed interpretations, over-identifications with the patient).

References

Auld, F., Jr. Vicissitudes of communication in psychotherapy. In J. M. Shlien et al. (Eds.), *Research in Psychotherapy*, Vol. 3. Washington, D.C.: American Psychological Association, 1968. Pp. 169-78.

Auld, F., Jr., and Dollard, J. Measurement of motivational variables in psychotherapy. In L. A. Gottschalk and A. H. Auerbach (Eds.), *Methods of research in psychotherapy*. New York: Appleton-Century-Crofts, 1966. Pp. 85-92.

Auld, F., Jr., and White, A. M. Rules for dividing interviews into sentences. Journal of Psychology, 1956, 42, 273-81.

———. Sequential dependencies in psychotherapy. *Journal of Abnormal and Social Psychology*, 1959, 58, 100-104.

Bloomfield, L. *Language*. New York: Holt, Rinehart & Winston, 1933.

Dollard, J., and Auld, F., Jr. *Scoring human motives: a manual*. New Haven, Conn.: Yale University Press, 1959.

Dollard, J., Auld, F., Jr., and White, A. M. *Steps in Psychotherapy*. New York: Macmillan, 1953.

Dollard, J., and Miller, N. E. *Personality and psychotherapy*. New York: McGraw-Hill, 1950.

Dollard, J., and Mowrer, O. H. A method of measuring tension in written documents. *Journal of Abnormal and Social Psychology*, 1947, 42, 3-32.

Fries, C. C. *The structure of English*. New York: Harcourt, Brace, 1952.

Goldenberg, G. M., and Auld, F., Jr. Equivalence of silence to resistance. *Journal of Consulting Psychology*, 1964, 28, 476.

Hampton, P. A study of hidden motives and conflicts in university counseling. *In VII Congreso Interamericano de Psicología*. Mexico, D. F.: Sociedad Interamericano de Psicología, 1963. Pp. 437-41.

Klein, L. S. Correlation of resistance with GSR of patients in psychotherapy. Unpublished doctoral dissertation, Wayne State University, 1965.

Snyder, W.U. *Dependency in psychotherapy*. New York: Macmillan, 1965.

Tourney, G., Bloom, V., Lowinger, P. L., Schrorer, C., Auld, F., and Grisell, F. A study of psychotherapeutic process variables in psychoneurotic and schizophrenic patients. *American Journal of Psychotherapy*, 1966, 20, 112-24.

White, A. M., Fichtenbaum, L., and Dollard, J. A measure for predicting dropping out of psychotherapy. *Journal of Consulting Psychology*, 1964, 28, 326-32. (a)

________. Evaluation of silence in initial interviews with psychiatric clinic patients. *Journal of Nervous and Mental Disease*, 1964, 139, 550-57. (b)

________.A content measure of changes attritutable to psychotherapy. *American Journal of Orthopsychiatry*, 1966, 36, 41-49. (a)

________. Measuring change: a verbal and nonverbal content analysis method. *Psychotherapy*, 1966, 3, 107-113. (b)

White, A. M., Fichtenbaum L., Cooper, L., and Dollard, J. Psychological focus in psychiatric interviews. *Journal of Consulting Psychology*, 1966, 5, 363.

A System for the Analysis of the Content of Clinical Evaluations and Patient-Therapist Verbalizations

Timothy Leary and Merton Gill

1. Rationale for Development of the System

Leary and Gill's major goal was to devise a means "for the intensive, detailed study of the process of psychotherapy" (1959, p. 62). They were dissatisfied with the content-analysis systems available, primarily because none of the systems was sufficiently comprehensive.

> Other people had studied the content of the patient-therapist verbalizations in nonclinical categories (Mowrer, 1957; Gottschalk and Hambridge, 1955) and there had been some studies which used some of what we called clinical categories (Dollard and Mowrer, 1947), but there had been none which had used what we regarded as a comprehensive set of clinical categories, though Strupp's system (Strupp, 1957) comes closest to doing so. (Leary and Gill, 1959, p. 63)

Besides a comprehensive system that would encompass most of the events occurring in psychotherapy, the authors wanted a system that would be clinically relevant, that is, a system whose major features would be factors similar to those used by experienced clinicians in conceptualizing the psychotherapy process. To accomplish this goal, the authors decided

> to have . . . a group of clinicians—and there were twelve of us of mixed Sullivanian and Freudian training sitting in a circle around the recording machine—listen to tape-recorded interviews and freely and independently write down what we felt was going on. . . . We evolved a model which covered everything our clinicians said in their evaluations. . . . One [aspect of the model] is a view of the nature of psychological functioning—the constituents which go to make up this functioning and their interrelationships.

> The other [aspect] is a view of the psychotherapeutic interaction—both intellectual and emotional—between patient and therapist, and of how this interaction facilitates or hinders changes in the patient's psychological functioning in terms of both insight and clinical improvement. We arranged the components of the model—constituents and relationships—in a group of what we labeled "clinical categories" and developed groups of variables for each category. The clinical categories thus became the comprehensive set of the dimensions of the process of psychotherapy. Now we could code any clinical evaluation, and count the entries in the various categories, so we could compare clinical evaluations with each other. We called this a count of the content of clinical evaluations. (pp. 62-63)

By this procedure Leary and Gill had accomplished their first goal, which was to develop a comprehensive coding system for analyzing the assessments of clinicians observing the psychotherapy interaction. Their next step had to do with the raw data of therapy itself, that is, the recorded interactions of patient and therapist (in contrast to clinicians' interpretations of that raw data).

> Our second goal [was] to find some other way of analyzing the raw data which would give us some measurement of the psychotherapeutic process. . . . We wanted our second method to be quantitative and to serve two functions. First, it was to be a measurement of the process of psychotherapy, for the validity of which our clinical evaluation would be the criterion. Second, we would also use it in the reverse direction, to give us clues to the validity of the evaluation. . . . An obvious possibility for a method of measurement suggested itself. Why not study the patient-therapist verbalizations on the same categories we had developed for the clinical evaluations? We knew that in insight-oriented therapy—the kind which especially interested us—patient and therapist come progressively to talk more and more about the same things an evaluating clinician talks about. . . . Of course, we found that our clinical categories covered sometimes more, sometimes less of the patient-therapist verbalizations. That part which was not covered we called "nonclinical." We decided we could more usefully study this nonclinical content if we made some kind of systematic classification of it, so we devised a scheme for classifying all the nonclinical statements too. (p. 63)

The model they developed they called a "combined psychological and psychotherapeutic model."

> Its psychological aspect is a much simplified form of the psychoanalytic model made explicit by Rapaport, in addition to which it includes intrapersonal communication between the topographical levels of the psyche—defining topographic in the psychoanalytic sense of relationsip to consciousness. Its psychotherapeutic aspect deals with the interpersonal communication—both emotional and intellectual—between patient and therapist, and how this facilitates or inhibits changes in the intrapersonal communication and in behavior. . . . Although the model is derived from the psychoanalytical one, it is implicit in the evaluations of most clinicians—not only those analytically trained. (p. 65)
>
> In conclusion, research into the process of psychotherapy requires study of the raw data both by clinical evaluation and by other less inferential methods so that each can be used in the validation of the other. (p. 94)
>
> We were urged on by the conviction that because our point of departure was something real and important about psychotherapy—what a clinician had to say about it—we were dealing with something significant and not just building an elaborate but meaningless scheme. (p. 64)

In summary, Leary and Gill present a system designed to be comprehensive of the psychotherapy interaction; relevant to both the recorded verbalizations of patient and therapist and to interpretive assessments of that interaction by clinicians; derived from a neo-analytic framework; and hopefully possessing all the characteristics of reliable measurement procedures.

2. Description of the Scoring System

The authors define first the psychoanalytic model, and then the category scoring system derived from that model. Focusing first on clinical evaluations of psychotherapy interviews, Leary and Gill state that clinicians discuss primarily two kinds of topics.

> One kind has to do with the patient's psychological functioning. . . . The other has to do with the emotional and intellectual interactions between patient and therapist and how these either facilitate or hamper insight on the one hand, and therapeutic progress on the other. (1959, p. 64)
>
> We are seeking a way of classifying every statement consisting of a subject and a characteristic, and . . . both of these are to be hierarchically ordered in terms of their probable importance in producing insight. (p. 70)

The model they evolved consists basically of (1) four constituents (psychological processes), (2) distinctions of three topographical levels at which these constituents can be said statically to reside, and (3) description of movements between the various topographical levels. The four constituents include motives, affect, thought, and action; the three topographical levels are unconscious, conscious, and overt behavioral expression.

> The model takes its point of departure from motives, which therefore form one of its four principal constituents. The other three are drawn from the three possible fates of motives. In the cognitive model the fate to the motive is action, in the affective it is affect, and in the cognitive it is thought. . . . Clinicians talk not only about these four major constituents but they also describe three of them—motives, affects, and ideas—topographically, that is, whether they are conscious or unconscious; and they discuss whether or not these three remain intrapsychic or reach overt behavioral expression—motives in action, affects in affect, and ideas in speech. We will call the unconscious, conscious, and overt behavioral expression the three levels of our model. . . . Hence, the patient's ideas which the clinician will mainly discuss are . . . the ideational representation in the patient of his motives, affects and actions, or the patient's ideas about these three. (p. 65)

Finally, the authors describe the movement that can occur between the various levels of the model.

> Any constituent of the model which is described as static, we will say is at one of the levels. Speaking loosely—in that the topographical position of the constituents is only a reflection of the mental dynamics—we may say that the constituents of the model can move from one level to another. Movement between levels may take place either in the discharge direction — unconscious → conscious → overt expression — or in the reverse direction. What we may call a partial movement toward discharge may take place if the content of the constituents is altered—for example, if the hostility is expressed to someone other than the one for whom it was originally intended. Such partial movements, as well as inhibition of movements, are conceptualized as the clinically familiar defense mechanisms. . . . The therapist in insight-oriented psychotherapy—and the patient too insofar as he is in part cooperating—attempts by various maneuvers to diminish these inhibitors of discharge into consciousness and overt expression, whether action, affect expression, or speech. (p. 66)

The authors' scoring system derived from their psychoanalytic model and consists of four major groupings of categories, each with subcategories. It consists of Clinical Categories, Nonclinical Categories, Special Clinical Categories, and Modifiers by Which Statements are Qualified. Table 3.3 presents a synopsis of Leary and Gill's system of content-analysis.

CLINICAL CATEGORIES

"The model presents us with a hierarchy which we may designate as static condition (at a level), movement, cause of movement. It is from this hierarchy that we derive the first group of clinical categories to be used in coding." (Leary and Gill, 1959, p. 66) From the table it is apparent that the fifth category (constituents) designates a constituent at a level; the second (admission into speech), third (admission into awareness), and fourth (discharge) represent movements between levels; and the first (intellectual interventions) reflects interventions which facilitate or hinder movement towards awareness and speech.

> Under each of these five categories we have a list of variables to permit a more differentiated analysis of content. For the first category, our variables are the different kinds of insight-oriented interventions a therapist or patient can make, for example, clarification and interpretation. For the second, third, and fourth categories our variables designate three specific types of movement from one level to another: (A) movement in which what is believed to be the original content of the constituent is unaltered, for example, expression and awareness; (B) complete obstructions of movement, for example, inhibition and denial; and (C) partial movement made possible by altering some component of the original motive or affect, for example, reversal and displacement. For the fifth category, that of the psychic constituent, we have three groups of variables—derived motive, action, or idea; bodily motive, action or idea; and affect. (p. 68)

NON-CLINICAL CATEGORIES

> The great bulk of what clinicians evaluating a psychotherapy say is subsumed under the categories already presented. But much patient-therapist talk is not. . . . We wanted to devise a classification of this "nonclinical" part of patient-therapist verbalizations. We settled not on one which we developed empirically, but rather one which follows from man's imbeddedness in the biological, social, and material worlds, one which the division of the sciences follows too. (Leary and Gill, 1959, p. 70)

These categories are subdivided into those dealing with the *subjects* of a statement (the basic unit being rated), and those dealing with *characteristics* imputed in the statement as belonging to the subjects.

"Beginning with clinical and proceeding to nonclinical talk we order the subjects talked about, the patient, the therapist, or the clinician, in increasing distance from what is important to the person whose statements are being coded" (p. 70). That is, from the self in therapy, through people personally known to the speaker, to impersonal talk. "As for characteristics of subjects, after the five clinical categories already defined, the nonclinical characteristics follow the same sequence suggested for impersonal subjects: biological (somatic), social . . . and physiochemical or inanimate characteristics" (p. 70). The nonclinical categories are numbers nine, ten, and eleven in their coding system.

SPECIAL CLINICAL CATEGORIES

> Although any unit consisting of a subject and a characteristic of that subject can be subsumed under the categories already proposed, our study of our sample of clinical evaluations as well as our clinical experience shows that three categories are of sufficiently distinctive relevance to insight-oriented psychotherapy to be pulled out of their general class and given a specific designation. (Leary and Gill, 1959, pp. 70-72)

The sixth category, psychological symptomatic, includes whatever a clinician designates as a symptom; the seventh, psychotherapeutic, reflects statements about therapy which do not fall in one of the first five clinical categories; and the eighth, vocal-kinetic, focuses on paralanguage and motoric aspects of the patient's communication from which the clinician infers at least some of his evaluations.

The authors summarize that their matrix is complete.

> We repeat that it is employed to code statements expressed both in patient-therapist verbalizations and in clinical evaluations. While any particular statement . . . may appear anywhere in the matrix, clinical evaluation statements are likely to fall into the first eight categories, and patient-therapist verbalizations, much more frequently than clinical evaluations, will fall into categories nine through eleven. The logic of this matrix is such that . . . it can subsume any verbalization of patient, therapist, and evaluator. Our experience so far in using the matrix corroborates this logic. (pp. 72-73)

MODIFIERS BY WHICH STATEMENTS ARE MODIFIED

> Up to now the description of our system has proceeded as though all statements were simple declarations. This is of course unjustified, because statements are qualified in many different ways which result in changes in clinical meaning sufficiently important to warrant the introduction of these modifiers into a scheme of classification. A statement may be presented for example as conditional, as a question, or dealing with something which occurred in a dream, as equivalent to some other statement, and with many other kinds of modifications. We will call these qualifications as a general class "modifiers." (Leary and Gill, 1959, p. 74)

Modifiers are subsumed under three groups. Attitudinal modifiers include grammatical modes, for example, conditional, interrogative and negative; evaluative attitudes, for example, desirable and undesirable; and states of consciousness, for example dreams and fantasy. Dynamic modifiers reflect the interaction of psychic forces and describe whether the constituent is unconscious, in awareness, or overtly expressed. Connective modifiers consist of various kinds of connections between propositions, a specification of a statement in relation to another statement; they are divided into three kinds: simple, casual, and change-improvement.

Leary and Gill, in several places, emphasize the tentative nature of their categories, and they state that varying amounts of "care and completeness" have gone into definition of the categories of their system. They caution that "only extensive experience can show how effectively and usefully [our system] differentiates the material" being coded. (p. 72)

3. Data Collection Context

The data to which the coding system is applied is of two sorts: the verbal evaluations of clinicans who observe or audit tape recordings of the psychotherapy interaction; and samples of the actual patient-therapist verbalizations taken from recordings of live psychotherapy interactions. For the former task the clinicians are instructed to evaluate freely, "that is, they were asked to say whatever they wanted to in their own words—and that is what clinicians prefer to do." (Leary and Gill, 1959, p. 79) Hence, in both cases the data begin coded is from the live, naturalistic setting: either the uninhibited, free individual assessments by clinical evaluators or verbalizations taken from recorded psychotherapy interviews.

4. Data Form

The coding system has been applied exclusively to typewritten transcriptions of either clinical evaluations or of the psychotherapy interaction (patient-therapist verbalizations). Since the authors' system is unique vis-a-vis coding clinical evaluations, an excerpt is chosen to show the kind of assessment one clinician made of a psychotherapy interaction, in the exact form in which it would be unitized and subsequently coded. The excerpt is from a clinician's evaluation of the third 10-minute segment of a first psychotherapy session.

> T moves abruptly to requesting information of P's difficulty. / P momentarily shocked. / Embarassed / —regains poise. / becomes intellectual / and controlled talking about sexual life. / Tries to be calm / but occassionally embarassment comes through. / P's defensiveness more obvious as rationalization. / T tends to encourage / P to return to generalization. / (Leary and Gill, 1959, p. 82, Table 11)

5. Choice of Units

The authors outline three separate unit issues in regard to application of their category system. The first problem has to do with the segment of therapy material to be given the clinician, on which he is to make his evaluation. The second concerns the segment of material across which one summarizes the various counts of patient-therapist verbalizations. The third issue deals with the segment to be coded, or the unit to be used in making the various content counts.

THE UNIT GIVEN THE EVALUATOR

> The natural unit of psychotherapy for the clinician is the session. But psychotherapy can be divided into units which for various research purposes may be more useful than the session. . . . In our own research thus far we have asked the clinicians to evaluate consecutive ten-minute segments of an interview, and then to make a summary evaluation of the interview as a whole. (Leary and Gill, 1959, p. 76)

The "scoring unit" (in this case "assessment unit") for the evaluator's task, then, is a ten-minute segment, and also the entire interview.

UNIT FOR SUMMARY ANALYSIS

> After the statements have been coded and counted, into what temporal units will they be combined for summary and tally analyses? We have settled on the ten-minute units so that our patient-therapist content count summaries cover the same unit which the clinician is evaluating. (Leary and Gill, 1959, p. 76)

The "summarizing unit," then, for both coders and evaluators, is the ten-minute segment.

UNIT FOR CODING

> Since coding of clinical evaluations or of patient-therapist content should be such that it can be executed by technicians, and because the coding must be as objective as possible, the unit should be such as to involve the least amount of inference. (Leary and Gill, 1959, p. 76)

> Our unit for coding both clinical evaluations and patient-therapist content is the shortest verbalization which can be understood to be a combination of subjects—whether a person or impersonal—and some characteristic or attribute of that subject. (p. 63)

The authors call this unit a statement.

Thus, the basic "scoring unit" is the statement, either patient's, therapist's, or evaluator's. For the clinical evaluation data, the statements coded are a particular evaluator's written descriptions of consecutive ten-minute segments of psychotherapy sessions. For the patient-therapist interaction data, the statements coded are typescripts of patient and therapist verbalizations occurring in a particular ten-minute segment of psychotherapy sessions.

Leary and Gill are not explicit about the "contextual unit" for their system. Apparently the interview segments are coded with the other participant present, and are scored sequentially within a segment (that is, in the P-T-P-T-P-T-P order).

They have, however, considered the issue of whether the ten-minute units to be coded or evaluated should be presented sequentially or randomly:

> It is possible to give clinicians or technicians the interview material in its original sequence or in randomized order. The latter approach is necessary only when the research design aims at preventing the listener from knowing what section of therapy is being considered. Where it is the intention to have the clinicians evaluate interview material as they do in their usual clinical work, it is

> essential that they be exposed to the raw data in the original sequence. Since technicians simply code the content, they can be given data in nonsequential order where this is convenient. (p. 77)

Apparently, then, the clinicians evaluate the segments in consecutive order. The technician scorers, of both the clinical evaluations and patient-therapist verbalizations, seem to code the segments primarily in sequential order, although sometimes in random order. The authors present no empirical data comparing the differential effects on their category scores of random versus sequential coding by the technicians.

6. Participant-Context Restrictions

Technicians code all the "statements" in the ten-minute segments of clinical evaluations of patient-therapist verbalizations. The authors do not explicitly consider whether, in the scoring of the latter segments, it makes a difference, in scoring either patient or therapist statements in a segment, if the other participant's verbalizations are present or not.

7. Type of Sampling Indicated

The authors do not consider sampling from the point of view of either random or systematic approaches. Apparently, sampling is not involved. Their coding system has been applied to date to the entire session, admittedly arbitrarily separated into consecutive ten-minute segments.

They do, however, contrast "arbitrary" and "meaningful" units of psychotherapy.

> Basically, the choice in process research is between arbitraty units or meaningful units. Arbitrary units are temporal (minutes, sessions, blocking of sessions), grammatical (the word, the clause, the sentence), or typographical (the page). Meaningful units require a proper definition of a critical event, and the ways of determining the beginning and ending of such an event. Meaninful units seem a rational division of the process, but arbitrary units can be more easily and reliably determined. In meaningful units it is often impossible to obtain agreement as to when a unit begins or ends. And the fact that there are many levels and categories in which events occur makes it difficult to determine which is the critical variable. . . . We have not yet found a satisfactory way of reaching good interjudge reliability in classifying meaningful units. (Leary and Gill, 1959, p. 76)

In applying their system, therefore, the authors do not sample; and the units they have picked are arbitrary ones—in one case a grammatical one (the statement), and in the other two cases a temporal one (ten-minute segments).

8. Sample Location Within the Interview

Since the entire session is coded, in consecutive ten-minute segments, the issue of sampling from a particular session has not been considered by the authors to date. They do not present any data regarding the trend of their category scores over the consecutive ten-minute segments of particular sessions—that is, they do not consider the issue of differential effects of segment location within the interview on the resulting category scores.

9. Sample Location over Therapy Interviews

The authors do not explicitly consider this issue, since apparently they do not sample across interviews either. The scoring system, instead, is applied to the total content of each therapy interview from initiation to termination. The authors, therefore, have not dealt with the issue of how representative of the total therapy case are scores derived from interviews at various stages (early to late) of the treatment continuum.

10. Clinical Sophistication of Judges

Obviously, experienced clinicians are required to obtain clinical evaluations of the psychotherapy interaction. However, the authors make it clear that naive judges suffice for coding either the clinical evaluations or patient-therapist verbalizations on the various categories of their system.

> Our technicians are not psychologists, are not necessarily college graduates. They are trained like mail clerks to recognize certain addresses (which are the sentences and phrases which the clinicians are sending them), and they file them in the appropriate letter box. It has not proven to be an impossibly demanding task. (Leary and Gill, 1959, p. 118)

11. Training Required of Judges

Since the authors do not spell out their training procedure in any detail, it is difficult to determine how much training is necessary. At one point they indicate that degree of intercoder agreement is a function of amount of training, so that some training is clearly required. At another place, they suggest that training can be accomplished in a two-week period, apparently involving about eighty hours: "We have just trained a new technician, a high school graduate, in about two weeks, so that her reliability is now up to the average of our technician groups." (Leary and Gill, 1959, p. 118)

12. Training Manual

There is no training manual available. The authors have not to date spelled out in any detail the procedures they use in training technicians, or whether or not it is standardized and self-administrable.

13. Interrater and Intrarater Reliabilities Reported

Leary and Gill discuss reliability aspects of their coding system. The first has to do with the reliability of the unitization process. Regarding this reliability they state that "we have not yet worked out exact rules for determining what constitutes a statement, but we have found that even in the absence of such rules agreement among coders is high. The general rule is to code as a statement any and every verbal grouping which can be understood as a subject with its characteristics" (1959, p. 77).

The second aspect of reliability has to do with the consistency with which independent coders score a statement in the same category of the coding system, that is, with interscorer agreement. The authors have assessed this for technicians coding what the clinician has said about a particular ten-minute segment. "The intertechnician agreement as to order, variable, and level has been quite high (averaging 90 percent). The agreement is a function of how well-defined the orders and variables are. Intertechnician agreement has not been a problem" (p. 11). The authors report a study in which percentages of agreement in coding were obtained for clinical evaluations "between the codings of judge (one of us) which were used as a criterion, and the codings by technicians working independently" (p. 77). In three separate studies involving four coders and 572, 544, and 2,777 separate coding decisions respectively, the percentages of agreement ranged from 77 to 99. "The coder's reliability changes from clinician to clinician and from unit to unit. Some clinician's evaluations are more difficult to rate because of the vagueness or complexity of their language" (p. 77).

Regarding the reliability of the coding of patient-therapist verbalizations, "we report only one set of figures, based on the coding of 584 statements in one fifty-minute session. Agreement as to subject category was 99 percent; characteristic category, 87 percent; and for variable, 97 percent." (p. 77)

In reporting these figures the authors point out that

> . . . The rules for determining "agreement-nonagreement" were rigidly defined. Failure to score the event or adding an extra score were counted as misses. For decisions as to category level, the code was either "right or wrong"—with no half scores or near misses credited. On fifth-category interpersonal variables, for which . . . the Kaiser interpersonal circle was used, scores in the same octant of the circle were considered hits—all others misses. (p. 77)

The final aspect of reliability the authors address has to do with agreement among the expert clinicians in judging what is going on in the therapy session.

> One thing that tends to lower the interclinician agreement is that they talk about different aspects of the therapy process. . . . So, if anything, we tend to get higher interclinician agreement when we use longer time units. (p. 177)

> Because our freely obtained individual clinical evaluations are not comprehensive we use pooled clinical evaluations as our basis for comparison with counts of patient-therapist content. . . . We [have studied] interclinician reliability by comparing the pooled evaluations of the group split in half. . . . But it is clear there are many ways in which such a method could lead one astray. We are banking on the assumption that the clinicians generally agree that some of their apparent differences actually complement one another because they are made at differing "depth," and that idiosyncratic evaluations will not carry much weight in comparison with the mass of pooled evaluation. (p. 80)

> A satisfactory demonstration of reliability of the clinical evaluations is, of course, essential before one can place much confidence in them in using them for comparison with a measurement of the raw date of psychotherapy. (p. 79)

14. Dimensionality Considerations

To date the authors have not presented any data or discussion regarding the intercorrelations present among the various categories in their system. At the empirical level the dimensional structure of their system remains unknown.

15. Validity Studies

The only validity data presented so far for the coding system is that found in the authors' 1959 paper. The data presented there are examples of applications of the system to particular case samples. For example, the authors provide a sample clinical evaluation of a ten-minute unit of therapy, an excerpt (scored) from the first few minutes of a ten-minute segment of patient-therapist verbalizations, the summary and tallying procedures for scoring both examples, and a comparison of the separate analyses of the clinical evaluations and the patient-therapist verbalizations.

> Further details of the collection, classification and analysis of data will be discussed in future publications. . . . We are presently engaged in a study we hope will teach us the ways in which our two counts can be usefully compared. We have obtained free clinical evaluations of each unit of a psychotherapy consisting of 17 interviews; and we are coding clinical evaluations, and the patient-therapist content of this therapy, and studying the pattern of scores and indexes as they vary from unit to unit and session to session. The next step which the research calls for seems clearly the working out of a method of obtaining comprehensive clinical evaluations so that their reliability can be properly studied. And then we plan to make one more study devoted to the method of analysis before applying the system to the study of specific problems in psychotherapy. We will compare our system of analysis with others developed to quantify the process of therapy. (Leary and Gill, 1959, p. 94)

To this reviewer's knowledge, Leary and Gill have not published anything further regarding their content-analysis system since their 1959 paper. It is clear from that paper that the authors considered their category system still under development, and not yet a final product.

> How can we be sure that our system studies what it is supposed to study—that it is valid? How do we know it measures what "really" goes on in psychotherapy? It is exactly in order to be able to make a step forward towards answering this question that we have laid so much stress on the desirability of studying the raw data of psychotherapy by two different methods—the clinical evaluation and the count of the patient-therapist verbalizations. . . . We must nevertheless admit that the clarification of what constitutes validity in this research, let alone what methods may be used to

demonstrate validity, are problems for the future. . . . [We] stress again that the development of useful methods of comparing the two kinds of analysis of the raw data is a task for the future. (pp. 80-81)

References

Dollard, J., and Mower, O. H. A method for measuring tension in written documents. *Journal of Abnormal and Social Psychology,* 1947, 42, 3-32.

Gottschalk, L. A., and Hambridge, G., Jr. Verbal behavior analysis. I. A systematic approach to the problem of quantifying psychologic processes. *Journal of Projective Techniques,* 1955, 19, 387-409.

Leary, T. *Interpersonal diagnosis of personality.* New York: Ronald Press, 1957.

Leary, T., and Gill, M. The dimensions and a measure of the process of psychotherapy: a system for the analysis of the content of clinical evaluations and patient-therapist verbalizations. In E. A. Rubinstein and M. B. Parloff (Eds.), *Research in psychotherapy.* Vol. 1. Washington D. C.: American Psychological Association, 1959. Pp. 62-95.

Mowrer, O. H. *Psychotherapy: theory and research.* New York: Ronald Press, 1957.

Rapaport, D. The conceptual model of psychoanalysis. *Journal of Personality,* 1951, 20, 56-81.

Strupp, H. A multidimensional system for analysing psychotherapeutic techniques. *Psychiatry,* 1957, 20, 293-306.

A Communication-Interaction Category System

Henry L. Lennard and Arnold Bernstein

1. Rationale for Development of the System

Lennard and Bernstein, for the last decade or so, have brought to bear on psychotherapy investigation a perspective emphasizing the social-dyadic communicational nature of psychotherapy. "Psychotherapeutic intervention has traditionally located pathology within the individual and has focused its attention on the management of intrapsychic variables. . . We shift the perspective from the individual and his intrapsychic states to the interactional environment within which his behavior is inevitably embedded." (Lennard and Bernstein, 1969, p. 3).

The basic idea prompting this research was to apply concepts and methods developed within the framework of the social sciences—especially concepts pertaining to the study of face to face interaction and methods pertaining to the analysis of communication—to

> the study of psychotherapy. . . . Our conviction [is] that social science concepts designed to describe phenomena of interaction and systems of relationships can make a major contribution to the understanding of therapy. . . . Social science concepts and methods can help to identify those factors in the therapeutic interaction which arise from the fact that therapy is a social situation, that is, an interaction system. . . . From the perspective of the social sciences, the focus in the study of therapy can be upon therapy as a system of action (verbal communication), upon therapy as a system of expectations, and upon the interrelationships between communications and expectations. (Lennard and Bernstein, 1960, pp. 1-4)

To label this new perspective, the authors coined the term "clinical sociology," which refers to any "application of social research methodology and sociological theory to the data of the clinical situation and to subject matter traditionally falling within the fields of pyschiatry and clinical psychology" (Lennard and Bernstein, 1969, p. 3).

A second major aspect of their approach involves an emphasis on the linguistic aspects of human communication.

> To encompass the total interaction that takes place between a therapist and a patient is almost impossible. Since, however, there seems little doubt that language is the main instrument of therapeutic communication, we have concentrated our attention upon it. An analysis of the role of visual cues, gestures, the physical situation, and other variables was not undertaken. Our research addressed itself specifically to a description in quantitative terms of the verbal interaction that takes place in the course of psychotherapy. . . . [As a result] the methodological armamentarium available in the social sciences for the systematic, quantitative study of communication can be brought to bear upon the study of psychotherapy. (Lennard and Bernstein, 1960, pp. 2-3)

A third major emphasis of the authors is on the formal (noncontent) aspects of linguistic communication, of which the participants in psychotherapy are usually unaware.

> Let us conceive of therapeutic interaction as a sequence of activities including verbal statements and other behavior. Therapist communication follows upon patient communication, and patient communication follows upon therapist communication. The attention of both therapist and patient is focused on limited aspects of

> the communication sequence. . . . It appears to us that most of what occurs . . . must of necessity lie outside the cognizance of the participants in the therapy group. (p. 7)

> It is the inability of informants to report on what we wish to study that is the most serious drawback of the interview approach for our purposes. For it is just as difficult for a person engaged in interaction to be simultaneously aware of the multiple aspects of interaction process as to monitor nuances of grammar and syntax of speech while engaged in a heated political discussion. The temporal vicissitudes of interaction process are especially resistant to awareness. (Lennard and Bernstein, 1969, p. 47)

> If in our study of interaction processes we tend to place greater emphasis upon the formal and process characteristics of interactions than upon their contents, it is because these characteristics are not usually accorded the attention they deserve, but also because we suspect that Hare (1961) may be right when he argues that the *form* of interaction frequently turns out to be a major factor, even in research devoted to content. (p. 44)

> It is not our intention, in introducing this new perspective of the psychotherapy relationship, to replace the more traditional psychodynamically oriented approaches with a totally new theory of treatment, but rather to add another set of dimensions to those already formulated. It does not appear to us that consideration of the contextual properties of the system in which psychotherapy ordinarily occurs, nor attention to role-learning, contradicts in any significant way the more traditional ways of looking at psychotherapy, but rather that it places them within a broader frame of reference. (p. 170)

2. Description of the System

Table 3.4 presents Lennard and Bernstein's six broad categories of Interaction Analysis. These include units of interactional quantity or productivity, categories of therapist informational specificity, grammatical forms of propositions, affective content of propositions, interaction process categories, and role system reference categories.

Some additional higher order or derived measures are used by the authors in their various studies. (1) Appropriateness or relevance of a response. "By identifying the reference category for a patient's response, it is possible to get a rough estimate of its relevance to the preceding therapist communication. If a patient statement falls into the same reference category as the therapist statement that precedes it, it is treated as evidence that communication regarding a given content is continuing" (Lennard and Bernstein, 1960, p. 93). Correlations are calculated between percentage of therapist propositions and percentage of patient propositions which are of the same kind, that is, which are classified in the same category. By this procedure an *Index of Similarity* is provided expressing "the fact of an increasing correlation over time between patient and therapist with respect to the following three kinds of communicative sets: (*a*) primary system references, (*b*) evaluative communications, and (*c*) affective communication" (p. 91). Furthermore, an *Index of Responsiveness* can be determined by "comparing the character of a response [by the patient or by the therapist] with the character of the immediately preceding statement. . . . [The index] is the ratio between the frequency of similar responses and frequency of dissimilar responses" (p. 94). (2) *Equilibrium* refers to "a state of a system such that there is a zero change of the units relative to each other . . . the tendency of the system to maintain a steady state" (p. 16). (3) *Differentiation* has two meanings: either "a temporal or phase phenomenon in which the behavior of the participants is seen to differ systematically over time (T_1, T_2, T_3, . . T_n)," or "specialization of the behavior of participants at a given point in time, (T_1, T_2, or T_3)" (pp. 17-18). (4) *Socialization* in psychotherapy refers to "the learning of a social role . . . to acquire the set of role expectations which are reciprocal to those of the therapist . . . to be inducted into the patient role" (pp. 24-25). The socialization process involves four factors: (*a*) activeness or learning who is to perform and how much of the verbalization is to be done by each; (*b*) differentiation of performance through time; (*c*) selectivity or what communications are appropriate and relevant; and (*d*) timing or expectations concerning the total time duration of the psychotherapy relationship. Finally, *Deutero-learning* refers to learning how to learn.

> In therapy the patient not only "learns" a set of expectations appropriate to the therapeutic relationship, and how to behave in accordance with such expectations; but in learning this . . . he acquires insight into the principles underlying the learning of role expectation in general. These principles are then available for use in learning or relearning other patterns of expectations governing relationships in which he participates. (Lennard and Bernstein, 1960, p. 28)

For greater detail regarding each of these constructs and the actual statistical indexes used for their measurement, the reader is referred to Lennard and Bernstein's two volumes (1960, 1969).

3. Data Collection Context

In 1953 Lennard, wanting to apply social science concepts and small-group theory to actual psychotherapy data, needed to find verbatim records of psychotherapy hours. Since no appropriate recordings were available at that time, he set about collecting his own therapy data. He recorded eight therapy cases, four therapists with two patients each, for a period of eight months apiece. Three of the therapists were associated with analytic institutes, the fourth was a clinical psychologist. All four worked within a psychoanalytic framework. The therapists were free to accept or reject patients on the same basis as they would in their practice. The patients were all referred from clinics in the New York City area. "More than 500 sessions were thus [tape] recorded. Over 120 of these sessions were subjected to an intensive analysis that resulted in the classification of more than 40,000 verbal propositions along several dimensions" (Lennard and Bernstein, 1960, p. 3l). "Patients and therapists were interviewed prior to therapy, and were given questionnaires to fill out at intervals during treatment. The interviews and questionnaires sought information on role expectancies of therapists and patients. . . . In addition, therapists and patients executed an 'inventory of values' " (p. 37). Analysis of this data represent the focus of the authors' 1960 volume.

In their 1969 volume, Lennard and Bernstein extend the application of their interaction system to the study of psychotherapy of schizophrenics and to an analysis of family group functioning. Using the same scoring systems, the authors first analyzed "nineteen tape recordings of the first four sessions of therapy of five schizophrenic patients (three therapists) in the adult ward of Rockland State Mental Hospital and [compared] them with the findings of the first four sessions of our eight psychoneurotic (1960) office patients" (p. 153).

> [Secondly,] we collected and studied interactional protocols from different groups of families, one group that we treat as "control" families, and one group that we treat as "disturbed" families. The so-called normal families are those in which no member has been identified as a patient. (Lennard and Bernstein, 1969, p. 4).

The analyses presented include comparisons between interaction patterns in family versus therapy contexts, German versus American family contexts, and "normal" versus "disturbed" family contexts. Our primary purposes were to construct and refine a

> research methodology applicable to the study of human interaction processes and to discover some of the more general principles governing the operation of social systems in general. (p. 66)
>
> The justification for the parallel study of family and therapy contexts arises from the premise that these two types of systems bear a special relation to each other. The same concepts and methods that apply to the description of therapy systems are also useful for the description of interaction in family systems, because both types of systems or contexts are actually subclasses of the more general category, human interaction systems. Therapy contexts are possibly able to induce changes in individuals by virtue of the same principles and processes that operate in family systems. (p. 4)

4. Data Form

The data presented judges for coding take the form of typescripts of therapy or family interaction tape-recorded sessions. The authors have not considered the differential effects on their category scores of judges rating audio or video representations, in contrast to the typescripts.

> After the session was tape-recorded, it was transcribed verbatim, the typescript noting any and all sounds made by either of the participants including all silences timed to the second, giggles, laughs, sighs, sobs, stuttering, coughs. Any marked change in the voices was noted by underlining. . . . Each verbal statement made by either a therapist or patient was then classified, coded, and punched onto an IBM card. . . . Pages in our typed manuscripts were prepared uniformly and thus could be used as a rough standard approximation of the number of words produced or the volume of a session. (Lennard and Bernstein, 1960, p. 37)
>
> Since an exchange contains both a patient's statement and a therapist's statement, half of each IBM card was devoted to coded information about the therapist's statement and half to coded information about the patient's statement. (p. 42)

5. Choice of Units

Lennard and Bernstein report (1969) that in their various studies they "worked with a variety of units, both natural and arbitrary. However, we propose that a distinction between a 'primary' and 'derived' unit is more appropriate" (p. 57). The three primary units employed are the proposition, statement, and interaction or exchange. The basic and smallest unit the raters score on the transcript is the therapist or patient proposition ("a verbalization containing a subject and predicate whether expressed or implied"). "This is the smallest unit we employed in segmenting interaction process for the purposes of categorization and quantification" (p. 57). The proposition, then, is the basic "scoring unit" in the system. The next larger unit analyzed is the statement ("an uninterrupted sequence of propositions from either the therapist or patient")—that is, either a particular P or T in the P-T-P communication sequence. The last primary unit used is the interaction or exchange. The exchange for an interpersonal dyad (individual therapy) is "a therapist statement followed by a patient statement, or vice versa" (p. 57). For family or group interaction analysis, the exchange is defined as a "statement of one family [group] member followed by a statement of another family [group] member" (p. 57). Thus, Lennard and Bernstein employ three distinct "scoring units": the first and most elementary is the "proposition," the second is the "statement," and the third is the "interaction or exchange."

The authors do not explicitly define the "contextual unit" for their system. Apparently the scoring is done seriatum, so that, in rating a particular therapist or patient proposition, the judge is cognizant of the preceding interaction of the interview. Evidently, also, the authors have not considered the effects of alternatively presenting individual propositions in a random order to the judges.

The various derived units discussed in the previous section are all "summarizing units," since they represent summarizations or combinations of numerical scores and measures designed to summarize the interaction process data, for example, "when psychotherapy interaction data are summarized for subperiods within a session, or for the session as a whole" (p. 58).

The comparative unit size problem for the authors' scoring system would deal primarily with their various derived units. What would be the differential effects on the scores obtained of different sizes or lengths of typescript material (for example, two-, four-, eight- or sixteen-minute protocol sample)? Are the various category scores obtained for these different length samples equivalent? The authors have not discussed or empirically assessed this issue.

6. Participant-Context Restrictions

The authors do not explicitly consider the participant-context issue. Apparently the scoring is done seriatum, so that, in rating a particular therapist or patient proposition, the judge is aware of the preceding interaction in the interview to that particular point. This would include the other participant. Lennard and Bernstein have not explicitly considered or empirically assessed the differential effects on their category scores of coding patient propositions with and without the therapist's preceding and subsequent statements being present or vice versa.

7. Type of Sampling Indicated

In the several studies reported in their two volumes, Lennard and Bernstein have consistently scored the entire sessions constituting their study samples. Hence, they have not considered the sampling problem, nor the differential representativeness of their data that might result from random in contrast to systematic sampling procedures.

8. Sample Location Within the Interview

Since they have typically scored the entire therapy session, the authors have not considered the differential effects on their scores of using samples extracted from different locations of a particular interview hour. Hence, there is no data regarding the representativeness of category scores obtained from various subsamples of particular sessions.

9. Sample Location over Therapy Interviews

For their first study (1960), Lennard and Bernstein analyzed eight therapy cases over a period of eight months each. They did not analyze all the sessions for each of the eight cases, but took a sample (120 of the 500 recorded sessions). The authors did not specify how this sample was extracted, that is, whether randomly, systematically, or in some other fashion. Hence, they have not considered where, along the interview continuum from initiation to termination, samples can be taken that will yield category scores representative of patient and therapist interaction over the entire therapy case. In their 1969 volume they collected recordings of the first four sessions of therapy for five schizophrenic patients. To the extent that they were interested in characterizing interaction in the early phase of therapy (the first five interviews) for these cases, sampling is not an issue, since they scored each interview for each case. To the extent that these early interviews were considered representative of the entire therapy interaction, the sampling problem is crucial and needs to be assessed empirically. Lennard and Bernstein (1960) do present some data that suggest that different scores are obtained from individual in contrast to the total series of interviews.

> Insofar as [the particular category] Differentiation is concerned, does the single session represent a minature of therapy as a whole, or do variations in the length of interaction between participants eventuate in variations between the macro- and micro-patterns of Differentiation? . . . The phase movement within the individual session, as assessed by the Bales Interaction Process Categories, did not replicate the long-term trend, and thus did not resemble the pattern found by Bales in his small one-session problem-solving groups. The emergent picture of phase movement within the session is almost the reverse of that postulated. (pp. 73, 78)

10. Clinical Sophistication of Judges

In neither volume do Lennard and Bernstein discuss how many judges made the codings for their category system, or what level of clinical experience or sophistication these judges possessed. Apparently, the authors have also not considered or assessed the differential effects on their category scores of using judges of various levels of clinical sophistication.

11. Training Required of Judges

The authors do not discuss whether or to what extent training is required of judges before they code the experimental materials. In neither volume do they refer to or outline anything resembling a standardized training procedure for coders.

12. Training Manual

A training manual is not available. The authors' two volumes provide extensive descriptions of the various categories of the system and provide examples and some rules for scoring. However, the authors do not present a standardized training procedure for training judges to score the system.

13. Interrater and Intrarater Reliabilities Reported

It is not clear whether the scores used in Lennard and Bernstein's analyses are the scores of one judge or some composite or average of the scores of two or more judges independently scoring the transcript protocols.

The authors do provide some limited data regarding interjudge reliability. In regard to the reliability of the unitization process (that is, breaking down the transcripts into patient and therapist propositions), the authors report one study where the same therapy session was unitized independently by two different coders. The number of resulting propositions coded were quite similar, 332 and 334 respectively, "a difference of less than one percent" (Lennard and Bernstein, 1960, p. 41).

In regard to the entire category system, the authors report reliability figures for only one subsystem, the Scale of Therapist Informational Specificity. In this study two coders independently scored a therapy session chosen at random. The results showed that "they agreed as to category in 171 out of 208 decisions. In other words, they independently placed a therapist statement into the same category in 82 percent of the cases" (p. 43).

14. Dimensionality Considerations

The authors have not discussed nor do they present data regarding the extent to which scores for the various categories intercorrelate when applied either to patient or to therapist propositions. The questions of redundancy or independence of the various scoring categories remains unanswered.

15. Validity Studies

The authors summarize their findings to date with the category system in their 1960 and 1969 volumes. Some examples of their findings are presented here as representative.

> [1] When we examined psychotherapeutic communication from the point of view of system referent, we discovered that there was a very consistent downward trend, over the life of therapy, in the frequency of primary system references. . . . In other words, as therapy progressed, discussion about therapy itself and the reciprocal therapist-patient roles decreased. (Lennard and Bernstein, 1969, p. 69)
>
> [2] Both the therapist and the patient tend to increase their communications about affect. This means that, as therapy proceeded, the therapists increased the frequency with which their propositions inquired into and solicited patient verbalization about feelings, and also that our patients began to verbalize more voluminously about feelings. (p. 70)
>
> [3] From the first to the second phase of an individual session, just as was the case over the life of therapy, decrease in primary system communication is accompanied by an increase in communication about affect. (p. 77)
>
> [4] For the group of patients and therapists we studied, the

patients averaged about four times as much verbal material as the therapists. This difference in relative volume of total output remained essentially the same throughout therapy for the group of sessions studied. (p. 83)

[5] For each dimension of communication (primary system, evaluations, affect), there is over time an increase in correlation, with an especially marked increase in the correlations for affective propositions. These findings suggest that there is over time an increase in similarity of patient and therapist behavior with regard to these three areas. (p. 93)

[6] The interaction rate for each therapist-patient pair varied very little from session to session. . . . The pace of interaction, therefore, seems to be fairly stable and varies very little over time for any given therapist-patient pair. . . . There is a trend, shown by all pairs, toward stabilization at a lower interaction rate after the first or second month of therapy. (p. 103)

[7] The sessions exhibiting most silences were succeeded by sessions characterized by a higher percentage of therapist evaluative acts and therapist acts of high informational specificity. (p. 105)

RELATED SCALES OR CONSTRUCTS

The Interaction Chronograph measures of Matarazzo and Saslow (see below, this chapter) are very similar to some of the categories used by Lennard and Bernstein, and some of their respective findings are quite similar. Siegman and Pope (see Chapter 4) developed an empirical scale of therapist specificity-ambiguity which is very close empirically to Lennard and Bernstein's Categories of Therapist Informational Specificity. Of course, Lennard and Bernstein's system shows similarity to Bales' Interaction Process Analysis system in that they modified his categories to form one of the subcategories of their system.

References

Hare, A. P. Review of H. L. Lennard and A. Bernstein, *Anatomy of psychotherapy. American Sociological Review* 1961, 26, 288.

Lennard, H. L. Some aspects of the psychotherapeutic system. In H. Strupp and L. Luborsky (Eds.), *Research in psychotherapy*. Vol. 2. Washington, D. C.: American Psychological Association, 1962. Pp. 218-36.

Lennard, H. L. and Bernstein, A. *The anatomy of psychotherapy: systems of communication and expectation*. New York: Columbia University Press, 1960.

———. *Pattern in human interaction*. San Francisco: Jossey-Bass, 1969.

A Speech Interaction System

Joseph D. Matarazzo

1. Rationale for Development of the System

In collaboration initially with G. Saslow, R. Matarazzo, and J. Phillips and more recently with A. Wiens and others, J. Matarazzo has been concerned since 1955 with the analysis of interview material, focusing on the formal or interactional components of communication. He assumes that "the very essence of diagnostic interview and psychotherapy material—interview content—is carried by durations of communicative action (utterances) and silence. Nevertheless, only in the very recent past have investigators seemed to concern themselves with the form (and other normative characteristics) of the distributions of these two basic and highly stable interview variables." (Matarazzo, Weins, and Matarazzo, and Saslow, 1968, p. 353)

Both the rationale and methodology derived initially from Chapple's Interaction Chronograph method (Chapple, Chapple, and Donald, 1939; 1946) and his interaction theory of personality.

> The basis of Chapple's interaction method is an analysis of the time variable during the interview. After considerable work in the field, Chapple arrived at his conclusion that time was an important variable for describing human relations. He and his early collaborator, Arensberg, found that their field work as anthropologists was unduly hampered by the lack of precision and communicability of the various "subjective" variables which anthropologists (and other behavior scientists) were then using to describe human relations, in the family, tribe, interview-situation, etc. (Matarazzo, Saslow and Matarazzo, 1956, pp. 349-50)

> From an examination of our previous studies in evaluation of personality, we concluded that one measurable factor that seemed highly significant was time. The question then arose: What traits of personality express themselves in time? (Chapple and Donald, 1946, p. 199)

> We all know, as a matter of observation, that people have different rates (timing) of interaction. Some of our friends or acquaintances seem to talk and act very speedily as compared to ourselves; others are slow and deliberate. These characteristics of individuals are something we intuitively recognize, and we often are at variance

> with the rates at which others act. (Chapple and Arensberg, 1940, p. 31)
>
> If the reader sharpens his powers of observation, he will see that in many cases people whom he does not like or cannot get along with say exactly the same things that the people he does like say. So actors frequently take a short play, play it first as a tragedy and then, using the same words, play it as a comedy. Here the language is seen as unimportant, and the timing is the factor which makes the difference in its effect on the audience. (Chapple and Arensberg, 1940, p. 33)
>
> [Chapple, thus,] has taken the (behavioristic) position that personality can be assessed without recourse to intrapsychic and other currently popular psychodynamic formulations, and further that this assessment involves merely the process of observing the *time relations* in the interaction patterns of people. Accordingly, Chapple has indicated that this method, because of its objectivity, can lead to a *science* of personality. (Matarazzo et al., 1956, p. 350)

Utilizing Chapple's rationale, Matarazzo and Saslow set out to apply his measurement methodology to the study of clinical interviews, in both naturalistic and experimental settings.

> Many investigators have used the interview as their instrument of assessment (change in behavior). The advantages of the clinical interview are its obvious flexibility and uniqueness, so that every patient has an opportunity to manifest his own, presumably learned, interpersonal behavior patterns. Its major disadvantage as a research instrument is its notorious unreliability. . . . It has long seemed to us that some standardization of the interviewer's behavior in the clinical interview, combined with suitably pecise recording of predefined variables, could enable one to surmount its major handicap of unreliability while preserving its dynamic nature (spontaneity, richness, multidimensionality, transference potentialities, etc.). Chapple laid the groundwork for just such an approach. (Saslow and Matarazzo, 1959, p. 125)

Thus, the two major goals of this research program were defined: First, to develop a standardized interview format, an experimental analogue of the clinical interview, for studying dyadic interaction; and secondly, to modify and use Chapple's interaction chronograph procedure for measuring the basic temporal factors of participants' behavior in the interview.

2. Description of the Scoring System

The earliest research, summarized in Saslow and Matarazzo (1959), concerned itself with a series of five studies designed to test one of the critical questions on which any long-term research program on the interview such as they proposed would depend: Is the interview speech behavior of an interviewee sufficiently *reliable* or *stable* for him so that such speech behavior could form the basis for further study? In answering this question, Matarazzo and his colleagues initially employed Chapple's Interaction Chronograph and the ten speech variables which it generated (Matarazzo et al., 1956). However, a subsequent factor analysis (Matarazzo, Saslow, and Hare, 1958) revealed that many of these ten variables were redundant and that two variables (speech and silence durations), and possibly a third (a speaker's interruption of his partner, or similar "maladjustment" in synchrony), more than adequately recorded what previously had required ten separate measures. The authors then developed their own successor to the Chapple chronograph, the Interaction Recorder (Johnston, Jansen, Weitman, Hess, Matarazzo, and Saslow, 1961; Wiens, Matarazzo, and Saslow, 1965). Recently, the system has been expanded into a Group Interaction Recorder, which records a whole group of interacting participants (up to twenty-four persons) involved in group psychotherapy or sensitivity training sessions (Morris, Johnston, Bailey, and Wiens, 1968). However, when only several channels of this latter twenty-four-channel recording device are used it, too, is a two-person Interaction Recorder.

The basic unit in the recording system is the length of each interviewer's and interviewee's speech and silence units as they occur in ordinary conversation and are recorded on the Interaction Recorder. (Weins et. al., 1965) The Interaction Recorder is an electronic device which time-records on paper or magnetic tape an account of the time when either person in an interview is speaking or silent. These recordings are binary coded and acceptable to a modern computer. An interview is recorded "live" through a one-way mirror by an observer who depresses (on the Interaction Recorder) either the interviewer or interviewee key, depending upon who is talking. Both keys are depressed if both participants are talking at the same time. Each key is released at the completion of an utterance, providing for a sequential analysis of the interview, which is automatically provided by the computer print-out.

Three speech variables are derived from the interview data: (1) *mean speech duration*, the total time in seconds the interviewee (or interviewer) speaks divided by his total number of speech units; (2) *mean speech latency*, the total latency time (the period of silence separating two different speech units) divided by the number of units of interviewee (or interviewer) latency; and (3) *percentage interruption*, the total number of times the interviewee (or interviewer) speaks divided into the number of these same speech units which were interruptions of his partner. Hence, the system has as its basic units the duration of each interview participant's speech, his reaction time before each unit of speech, and the number of these units which are interruptions of his conversational partner. Table 3.5 presents the scoring system in more detail.

3. Data Collection Context

By far the majority of the authors' studies using the Interaction Recorder focused on interview behaviors occurring in a live, clinical, but nominally standardized interview. Examples of the real life interviews they have utilized are (1) initial psychiatric interviews with inpatients and outpatients; (2) employment interviews with applicants applying for civil-service positions, etc., (3) interviews with administrators. However, in one major investigation, built upon years of preliminary research, they studied seven full psychotherapy cases involving naturally occurring, live psychotherapy interviews (Matarazzo et al., 1968). In all studies but the latter, the authors have shown that interview research such as theirs can be carried out by employing a basic research design which divides the real life interview into three parts, each typically lasting fifteen minutes: A baseline period, an experimental period, and a return to the baseline period. The interviewer is instructed to interview in his normal manner in Periods 1 and 3, and to introduce a planned change in his own speech behavior in Period 2. Thus, for example, in a 5-10-5 study, the interviewer conducted his nondirective interviewing in Periods 1 and 3—utilizing open-ended utterances of approximately 5-seconds duration—but doubled these utterances to approximately 10 seconds in the experimental period. The effect was a similar *increase* in the interviewee's average speech durations in Period 2. Other tactics utilized by the authors and similarly investigated were head nods, the use of mm-hmm and similar verbal reinforcers, increases in the interviewer's own reaction time, etc. (See a review of these studies in Matarazzo et al., 1968.)

4. Data Form

The typical form of interview material judged by the observer who presses the key of the Interaction Recorder has been the in-progress, live interview observed through a one-way vision mirror. However, a recent study indicates that the same speech measures can be taken directly from tape recordings of interviews yielding scores equally reliable and equivalent to those obtained by an observer of the live interview. Three observers were used for this study (Wiens, Molde, Holman, and Matarazzo, 1966), an experienced observer, who recorded live from behind a one-way mirror, and two beginning students who later recorded from tape recordings of the same interviews.

> When our overall findings are reviewed, . . . it is apparent that comparable data were obtained among the different observer-recorders (whether they recorded "live" or from "tape"). . . . This comparability was evident in the high correlations (0.94 to 0.99 for the two interviewee speech measures and also for one of the two interviewer speech measures) and similar mean values for the different observers when they recorded the interviewee's duration of utterance and latency, and the interviewer's duration of utterance. Even when the more difficult variable, interviewer latency, was dealth with—with numerical values of less than one second and undoubtedly involving individual differences in observer reaction time—gross comparability for all practical purposes was evident in mean values that ranged from 0.55 to 0.75 seconds, and in correlations between observers that were significant in two out of three cases. Nevertheless, reliability is less for this variable and it may be necessary to utilize some recording aids that will enhance comparability of data recorded for this variable and thereby decrease to a considerable degree the variance among observers, "live" or "tape." We conclude from our findings that it is feasible to collect data initially by tape-recording interviews and subsequently recording them on the Interaction Recorder or similar devices for analysis of speech and silence duration characteristics. (pp. 258-59)

For individual investigators not wishing to utilize an electronic recording system, the authors point out that a study of theirs (Matarazzo, Holman and Wiens, 1967) has shown that

> . . . a word count from a typescript of an interview is all that an investigator needs to derive [our] variables . . . since the correlation between average duration of utterance for each speaker as recorded by stopwatch or other chronographic device and the average number of words spoken per utterance by this same person in that interview is of the order of 0.92. Thus, any investigator can now tape record a therapy interview, transcribe it, count the number of words spoken in each utterance by each

> speaker, compute the mean number of words per utterance for both speakers, and therby have data for his own cases comparable to [ours]. (Matarazzo et al., 1968, p. 391)

5. Choice of Units

The authors define their basic speech unit as the "utterance," which is "merely what an experienced or naive observer would record if he used the conventions appropriate to ordinary conversational behavior in our society" (Matarazzo el al., 1968, p. 353).

> [The utterance is] separated at either end by two silence periods–one silence following the other participant's last comment (that is, the speaker's latency), the second silence following the speaker's own comment and preceding the listener's next comment (that is, the listener's latency). Pauses for breathing, for choosing words, for reflection, etc., are included in the speech unit when the context clearly suggests that the speaker has not yet completed that utterance. . . . However, pauses (again determined by context) which precede the introduction of new ideas or thoughts by the same individual, without an intervening comment by the other interview participant, signal the onset of a new speech unit. (Wiens et al., 1966, p. 253)

Matarazzo and his colleagues do not explicitly discuss the different units involved in process measurement. From the preceding paragraph, and the published references the authors use as examples of their scoring unit (Rogers' and Wolberg's transcribed verbatim speech units for therapist and patient), it is clear the "scoring unit" for their system is the utterance, for both patient and therapist. The "contextual unit," however, is not specified. Presumably, in scoring a particular utterance in a session, the observer has as context the preceding interview interaction to that point. Furthermore, in making decisions about interruptions, silences, and other variables in the system, the observer must keep in mind some part of the immediately succeeding interaction. Apparently, then, the most relevant context (which would define the "contextual unit" for the system) is the interaction immediately preceding and immediately following the utterance, all of which occurs in a matter of seconds. Finally, the most frequently employed "summarizing unit" seems to be the total session. An individual's score on a particular variable is calculated for the entire session, and represents an average of his scores for the numerous individual utterances occurring within that session. The evidence the authors have published on observer reliability in recording their scoring unit would seem to add substance to their claim that their scoring unit is reliably and objectively described. (Phillips, Matarazzo, Matarazzo, and Saslow, 1957; Wiens et al., 1966)

6. Participant-Context Restrictions

Some of the Interview Speech Interaction measures by definition (for example, latency) require assessment of the verbal interaction of both participants. However, in a monologue situation, some of the measures (for example, duration of utterance or latency between successive utterances) could easily be obtained. Goldman-Eisler, Hargreaves, and Starkweather, among other investigators, have done just this type of analysis of such single-person speech behavior (for example, during a lecture, reciting a standardized passage, etc.).

7. Type of Sampling Indicated

The authors typically have applied their system to entire interview sessions (either a 45- or 50-minute standardized experimental interview or live therapy sessions). However, they have concerned themselves with the issue of the kind of sampling necessary, random or stratified. Their results show that their speech measures derived from a 15-minute segment of a 45-minute interview correlate between 0.70 and 0.90, with comparable measures based on the whole 45-minute interview (for example, Matarazzo, Wiens, Saslow, Allen, and Weitman, 1964, p. 112). Interview samples shorter than 15 minutes are not recommended; ten-minute samples were found by the authors and others to be less reliable. (Matarazzo, 1962, pp. 497-99)

8. Sample Location Within the Interview

The authors have not specifically addressed themselves to the problem of from where (in the hour) samples of interaction can be extracted that will yield speech scores representative of therapist and patient behavior during the entire interview hour. However, the research referred to in the last section would suggest that, when samples must be utilized, a 15-minute segment can be taken from any part of the interview.

9. Sample Location over Therapy Interviews

In the one study of live psychotherapy to date (Matarazzo et al., 1968), the authors studied seven psychoneurotic patients whose total therapy interviews ranged from 11 to 50, with an average of 23 sessions. Since speech measures were obtained by an observer who witnessed each live therapy session for each case, the issue of where and in what manner (randomly or systematically) to sample over the continnum from initiation to termination did not rise. Apparently, the issue has not been discussed or empirically assessed to date. Whether the different sampling procedures yield different results for the speech variable scores in different phases of psychotherapy remains an unanswered question. However, the authors have published a number of graphs for a whole therapy (up to 50 sessions); these clearly reveal marked changes from session to session in the speech behavior of both the patient and the therapist. (Matarazzo et al., 1968) Interesting correlates of these session-to-session changes were described in the same study.

10. Clinical Sophistication of Judges

It seems quite likely that clinical sophistication is totally unrelated to one's skill as an observer and recorder for the Interview Speech Interaction procedure since only the temporal factors of the interaction are considered. Several studies have, in fact, revealed that even the most inexperienced observers can generate data comparable to a highly skilled, clinician-observer (Wiens, Molde, Holman, Matarazzo, 1966; Matarazzo, Holman and Wiens, 1967).

11. Training Required of Judges

The authors report an early study where two observers made simultaneous but independent live recordings of the same standardized interviews. "One of the Os had had approximately two years of experience (involving many hundreds of interviews) observing the standardized interview in an employment setting. The second O was relatively inexperienced, having recorded only some ten practice interviews, and these in a psychiatric rather than a department store setting" (Saslow and Matarazzo, 1959, p. 132; see also Phillips et al., 1957). The results were striking evidence that one obtains reliable and equivalent interview speech scores from an inexperienced observer. The intrarater reliabilities for nine speech scores for the inexperienced observer ranged from 0.71 to 1.00, with eight of the nine variables having coefficients above 0.94. The means and standard deviations of each measure for the two Os were almost identical, and the scores for the two observers ranged in intercorrelation from 0.94 to 1.00. The authors' most recent studies show that observers having no more than several hours practice with this procedure can apply the system as well as others who have had extensive experience. (Wiens et al., 1966; Matarazzo, Holman, and Wiens, 1967)

12. Training Manual

Matarazzo and Wiens (1972, in press) have recently put most of the published research of this group in book form. In addition to a definition of each of the three speech variables, the book contains a verbatim transcript of an interview which clearly delineates each speech unit, and also identifies interruptions as scored in this system.

13. Interrater and Intrarater Reliabilities Reported

The authors have given considerable attention to the reliability of various aspects of their scoring and interview procedure. In the study described in this section, very high *interobserver* consistency was obtained for two observers independently recording the same interviews. From this study the authors conclude that "the observation and recording of interaction patterns during the partially standardized interview is a highly reliable undertaking . . . the observer's task is largely a mechanical one once he has read, understood, and practiced the published rules as to what constitutes an action and an inaction." (Matarazzo, Saslow, and Matarazzo, 1956, pp. 362-64) Observer response-sets or biases "appear to have little effect upon the interview interaction record finally obtained." (Saslow and Matarazzo, 1959, p. 135) Later research confirmed and extended these results. (Wiens et al., 1966; Matarazzo, Holman, and Wiens, 1967)

This research group also has examined various aspects of reliability vis-a-vis their standardized interview procedure. Their results show that a single interviewer "is able both to learn and to follow the rules of the standardized interview to a reasonably high degree." (Saslow and Matarazzo, 1959, p. 137) A related but separate question is: How reliably can two interviewers carry out the standardized interview with a given sample of subjects? Results from another study indicated that two interviewers can perform comparably in the standardized format. The authors conclude that "the ability to learn and follow the rules is not limited to one interviewer. . . .Interviewers can, with a little practice, become research instruments of considerable reliability." (Saslow and Matarazzo, 1959, pp. 138-39)

A final aspect of reliability has to do with the interviewee's interaction patterns as they occur in the standardized interview. The results of various studies suggest that

> interviewee interaction patterns have the following characteristics. First, there are wide individual differences in interaction patterns among subjects. Second, the interviewee interaction characteristics for any given subject are highly stable across two different inter-

> viewers when the latter standardize their interviewing behavior along the minimal predefined dimensions of our standardized method; and at the same time, these interviewee characteristics are modifiable by planned changes in the intrainterview behavior of either interviewer. Third, the marked stability and modifiability of an individual's interaction patterns, found for our first sample of subjects, were cross-validated in a second sample. And fourth, the stability and modifiability were equally striking when only a single interview was used and the test-retest interval was extended to several days, five weeks, and eight months, in contrast to the first two studies which employed a test-retest interval of a few minutes. (Matarazzo, Saslow, and Hare, 1958, p. 419)

The authors conclude that the interaction variables reflect stable and invariant personality characteristics under the real-life but minimally standardized interview conditions in which subjects were studied.

> Thus, we have studied and established as having extremely high reliability the following aspects of interview interaction behavior: the reliability of the interviewer who serves as the independent variable by conducting the standardized interview; the reliability of the interviewee interaction patterns, the dependent variables; the reliability of the observer who observes the interviewer-interviewee interaction and records his observations by pressing separate keys for each participant; and finally, the reliability of the scorer who scores the final interaction chronograph record. (p. 419)

14. Dimensionality Considerations

Matarazzo, Saslow, and Hare (1958) conducted a factor analysis of twelve of the interview interaction measures recorded by the earlier-employed Chapple Interaction Chronograph. This factor analysis of the data of sixty subjects, as well as a replication study, revealed the presence of four independent factors: two major (speech and silence) and two weaker (initiative and interuption-maladjustment).

> The results indicate that as viewed from an interaction chronograph framework, doctor-patient interactions (and possibly most other two-person interactions) consist of two very stable factors for any given individual: (*a*) how long on the average he or she waits or remains silent before communicating (response latency), and (*b*) the number and average duration of each of these communicative interactions. A third [weak] factor [is] the frequency

> with which one initiates or starts again with another communication unit of his own when his partner has not answered him. . . . A fourth [also weak] factor [is] the efficiency with which a member of the communicating pair synchronizes and adjusts (or maladjusts) to his partner. (pp. 427-28)

> As a result of this study, we have stopped analysing all [fourteen of the] Chapple variables and their numerous derivative variables, and have focused our attention, instead, on the two strongest factors, speech and silence [latency] duration [for patient and therapist]. Together these . . . account for about 88 percent of the variance of the 14 interview interaction measures recorded by the Interaction Chronograph. (Matarazzo, Wiens, and Saslow, 1965, p. 190)

15. Validity Studies

This has been a vigorous research group, with a total of almost three dozen research papers by Matarazzo and his colleagues appearing in the past 15 years. The various studies of interaction process in the author's quasi-experimental interview as well as their later study of psychotherapy interviews and their current saliency studies are summarized in several places (Matarazzo, 1965; Matarazzo, Wiens, and Saslow, 1965; Matarazzo, Wiens, Matarazzo, and Saslow, 1968; Saslow and Matarazzo, 1959; Matarazzo and Wiens, 1972 in press: Jackson, Wiens, Manaugh, and Matarazzo, submitted for publication). Their earlier reliability studies revealed that: (1) there are *wide individual differences* across persons in speech, silence, and interruption behavior; and (2) despite these individual differences, the speech behavior of any given individual is *highly stable*, for him, from one interview situation to another, providing the interviewer maintains a fairly consistent interviewing style. Subsequent studies in this program of research indicated that these objective, noncontent dimensions of interviewee speech also show a number of modest personality and other validity correlates, and are subject to control by the interviewer. Thus, in one study involving real-life employment interviews, Matarazzo et al. (1968) found that by doubling or halving the duration of each of his own single speech units in each of three 15-minute periods of an otherwise free 45-minute interview, the interviewer was able to influence the mean speech duration of twenty job applicant interviewees in the three comparable periods of the interview. The positive results of this study were cross-validated in two additional studies in which the interviewer unobtrusively controlled his single speech unit durations to approximate roughly 10-5-10-second and 5-15-5-second durations in the three parts of his planned interview. These findings have since been independently confirmed in analogous studies by Simpkins (1967) and Lauver, Kelley, and Froehle. (1971)

That such interview-control effects are not limited to face-to-face employment interviews was revealed in another study (Matarazzo, Wiens, Saslow, Dunham and Voas, 1964) in which the authors discovered that the speech behavior of an orbiting astronaut could be "controlled" by changes in the speech behavior of the ground communicator. In an ingenious extension of this study, Ray and Webb (1966) showed that how much or how little President Kennedy talked in response to a reporter's questions in his 1961-1963 series of press conferences was clearly related to the length, or shortness, of the question posed by the reporter. Effects such as these clearly are out of the realm of conscious awareness.

Research carried out by the Matarazzo group on their silence measure also demonstrated that planned changes in the interviewer's own latency (reaction time before he answers his conversational partner) also quite dramatically produced the predicted increases and decreases in the corresponding latency behavior of the interviewee. (Matarazzo and Wiens, 1967) The third speech variable, frequency of an interviewer's *interruption* of the interviewee, also revealed that with surprising regularity the corresponding interruption rate of the interviewee could be brought under the control of the interviewer. (Wiens, Saslow, and Matarazzo, 1968)

Concurrent with these studies the research program was extended to a study of a situation, psychotherapy, in which the two conversational partners met not merely for one encounter (a single employment interview), but for a series of encounters. The authors studied three psychotherapists who were paired with two patients, two patients, and three patients respectively (that is, seven patient-therapist individual psychotherapies). The results of this research (Matarazzo, Wiens, Matarazzo, and Saslow, 1968) revealed a heretofore unsuspected "synchrony" or "tracking" over sessions in the speech behavior of one speaker in relation to the speech behavior of his conversational partner. That is, the study of one person's durations of pauses before answering his conversational partner showed sizable differences in average pause length from one day to the next and also a remarkable correlation between one person's session ups and downs in pause lengths and similar increases and decreases in the same variable in his conversational partner on these same days. Frequency of interrupting behavior likewise showed this "tracking" or "synchrony" across numerous face-to-face encounters.

It appeared to Matarazzo that in order to increase their knowledge in this area (for basic personality theory and study) even further, the results of this first decade of research on speech and silence measures should next be applied in natural settings in order to better test their potential as indexes of underlying attitudinal, mood, and motivational states. That such an application was now tenable was suggested by an earlier study that revealed that an experimentally induced "expectancy" in an interviewee that he would talk to either a "cold" or "warm" interviewer markedly influenced the interviewee's latency before answering the interviewer in an otherwise free employment interview. (Allen, Wiens, Weitman, and Salsow, 1965) Likewise, a study by Craig (1966) revealed that the increased accuracy of an interviewer's statements about an interviewee's underlying personality and attitudinal attributes very clearly affected (increased) the length of the subsequent verbal responses by the interviewee.

These two studies, and a third one (Wiens, Matarazzo, Saslow, Thompson, and Matarazzo, 1965) which demonstrated that "supervisory" versus "nonsupervisory" status was reflected in the speech characteristics of these two classes of interviewee-respondents, all suggested to Matarazzo and his group that speech and silence indexes deserved to be examined for their potential (theoretical and practical) to reveal a respondent's underlying moods, attitudes, or motivational characteristics in real life situations. If these speech measures were found to be viable indexes of such motivational characteristics, that finding would be an important contribution to psychological science, especially personality theory.

Contribution to basic personality theory is thus the primary purpose of the new direction the group began to take in 1967. This basic goal served as the framework for five studies completed since then. In the first, (Manaugh, Wiens, and Matarazzo, 1970) they learned, despite their initial methodological attempts to control for such an effect, that four groups of young college students, interviewed one at a time, showed *differential* and statistically significant changes in their speech and silence behavior when discussing a topic (their individual *educational* background) which was *salient* in their current collegiate life situation relative to discussion of two less-salient topic areas (their family background and their occupational background).

In a follow-up study (Matarazzo, Wiens, Jackson, and Manaugh, 1970) designed to remove or otherwise control for this differential content saliency in four similar groups of undergraduate subjects, they utilized interviews involving discussion of two presumably (a priori) *equally* salient interview content categories, each subject's *college major* and his *present living setting* (home, dormitory, apartment, etc.). Contrary to expectation, the overriding result of this study, consistent with that of its predecessor, was the finding, again in both the two control and two experimental groups, that *college major* was a content topic of apparent higher intrinsic saliency (as revealed by differences in their speech behavior) for these eighty subjects than was *living setting*.

Concurrent with the execution of these first two studies, they conducted and published another study, (Matarazzo, Wiens, Jackson, and Manaugh, 1970), a variant of the first study. Sixty job applicants for the position of patrolman in Portland, Oregon were each given a 45-minute interview unobtrusively divided into three 15-minute segments. During each segment, a different content area (education, occupation, and family history) was discussed. The results, when compared with twenty job applicants in a control group, showed that their noncontent dimensions of speech behavior again *were* differentially affected by the content being discussed by the interviewer. The *job applicants* spoke with a statistically significantly shorter reaction time and with a longer mean utterance during content conditions involving a discussion of their *occupational* histories. These results, cross-validated on a second group of thirty applicants, were interpreted to suggest that the content category *occupation* was tapping a higher level of saliency in these job applicants in this content area than was either the content category of education or family. This finding was consistent with their twice-confirmed finding in the first two studies in which education (or its derivative, college major) was found to be a content area with differential sensitivity or saliency in interviewees who were current college students.

These studies led to the postulation that discussion of the topic area *education* with college student interviewees and the topic area *occupation* with job applicant interviewee tapped in each group an already present, differentially viable (salient) motivational state appropriate to each subject's own life space as this motivational or personality-emotional state was being revealed in each subject's interview, noncontent speech behavior.

As a more direct check of this hypothesis, the research group developed an approach which would allow them to abandon further searches for evidence of saliency in the speech of target *groups* of subjects (collegiate versus job applicant groups) but, instead, would allow them to search for interview content areas which are salient for each individual himself. Jackson, Manaugh, Wiens, and Matarazzo (1971) developed a questionnaire-type scale, the Topic Importance Scale, or TIS, which consists of forty-five items. Each individual is to rate on a 7-point scale, for four separate subdimensions, the importance to him of each of these forty-five topic areas. For example, his interest in drugs, the Vietnam War, marriage, goal in life, feelings about himself, etc. The first results with this scale revealed (1) the TIS saliency ratings show the usual and necessary levels of reliability; and (2) the TIS saliency ratings show early evidence of being *valid* indexs of "saliency" as revealed by their potential to differentiate: (*a*) married from unmarried subjects; (*b*) draft-exempt from draft-eligible subjects; and (*c*) subjects majoring in different undergraduate disciplines. These TIS saliency results were obtained by comparing subgroups of subjects differing in the ways indicated by these initial validity studies.

As a more direct study of the validity of the TIS to reflect or mirror the content area(s) of highest saliency in the *individual* case, Matarazzo and his research group have completed two studies directly relating an individual's areas of high (or low) saliency, as a motivational state, to the speech behavior of this same subject in an interview situation not related to the independently obtained saliency ratings. The two studies tested this relationship between duration of utterance, reaction time, and interruption and the saliency of the content being discussed by an interviewee first in terms of group differences and subsequently for each individual subject studied uniquely. In the first study, forty male college students were interviewed in a 30-minute interview about one topic of known high saliency (goals in life) and one of known low saliency (interior decorating) for 15 minutes per topic. In the second study, fifty male college students were interviewed about two topics which were specifically selected to be of high or low saliency for each interviewee based on his own TIS saliency ratings months earlier. The results of both studies indicate that interviewees talk with a longer average duration of utterance (but content-specific either high or low latency) when talking about a high saliency topic relative to a low saliency topic.

It is clear that the authors' earlier psychotherapy research, despite the interesting synchrony obtained, had failed to yield clues for a full understanding of the empirically observed ups and downs from one session to another in a patient's speech behavior. Their recent development of a content saliency measure may permit them and others to next relate in a more effective way the content of an interview with the formal speech and silence measures they have so extensively studied.

RELATED SCALES OR CONSTRUCTS

The Speech Interaction System variables (duration of utterance, silence, and interruption) are very similar to some of the category scores used by Lennard and Bernstein (see above, this chapter), particularly to the latter authors' units of quantity. Some of the findings of the two groups are quite consistent.

Very recently Jaffe and Feldstein (1970) outlined final development of a completely automated technique of interaction chronography that feeds directly into a computer system. The Automatic Vocal Transaction Analyser (AVTA) is based on audio pickup of interview interaction from a two-channel tape recorder.

> AVTA is a two-channel speech detector and analog to digital converter designed to bridge the gap between live and tape-recorded interviews and an on-line digital computer. As a two-channel A to D converter it has much in common with other interaction chronograph systems in which the subjects' behaviors are tracked either manually or by means of a voice-actuated relay. Its unique feature is a network which electronically cancels the unintended "spill" of each speaker's voice to one channel of the audio-tape even though ordinary microphones are used and the speakers are conversing at close range in a face-to-face situation. This particular feature eliminates the need to separate the participants by isolation booths, or by use of throat or bone microphones, or other such solutions to the "cross-talk" problem. The goal was, of course, maintenance of as natural a dialogic context as possible. (p. 123)

The authors conclude that "we have completely automated the technique of interaction chronography. The complete process, from microphone input to computer generated statistical summary, is accomplished in a single operation without human intervention." (ix)

Since analyses of interaction processes occurring in psychotherapy have shown results having clear relevance to psychotherapy theory and other research, perhaps the day will come when all interview researchers will record their interview materials on two-channel tape recorders hooked into an AVTA system, which would permit easy comparison of interaction variables with the other measures that a particular researcher employs. Importantly, investigators wishing to do research in this area, especially graduate students, not having access to the Matarazzo Interaction Recorder or Jaffe's AVTA, can tape-record sessions and then use either a word count or stopwatch as described by Wiens, Molde, Holman and Matarazzo (1966) and Matarazzo, Holman, and Wiens (1967), or any of a number of inexpensive recording devices costing only a few dollars. Examples of the latter have been described by Kasl and Mahl (1956) and Lauver (1970) among others. Simple word count as a measure of utterance duration has also been used by Pope and Siegman (1966), and Ray and Webb (1966).

Three recent studies have concerned themselves with direct attempts to relate the Matarazzo research group's speech measures (as potential process variables) to process variables measured through content analysis in other systems. In the first of these studies, Kiesler, Mathieu and Klein (1967) failed to find a correlation between their own process variable, Experiencing, and Duration of Silence in

120 eight-minute segments of patient and therapist verbalizations. Pierce and Mosher (1967), on the other hand, found a good relationship between an interviewer's level of Empathy (as later independently rated by judges) and his own silence and interruption behaviors in the same interview segment. Truax (1970) recently reported finding a similar relationship between duration of therapist talk (utterance) and his independently rated level of Accurate Empathy (as well as the patient's level of overall improvement during therapy). That is, therapists who talked more per session (and over all sessions) were rated as showing higher levels of Accurate Empathy and their patients also showed greater degrees of overall improvement than was the case with therapists who talked less. Inasmuch as duration of utterance, as a measure, can be derived quickly and inefficiently from a tape-recording merely by counting the words in an utterance, and latency and interruption derived almost as easily, these last studies indicate that studies simultaneously utilizing process measures from *each* of these systems are now possible. These findings by Pierce and Mosher and by Truax suggest that these predicted studies will unearth a number of still other important relationships between the process measures in these heretofore disparate systems of analysis.

References

Allen, B. V., Wiens, A. N., Weitman, M., and Saslow, G. Effects of warm-cold set on interviewee speech. *Journal of Consulting Psychology*, 1965, 29, 480-82.

Chapple, E. D. Quantative analysis of the interaction of individuals. *Proceedings of the National Academy of Science*, 1939, 25, 58-67.

———. *The Interaction Chronograph manual.* Noroton, Conn.: E. D. Chapple Co., 1956.

Chapple, E. D., and Arensberg, C. M. Measuring human relations: an introduction to the study of the interaction of individuals. *Genetic Psychology Monographs*, 1940, 22, 3-147.

Chapple, E. D., and Donald, G., Jr. A method for evaluating supervisory personnel. *Harvard Business Review*, 1946, 24, 197-214.

Craig, K. D. Incongruencies between content and temporal measures of patients' responses to confrontation with personality descriptions. *Journal of Consulting Psychology*, 1966, 30, 550-54.

Jackson, R. H., Manaugh, T. S., Wiens, A. H., and Matarazzo, J. D. A method for assessing the saliency level of areas in a person's current life situation. *Journal of Clinical Psychology*, 1971, 27, 32-39.

Jackson, R. H., Wiens, A. N., Manaugh, T. S., and Matarazzo, J. D. Speech behavior under conditions of differential saliency in interview content (Submitted for publication).

Jaffe, J., and Feldstein, S. *Rhythms of dialogue*. New York: Academic Press, 1970.

Johnston, G., Jansen, J., Weitman, M., Hess, H. F., Matarazzo, J. D., and Saslow, G. A punched tape data preparation system for use in psychiatric interviews. *Digest of the 1961 International Conference on Medical Electronics* (July 1961), p. 17.

Kasl, S. V., and Mahl, G. F. A simple device for obtaining certain verbal activity measures during interviews. *Journal of Abnormal and Social Psychology*, 1956, 53, 388-90.

Kiesler, D. J., Mathieu, P. L., and Klein, M. H. Patient experiencing level and Interaction Chronograph variables in therapy interview segments. *Journal of Consulting Psychology*, 1967, 31, 224.

Lauver, P. J. Inexpensive apparatus for quantifying speech and silence behaviors. *Journal of Counseling Psychology*, 1970, 17, 378-89.

Lauver, P. J., Kelly, J. D, and Froehle, T. C. Client reaction time and counselor verbal behavior in an interview setting. *Journal of Counseling Psychology*, 1971, 18, 26-30.

Manaugh, T. S., Wiens, A. N., and Matarazzo, J. D. Content saliency and interviewee speech behavior. *Journal of Clinical Psychology*, 1970, 26, 17-24.

Matarazzo, J. D. Prescribed behavior therapy; suggestions from interview research. In A. J. Bachrach (Ed.), *Experimental foundations of clinical psychology*. New York: Basic Books, 1962. p. 471-509.

________. The interview. In B. B. Wolman (Ed.), *Handbook of clinical psychology*. New York: McGraw-Hill, 1965. Pp. 403-50.

Matarazzo, J. D., Holman, D. C., and Wiens, A. N. A simple measure of interviewer and interviewee speech durations. *Journal of Psychology*, 1967, 66, 7-14.

Matarazzo, J. D., Saslow, G., and Hare, A. P. Factor analysis of interview interaction behavior. *Journal of Consulting Psychology*, 1958, 22, 419-29.

Matarazzo, J. D., Saslow, G., and Matarazzo, R. G. The interaction Chronograph as an instrument for objective measurement of interaction patterns during interviews. *Journal of Psychology*, 1956, 41, 347-67.

Matarazzo, J. D., and Wiens, A. N. Interviewer influence on duration of interviewee silence. *Journal of Experimental Research in Personality*, 1967, 2, 56-59.

________. *The interview: an analysis of speech behavior.* Chicago: Aldine-Atherton, 1972.

Matarazzo, J. D., Wiens, A. N., Jackson, R. H., and Manaugh, T. S. Interviewee speech behavior under conditions of endogenously-present and exogenously-induced motivational states. *Journal of Clinical Psychology*, 1970, 26, 141-48. (a)

________. Interviewee speech behavior under different content conditions. *Journal of Applied Psychology*, 1970, 54, 15-26. (b)

Matarazzo, J. D., Wiens, A. N., Matarazzo, R. G., and Saslow, G. Speech and silence behavior in clinical psychotherapy and its laboratory correlates. In J. M. Schlien, H. F. Hunt, J. D. Matarazzo, and C. Savage (Eds.), *Research in psychotherapy*. Vol. 3. Washington, D. C.: American Psychological Association, 1968. pp. 347-94.

Matarazzo, J. D., Wiens, A. N., and Saslow, G. Studies in interview speech behavior. In L. Krasner and L. P. Ullmann (Eds.), *Research in behavior modification: new developments and clinical application.* New York: Holt, Rinehart & Winston, 1965. Pp. 179-210.

Matarazzo, J. D., Wiens, A. N., Saslow, G., Allen, B. V., and Weitman, M. Interviewer mm-hmm and interviewee speech durations. *Psychotherapy: Theory, Research and Practice*, 1964, 1, 109-14.

Matarazzo, J. D., Wiens, A. N., Saslow, G., Dunham, R. M., and Voas, R. B. Speech durations of astronaut and ground communicator. *Science*, 1964, 143, 148-50.

Morris, R. L., Johnston, G. L., Bailey, D. D., and Wiens, A. N. A twenty-four channel temporal-event digital recording system. *Medical Research Engineering*, 1968, 7, 32-37.

Phillips, J. S., Matarazzo, J. D., Matarazzo, R. G., and Saslow, G. Observer reliability of interaction patterns during interviews. *Journal of Consulting Psychology*, 1957, 21, 269-75.

Pierce, W. D., and Mosher, D. L. Perceived empathy, interviewer behavior, and interviewee anxiety. *Journal of Consulting Psychology*, 1967, 31, 101.

Pope, B., and Siegman, A. W. Interviewer specificity and topical focus in relation to interviewee productivity. *Journal of Verbal Learning and Verbal Behavior*, 1965, 4, 188-92.

________. Interviewer-interviewee relationship and verbal behavior of interviewee in the initial interview. *Psychotherapy: Theory, Practice & Research*, 1966, 3, 149-52.

Ray, M. L., and Webb, E. J. Speech duration effects in the Kennedy News Conferences. *Science*, 1966, 153, 899-901.

Saslow, G., and Matarazzo, J. D. A technique for studying changes in interview behavior. In E. A. Rubenstein and M. B. Parloff (Eds.), *Research in psychotherapy*: Vol. 1. Washington, D.C.: American Psychological Association, 1959. Pp. 125-59.

Simpkins, L. The effects of utterance duration on verbal conditioning in small groups. *Journal of Social Psychology*, 1967, 71, 69-78.

Truax, C. B. Length of therapist response, accurate empathy, and patient improvement. *Journal of Clinical Psychology*, 1970, 26, 539-41.

Wiens, A. N., Matarazzo, J. D., and Saslow, G. The Interaction Recorder: an electronic punched paper tape unit for recording speech behavior during interviews. *Journal of Clinical Psychology*, 1965, 21, 142-45.

Wiens, A. N., Matarazzo, J. D., Saslow, G., Thompson, S. M., and Matarazzo, R. G. Interview interaction behavior of three groups of nurses: supervisors, head nurses, and staff nurses. *Nursing Research*, 1965, 14, 322-29.

Wiens, A. N., Matarazzo, R. G., Saslow, G., Thompson, S. M., and Matarazzo, J. D. Speech interaction patterns of ward nursing personnel before, during, and after brief sensitivity training. *Journal of Applied Behavioral Science*, 1967, 3, 418-19.

Wiens, A. N., Molde, D. A., Holman, D. C., and Matarazzo, J. D. Can interview interaction measures be taken from tape recordings? *Journal of Psychology*, 1966, 63, 249-60.

Wiens, A. N., Saslow, G., and Matarazzo, J. D. Speech interruption behavior during interviews. *Psychotherapy: Theory, Research and Practice*, 1966, 3, 153-58.

A Content-Analysis Method for Studying Psychotherapy

Edward J. Murray

1. Rationale for Development of the System

Murray attempted to develop a content-analysis system for measuring patient and therapist behavior in the interview. His basic focus was on the meaning properties of verbal phenomena, particularly as these verbal events manifested underlying emotional events.

> The observable events in psychotherapy may be grouped as physiological, gross behavioral, and verbal. . . . A full understanding of psychotherapy would require information on all the observables. The present [system] is aimed at an understanding of the verbal phenomena in psychotherapy with respect to the underlying emotional processes. . . . The phenomena of greatest interest in psychotherapy are emotional in nature. . . . The meaning functions of verbal behavior were selected for study. Although there have been interesting studies on the grammatical and formal properties of the verbal behavior of the patient in psychotherapy, the content of the patient's speech seems more related to the major theories of personality. (Murray, 1956, p. 1)

> [Hence,] the method is a way of obtaining measures of the manifest content of the verbal behavior of the patient, and also of the therapist, with respect to underlying emotional processes in terms of psychoanalytic theory and learning theory. . . . [It is] limited to the conscious part of therapy. In all but a few specified instances the patient's words were taken at face value. (p. 2)

Murray cautions that since the system is based only on verbal behavior, "some interpretation is needed to relate it to the underlying emotional processes." Furthermore, since it concentrates on motivation and conflict, "the method has ignored various cognitive processes such as insight." Finally, he warns that "the method is a laborious one and imposes limits on the size of samples that can be reasonably studied" (p. 24).

2. *Description of the Scoring System*

Murray's content scoring system is presented in Table 3.6. It contains two major subdivisions, one for patient and the other for therapist statements.

The system of patient content categories was defined in terms of manifest motivations and conflicts. Statements of the patient are first put in one of four main *drive categories*, and then into one of three subcategories under each drive. The four main drives are sex, affection, dependence, and independence.

> Sex referred to all erotic needs including sexual play, intercourse, masturbation, and perversions. It also referred to sexual curiosity and interest, as well as bodily functions related to sex. Affection referred to needs for love, human warmth, friendship, acceptance, etc. Dependence referred to needs to be taken care of, helped, nurtured, etc. Independence included needs to be independent,

> self-assertive, mature, successful, and competitive. (Murray, 1956, p. 5)

In addition, there are unspecified, hunger, and maternal drive categories.

> [The patient's statements are then put into] one of three subcategories under each drive . . . according to whether the patient was: (1) simply expressing a need, describing past gratifications of that need, and making plans for the future gratification of that need (approval), or (2) describing a partial or complete blocking of that need by internal factors such as anxiety, fear, and guilt (anxiety), or (3) complaining about and getting angry about frustration of that drive by external, environmental factors (frustration). (p. 6)

Several special patient categories were also used. These were: disturbances of free association, simple agreement with the therapist, simple disagreement with the therapist, intellectual defenses, and generalized anxiety. Finally, each statement, in addition to being placed in a content category, was rated as to the referent, for example, self, mother, uncle, therapist.

> The various categories may be combined for various purposes of analysis, since they are defined in such a way as to be comparable. Thus, sex frustration, affection frustration, dependence frustration, independence frustration and drive-unspecified frustration may be combined to give an overall measure of frustration. (p. 6)
>
> While the main interest in developing the method was in the patient-content categories, it was thought desirable to devise at least a preliminary set of categories for therapist remarks, so that something would be known about the stimuli presented to the patient. (p. 8)

The therapist's remarks were grouped into two general classes: active and passive remarks.

> The active remarks included all clearly interpretive, evaluative, and manipulative responses. The subcategories of active remarks consisted of: instructions to free associate, labels, discriminations, similarities, strong approvals, demands, and directions. These subcategories were drawn from the learning theory analysis of psychotherapy by Dollard and Miller (1950) and from the examination of verbatim transcripts. Passive remarks refer to those remarks which are primarily designed to acknowledge that the patient is talking.

> The subcategories consist of: mild probings, mild approvals, and "Mm" . . . . All other therapist remarks were scored as irrelevant. (p. 8)

3. Data Collection Context

Murray has limited application of his system to a few case studies. In one case this idiographic focus characterized eight complete therapy hours for one patient, in another 110 complete therapy hours from seven cases were scored.

4. Data Form

The scoring system has been applied exclusively to typed transcripts of tape-recorded therapy sessions. Murray has not considered applications of his system directly to either audio or videotape recordings of psychotherapy interviews.

5. Choice of Unit

The basic unit scored for the patient was the "statement or meaning phrase" (Murray, 1956, p. 4), which usually takes the grammatical form of a sentence. "The simple sentence is the basic unit of scoring. In its purest form the sentence contains a subject and predicate" (p. 26). All of the following statement units are scored: simple sentences, incomplete sentences, slightly complex sentences, and conjunctival sentences. The unit scored for the therapist was the T in the P-T-P communication sequence, that is "everything a therapist said in between patient statements" (p. 8). The basic "scoring units" of the system, then, are clearcut: for the patient, "the sentence," and for the therapist, "the statement," which is defined as everything a therapist said in between patient statements.

Murray does not specify the "contextual unit" for his system. Apparently the same judges score both patient and therapist categories. The sequence in which the codings are made, that is, for example, whether all patient units in successions are first scored, and then all therapist units in succession, is not indicated. Since the ratings are made from typescripts, the judges, in coding the scoring units, presumably have available as the contextual unit all the preceding and some of the subsequent patient and therapist statements. The "summarizing unit" for the system is the hourly (session) total for the various patient and therapist categories. That is, the scores for the numerous scoring units within a session are combined to provide a total score for that session.

6. Participant-Context Restrictions

As mentioned above, the same judges score all the patient and therapist categories. Judges are apparently cognizant of all preceding and some succeeding statements of the other participant. Murray has not considered or empirically assessed what differential effects on his category scores might result from applying his system both with and without the presence of the other participant's verbalizations.

7. Type of Sampling Indicated

Sampling issues have not been considered to date by Murray. His attempts seem to emphasize the desirability of scoring the total psychotherapeutic interaction.

8. Sample Location Within the Interview

In none of his studies has Murray sampled portions of the interview hour. He has, instead, scored the entire session. As a result, whether samples taken from different locations in particular interviews would yield category scores differentially representative of single therapy hours is unknown.

9. Sample Location over Therapy Interviews

Murray has not explicitly considered this issue, although in each of his studies he clearly sampled from the therapy hour and did not rate every hour to termination. In one study he scored eight therapy hours of a case of Rogers, but he does not indicate which hours were selected, nor does he provide any rationale for their selection. Another study scored 110 therapy hours from seven cases. In this study, Murray seems to have scored all the interviews for three cases, a random selection of six hours from another, "every third consecutive hour over a series of 69 hours" for another, and in the final two cases 17 and 8 "consecutive" hours. Murray does not conceptually or empirically contrast these various sampling procedures.

10. Clinical Sophistication of Judges

Murray gives minimal attention to judge sophistication. Apparently the rating task would require some level of clinical sophistication and experience as well as some grounding in psychoanalytic and learning theory. However, Murray does report that "a preliminary study showed that with training even a relatively psychologically naive person could score therapist remarks reliably" (Murray, 1956, p. 8). From an examination of the system (Table 3.6), it seems that relatively unsophisticated judges might reliably apply the entire system if they were provided with standardized training procedures. The question should be put to empirical test.

11. Training Required of Judges

Murray does not explicitly discuss training. It would seem that judges would need considerable practice in applying the system, as well as examples of standardized criteria to help resolve discrepancies in their understanding and applications of the system.

12. Training Manual

There is no manual available to date. Murray's 1956 publication presents the scoring system in detail, including rules for scoring. There is little other methodological presentation, and standard procedures for training judges are neither discussed or presented.

13. Interrater and Intrarater Reliabilities Reported

Two interrater reliability assessments have been considered by Murray. The first has to do with the reliability of the unit-determining process. Before patient or therapist statements are scored, the transcript is marked off in scoring units. In one study two judges independently unitized six typescripts. "In the vast majority of cases both [judges] . . . scored precisely the same string of words as a unit" (Murray, 1956, pp. 4-5). The ratio of the number of exact agreements to the total number of instances ranged from 0.92 to 0.94.

In discussing interrater ability to apply the scoring system consistently, Murray points out that the reliability he assesses is "in terms of data pooled for the hours, and not in terms of exact agreement between judgments of individual . . . statements" (p. 6). In one study two judges independently scored the patient's statements in 15 therapy hours, and the hourly totals in each patient category were compared. The range of Pearson correlations obtained were: Categories of Drive 0.58 to 0.92, Drive Components 0.77 to 0.89, and Special Categories 0.67 to 0.98. These values generally show moderately high interjudge agreement. "Two of the subcategories,

Dependence-Frustration and Independence-Frustration, showed little interjudge agreement and were excluded from general use" (p. 7). It is important to reiterate, though, that these reliability figures are for Murray's "summarizing" units and not for the basic "scoring" units (sentences and statements).

Another study looked at the interjudge reliability of scoring the therapist categories. Two judges, one relatively naive, independently scored the therapist statements in the same previous 15 therapy hours. That range of Pearson coefficients obtained were: Active therapist remarks, 0.54 to 0.97; Passive therapist remarks, 0.46 to 0.99; and Not Classifiable, 0.64. These values show moderately high interjudge agreement for the therapist categories using summarizing units. "The subcategories of discrimination and similarities had no frequency in the reliability sample. . . . [They] also had very little freqency in all of the cases studied to date" (p. 8).

14. Dimensionality Considerations

Murray has presented to date no data clarifying how the various patient and therapist categories of his system might intercorrelate with each other. As a result, the dimensional nature of the system remains unknown, as does the extent to which his individual categories assess unitary factors.

15. Validity Studies

> The three case studies made with the aid of the method have all produced theoretically meaningful results. The first study (Murray, 1954) led to an hypothesis about displacement which was verified in the animal laboratory (Murray and Berkun, 1955). The second study (Murray, Auld, and White, 1954), yielded results which were in essential agreement with a detailed clinical analysis made of the same case. The last case study fits in with expectations of learning theory (Dollard and Miller, 1950) concerning the effects of approval and disapproval on human behavior. . . . Therefore, it is concluded that the method appears to be of some use and to have some validity. (Murray, 1956, p. 24)

Other studies employing Murray's scoring system to various degrees are Bandura (1965), Bandura, Lipscher, and Miller (1960), Caracena (1965), Murray (1962), Varble (1968), and Winder, Ahmad, Bandura and Rau (1962).

References

Bandura, A. Behavioral modifications through modeling procedures. In L. Krasner and L. P. Ullman (Eds.), *Research in behavior modification*. New York: Holt, Rinehart & Winston, 1965.

Bandura, A., Lipscher, D. H., and Miller, P. E. Psychotherapists' approach-avoidance reactions to patients' expressions of hostility. *Journal of Consulting Psychology*, 1960, 24, 1-8.

Caracena, P. F. Elicitation of dependency expressions in the initial stage of psychotherapy. *Journal of Counseling Psychology*, 1965, 12, 268-74.

Dollard, J., and Miller, N. E. *Personality and psychotherapy*. New York: McGraw-Hill, 1950.

Murray, E. J. A case study in a behavioral analysis of psychotherapy. *Journal of Abnormal and Social Psychology*, 1954, 49, 305-10.

_______. A content-analysis method for studying psychotherapy. *Psychological Monographs*, 1956, 70 (113).

_______. Direct analysis from the viewpoint of learning theory. *Journal of Consulting Psychology*, 1962, 26, 226-31.

Murray, E. J., Auld, F., and White, A. M. A psychotherapy case showing progress but no decrease in the discomfort relief quotient. *Journal of Consulting Psychology*, 1954, 18, 349-53.

Murray, E. J., and Berkun, M. M. Displacement as a function of conflict. *Journal of Abnormal and Social Psychology*, 1955, 51, 47-56.

Murray, E. J., & Miller, N. E. Displacement: steeper gradient of generalization of avoidance than approach with age of habit controlled. *Journal of Experimental Psychology*, 1952, 43, 222-26.

Varble, D. L. The relationship between the therapists' approach-avoidance reactions to hostility and client behavior in therapy. *Journal of Consulting Psychology*, 1968, 32, 237-42.

Winder, C. L., Ahmad, F. A., Bandura, A., and Rau, L. C. Dependence of patients, psychotherapists' responses, and aspects of psychotherapy. *Journal of Consulting Psychology*, 1962, 26, 129-34.

A Nondirective Classification System for Therapist and Patient Responses

William U. Snyder

1. Rationale for Development of the System

Snyder's basic purpose in developing his coding system in the mid-1940's was to derive a quantitative measure of psychotherapy that would permit him to test various hypotheses about nondirective or relationship therapy.

> Many of the notions developed in the material so far published have been observations deduced through a keen insight, and from empirical relationships. Numerous clinicians have been quite impressed on the basis of their experience with the results they are

> able to obtain by following nondirective principles. It is therefore desirable that scientific techniques and mathematical checks be applied to treatment interviews in such a manner as to demonstrate whether or not some of the proposed hypotheses are consistent with fact. Persons with a critical point of view, including many of the nondirective counselors, are interested in knowing whether the apparent observations are supported by measurable data. (Snyder, 1945, p. 194)

His second goal was to develop a system that would permit him to contrast nondirective (relationship) with more traditional directive psychotherapeutic procedures. He paraphrases Rogers' (1942) earlier theoretical statement in distinguishing nondirective and directive therapies.

> First, there is the assumption that "the client has the right to select his own life goals even though these may be at variance with the goals that the counselor might choose for him." The directive counselor assumes that the counselor is in a position to know the best thing for the client to do, and to want to do, and he orients his actions around this philosophy. Obviously it is implicit in this notion that the counselor is an authority or "expert." . . . Another assumption of nondirective therapy is that the client will, if given the opportunity, choose for himself the goal most likely to produce the truest happiness. The desire of the therapist, therefore, is merely to create a situation in which the client is able to evaluate his goals in terms of their probable ultimate outcomes. The nondirective therapist does not in any sense superimpose upon his client his own standards or morals, or those of the society he prefers. . . . A third principal tenet of nondirective psychotherapy is that the client should be brought by means of the counseling situation to a position where he is able to operate independently, and if possible in a reasonably short time. (p. 193)

Some of the more specific questions Snyder desired to examine by use of his system were the following:

> (1) How can such unstructured material as psychotherapeutic interviews be made into measurable data; (2) are the people who think they are using nondirective methods really doing so; (3) are the advocates of nondirective therapy correct in assuming that it is their nondirective techniques which produce the responses that indicate a therapeutic process, or whether it is their more directive techniques; (4) does the client really show insight in the process of changing attitudes; (5) if the counselor is recognizing feelings, as

he believes he is, what are those feelings; (6) do the feelings themselves change during the treatment process and are there any differences in the objects toward which they are directed; (7) is there a difference in the nature of the feelings which correlate with certain types of content material; (8) is there a difference in the nature of the feelings which are sequels of certain counselor statements; (9) what is the client's attitude toward the counselor during and after the treatment process; (10) what is the client's attitude toward the treatment process during its progress and after it is completed; (11) does the frequency of various types of counselor or of client statements vary throughout the treatment process in any clearly recognizable patterns; (12) does the discussion of plans follow, as is proposed, the understanding of and insight into the problem? (pp. 194-95)

2. Description of the Scoring System

Snyder, in developing his system, built upon the previous work of Porter (1943, 1950), who was the first nondirective therapist to report a content-analysis system. Porter's system, however, unlike Snyder's, was devoted exclusively to categories for the therapist's behavior and ignored the client's activities. Snyder's system, for some time after its initial publication, was the most influential nondirective content analysis available.

The categories of Snyder's scoring system have changed over the years with research experience with the system. The earliest form is presented in the 1945 report, the latest in Snyder's 1963 volume. Unfortunately, in presenting the latest form of his system, Snyder simply lists the various categories used without including definitions or examples. One assumes that the definitions in the 1963 version are similar to those presented in his 1945 version. As a result, we will present and discuss briefly here both forms of his system, letting the reader himself extrapolate from the earliest to the lastest versions.

Snyder draws the perspective for his 1945 version as follows.

> In order to make some sort of measurable data out of the material recorded in [psychotherapy] interviews, it was necessary to devise a scheme of categories into which the various statements might be classified. In the use of any subjective material such analysis is requisite. . . . Previous attempts to objectify such subjective material have been made by Porter, Covner, Rogers, Royer, Sargent, and others, in the order mentioned. The method used in each of these cases was that of constructing a system of categories into which the specific statements could be classified by a trained or untrained classifier. None of the methods used was considered

> entirely satisfactory for the present investigation, and a new one resembling in nature some of the others but considerably modified was finally devised. (1945, P. 197)

Snyder's system of counselor and client categories, of both the 1945 and 1963 versions, is presented in Table 3.7.

> In making this analysis, it appeared that the statements of counselors could usually be observed to break down into one of sixteen types, classified with reference to the subject matter being discussed. The small percentage of counselor statements not so classifiable (less than one percent) could be labeled unclassifiable. (p. 198)

The five headings under which the seventeen categories are subsumed are: lead-taking categories; nondirective response-to-feeling categories; semidirective response-to-feeling category; directive counseling categories; and minor categories. The categories are listed in Table 3.7 together with brief definitions of each.

> In the case of statements made by the client or counselee, it was found that a two-dimensional type of significance seemed to exist. First, there was a content significance, or what one might call a subject-matter heading. Second, it was noted that in the case of many statements intense feeling was either explicit or clearly inferred. For example, in a statement like, "I don't like that sort of behavior," a client is stating a problem and is expressing also a negative feeling with reference to external objects. It was decided, therefore, that a two-dimensional type of classification was necessary for many of the counselee responses.(pp. 199-200)
>
> In the first dimension, that of the content of the material, eleven categories and an "unclassifiable" heading were found desirable. (p. 200)

The four headings subsuming these twelve categories are: problem, simple response, understanding or action-taking, and minor. "In the case of the second or 'emotions' dimension, nine categories were decided upon. . . . These are the possible inter-relationships of positive, negative, and ambivalent attitudes towards the self, the counselor, or toward external objects or persons" (p. 200). The three major headings for the client categories are, therefore, positive attitudes, negative attitudes, and ambivalent attitudes. "It should be clearly indicated that while all counselee's statements were assumed to possess content significance, only a part of them contained feeling believed to be measurable. Therefore, counselee statements could be classified either in the one dimension or in both dimension" (p. 200).

The version Snyder presents in his 1963 volume shows some changes from his 1945 presentation.

> These codings of the therapist's responses are based on several modifications of our own previously published system (1945). We have added some new categories, dropped a few, and subdivided others. The most important subdivisions are in the category of interpretation, where we have applied the Raush et al. (1956) scheme for classifying depth of interpretation. . . . Our coding of client responses are modified from those proposed by Dollard and Auld (1959) based on Murray's need system. We found it important to classify both the client's principal affect theme and the principal object or source of his affect. . . . We also classified the affect themes as plus or minus, depending upon whether or not the client perceived the need of pressure as being fulfilled or satisfied within himself, that is tension-reducing versus tension-building. . . . We also had a parallel classification of the affect themes which constituted descriptions of therapeutic activities which these affect themes also represented. . . . These latter classifications were reported only when they were apparent, that is, not in all cases. The objects (or sources, in some cases) of the affect were classified into major and minor categories. . . . In addition to the above, in many client classifications an arrow was used to indicate a transition from one affect theme to another, usually perceived as being in a causal relationship. (1963, pp. 21-24)

Unfortunately the author presents no further information regarding definitions, rules for scoring, or examples of scorings than that presented in Table 3.7 regarding his 1963 version. The reader will have to make his own extrapolations from the two versions. Consequently, the discussion that follows will apply exclusively to Snyder's 1945 version, unless explicitly stated otherwise.

3. Data Collection Context

Snyder has applied his coding system to typescripts taken from tape recordings of live psychotherapy interviews. He has tended to focus on intensive and relatively exhaustive study of a few cases (in 1945, six cases; in 1963, two cases), rather than study larger numbers of therapy cases. His studies are clearly in the correlational-naturalistic tradition.

4. Data Form

In his later studies, Snyder's coding system has been applied to typewritten transcriptions taken from tape-recorded psychotherapy interviews. It is historically interesting that in his 1945 study Snyder used typescripts made not only from tape-recorded therapy interviews but also from stenographic recordings of the live interview (a stenographer was seated in a different room from that in which the interview took place, and listened to the interview by means of a public address system operating through a concealed microphone), as well as from counselor transcriptions (these protocols were based on the note-taking of the counselor followed by his immediate recall and transcription from notes).

Snyder used a "condensed interview" modification of the typescript protocol for the analyses and other presentations of his coding scores in 1963. The frequencies of category scores for patient and therapist are based on condensed transcripts rather than on the unedited originals. "Most of our interviews have been somewhat condensed. Sometimes a client, or the therapist, repeats himself unnecessarily, and this repetition has been eliminated in order to save space. Casual, trivial conversations or digressions have usually been omitted or summarized in a short sentence. Connective phrases have been eliminated, although the idea itself has usually been included" (1963, p. 22).

Snyder has not discussed or empirically considered the differential effects on his category scores of coding audio or videotape recordings directly, in contrast to his typescripts.

5. Choice of Units

Snyder attempted to define meaningful (rather than arbitrary) units for his coding analysis. The basic "scoring unit" he settled on was the "idea," defined as a clearly indicated change in the subject matter or attitude of the client or therapist's thinking. From inspection of the verbatim transcripts presented in his 1963 volume, it seems that the idea-unit, in terms of grammatical structure, can vary anywhere in size from a phrase or a sentence to a group of sentences. Its limits are defined by the initiation of the other participant's response. Hence the idea-unit may be the entire P or T in the P-T-P communication sequence, or various sentence or phrase breakdowns of a particular P or T.

One very significant question that has faced every person who has attempted to objectify spoken or subjective statements has been

> the question of determining the boundaries of the units of the material; that is to say, determining the boundaries of "ideas." Covner attempted to break each speech into "ideas" which he defined as a clearly indicated change in the subject matter or attitude of the client's thinking. Royer and Sargent avoided this problem by considering each section of material between two counselor statements as a single idea. They were faced with the problem however, that at times this was observably not a true recognition of what was happening, and they used the arbitrary method of breaking the passage into two or at times three units. This break was made only rather occasionally, and then with the mutual agreement of two classifiers. For the present study it was felt that Covner's attempt to classify ideas was preferable to the other method. Covner checked the reliability of the breakdown of ideas and determined that there was a rather high consistency in the way these ideas could be differentiated. The present writer felt that to interject the question of reliability of breakdown into this material would complicate the problems under study. It was therefore decided that the breaks between ideas should be arbitrarily decided by the (single) classifier, and that the study would not attempt to predict results determined from the unmodified data, but only results based on the breakdown of ideas which was made. (Snyder, 1945 pp. 201-202)

Unfortunately, as was pointed out in Chapter 2, this decision inextricably confounds scoring reliability with the unknown reliability of Snyder's unitizing process.

In order to compare patient and therapist responses in interviews, Snyder (1945) adopted another scoring unit called the "sequel," after Sargent who first adopted the procedure. "Sargent was the first person to make a statistical treatment of the type of client response which follows a counselor's statement" (p. 195). Sargent considered as a sequel all the material between two counselor statements. Snyder modified Sargent's definition of sequel for his study to put it in line with his basic unit, "the idea."

> The present writer . . . classified ideas on the basis of much smaller units [than did Sargent]. As a result, two or three, and sometimes as many as ten, client ideas would follow two or three or even more counselor ideas. To ignore all but the first of such client ideas would be a misrepresentation of the probable situation that actually occurred. By the same token, to assume that all the ideas which occurred between two counselor statements followed only the last ideas previously expressed by the counselor would not

seem to be justified by common sense. After considerable thought, it was decided to call each idea between two counselor statements a sequel to *every idea* expressed in the previous counselor statement. While such a procedure may not have been justified in every case, it seemed a much more justifiable method of measuring sequels than any of the possible alternates. As a result of this method more sequels were indicated than actual items. It was felt, however, that they were logically measured only in the way chosen. (p. 204)

Importantly, by defining sequel units, Snyder was able, through his coding system, to calculate not only the total frequencies of each type of category of counselor and client responses but also could provide a breakdown of types of client responses which follow the various counselor statements and the frequencies of each.

Snyder does not specify exactly either his "contextual" or "summarizing" units. Since coding of the typescript data is done sequentially, apparently his contextual unit is all therapist and patient verbalizations preceding, as well as some following, occurrences of a particular "idea" scoring unit. He has not considered the differential effects of coding responses in a random order, in contrast to his usual sequential data processing. Apparently the summarizing unit is the total session; that is, various codings of ideas and sequels occurring within a particular interview are averaged to provide total scores for the session.

6. *Participant-Context Restriction*

Since coding of the typescript data is done sequentially, evidently the categories are scored routinely with the presence of the other participant's verbalizations. Snyder has not considered or empirically assessed different effects on his category scores of coding a particular participant (for example, patient) without the other's (for example, therapist's) responses being present, in contrast to his usual coding done in participant context.

7. *Type of Sampling Indicated*

In his studies to date, Snyder has coded the entire contents of the interview sessions he has studied. As a result, he has not considered the issue of differential effects on his category scores of random versus systematic sampling procedures.

8. Sample Location Within the Interview

Since he has coded entire interviews, Snyder has not considered what size and from where in particular sessions samples can be extracted (randomly or systematically) that will yield category scores representative of therapist and patient behavior in the total hour.

9. Sample Location over Therapy Interviews

Snyder used different procedures for analyzing case data in his 1945 report and in his 1963 volume. In the earlier study he analyzed six cases of psychotherapy with four different counselors. A total of forty-eight interviews were analyzed, with the number per case varying from five to thirteen. For some of the cases all interviews were coded (each from initiation to termination); for others sampling of the interviews occurred that apparently attempted to represent the entire interview series, but especially weighted sessions near initiation and near termination.

> Four of these cases are analyzed completely. In one case seventeen interviews occurred, but only the first ten are analyzed. The last seven interviews of this case were not analyzed because in the opinion of three experienced counselors treatment was believed to have been successful by the end of the tenth interview. In one case there were a total of twenty-one interviews of which only thirteen were analyzed for this study. The other eight interviews were excluded from analysis in order to keep the material somewhat less cumbersome. The basis on which the thirteen interviews were selected was that all initial and closing interviews were included . . . . Also, all stenographically recorded interviews were analyzed. In addition, wherever there was a marked gap, several interviews were selected at random so as to give a rather smooth cross-section of the entire case. In no situation were more than two consecutive interviews omitted. (Snyder, 1945, pp. 196-97)

Snyder's 1963 volume focuses on the intensive study of two "dependency" cases. The scored transcripts are presented for each case of each therapy session from initiation to termination—twenty-nine interviews for Quinn and twenty interviews for Jones. Hence, for this study there was no sampling of sessions across the interview series.

In summary, it seems that Synder prefers to code every interview in each case being studied, that is, he prefers not to sample across the interview series. However, in studies where this is not economically feasible he seems to prefer sampling representatively from the various stages of the case (early, middle, late), with more weight given to earlier and later interviews. Within this restriction, choice of particular interviews to be sampled seems to be randomly determined.

10. Clinical Sophistication of Judges

In most of the studies to date an experienced clinician (Snyder) has made both the unitization judgments and categorization of the units. In one study he reports using a second coder, "an individual who had not previously had experience in the classifying of psychotherapeutic interviews." The author has not emperically determined whether clinically naive judges could perform the same codings as reliably.

11. Training Required of Judges

To date, Snyder has not considered the extent to which coders need to be trained in order to perform equivalent and reliable scorings except in the out-of-print 1953 volume. However, one study suggests that systematic and extensive training may be unnecessary. For this study, Snyder (1945) used a second coder, "an individual who had not previously had experience in the classifying of psychotherapeutic interviews" (p. 202), who scored four interviews which had previously been coded by Snyder.

> The second classifier was given the definitions of the categories . . . and was allowed to read through two of the interviews classified by the principal classifier and to study the classifications made. He then proceeded to make classifications of four interviews selected as typical. The classifier was able to match the scores of the first classifier with reliabilities ranging from O.52 to O.78. . . . Consequently, it may be said that the second classifier was able to match the scores of the first classifier with a reliability at least equivalent to that found in the average standardized test. In view of the fact that the second classifier was so weakly indoctrinated in the methods which the first classifier was using, it is perhaps remarkable that he was able to achieve as similar scoring as occurred. (pp. 202-203)

12. Training Manual

There is no training manual. The author does not discuss or present any detailed procedure for training judges to score with his system, and he does not present any detailed rules (other than the category definitions) for scoring interview protocols.

13. Interrater and Intrarater Reliabilities Reported

Snyder (1945) checks on the reliability of his category codings by assessing both intrarater and interrater agreement. For the former,

> [a recheck was made] by the classifier himself in which he attempted to rescore certain interviews without recall of previously made classifications. Four of the interviews were rescored after an interval of more than a month, during which time numerous other interviews had been scored. Two of the interviews chosen for rescoring were phonographically recorded ones, and two were interviews recorded from the counseler's notes. Precautions were taken to avoid initial or terminal interviews on the basis of the assumption that such interviews might tend to be more specialized in character and therefore more clearly classifiable with regard to any particular category. The general conclusion which may be made is that the classifier was able to demonstrate a reliability ranging from O.76 to O.87 using the test-retest method. . . . It can therefore be said that a high degree of reliability existed in the scoring of items insofar as they were checked by the test-retest method. (p. 202)

The study checking on interrater agreement was reported in the above section. A second coder independently scored four interviews. The interobserver coefficients ranged from O.52 to O.78. Apparently, then, the codings required of the system can be made with a relatively good degree of intra- and interjudge agreement.

14. Dimensionality Considerations

Snyder neither discusses nor presents data concerning the intercorrelations present among his various patient categories and among the therapist categories. It is not possible, therefore, to ascertain how many and which dimensions are operative in his category scores matrix.

15. Validity Studies

Validity data is presented in the 1953 and 1963 volumes as well as in his 1945 and 1959 reports. For the 1963 study the analyses are restricted to the two cases of dependency being intensively studied. Data analyses are very briefly presented, covering only fourteen pages of the 424-page volume. Samples of the findings presented are:

[1] For both clients a high correlation indicated that when they discussed the therapy relationship, the therapist responded with a discussion of the same topic. With Quinn, the therapist also handled resistance and dependency with a discussion of the relationship, and in addition he dealt with resistance by means of interpretation. With Jones, anxiety was very frequently met with reassurance or other supportive procedures. (1963, p. 32).

[2] While [supportive] methods constituted about 15 percent of this therapist's total counseling, the percentages changed markedly when the therapist was dealing with expressions of dependency on the part of the client. In terms of expressions of dependency directed toward persons other than the therapist, the supportive procedures dropped to about 8 percent in both cases (Quinn and Jones). But when dependency was directed toward the therapist, the expressions of support rose to 34 percent in the case of Quinn and to 25 percent in the case of Jones. (p. 36)

The 1945 study was an investigation of the nature of nondirective psychotherapy, based upon an analysis of forty-eight therapeutic interviews made by four counselors in the treatment of six different cases. Some illustrative findings from that study are:

[1] In typical nondirective psychotherapy the clarification of feeling comprises about half of the statements made by a counselor. The amount of such clarification in the early stages of treatment comprises 44 percent of all responses and in the late stages of treatment, 26 percent. (p. 22)

[2] Understanding and insight on the part of the client comprises 12 percent of his responses at the beginning of treatment, 28 percent in the middle, followed by a slight drop, and 30 percent at the end of treatment. (p. 221)

[3] Statements of the client's problem most frequently follow nondirective leads by the counselor. Occasionally a simple restatement of what the client has said may bring about further statement of the problem. Approval and encouragement produce statement of the problem in some cases. A client's statement of the problem is seldom produced by a counselor's structuring of the situation, direct questions, or clarification of feeling. It is almost never produced by interpretation, persuasion, or disapproval and criticism.(p. 221)

[4] Feelings associated with statement of the problem are usually negative. Those associated with understanding and insight and discussion of plans are positive or occasionally ambivalent. . . .

> During treatment there is a marked tendency for the client's feelings to change from a negative to a positive affective tone. In two of the six cases clients changed from a negative to an ambivalent attitude, apparently never quite reaching a positive attitude during the counseling process.(p. 222)

Snyder's conclusions from this 1945 study are historically interesting. His first claim is simply that "the results of the present study show that nondirective counseling can be subjected to scientific investigation" (p. 223). His remaining conclusions manifest the defensive stance the new nondirective school of psychotherapy must have felt in the mid-1940's.

> The method used by the nondirective counselors whose work was studied in this investigation is essentially similar to the principles which have been defined by Rogers for nondirective counseling. On the whole the counselors are conducting their interviews very much in the manner they state they are. The facts of the present study clearly support the theory that it is the nondirective elements of this type of treatment which produce the favorable change in the client's behavior. What directive elements exist are unfavorably received. (pp. 222-23)

References

Dollard, J., and Auld, F., Jr. *Scoring human motives: a manual.* New Haven, Conn.:Yale University Press, 1959.

Porter, E. H., Jr. The development and evaluation of a measure of counseling procedures. Unpublished doctoral dissertation, Ohio State University, 1941.

________.The development and evaluation of a measure of counseling interview procedures. *Educational and Psychological Measurement,* 1943, 3, 105-26; 215-38.

________.*An introduction to therapeutic counseling.* Boston: Houghton Mifflin, 1950.

Raush, H. L., Sperber, Z., Rigler, D., Williams, J. V., Harway, N. I., Bordin, E. S., Dittman, A. T., and Hays, W. A dimensional analysis of Depth of Interpretation. *Journal of Consulting Psychology,* 1956, 20, 43-48.

Rogers, C. R. *Counseling a psychotherapy.* Boston: Houghton Mifflin, 1942.

Royer, A. E. An analysis of counseling procedures in a nondirective approach. Unpublished doctoral dissertation, Ohio State University, 1942.

Snyder, W. U. An investigation of the nature of nondirective psychotherapy. *Journal of General Psychology,* 1945, 33, 193-223.

________. (Ed.). *Group report of a program of research in psychotherapy.* State College: Pennsylvania State College, 1953.

________.Some investigations of relationship in psychotherapy. In E. A. Rubinstein and M. B. Parloff (Eds.), *Research in psychotherapy.* Vol. 1. Washington, D. C.: American Psychological Association, 1959. Pp. 247-59.

________.*Dependency in psychotherapy: a casebook.* New York: Macmillan, 1963.

4

Major Process Systems for Analyzing Therapist Interview Behaviors

The systems presented in this chapter focus on measuring one or more aspects of therapist behavior in psychotherapy interviews. Two of the systems are multidimensional (Strupp and Truax), while the other three focus on assessing unitary therapist variables. All the systems involve rating scales representing ordinal measurement. Two of Strupp's five scales are the only nominal systems present in this chapter.

The systems are presented in alphabetical order by author. Chronologically, Harway, Dittman, Raush, Bordin, and Rigler's Depth of Interpretation Scale, appearing in 1955, antedates the others. Strupp's multidimensional system was first published in 1956, Howe and Pope's Therapist Verbal Activity Level scale in 1961, Siegman and Pope's Therapist Specificity scale in 1962, and Truax's Therapist Conditions scales in 1967.

Two of the systems (Howe and Pope, and Siegman and Pope) are empirically derived, and relate more to general clinical lore than to a particular theory. Two of the systems derive directly from psychoanalytic theory (Strupp, and Harway et al.), while the final system (Truax) is a direct offshoot of Rogerian theory.

The remainder of the chapter presents an intensive analysis of these five therapist systems: (1) Howe and Pope's Therapist Verbal Activity Level scale; (2) Harway et al.'s Depth of Interpretation scale; (3) Siegman and Pope's scale for measuring Therapist Specificity; (4) Strupp's multidimensional system measuring Type of Therapeutic Activity, Depth-Directedness, Dynamic Focus, Initiative, and

Therapeutic Climate; and (5) Truax's three therapist conditions scales of Accurate Empathy, Nonpossessive Warmth, and Self-Congruence.

The Depth of Interpretation Scale

Norman I. Harway, Allen T. Dittmann, Harold L. Raush, Edward S. Bordin, and David Rigler

1. Rationale for Development of the Scale

Bordin and his colleagues have been involved in the study of psychotherapy for a considerable period of time. They have focused on the development of various scaling instruments for assessing key psychoanalytic constructs of psychotherapy from interview data. In addition to interpretation, and Bordin's free-association scale presented elsewhere in this volume, they have addressed themselves to constructs of therapist ambiguity and warmth as well as to patient resistance.

"In these studies we have attempted to select variables which have theoretical and practical relevance over a wide variety of therapeutic approaches" (Harway et al., 1955, p. 247). However, definitions of the constructs chosen make it clear that their approach has a psychoanalytic emphasis. Bordin (1959) draws this perspective:

> Whether we deal with observations of "live interviews," electrical recordings, or typescripts, the data before us is infinite in quantity. Blind explorers will either lose themselves in a morass of detail or soon become so baffled that they will turn to less frustrating areas of research. This complexity has forced us to set great store by the selectivity that theory permits. As is evident from our research, we are most heavily influenced by psychoanalytic theory. . . . As Freud and Rogers, among others, have demonstrated, theories of psychotherapy cannot be divorced from theories of personality development. We are encouraged to pursue further those attributes of therapeutic relationships which have either direct translations to or indirect implications for the development of personality. Our ideal is to be able to build a network of relationships which can be traced not only through the therapist's office but also through the laboratory, the home, and school. (p. 236)

The authors decided to focus on interpretation since "one of the major activities of the psychotherapist in the course of treating his patient is to engage or avoid engaging in interpretive behavior" (Harway et al., 1955, p. 247).

> In the case of depth of interpretation, we have chosen a definition and a mode of differentation which permits us not only to distinguish between interpretations of superficial as against those of moderate depth, such as would be necessary to test the differences in views between Fenichel and Rogers, but also makes possible the distinction between moderate and deep interpretations such as might be involved in differentiating the views of Fenichel and others like Berg or Rosen, (Bordin, 1959, p. 238).

2. Description of the Scales

The authors define interpretation as "any behavior on the part of the therapist that is an expression of his view of the patient's emotions and motivations—either wholly or in part" (Harway et al., 1955, p. 247). The concept of depth of interpretation refers to a "description of the relationship between the view expressed by the therapist and the patient's awareness. The greater the disparity between the view expressed by the therapist and the patient's own awareness of these emotions and motivations the deeper the interpretation" (pp. 247-48).

The Depth of Interpretation Scale is presented in Table 4.1.The seven-point scale ranges from superficial interpretations embodied in restatements of what the patient has just said to deep interpretations characterized as completely beyond the patient's conscious grasp.

In developing the scale the authors followed Thurstone's method of equal-appearing intervals.

> Seventy statements descriptive of therapist activity were sorted by two groups of judges, one experienced, the other naive. The experienced group consisted of fourteen staff members and advanced graduate students in clinical psychology, each with at least 100 hours of experience in psychotherapeutic practice. Eleven undergraduate students in the first course in psychology composed the "naive" judges. Judges with disparate experience were used in hope of identifying items highly communicable to a wide range of possible raters. . . . Seven of the statements had been originally selected so as not to fit the requirements of our definition; while descriptive of therapist activity, they did not give any indication of patient awareness or of the relation of the therapist's activity to the patient's awareness (for example, "Questioning designed to gain information," "Therapist suggests that the patient desires to

> terminate therapy"). These seven statements offered an internal check. If they scaled along with our bona fide statements, the meaning of the resulting scale would be open to question. None of these "spurious" statements met our criteria for inclusion in the scale. By this procedure a seven-point graphic scale was obtained. Nine statements were selected to exemplify points on this scale. (Harway et al., 1955, p. 248)

In subsequent studies with the scale "the definition of depth of interpretation and the scale were presented with the statement that the nine items on the scale are not inclusive of all possible descriptions of depth at these points . . . but are merely examples of types of things that could occur and where they would fall on the scale" (p. 249). Since the scale is graphic in form, raters are permitted to check anywhere on the continuous line between 1 and 7 the point they feel is most descriptive of a particular therapist statement. Raters are further instructed "to rate each unit, but to indicate those units or responses which they did not feel were reliable on this particular scale. The ratings of responses so indicated were considered as 'forced' ratings, and were not used in computing the means for the response unit scores, nor were they used in computing interrater agreements in rating" (p. 250).

3. Data Collection Context

To date the authors have applied the scale to various samples of psychotherapy interviews. They have not primarily been concerned with relating therapist depth of interpretation to patient interview behavior or to measures of patient out-come.

> The heart of construct validity is to be found in demonstrable relationships between any given variable (in this case, depth of interpretation) and other observations drawn either from within or outside the therapeutic process. We achieve the greatest degree of confidence in the validity of a given measure when we can verify predictions formally derived from the specific assumptions about the concept in question. Our research strategy has been to give considerable attention to the internal analysis of our measures and to test assumptions about the condition of measurement before moving to a greater stress on external validity. Consequently, we have accumulated relatively less data at this level of construct validity. (Bordin, 1959, p. 241)

The upshot is that to date the scale has been studied primarily in terms of its methodological, measurement, and dimensionality characteristics.

4. Data Form

In one study, Harway et al. (1955) compared the effects on DI ratings of presenting to raters typescripts in contrast to tape-recorded samples of therapy interviews. Their findings indicated that "there is no difference in the ratings of interviews under different methods of presentation of the interview. . . . For evaluations of this particular variable, then, we can in the future present typescripts to our raters and enjoy the practical advantages stemming from the easier administration permitted by this method" (p. 251). The primary data form used for obtaining DI ratings has been typescripts transcribed from tape-recorded therapy interviews. To date the authors have not empirically assessed the differential effect, if any, of video presentation of the data. The above findings suggest that likely no differences would emerge.

5. Choice of Units

Apparently the unit most frequently presented to judges consists of three consecutive patient-therapist exchanges ending with a therapist's remark, that is, P-T-P-T-P-T. "Only the final therapist response was to be judged; the preceding section served to provide context" (Raush et al., 1956, p. 44). Thus, the "scoring unit" is the final therapist statement in the sequence.[1] The "contextual unit" consists of the "three consecutive patient-therapist exchanges"; the judges use these verbalizations to score the final therapist statement.

The authors do not explicitly define the "summarizing unit" for their studies. They seem to use three different DI scores in their data analyses. When the interview is the unit rated, only one overall DI score is obtained from each judge. On the other hand, "when the [therapist] response was the unit rated, there were . . . as many scores for each rater as there were responses. . . . [In this case] the response unit ratings, for a single judge, were averaged to give a rating for the interview as a whole" (Harway et al., 1955, p. 249). Finally, they seem also to have used an average DI score for each rater over a unit of ten consecutive therapist responses. For most studies the DI rating of two judges are averaged and the mean score is used in data analyses.

1. In some other studies, *each* successive therapist response has been rated for depth of interpretation (for example, Harway et al., 1955). In these cases each therapist statement is the scoring unit.

6. Participant-Context Restrictions

The authors have been particularly concerned about participant context, since their construct definition demands that patient's verbalizations be present together with subsequent therapist statements in order to assess depth of interpretation.

> The concept of interpretation, and the specific definition used in this study, imply that knowledge of both patient and therapist activity is necessary for a correct appraisal of the interpretive level. . . . [Hence,] removal of the patient response should lead to different results from those obtained when the patient responses are included in the information given to raters. (Harway et al., 1955, p. 251)

In one study the authors empirically assessed the effect of participant-context versus no-context (patients statements omitted) on subsequent ratings of depth of interpretation. The findings indicated that "the expected difference did not occur. Furthermore, the reliabilities of the two methods are comparable, and the cross correlations indicate that the methods are equivalent. . . . Such a finding casts doubt on the validity of our measurements or on the adequacy of the definition of the concept" (p. 251).

The authors subsequently considered a third alternative explanation. "It seems possible that the raters were obtaining information as to the patient's behavior from the sequence of the therapist's response" (p. 251). To check this possibility another study was run in which one group of judges rated therapist responses in sequence while another group rated therapist responses in a random order. The results showed that the reliabilities for the random order ratings were lower than for the sequential order ratings, and that none of the cross-context correlations differed significantly from zero.

> These data suggest that the sequence did give the judges enough information about what the patient's behavior may have been to allow them to make ratings equivalent to those of judges who actually had read the intervening patient responses. Randomizing the sequence of therapist responses probably randomized the judges' hypotheses about the level of awareness demonstrated by the intervening patient behavior. (p. 252)

The authors conclude from these two studies that "we have illustrated . . . that it is possible to check on the validity of measurement by examining the consistency of the measurements with the definition of the variable" (p. 253).

The final analysis seems to be that to obtain valid DI ratings, either the therapist responses to be rated need to be presented with the previous patient statements intact (the P-T-P-T-P-T unit); or if the therapist statements alone are to be rated, the responses need to be presented in the sequential order in which they occurred in the interview.

7. Type of Sampling Indicated

The authors have not explicitly discussed whether their construct of depth of interpretation would require systematic versus random sampling of therapist interview statements. To the extent that their construct is derived from psychoanalytic theory, one might expect that some prior editing of different content areas of patient talk is indicated, and would define various domains from which samples of therapist statements could be systematically extracted. To the extent that the scale is designed to have "theoretical and practical relevance over a wide variety of therapeutic approaches," one might opt for a random sampling of therapist statements.

8. Sample Location Within the Interview

The authors have not addressed the issue of where, in particular interview sessions, samples should be extracted in order to obtain depth of interpretation ratings representative of the total session. One study suggests that sampling may indeed be an important issue. In this study, depth of interpretation ratings were independently made both to each individual therapist statement and to the therapists statements encompassing the entire session. The DI ratings obtained for each session by averaging the individual-therapist-statement ratings were then compared to the single overall DI rating made for the session as a whole. Significant differences were obtained. "For each interview . . . the evaluation based on the interview unit was 'deeper' than the mean of the response unit ratings . . . . Apparently, the judges' perceptions of the depth of an entire interview are strongly determined by the therapist's deeper responses" (Harway et al., 1955, p. 251). Clearly one of these scoring alternatives would need to be standardized for any particular study.

9. Sample Location over Therapy Interviews

To date studies applying the scale have predominantly included only single interviews drawn from a particular patient-therapist case. The authors consequently have not discussed the problem of where over the entire interview series and in what manner one should sample in order to obtain depth of interpretation ratings representative of the therapist statements from initiation to termination of therapy. Clearly, the decisions made will depend on the particular theoretical questions being asked, but would also need to be checked empirically.

10. Clinical Sophistication of Judges

DI judges have been clinically sophisticated, either clinical psychologists or psychoanalysts with some experience in psychotherapy. The authors emphasize the necessity for clinical experience vis-à-vis DI ratings.

> Many research workers, particularly those of a psychoanalytic bent, will accept as observers only those who have gone through formal therapeutic training, including personal therapy, and who have considerable experience as therapists. The issue of the qualifications of the observer would seem to apply especially to depth of interpretation. Here the observer is asked to judge the patient's level of awareness of those emotions and motivations which have been the object of the therapist's interpretative remarks. Surely the observer would need both professional sophistication and personal freedom to be sensitive to the feelings of others. If we cannot find differences between ratings obtained from sophisticated and unsophisticated observers, surely our confidence in the meaningfulness of depth of interpretation ratings would be shaken. We were relieved to discover that naive observers, namely undergraduates drawn from the first course in psychology, did not attain as much agreement among themselves as more expert raters, clinical psychologists who met the criterion of having had a minimum of 100 hours of experience as therapists. At the other extreme of the continuum of experience and personal therapy, we compared clinical psychologists and psychoanalysts in terms of ratings of depth of interpretation. Here we found relatively little difference between the groups. (Bordin, 1959, p. 240)

Thus, the authors clearly intend that DI ratings should be restricted to professional judges with some level of therapeutic experience. It seems fair to suggest, however, that perhaps unsophisticated judges might be employed if relatively extensive standardized training procedures were required of DI judges before experimental ratings were performed. The definitions of the scale stages seem relatively straightforward and at a low inferential level. Whether, for example, undergraduates could then obtain equivalent DI ratings, if trained in use of the scale could be empirically assessed. Fisher's results (1956) reported below are consistent with this suggestion.

11. Training Required of Judges

The authors have intentionally not established training procedures for judges who are to apply their scales. This has been particularly true for depth of interpretation ratings. In a personal communication (April, 1969), Bordin states:

> Our general approach with regard to the training of raters is to feel that it ought to be possible for raters to achieve acceptable levels of agreement without extensive training. We're inclined to use sophisticated clinicians as raters and to feel that extensive training runs the risk of shaping raters' responses, inadvertently, around artificial aspects of responses as they try to solve the problem of reaching agreement. The result is that you get high levels of agreement but have moved the attribute being rated from what it was originally intended to be to some more artificial characteristics.

12. Training Manual

There is no training manual. This is consistent with the author's expressed desire to develop measures that can be applied by sophisticated clinicians with little training required. The best sources for information on use of the scale are Harway et al. (1955) and Bordin (1959).

13. Interrater and Intrarater Reliabilities Reported

The authors report several studies of interjudge agreement. "Almost all the reliability coefficients based on the ratings of two raters working on the same interview and presentation conditions were satistically significant. The median coefficient for the main study was 0.40. Reliabilities of this order are disappointing."(Harway et al., 1955, p. 252) However, the authors found that if they modified the unit being rated the situation improved. When the unit rated was increased from the single therapist statement to a unit of ten consecutive therapist responses, interjudge agreement improved to 0.74 as compared to 0.36 for the single response units" (p. 252). Hence, the authors seem to recommend the use of a ten-response therapist unit; or if single therapist responses are to be rated, they recommend increasing the number of judges in order to insure adequate interrater reliability.

14. Dimensionality Considerations

The authors have made dimensionality concerns the major focus of their studies to date. They take pains to spell out the rationale for this concern.

> A rating scale such as we have used and such as is common in other clinical studies forces judges to respond as though they were dealing with a single dimension, irrespective of the true complexity of the variable. If we demonstrate that depth of interpretation is in fact unidimensional, we can proceed to use the scale and to make more confident inferences about its relationship to other variables. . . . If we uncover evidence of more than one dimension, but we judge that these dimensions can be incorporated into a revised notion about depth of interpretation, then our study will have brought about a modification in our concept or theory. Also by being able to identify these dimensions we may be able to achieve better agreement among raters. Finally, if more than one dimension is revealed, any of the additional ones may prove irrelevant from our point of view, and might be susceptible to elimination through refinement of the scale or through training of judges. In summary, our specific purpose . . . is to find out what attributes judges use in dealing with depth of interpretation, to what extent they agree as to the attributes, and to what extent any of these attributes correspond to our definition and scale of depth of interpretation. (Raush et al., 1956, p. 43)

The methodology the authors use for this dimensional unraveling is generally based upon the psychophysical method of similarities and upon Coombs' Unfolding Technique.

> Bennet (1951) has developed techniques which enable us to estimate the number of dimensions in data that are collected by methods developed by Coombs (1953). Hays (1954) has expanded the procedure so as to provide information on the ordering of the stimuli on the several dimensions. These methods enable us to investigate the underlying factors entering into judgments of behavior by providing a set of dimensions which best account for a given set of judgments. (Raush et al., 1956, p. 44)

The reader who wishes further detail regarding this procedure can consult the above article as well as the original sources.

Applying this procedure in several studies, the authors found that three dimensions consistently emerged for depth of interpretation ratings. "In each of the four studies, involving a sample of stimuli from five interviews with different patients and therapists, depth of interpretation was consistently the primary dimension." (p. 47) Hence, although depth of interpretation was shown to be treated by judges not as a unitary dimension but as at least three dimensional, the primary dimension nevertheless was DI; the secondary dimensions varied depending on the judges and stimuli used. These findings "permit us to state with confidence that more variability in our data can be attributed to the depth of interpretation dimension than to any of the other dimensions operating. . . . [Consequently,] pooling judgments may maximize its [DI's] contribution and reduce the effect of secondary factors, specific to the ratings of individual judges." (p. 47)

15. Validity Studies

Apparently the only study examining the external validity of the scale is that of Speisman (1959), who investigated therapist depth of interpretation as related to patient verbal resistance in psychotherapy. Speisman recorded all responses in a sequence of five consecutive interviews from a single case as well as a block of eleven successive patient-therapist responses randomly selected from twenty-one other cases. The sample of patients was characterized as psychoneurotic, and the psychologist and psychiatrist therapists were of various orientations (Adlerian, nondirective, neoanalytic, eclectic) of one to ten years of experience. The therapists' responses were rated as either superficial, moderate, or deep interpretations by the Depth of Interpretation Scale. The subsequent patient responses were classified into various positive and negative categories of resistance. Speisman's results showed that both superficial and moderate interpretations were followed by more patient exploration and less resistance than were deep interpretations. Therapist shifts from deep to not deep interpretations were followed by increased patient exploration and decreased resistance, while higher resistance followed the reverse shift. Speisman concluded that his results offer confirmatory support for Fenichel's psychoanalytic dictum to "interpret just beyond the preconscious."

RELATED SCALES OR CONSTRUCTS

Fisher (1956) suggests an alternative explanation of depth of interpretation from that of the scale authors: "A rather common way of estimating depth clinically seems to be based upon the patient's subsequent reaction to an interpretation. If the patient strenuously rejects an interpretation, it must perforce be deep; an avidly accepted interpretation suggests shallowness." (p. 252) Some problems arise if depth of interpretation is considered, as the scale authors do, in relation to the degree of awareness on the patient's part. "[As] therapy progresses, it is generally claimed that patients tend to acquire increased awareness. Hence, an interpretation given late in therapy might not be as deep as if it were given very early." (p. 252)

On the other hand, "if we equate depth with perceived plausibility, it becomes possible to understand why many therapists verbalize their definition of depth in terms of the patient's response to an interpretation. . . . While the concept of depth assumes truth-content of an interpretation, this limitation disappears when a dimension of 'perceived truth' or plausibility is used." (p. 254) Fisher then describes his plausibility construct.

> Depth can be considered a form of "distance" . . . (that is, the discrepancy between two persons' opinions. If A expresses an opinion quite similar to that held by B, the distance is small; if A expresses a judgment markedly different from B's belief, the distance is large). . . . It is self-evident that, other things being equal, plausibility is a necessary monotonic correlative of distance, larger distances being more implausible than smaller distances. . . . A "deep" (implausible) interpretation is one with a larger distance; a "shallow" (plausible) interpretation has little distance; a therapist statement which has zero distance is not an interpretation. . . . Thus a new and unified working definition is suggested, where interpretation is an implicit or explicit judgment about the patient's motivational and emotional behavior where the distance is greater than zero; the magnitude of the distance is a measure of the interpretation's depth. (p. 255)
>
> Fisher submitted this hypothesis to empirical test.
>
> Four groups of judges, three of which differed in therapeutic experience, were asked to rate a series of 60 psychotherapeutic interpretations. Two groups rated for "depth" (in the usual sense of the term); two groups rated for "plausibility" (from the patient's point of view: Do these statements seem true or false to the particular patient?). High intergroup agreement was obtained on both depth and plausibility scales. When mean plausibility ratings were correlated with mean depth ratings, a sufficiently high relationship was found to suggest that two scales may be measuring the same underlying construct. Plausability ratings of therapeutically naive graduate students correlated 0.88 with depth ratings from experienced psychologists and 0.86 with psychiatrists' depth

ratings, implying that advanced training in therapy and psychodynamics may not be prerequisite for a knowledge of what is "deep" or "shallow." (p. 255)

References

Bennett, J. F. A method for determining the dimensionality of a set of rank orders. Unpublished doctoral dissertation, University of Michigan, 1951.

Bordin, E. S. Inside the therapeutic hour. In E. A. Rubinstein and M. B. Parloff (Eds.), *Research in psychotherapy*. Washington, D. C.: American Psychological Association, 1959, pp. 235-46.

Coombs, C. H. Theory and methods of social measurement. In L. Festinger and D. Katz (Eds.), *Research methods in the behavioral sciences*. New York: Dryden Press, 1953, pp. 471-535.

Fisher, S. Plausibility and depth of interpretation. *Journal of Consulting Psychology*, 1956, 20, 249-56.

Harway, N. I., Dittmann, A. T., Raush, H. L., Bordin, E. S., and Rigler, D. The measurement of depth of interpretation. *Journal of Consulting Psychology*, 1955, 19, 247-53.

Harway, N. I., and Iker, H. P. Content analysis and psychotherapy. *Psychotherapy: Theory, Research and Practice*, 1969, 6, 97-104.

Hays, W. L. An extension of the unfolding technique to r-dimensions. Unpublished doctoral dissertation, University of Michigan, 1954.

Raush, H. L., Sperber, Z., Rigler, D., Williams, J., Harway N. I., Bordin, E. S., Dittman, A. T., and Hays, W. L. A Dimensional analysis of depth of interpretation. *Journal of Consulting Psychology*, 1956, 20, 43-48.

Speisman, J. C. Depth of interpretation and verbal resistance in psychotherapy. *Journal of Consulting Psychology*, 1959, 23, 93-99.

An Empirical Scale of Therapist Verbal Activity Level in the Initial Interview

Edmund S. Howe and Benjamin Pope

1. Rationale for Development of the Scale

Howe and Pope's basic concern centers on the question: What kind of therapist activity level leads to the most productive and fruitful initial interview session with therapy patients? Their basic assumption is that the therapist's mode of verbalization in the initial interview has an important bearing upon achievement of his diagnostic or other goals; and that the initial interview is diagnostically fruitful only if it is projective. This assumption derives from the "increasing adoption of the projective interview, in which it is now commonly accepted that one is apt to discover more information of a relevant nature either by remaining silent or at most by asking rather vague, nonleading questions onto which the patient may project his own referents, and his own interpretation of what is meant." (Howe and Pope, 1961a, p. 510) In other words, the most useful patient information is elicited when the therapist remains inactive, that is, silent, or at most asks rather vague, nonleading questions. Maintenance of a low verbal activity level also enables the therapist to foster the development of transference reactions as well as to avoid shifting into a social relationship with the patient.

The author's efforts in developing the Therapist Activity Level Scale constituted "a preliminary basic step in a research program the aim of which is to evaluate the role played by, and the impact upon the patient of, the therapist's activity level in the initial interview." (p. 511)

2. *Description of the Scale*

Following Finesinger's (1948) principle of Minimal Activity, Howe and Pope state that the therapist's activity level is high when his verbal responses are relatively unambiguous, leading, and carry high inference; they are low when his verbal responses are ambiguous, nonleading, and carry low inference.

> These three attributes, Ambiguity, Lead, and Inference will be used to characterize what is meant by variations in activity level. It was assumed for the purposes of these studies that the three attributes are moderately (if not highly) intercorrelated, so that the three terms are to some extent interchangeable. Thus, ambiguity subjectively feels as though it would be negatively correlated with Lead and with Inference, whereas the last two would be positively correlated with each other. (Howe and Pope, 1961a, p. 511)

Consequently, the authors developed the following working definition of therapist activity level.

> A high-active response from the therapist is not, of course, necessarily one which has greater length. It does, however, have relatively low Ambiguity about it; it involves a marked degree of Lead by the therapist; and it carries a high degree of Inference. Conversely, a low-active response is highly ambiguous; it manifests a low degree of Lead by the therapist; and it carries a low degree of inference. Thus, compare the following three descriptive responses: (1) therapist gives a general, unfocused invitation for the patient to talk, (2) therapist asks the patient to describe the last

occasion when a pattern of symptoms occurred, (3) therapist explores the patient's feelings about something just reported by the patient. Going from one to two through three, the responses become less ambiguous, they show progressively more lead, and they connote an increasing degree of inference. (p. 511)

Development of the therapist activity level scale occurred in a series of stages. The authors first culled a sample of twenty published psychotherapy interviews (different types of patients, different phases of treatment, and therapists of different theoretical allegiance). They compiled from this sample a representative sample of fifty abstract descriptions of therapists' verbal responses. Thirty board-certified psychiatrists then rated each of the descriptive responses (typed on 3x5 cards) for activity level along an eleven-point scale, and also sorted duplicate sets of cards in three groups: responses primarily diagnostic, primarily therapeutic, and neither. Ebel intraclass reliabilities for the ratings were good ($r_{11} = 0.50$; $r_{kk} = 0.93$). Also, therapist responses judged primarily "therapeutic in purpose" were rated with a significantly high mean AL than those classified as "diagnostic in purpose."

In their next developmental study, ten new raters-four psychiatrists and six clinical psychologists-sorted the same fifty responses into six categories: simple facilitation, exploration, clarification, interpretation, supportive reassurance, and persuasiveness. This order represents a continuum of increasing therapist activity. The raters were given "a broad working definition of each category" (p. 512). The AL ratings of the fifty responses from the previous study were then correlated with these construct valid categories. The responses classified in these successive categories respectively showed increasingly higher mean activity levels, representing some construct validation of the scale.

A third study followed. Since the authors wanted to study therapist verbal behavior in the initial, rather than in the treatment, interview and "since initial interviews tend usually not to involve the more active types of therapist operations (for example, interpretative), twenty-five of the most active responses were removed from the original set of fifty" (p. 513), to which eleven more were added. This set of thirty-six responses (twenty-five of the fifty having lowest AL ratings and eleven new responses) were then rated along the 11-point Al scale by three groups of subjects: thirty psychiatrists, nineteen interested (planning to specialize in psychiatry) and eighteen not so interested (expressed low interest in specializing in psychiatry) freshman medical students. Interrater reliabilities for all three groups were quite high (Ebel's $r_{kk} = 0.93$). Data from the psychiatrist subjects in this study were used to form two parallel Activity scales. The two Therapist Activity Level Scales are presented in Table 4.2.

For the scales "each ordinal pair of items was matched in the basis of virtually identical mean Activity levels and of nonsignificantly different variances" (p. 514). Scale A and Scale B represent the final scale forms used in all subsequent studies of therapist verbal activity level by the authors.

Use of the two scale forms has led to different results in some cases. In one study application "the two Activity Scales not only led to different overall mean ratings of AL; interrater reliabilities also differed as a function of the particular scale. Scale A was more reliably employed for three of the interviews, Scale B being more reliably used with Interview IV" (p. 517).

3. *Data Collection Context*

The authors have applied their Scale A and Scale B forms of the Therapist Activity Level Scale primarily to transcriptions of initial psychotherapy interviews published in the literature. A major focus of their interest with these studies has been on methodological and dimensional problems with their scales. A few studies have looked at the intercorrelation of therapist activity level with different measures of patient responses occurring subsequently in the interview.

4. *Data Form*

The exclusive data form to which the Activity Level ratings have been applied are typescripts of therapy interviews. The authors have not discussed or empirically assessed the differential effects on AL ratings of audio or visual recordings in contrast to the typescripts.

5. *Choice of Units*

The authors are not explicit about the exact unit scored other than stating that therapist statements are rated. Apparently the "scoring unit" involved is the T of the P-T-P communication sequence, that is, the entire therapist response intervening between two patient statements. They have not considered the differential effects on reliability or equivalence of AL ratings which might result from using different size therapist-statement units.

Howe and Pope do not specify the "contextual" or "summarizing" units for their scale ratings. Apparently this omission results from the fact that they have not applied their scale to therapy interviews, except in a few instances. Their primary focus has been on the scale items (therapists' statements) which they have presented to various samples of psychotherapist-judges, in order to examine the dimensionality of their scales. For these latter studies it seems the scoring, contextual, and summarizing units are identical: all involve the therapist "statement," which is the entire therapist response intervening between two patient statements.

6. Participant-Context Restrictions

Evidently, the usual scoring procedure is to rate therapists' statements without the presence of either the patient's preceding or subsequent verbalizations. One study, however, examined the participant-context issue for both forms of the Activity Level scale. Eight judges rated four initial therapy interviews on one of the two scales. For only two of the interviews the therapist responses were presented; for the other two interviews the entire typed protocol including subsequent patient responses was presented. There were no differences in AL ratings on either scale as the result of the context variable.

7. Type of Sampling Indicated

Since in their studies of initial interviews the entire session is rated, the authors have not explicitly considered the issue of random versus stratified sampling as it applies to their Activity Level scales.

8. Sample Location Within the Interview

For the same reason Howe and Pope have not considered what size and from where in the 50-minute session samples of therapist statements can be taken that will yield Activity Level ratings representative of total individual sessions.

9. Sample Location over Therapy Interviews

With their primary focus on the initial psychiatric interview, the authors have not been concerned about sampling over an entire therapy case from initiation to termination. They have not addressed the issue of from where and in what manner (randomly or systematically) samples can be drawn from the entire interview series that will yield activity level ratings representative of therapist behavior covering the entire case.

10. Clinical Sophistication of Judges

The authors have used professional psychotherapists (psychiatrists, clinical psychologists, psychoanalysts) as judges in the majority of their studies. However, in one of their scale development studies reported above they compared the activity level ratings of three groups of judges: thirty clinically sophisticated psychiatrists, nineteen interested (planning to specialize in psychiatry) and eighteen not so interested (expressed low interest in specializing in psychiatry) freshman medical students. Ebel intraclass reliabilities for all three groups were quite high: r_{11}s were 0.49, 0.42, and 0.42 respectively, and r_{kk} was 0.93 for all three groups. The high interest group's ratings correlated 0.87 and 0.74 with the psychiatrist and low-interest group respectively, while the low-interest group correlated 0.64 with the psychiatrists. The authors conclude that the "reliability of the rating procedure is but little altered by psychiatric interest and experience" of judges. (Howe and Pope, 1961a, p. 514)

11. Training Required of Judges

Apparently, no training on use of the scale is provided the judges before they are exposed to experimental data. They are given the scale, asked to study it, and then immediately apply it to the various typescript data.

12. Training Manual

There is no manual. The authors do not provide a standardized procedure for training raters to learn, master, and apply the Activity Level scales.

13. Interrater and Intrarater Reliabilities Reported

The authors report that the empirically derived Activity Scales (Scale A and Scale B), from data of several studies, yield ratings having "average reliability which is moderate (0.51) for untrained raters and very high (0.91) for well-trained raters. (Howe and Pope, 1961a, p. 517) They conclude that "the scales themselves are sufficiently meaningful and reliable to justify their application in further research on the initial as well as the therapeutic interview." (p. 518-19)

14. Dimensionality Considerations

The authors have placed considerable emphasis on the dimensionality problem as it relates to their Activity scales. After their earlier studies they felt that the rather low reliabilities obtained in some cases for their scale may have been because they assumed their dimension of study was multiple rather than unitary. To unravel the dimensionalities operative in activity level ratings, the authors have used a form of Osgood's Semantic Differential (Osgood, Suci, and Tannenbaum, 1957).

In the first of these dimensional studies (Howe and Pope, 1961b) the authors had thirty-five psychiatrists rate ten bona fide therapist verbal responses (from the original set of fifty) against forty seven-point semantic differential adjective scales chosen to correspond with the hypothetical variables of ambiguity, lead, and inference (stressfulness), and the three Osgood dimensions of evaluation, potency, and activity. For their task the raters were given the structure that each response was made during the initial interview. The matrix of intercorrelations obtained among the ratings for the forty semantic differential scales were factor analyzed. Nine factors were extracted, of which only three were interpretable. The first was Professional Evaluation (33 percent of total variance): "Its nature implies that the good therapist, the one who is thoroughly reputable and skilled, uses responses which are cautious, relaxed, muted, accepting, sensitive, and calm." The second factor, Precision/Potency (18 percent of total variance), "clearly refers to those attributes of therapist behavior variously referred to as activity, ambiguity, and the like" (p. 310), reminiscent of Osgood's dynamism factor. The third factor, Subjectivity/Objectivity, was difficult to interpret. The authors conclude that "regardless of what instruction one gives to a rater, he will, in the final analysis, rate according to certain internal mediating cues which only partly correspond with whatever explicit cues the experimenter is trying to communicate." (p. 301) Furthermore, "the results confirm . . . that raters do indeed tend to react to statements in the semantic differential rating situation with an attitude which is primarily evaluative, and that only in the second place, as it were, do they concern themselves with the degree of ambiguity, clarity, activity, precision, and focus of a response." (p. 310)

Howe, in a 1963 paper (see also Howe, 1965), summarizes the results of the various studies considering this dimensionality problem. He concludes that psychoanalysts' ratings of therapists' verbal exploratory responses on the Activity Level Scale have been factored consistently into three dimensions. Precision/Potency refers in part to the degree of ambiguity in the therapist statements. Professional Evaluation refers to the "proper" way for a therapist to behave. Objectivity/Subjectivity concerns the extent to which the therapist's statements credibly and objectively follow from issues previously raised by the patient, rather than emanating from intuitive, subjective guesswork by the therapist about what is relevant. "The three dimensions of judgment are orthogonal and hence independent . . . and anxiety-arousal emerges as a *non*evaluative judgment, correlated only with Precision/Potency—that is, the more precise therapist's statements are judged to be more anxiety-arousing." (Howe, 1963, p. 2)

Howe cautions that elements of spuriousness may exist in the semantic differential results in that only ten therapist statements were rated, and from the fact that semantic differential research yields repeated measures on the same subjects, which may undermine the assumption that independence among dimensions observed within the semantic differential situation necessarily implies independence in all situations. Another study examined these cautions, and found that in a nonsemantic differential situation the independence of the three dimensions observed in the semantic differential situation holds up for one of the initial interviews studies but not for the other. Hence, the semantic differential results should be interpreted with some caution.

Finally, Howe (1963) concludes:

> There is by this time no question in my mind that at least three demonstrable dimensions of verbal behavior exist. The occurrence of multi- rather than unidimensionality among ratings of the therapist's verbal responses appears to be well founded. The source of such ideas arose from a laboratory model, as it were, which at the moment we find only partly to hold up in more complex "live" conditions. It is perhaps time now to define *each* dimension operationally and to treat it as a rigorous independent variable in research on the therapy interview. (p. 6)

The work of Siegman and Pope on therapist specificity-ambiguity reported elsewhere in this volume is one result of Howe's move in this new direction.

15. Validity Studies

The authors' main concern with the therapist activity level scales has been to assess various methodological issues and particularly unidimensionality considerations regarding their instrument. However, one study (Howe and Pope, 1962) attempted to look at one aspect of patient interview behavior as a correlate of therapist verbal activity level. The specific hypothesis investigated was that discrete patient responses immediately following low-active (in contrast to high-active) therapist responses should be judged to carry greater diagnostic utility. Eight judges rated discrete patient responses from four initial interviews (Gill, Finesinger, Wolberg, and Rogers) for Diagnostic utility, along a four-point scale (zero, low, moderate, high). The Sequence of interviews rated by each judge, the Order in-which a given interview was rated, the Context variable (immediately preceding therapist response present or absent), and the Arrangement variable (statements presented seriatum versus randomly) were systematically varied and controlled. Analysis showed that neither the Context non Arrangement variables produced a significant effect for the Diagnostic Utility ratings. The four interviews were significantly discriminated from each other by the Diagnostic Utility ratings. Since eight raters had earlier performed the ratings of therapist Activity Level of discrete therapist responses from the same four interviews, for each of the interviews a block of 8x8 Pearson rs were computed, giving an index of relationship between therapist AL and the Diagnostic Utility of the following patient response. The ratings for each of the eight judges in the two groups were pooled, and the mean values of these pooled ratings were intercorrelated. The correlational findings supported the hypothesized relationship between AL and DU for only two of the four interviews. It was subsequently shown that for both significant relationships obtained, a verbal productivity factor (frequency of clauses per patient response) was responsible for the relationship. Mean DU per patient response was significantly correlated (0.47 and 0.36) with the number of clauses in that response. Mean Activity Level of the previous therapist response was insignificantly correlated (-0.20 and -0.23).

RELATED SCALES OR CONSTRUCTS

Howe (1962a) examined the similar construct and measure of Depth of Interpretation developed by Harway et al., (1955), described above. Several studies by Bordin and his colleagues had found Depth of Interpretation consistently to be the primary of three factors operating in the scale ratings. The secondary dimensions (emotionality or ambiguity) varied according to the particular raters and interpretive stimuli employed. From his results with the Therapist Activity Level Scale, Howe was concerned whether raters of Depth of Interpretation were employing, in addition to the cues implied by the scale itself, other types of cues not implied by the scale but unwittingly assumed by raters to be criteria of depth and actually utilized by them to degrees perhaps varying considerably from one rater to the next. His study examined the correlations between ratings of sixty-two interpretive responses of therapists made along the following dimensions: depth of interpretation, potential for anxiety-arousal, specificity-focus, therapeutic (skillfullness), and implausibility. His hypothesis was that responses rated deep (versus shallow) would be rated as strongly anxiety-arousing, as highly specific and focused, and as highly implausible. Each of forty-eight psychiatrist raters received for their task the sixty-two interpretive statements, and a case history and psychological test summary from a fictitious patient. Subgroups of judges rated the sixty-two therapist statements on *only one* of the above dimensions, attaining Ebel r_{kk} values ranging from 0.61 to 0.91. Results showed that: (1) despite their being culled from a fictitious interview, the statements as a group appear to have been considered at least moderately skillful; (2) depth emerges as the most reliably rated dimension, implausibility runs a close second; (3) depth, specificity, anxiety arousal, and implausibility show moderate to high intercorrelations (rs ranging from 0.45 to 0.75), indicating that, through whatever mediating mechanism, the separate groups of judges rating the respective nominal dimensions were in large part rating along the same functional dimension. The findings were supportive of Howe's hypothesis in that a deep interpretive statement was rated not only as relatively implausible but also as quite specific, and quite anxiety-arousing.

In his most recent study, Howe (1970) questioned whether psychotherapists' judgments of DI and potential for anxiety arousal (AA) of interpretive statements remain constant in the face of grammatical qualifications within interpretive statements. Four classes of qualifiers (intensive verbs, probabilistic adverbs, intensive colloquialisms, and probabilistic colloquialisms), each with four degrees of qualification, were inserted within sixty-four interpretive statements ranging in depth. Eighty AMA board-certified psychiatrists served as subjects. Forty subjects (DI group) rated the sixty-four statements for "depth—in the usual sense of the term"; twenty psychiatrists (AA group) rated "along a dimension of their potential for anxiety-arousal in the patient"; and twenty subjects (T group) rated along a scale of "how tentative or definite the statement seems." Howe concludes that the presence of different degrees of grammatical qualification in an interpretive statement has little influence on judgments of DI. On the other hand, the findings indicated that qualifications do produce small but systematic effects in the AA ratings: "the greater the degree of qualification and tentativeness, the less intense is the judgment of potential for anxiety arousal."

References

Howe, E. S. Anxiety-arousal and specificity: rater correlates of the depth of interpretive statements. *Journal of Consulting Psychology*, 1962, 26, 178-84. (a)

________. A study of semantic structure of ratings of interpretive responses. *Journal of Consulting Psychology*, 1962, 26, 285. (b)

________. Further data on the dimensionality of verbal exploratory behavior. Paper presented at the annual convention of the Eastern Psychological Association, New York City, April 1963.

________. Three-dimensional structure of ratings of exploratory responses shown by a semantic differential. *Psychological Reports*, 1964, 14, 187-96.

________. Further data concerning the dimensionality of ratings of the therapist's verbal exploratory behavior. *Journal of Consulting Psychology*, 1965, 29, 73-76.

———. Effects of grammatical qualifications on judgments of the depth and of the anxiety-arousal potential of interpretive statements. *Journal of Consulting and Clinical Psychology*, 1970, 34, 159-63.

Howe, E. S., and Pope, B. An empirical scale of therapist verbal activity level in the initial interview. *Journal of Consulting Psychology*, 1961, 25, 510-20. (a)

———. The dimensionality of ratings of therapist verbal responses. *Journal of Consulting Psychology*, 1961, 25, 296-303. (b)

———. Therapist verbal activity level and diagnostic utility of patient responses. *Journal of Consulting Psychology*, 1962, 26, 149-55.

Osgood, C. E., Suci, G. J., and Tannenbaum, P. H. *The measurement of meaning.* Urbana: University of Illinois Press, 1957.

An Empirical Scale for the Measurement of Therapist Specificity in the Initial Psychiatric Interview

Aron W. Siegman and Benjamin Pope

1. Rationale for Development of the Scale

Siegman and Pope (1965) developed their scale to study the relationship of specificity (the converse of ambiguity) and topical focus in the interviewer's verbal behavior to interviewee verbal productivity and verbal fluency. They emphasize the scale's derivation from social-interactional theory.

> Lennard et al. (1960) view the therapeutic dyad as an informational exchange system and designate specificity as the crucial variable in therapist informational output. The more specific a therapist remark is, the more it limits the range or array of possible patient responses, and the greater is its informational stimulus value. The model of the therapeutic dyad as an informational exchange system and the concept of therapist specificity as the crucial variable in the therapist informational output are both accepted as theoretical bases of the present research. Moreover, the finding of Lennard and his group of an inverse relationship between therapist specificity and patient productivity (Lennard et al., 1960) accords with [our finding of a] significant negative correlation between therapist specificity and patient clause units in immediately following responses. (p. 188)

Most psychotherapeutic systems, especially those modeled after psychoanalysis, tend to maximize rather than to minimize ambiguity, both by their very structure and by the nature of the therapist's communications. . . . There is an implicit assumption that the greater the ambiguity, the more the patient will reveal his basic

> motivations and conflicts. Briefly, it is assumed that ambiguity is productive of meaningful communication. (Siegman and Pope, 1968, p. 1)

Pope and Siegman (1965) postulate that "low interviewer specificity creates a condition of informational uncertainty which the interviewee strives to reduce through increased productivity." (p. 190) They assume further that interviewee productivity is reflected in the number of words he emits.

> Productivity is regarded as a basic measure of the efficacy of the interview, its success in evoking the verbal participation of the interviewee. It is recognized, of course, that in some instances verbose responses may be irrelevant to the purpose of the interview. Yet, it has been demonstrated that within the context of the initial interview (Howe and Pope, 1962) experienced clinicians tend to rate the more productive patient responses as more useful diagnostically than the less productive ones. (p. 189)

> Kenny (1961) defines ambiguity in projective test stimuli in terms of response variability. For example, TAT cards which elicit a variety of responses, that is, different themes or stories, are considered to be ambiguous, and conversely TAT cards which elicit stereotyped responses are considered to be unambiguous. (Siegman and Pope, 1968, p. 2)

Using a similar conceptual scheme, Siegman and Pope (1962) constructed an empirically derived scale for the measurement of interviewer ambiguity-specificity level.

Lennard et al. (1960) defined specificity as the amount of information carried by a verbal message. They developed an a priori Specificity Scale based on the assumption that as the therapist becomes more specific the patient will become less productive and less anxious, and that with increasing patient productivity the therapist's specificity will decrease.

2. Description of the Scale

Following the conceptual schemes developed by both Kenny as well as Lennard et al., Siegman and Pope defined the ambiguity-specificity level of an interviewer's remark "in terms of the limits it sets on interviewee's response alternatives. Thus, the interviewer remark, 'Just start by saying anything that occurs to you,' has a low specificity value because it does not limit the interviewee to a specific matter or proposition. On the other hand, the question,

'How old are you?' has a high specificity value because it limits the range of possible alternatives from which the interviewee can select his reply." (Siegman and Pope, 1968, pp. 2-3)

Their eleven-point empirical specificity scale is presented in Table 4.3. In developing their scale, Siegman and Pope (1962) culled thirty-nine therapist remarks from twelve initial interviews, conducted by different psychiatrists with patients ranging considerably in diagnosis. The thirty-nine therapist statements and the immediately preceding patient response were typed on cards and presented in random order to fourteen psychiatrists and residents for judgments. Their task was to rate each of the thirty-nine cards for therapist specificity described by the statement that "messages differ in the degree to which they limit the range of possible patient responses." (p. 516) Using Ebel's intraclass formula, they obtained estimates of the average intercorrelation among the fourteen judges ($r_{11} = 0.71$) and of the consistency of the average of the fourteen judges' ratings for the thirty-nine statements ($r_{kk} = 0.97$). Having determined that the specificity judgments were highly reliable,

> . . . the items were arranged in the order of increasing specificity, and grouped into categories of related types of statements, such as encouraging the patient to talk, asking the patient to elaborate, etc. Each category was then assigned a specificity score: the median of the mean specificity ratings which the judges assigned to the various statements of each particular category. (p. 516)

The result was the scale presented in Table 4.3

The authors report evidence that their empirical scale is associated strongly with Lennard et al.'s (1960) a priori Specificity Scale. "That the empirical scale does not depart from the concept of specificity on which the a priori scale was based is suggested by the following correlations (r) between previously obtained a priori scale ratings . . . and averaged empirical scale specificity ratings of therapist remarks in three interviews: Interview A, 0.90; Interview B, 0.89; Interview C, 0.62" (1962, p. 519).

3. *Data Collection Context*

Originally, the authors were interested in applying their scale to initial interviews in the naturalistic setting. Their first study dealt with an analysis of therapist ambiguity-specificity and patient productivity from typescripts of twelve initial therapy interviews. Because of problems of confounding that arose in this study, however, they subsequently focused on experimental interview studies.

For this latter purpose, Siegman and Pope used their Specificity

Scale to standardize and experimentally manipulate the level of specificity present in a series of questions asked by an interviewer in an experimental analogue interview. They were concerned with the relationship between specificity and topical focus in the interviewer's verbal behavior and interviewee verbal productivity. The dependent variables in their studies have been interviewee productivity as reflected in number of words, verbal fluency, and level of depth of self-disclosure as indicated by the Superficiality Index. For the latter measure, each clause unit is rated as either superficial (that is, factually descriptive) versus psychologically introspective or evaluational in nature. The Ratio consists of the number of superficial clauses divided by the total number of clause units, and has shown very high interjudge reliability (0.90 or better). The authors assume that the lower the Superficiality Index, the greater the informational relevance of the interviewee's response.

Siegman and Pope's experimental interview is based on a planned manipulation of specificity and topical focus as the independent variables. The interview is divided into two content segments, including a Neutral Topic (past school history) and an Emotional or anxiety-arousing Topic (family relationships). In each topic there is a "Low-High-Low" specificity order in which two low-specificity questions are followed by four high-specificity questions, and then again by low. On their eleven-point Specificity Scale, the low-specificity questions range from a scale value of 4.1 to 6.3; the high-specificity questions from 7.0 to 10.9. A detailed outline of the experimental interview may be obtained for a fee from the American Documentation Institute. (It is Document No. 8390 from ADI Auxiliary Publications Project, Photoduplication Service, Library of Congress; Washington, D.C., 20025. Remit in advance $1.25 for photocopies. Make checks payable to: Chief, Photoduplication Service, Library of Congress.)

4. Data Form

Apparently the scale has been applied only to typewritten transcripts of either initial psychotherapy interviews or of Siegman and Pope's experimental analogue interviews. To date the authors have not considered whether the scale can be applied to audio or videotape recordings as well.

5. Choice of Units

The unit to be scored for therapist specificity is the T of the P-T-P communication sequence, that is, "that portion of therapist speech occurring between two patient responses. In rare instances in which a therapist may be interrupted by a patient, and the therapist completes his statement ignoring the interruption, the completed statement is to be taken as the unit" (Siegman and Pope, 1962, p. 517). Hence, the "scoring unit" for their ratings is the particular therapist response (T).

In regard to the "contextual unit" for their scale, the authors indicate that ratings of therapist specificity are made with judges rating each therapist response sequentially as they progress through a particular protocol, after which they then rate another total interview protocol. Judges are asked "to rate the therapist statements in context in a number of interview protocols. It is . . . sugested that [they] work through the therapist statements sequentially, as they occur in each interview" (p. 518). Evidently, then, the contextual unit encompases all the therapist and patient verbalizations preceding the particular therapist response being scored.

Their "summarizing unit" is not specified, but apparently it is both the total specificity score for a particular therapist in an entire session (that is, the average of the specificity levels assigned to the numerous therapist statements occurring within a given session); as well as the average of the scale values independently assigned to a particular therapist statement by a group of judges.

For the Superficiality Ratio, the scoring unit is the clause. Interviewee responses are divided into clause units, which serve as the basic units scored for the Superficiality Index as well as for "productivity" and "diagnostic utility" ratings. The contextual and summarizing units for these variables would apparently be identical in nature to those used for the therapist specificity ratings.

6. Participant-Context Restrictions

Ratings of therapist specificity are made from the typescript protocol with preceding patient responses intact and, thus, are made in participant-context. The authors have not discussed or empirically assessed differential effects on their specificity ratings from having judges rate therapist statements without the patient's statements being present, in contrast to their usual procedure.

7. Type of Sampling Indicated

The authors have not considered this issue, since they have scored entire initial interviews. Whether randomly or systematically selected samples from particular interviews would yield representative therapist specificity ratings has not been determined to date.

The authors' decision to restrict their focus to initial interviews only was "prompted by the wish to avoid the long-term vicissitudes of the doctor-patient relationship and the cumulative impact of previous therapeutic sessions, as possible confounding variables. Moreover, the initial interview is concerned primarily with facilitating the patient's communication of information desired by the therapist" (Pope and Siegman, 1965, p. 191).

8. Sample Location Within the Interview

The authors have not considered where or in what manner samples can be extracted from particular interviews which would yield ratings of therapist specificity which are representative of the entire session.

9. Sample Location over Therapy Interviews

The author's theoretical focus has limited their interest to date to either naturalistic interviews or experimental analogues of initial interviews. As a result, they have not applied their specificity scale to more than one or two interviews for a particular patient-therapist dyad, nor have they considered the problems of where and in what manner to sample across the interview continuum from initiation to termination of therapy.

10. Clinical Sophistication of Judges

In the initial studies of the scale as well as in subsequent applications, the raters have been psychotherapy professionals (psychiatrists, psychiatric residents, clinical psychologists) of various but unspecified levels of clinical experience. The scale authors have not considered the judge experience issue explicitly, nor have they empirically compared the effects on specificity ratings of using naive versus clinically sophisticated judges.

11. Training Required of Judges

Siegman and Pope (1962) seem to imply that little or no training is required to perform the rating task, which is "to find the response category in the scale which best fits the therapist statement that you are rating. The scale value of the chosen category is then assigned to the therapist statement" (p. 518). In one study, in order to evaluate the effect of previous experience with the scale on subsequent ratings,

> [judges were] randomly assigned to three different groups which differed in relation to the order in which they rated the three interviews. Thus, 4 judges rated Interview A first, 4 judges rated

> the same interview second, and 4 judges rated it third. The other two interviews were similarly distributed between the judges. . . . [The results provided] no evidence for the position that experience (or training) with the scale, within the experience range of the present study, affects the rater's reliability. . . . The results indicate that the empirical specificity scale can be applied by untrained raters with at least adequate reliability. (pp. 517, 519)

12. Training Manual

There is no manual available. The authors have presented data indicating that reliable ratings can be obtained from untrained psychologist judges. To the extent that this conclusion is valid, a standardized training procedure would be superfluous.

The scale with examples may be obtained from the American Documentation Institute (Document No. 7283 from ADI Auxiliary Publications Project, Photoduplication Service, Library of Congress, Washington, D.C., 20025. Remit in advance $1.25 for microfilm or photocopies).

13. Interrater and Intrarater Reliabilities Reported

Twelve psychologists, in groups of four, applied the scale to typescripts of three initial psychiatric interviews. For the groups of four raters, Ebel intraclass reliabilities were calculated: The estimated average intercorrelation among the four raters (r_{11}) ranged from 0.59 to 0.82, while the reliability of the average of the four judges' ratings (r_{kk})ranged from 0.88 to 0.95 for the three groups of raters. When all twelve judges were considered as a group, the r_{11} values ranged from 0.59 to 0.76, while r_{kk} ranged from 0.94 to 0.97. This study (1962) indicated that, when four judges independently apply the specificity scale, average ratings of very high interjudge reliability are obtained.

14. Dimensionality Considerations

The authors implicitly assume that their scale is a measure of a unitary characteristic of therapist statements. To date they have not been concerned with the alternative assumption, that their scale may tap more than one dimension of therapist statements.

On the other hand, they clearly have been interested in this issue as it applies to the general construct of therapist ambiguity, and have demonstrated empirically, in their analogue interview studies, that various aspects of therapist ambiguity are related to interviewee productivity and level of self-disclosure (Superficiality Index).

In a naturalistic interview, the interviewer's ambiguity-specificity level may very well be confounded with some other variables. For example, interviewers may tend to be more general and less specific when they venture into potentially anxiety arousing areas. Following this lead, we classified the interviewer remarks into different content areas, and we found that they were in fact associated with different specificity levels. For example, inquiries about interviewee's background were associated with significantly higher specificity levels than remarks concerning interviewees' family relations. Consequently, the noted evidence of interviewee anxiety may not be a result of interviewer ambiguity but rather of his topical focus. It is clear, therefore, that if we wish to evaluate the effects of ambiguity per se, unconfounded by other variables, it is necessary to control for a host of other relevant variables. Therefore, in our subsequent studies we resorted to experimental analogues of the initial interviews. It was hoped that what would be sacrificed in generalizability to naturalistic settings would be gained in interpretability and theoretical significance. (Siegman and Pope, 1968, pp. 6-7)

In later analogue studies this point became even clearer. In addition to message ambiguity operationalized by therapist statements rated at different levels of the specificity scale, the authors built in a relationship ambiguity condition by placing a screen between the interviewer and interviewee. The screen eliminated interviewer nonverbal feedback, such as smiling, nodding, and other reinforcers. From their findings the authors conclude that "we now have a clear-cut reversal in the effects of the two types of ambiguity. While message or informational ambiguity is associated with an increase in interviewee productivity, the opposite is true in regard to relationship ambiguity. . . . We cannot speak of ambiguity in general, but must distinguish between different sources of ambiguity" (p.15).

15. Validity Studies

The author's major research interest has been to assess the effects of ambiguity in the interviewer's messages on the patient's subsequent verbal behavior. While they have shown interest in content variables, their major concern has been with noncontent variables, such as interviewee productivity, verbal fluency, silent pause ratios, and the Type Token Ratio.

Siegman and Pope conceptualize interviewer ambiguity in terms of informational uncertainty. They maintain that an ambiguous interviewer remark, by definition, is one which permits the interviewee to reply with a number of alternate responses. Consequently, the interviewee, being uncertain which of the response alternatives is the most appropriate, is likely to respond with several alternatives. This, then, produces longer interviewee responses to ambiguous than to specific interviewer probes. Moreover, uncertainty is likely to produce hesitant and nonfluent speech, manifested by a slow articulation rate, frequent and relatively long silent pauses, a high "ah" ratio, and a relatively long reaction time. These expectations were confirmed in two experimental analogue studies (Pope and Siegman, 1965; Siegman and Pope, 1965a, 1971), and in a naturalistic interview study using a psychiatric population (Pope et al., 1969). The relationship between interviewer ambiguity and patient productivity was also confirmed in an economically deprived population and in a group of schizophrenic patients (Hirshler and Nutt, 1967).[1]

Siegman and Pope considered the hypothesis that stress or anxiety is the mediating variable in the effects of interviewer ambiguity on patient verbal behavior. They conclude, however, that their findings contraindicate such an explanation.

> First, there is the finding that the relationships between interviewer ambiguity and interviewee verbal behavior are independent of the latter's anxiety level, either as measured by the Taylor Manifest Anxiety Scale or as manipulated via topical focus. Second, the effects produced by interviewer ambiguity on interviewee speech are distinct from those produced by anxiety. . . . Ambiguity is associated with a slowing down of interviewee's speech, but anxiety, if anything, is associated with an acceleration of speech. Anxiety arousal is associated with speech disruptions, as measured by Mahl's Speech Disturbance Ratio, while interviewer ambiguity has no such effect. (1971)

The authors maintain that their findings are best explained in terms of informational uncertainty and that there is no need to invoke the concept of anxiety.

Siegman and Pope find it necessary, however, to distinguish between message ambiguity and relationship ambiguity. The former, as pointed out earlier, refers to the ambiguity-specificity level of an interviewer's remark. The latter refers to uncertainty on the part of the patient about how the interviewer feels about him and his

1. Results from the experimental analogue studies indicate that the effects of interviewer ambiguity on the patient's verbal behavior are independent of the sequence of the interviewer's ambiguity-specificity level, that is, they occur when the interviewer begins with specific probes and proceeds to ambiguous remarks, or when he reverses this procedure. Finally, the effects of interviewer ambiguity are not limited to the first initial interview, but persist at least into the second of a series of two interviews.

responses. Relationship ambiguity was expermientally produced in a number of studies by eliminating interviewer nonverbal feedback, such as smiling, head nodding, and eye contact. Relationship ambiguity, like message ambiguity, was found to be associated with hesitant and nonfluent speech. Unlike message ambiguity, however, relationship ambiguity was found to have an inhibiting effect on patient productivity.

The authors conclude: "Perhaps by eliminating interviewer nonverbal feedback, we are eliminating the very conditions which maintain interpersonal communication" (Siegman and Pope, 1971).

Siegman and Pope also looked at the effects of interviewer message ambiguity on patients' vocabulary diversity, as measured by the Type Token Ratio, and on the predictability of the patient's responses, as measured by the Cloze technique. As expected, interviewer ambiguity was associated with high vocabulary diversity and with low predictability. The latter, however, was true only in some content areas (Siegman and Pope, 1966a, 1966b).

The authors also used experimental analogues of the initial interview in order to assess the effects on interviewee's verbal behavior of such variables as interviewee anxiety (Siegman and Pope, 1965a, 1971), interviewer warmth (Pope and Siegman, 1971; Siegman, 1971), interviewer status, duration of interviewer probes (Pope and Siegman, 1971; Siegman, Pope, and Blass, 1969), relationship imbalance (Siegman, Blass, and Pope, 1970), and interviewee expectations (Pope et al., in press). In another study they examined the relations between interviewee productivity and verbal fluency and a number of interviewee personality variables (Siegman and Pope, 1965b). Summary statements of their research can be found in Siegman and Pope (1971) and Pope and Siegman (1971).

RELATED SCALES OR CONSTRUCTS

Siegman and Pope derived their scale from Lennard et al.'s (1960) a priori scale of therapist specificity. Previous mention was made of the obtained correlation between Lennard et al.'s scale and the authors' empirical specificity scale ranging from 0.62 to 0.90. Additionally, the authors provide information regarding their scale's relationship to Howe and Pope's Therapist Activity Level Scale (see above).

> Correlations between the specificity and activity level scales in twelve initial interviews ranged from -0.05 to + 0.65, with 7 out of the 12 significant. In spite of some relationship between the two scales, [the authors] found that only specificity demonstrated negative correlations with patient productivity and speech disturb-

ance as they predicted. Although overlapping to some degree, it appears that activity level and specificity are sufficiently divergent to be dealt with as separate dimensions. (Siegman and Pope, 1962, pp. 519-20)

References

Hirshler, H. and Nutt, J. W. Interviewer specificity and client productivity: schizophrenic and culturally deprived populations. Unpublished master's dissertation, University of Maryland School of Social Work, 1967.

Lennard, H. L. and Bernstein, A. *The anatomy of psychotherapy*. New York: Columbia University, 1960.

Pope, B., Blass, T., Cheeck, J. A., Siegman, A. W. and Bradford, N. H. Interviewer specificity in semi-naturalistic interviews. *Proceedings of the 77th annual convention of the American Psychological Association*. Washington, D.C.: American Psychological Association, 1969. Pp. 577-78.

Pope, B. and Siegman, A. W., Interviewer specificity and topical focus in relation to interviewee productivity. *Journal of Verbal Learning and Verbal Behavior*, 1965, 4, 188-92.

________. Relationship and verbal behavior in the initial interview. In A. W. Siegman and B. Pope (Eds.), *Studies in dyadic communication*. Elmsford, N.Y.: Pergamon Press, 1971.

Pope, B., Siegman, A. W., Blass, T. and Cheek, J. Some effects of discrepant role expectations on interviewee verbal behavior in the initial interview. *Journal of Consulting and Clinical Psychology*, in press.

Siegman, A. W. The effect of interviewer warmth on interviewee productivity and attraction to the interviewer. Unpublished manuscript, University of Maryland, 1971.

Siegman, A. W., Blass, T., and Pope, B. Verbal indices of interpersonal imbalance in the interview. *Proceedings of the 78th annual convention of the American Psychological Association*. Washington, D.C.: American Psychological Association, 1970. Pp. 525-26.

Siegman, A. W., and Pope, B. An empirical scale for the measurement of therapist specificity in the initial psychiatric interview. *Psychological Reports*, 162, 11, 515-20.

________. Effects of question specificity and anxiety producing messages on verbal fluency in the initial interview. *Journal of Personality and Social Psychology*, 1965, 2, 522-30. (a)

________. Personality variable associated with productivity and verbal fluency in the initial interview. *Proceedings of the 73rd annual convention of the American Psychological Association*. Washington, D.C.: American Psychological Association, 1965. Pp. 273-74. (b)

________. The effect of interviewer ambiguity-specificity and topical focus on interviewee vocabulary diversity. *Language and Speech*, 1966, 9, 242-49. (a)

________. Effect of interviewer specificity and topical focus on the predictability of interviewee's responses. *Proceedings of the 74th annual convention of the American Psychological Association*. Washington, D.C.: American Psychological Association, 1966. Pp. 195-96. (b)

________. The effects of ambiguity and anxiety on interviewee verbal behavior. Paper presented at the Research Conference on Interview Behavior, The Psychiatric Institute, University of Maryland, Baltimore, Md.: April 1968. (Mimeographed)

________. The effects of ambiguity and anxiety on interviewee verbal behavior. In A. W. Siegman and B. Pope (Eds.), *Studies in dyadic communication*. Elmsford, N.Y.: Pergamon Press, 1971

Siegman, A. W., Pope, B., and Blass, T. Effects of interviewer status and duration of interviewer messages on interviewee productivity. *Proceedings of the 77th annual convention of the American Psychological Association*, Washington, D.C.: American Psychological Association, 1969. Pp. 541-42.

A Multidimensional System for Analyzing Psychotherapeutic Communications

Hans H. Strupp

1. Rationale for Development of the System

Strupp set out to develop a measuring instrument that would be sufficiently relevant to capture theoretically significant factors of therapist behavior in the interview, and also sufficiently general to assess therapist individual differences along these dimensions. "So far it has not been possible to make objective comparison between the techniques of, say, an orthodox Freudian and a neo-Freudian, an Adlerian and a Jungian, and so forth" (Strupp, 1960, p. 242). The system he developed is based upon an eclectic conception of the psychotherapeutic process, "although a preference for psychoanalytic formulations is evident" (Strupp, 1966, p. 5).

> By isolating common denominators from the techniques of therapists subscribing to a variety of theoretical orientations, the system attempts to build a bridge between divergent viewpoints by specifying their common and unique elements. (p. iv)

> It is hoped that the dimensions are sufficiently general to be of value in the analysis of therapeutic processes irrespective of the therapist's theoretical allegiance, while at the same time being sufficiently close to therapeutic thinking to be relevant to the study of therapeutic phenomena. (p. 12).

> Minimally, such a system should meet the following criteria: (1) It should take cognizance of the purpose and aims of psychotherapy as a unique form of social interaction and respect its complexities; it should show particular recognition of the therapist's role in the therapeutic process. (2) While being anchored to therapeutic operations, it should be sufficiently general to be applicable to the techniques of therapists whose theoretical positions may be divergent. In other words, it should stress the common denominators of

> different therapeutic approaches. (3) It should be primarily descriptive and nonevaluative, on the assumption that the relative effectiveness of therapeutic techniques must be evaluated on the basis of external rather than internal criteria. (4) It should meet the requirements of objectivity, reliability, and system. (Strupp, 1960, p. 246)

The system is designed for analysis of any psychotherapeutic procedures, including counseling and supportive therapy, "so long as the interaction is between two adults" (Strupp, 1966, p. 5).

> The system of analysis is a methodologic tool for abstracting and measuring selected aspects of therapeutic technique, aspects which are considered relevant to any psychotherapeutic procedure which stresses the development of insight on the part of the patient and emotional understanding of his difficulties in living. (Strupp, 1960, p. 243)

> Inevitably, the present system will be superseded by others yielding more precise and more sensitive measures, but technique measures of some kind must play a part in the comparative evaluation of therapeutic results. Before the effects of two drugs can be evaluated, it is indispensible to specify their respective ingredients. Similarly, before the merits of two forms of psychotherapy, say, psychoanalysis and intensive psychotherapy based on psychoanalytic principles, can be assessed, it will be necessary to specify the "ingredients." . . . This achievement, unfortunately lies far in the future. (p. 243)

2. *Description of the Scoring System*

Strupp's system is a variant of content analysis applied to the verbal behavior of the therapist and "is concerned exclusively with specifying important dimensions of the therapist's communications" (Strupp, 1966, p. 2). Strupp attempted to minimize nonverbal or other paralinguistic aspects of the therapist's communications, and emphasized instead relatively overt content characteristics, that is, the system deals with "the meaning of linguistic symbols, as distinguished from nonverbal communications" (p. 52). However, "even with these restrictions, it will be recognized that the degree of inference required for the assessments is frequently high" (p. 4).

Strupp makes the intensity-equals-frequency assumption that "the units of analysis have approximately equal weights, and that inferences can be made from cumulative frequencies" (p. 54). The constructs measured are limited in that they "refer to structural, dynamic, and attitudinal characteristics of the therapist's communications; they deliberabely disregard the question of appropriateness or therapeutic effectiveness" (p. 3). The therapist's communications are "regarded as indicators of certain characteristics of the therapist, such as the level of his experience and training, theoretical orientation, personal analysis, etc." (p. 56).

Strupp's multidimensional system is presented in Table 4.4. Since the emphasis of the scales presented is upon observable aspects of the therapist's technique,

> [the] observer asks in effect: *What* does the therapist do? and *How* does he do it? . . . The question, What does the therapist do? refers to what is generally described as technique. The observer . . . can make such determinations as these: Does the therapist ask for elaboration, specification, or further information? Does he restate or reflect the patient's feelings? Does he summarize? Does he interpret? Does he meet a patient's direct question with silence? Does he passively accept? etc. With regard to the how of therapy, observations can be made about the level of interpretive inference, the relative warmth or coldness of the therapeutic climate, the degree to which the therapist assumes the initiative, and the dynamic focus emphasized in the therapist's communication. (p. 4)

After some trial and error with various measurements, Strupp arrived at his present system, which consists of two sets of categories (type of therapeutic activity or communication and dynamic focus) and three dimensions (depth-directedness, initiative, and therapeutic climate or warmth-coldness) which are designed to quantify each communication by the therapist. The system "views each communication by the therapist as a multidimensional datum, on which five simultaneous assessments are made" (Strupp, 1960, p. 247).

TYPE OF THERAPEUTIC ACTIVITY

These categories were developed empirically by analyzing a variety of therapy protocols. Ratings are intended to be mutually exclusive in that each therapist communication is assigned to one category only. "These categories appear to be the minimum number necessary to characterize most therapeutic communications without duplicating information obtained from other components" (Strupp, 1960, p. 249). There are seventeen categories organized into eight major classes: facilitating communication, exploratory operations, clarification, interpretive operations, structuring, direct guidance, activity not clearly relevant to the task of therapy, and unclassifiable.

DEPTH - DIRECTEDNESS

The depth-directedness measure takes the form of a five-point intensity scale, which "embodies the conception that any communication by the therapist . . . carries with it an implication about, first, the patient's problem . . . and, second, the method or procedure best designed to bring about its alleviation or resolution" (Strupp, 1960, p. 251). A therapist's comment "which operates upon the manifest meaning of the patient's communication is at the 'surface,' whereas one that propounds a hypothesis, inference, conjecture, or interpretation is 'deep.' [Along] this continuum, defined by the two extremes, all therapeutic remarks find their place" (Strupp, 1966, p. 26). The assumption is made, then, that a quality of depth of interpretive inference is always implicit in a therapeutic remark. In this regard Strupp notes that comparable scales developed by Harway et al. (see above) and by Collier (see Chapter 6) are different in that they exclude from consideration all statements which are not clearly interpretations.

DYNAMIC FOCUS

The dynamic focus measure refers to "the frame of reference which the therapist adopts at a particular juncture, and which largely determines the content of subsequent communications by the patient. . . . Basically the therapist can do one of two things: he can accept the patient's formulation as it is presented, or he can introduce or superimpose a different frame of reference" (Strupp, 1966, p. 35).

> The therapist's understanding of the therapeutic process, in keeping with the particular theoretical formulations to which he subscribes, tells him what is "important" in the therapeutic situation and what is not, what he should focus on at a particular moment, and what is of no dynamic relevance, what is to be dealt with now rather than later, and so on. The way in which a therapist "sees" a situation is already an interpretation in terms of his particular framework—as well as a function of more personal factors. . . . Depending on his theoretical position, the therapist may be expected to engage in therapeutic activity congruent with his theoretical framework. An analysis of his focus alone may lead to an operational testing of his theoretical allegiance. (Strupp, 1960, pp. 252-53).

> Two major sectors serve to differentiate whether the therapist is "going along with" the patient (Sector A), or whether he introduces a different focus (Sector B). Once this distinction has been made, communications assigned to Sector B are subdivided into five categories. (Strupp, 1966, p. 36)

INITIATIVE

The initiative dimension takes the form of a four-point intensity scale, and refers to "the extent to which [the therapist] assumes the initiative and steers the patient in the direction of a more or less specific goal . . . the extent to which he accepts responsibility for directing the patient's verbalization in a given channel" (Strupp, 1966, p. 38). The concept has "a specific meaning which is related to goal-directedness or therapeutic directiveness. In intensive psychotherapy, (for example,) with reconstructive goals, the therapist assumes the initiative by directing the patient toward self-exploration, self-understanding, abandonment of defensive systems, and so on" (Strupp, 1960, p. 255). "Therapeutic statements may be regarded as ranging from a zero point (absence of initiative) through an area of 'mild' and 'moderate' initiative to an extreme of strong (authoritarian) directiveness. The intensity of the therapist's initiative (rather than its quality) is the measurement attempted by this scale" (Strupp, 1966, p. 40). With this scale, Strupp assumes that no matter what the therapist says or does, he gives the therapeutic situation a certain structure and defines its limits.

THERAPEUTIC CLIMATE (WARMTH-COLDNESS)

The final dimension takes the form of a five-point intensity scale. It reflects an "attitudinal-emotional continuum" and, unlike the other scales, goes beyond the symbolic structure of the communication and deals with the feeling tone. "There is a growing consensus which considers the existence of a warm, accepting relationship the sine qua non of effective psychotherapy" (Strupp, 1960, p. 256). The scale is bipolar:

> [It extends from] a zero point of neutrality to a positive pole in one direction and to a negative pole in the opposite direction. The positive end of the continuum includes all communications by which the therapist indicates acceptance, warmth, understanding, interest of a positive sort, tolerance, empathy, respect. . . . The negative pole of this scale is defined by signs of rejection, coldness, sarcasm, lack of sympathy, cynicism, hostility, brutality, derision, mocking, taunting, teasing, belittling, and so on. (Strupp, 1966, p. 116)

With this dimension, Strupp assumes that therapist communications exhibit varying degrees of emotional warmth which tend to define the climate of the therapeutic relationship. "Admittedly, the measurement neglects to some extent the way in which a therapeutic climate is fostered nonverbally; nevertheless, it is believed that, despite this restriction, useful inferences about the therapeutic climate can be made by considering simultaneously the structure of the verbal communication and its emotional overtones." (Strupp, 1960, pp. 256-57)

MORE RECENT SCALE DEVELOPMENT

Since about 1960, Strupp and his colleagues have expanded their measurement focus to attempt to handle some inadequacies noted from their applications of the original system. "Despite its demonstrated utility, we have come to feel that the system has some significant deficiencies. The main one is that it overemphasizes the structural aspects of the therapist's communications, and it is insufficiently sensitive to the attitudinal-emotional facets of his communications." (Strupp, Chassan, and Ewing, 1966, p. 364) In summarizing the film-analogue studies reported in his 1960 volume, Strupp comments:

> When the [original] system was . . . applied to the data collected in the course of this investigation . . . it emerged that differences in the degree of empathy shown by the therapist-respondents appeared to be a considerably more fruitful indicator of the total approach than structural differences, to which the system gives major emphasis. As a result, greater attention is being devoted in future research to the exploration of attitudinal and personality variables in the therapist. (Strupp, 1960, pp. 242-43)

With this realization, Strupp set out to design a system which would incorporate equally both technical and attitudinal components of therapists' communications.[1] His efforts built upon the empirical system developed by Bellak and Smith (1956). After some trial and error, modifications were made both in the Bellak and Smith scale items and in their rating procedure.

The system that evolved is presented in Strupp et al.'s 1966 report (p. 370). Basically, the therapist (or an observer), after each therapy session, rates thirty-five variables on five-point Likert scales,

1. In a personal communication (1971), Strupp states that "the multidimensional system was designed to get at the content of therapists' communications, whereas the scales in the 1966 article were used to discern themes during the therapeutic hour. The earlier system had nothing to say about the patient's contribution, whereas the latter attempts to assess dominant affects and themes in the patient's communications."

basing judgments on behaviors occurring in the just-completed session. The twenty-one patient variables rated are: dominance, dependence, resistance, anxiety, affect, sadism, masochism, hostility-anger, defensiveness, transference-positive, transference-negative, competitiveness-rivalry, depression, elation, insight, working through, oral strivings, anal strivings, phallic strivings, oedipal strivings, and genital strivings. The fourteen therapist variables rated are: intervention, interpretations, depth of interpretation, initiative, warmth, coldness, support, motivation-dedication-investment, positive attitudes, negative attitudes, countertransference problems, empathy, productivity of hour, and satisfaction with progress.

> Thus, the modified instrument was designed to provide information in each of the following areas: (1) the patient's feelings, attitudes, emotional reactions in the transference situation; (2) the frequency and kind of interventions by the therapist (technique); and (3) the therapist's feelings and attitudes toward the patient, about himself, and about the therapeutic process. (Strupp et al., 1966, p. 370)

Several studies with the new system are reported in the 1966 article. They examine the level of inference necessary for rating the various items of the scale system, the level of interjudge reliability attainable for the items, and an intensive application of the system to three cases of two experienced therapists. Interjudge agreement for these studies was poor: "the highest agreement (intraclass r) was obtained for Affect (0.648), Dependence (0.583) and Depression (0.504) items with most values being considerably lower. In eleven instances the obtained r was a negative value. . . . On the basis of these findings . . . the reliability of the ratings instrument appears deficient." (p. 376)

Although somewhat discouraged by the results to date, Strupp continues to work with his new rating system.

> Despite the inadequacy of the pilot experiments reported in these pages, it seems highly justified to persist in efforts to improve the agreement among judges or between the therapist and a pool of observers. The achievement of a solid consensus among observers of the psychotherapeutic process concerning the phenomena under scrutiny is obviously a task of the highest priority, upon whose satisfactory solution the comparative study of psychotherapy interviews . . . ultimately depends. (pp. 397-98)

Strupp et al. conclude:

Our efforts as yet are halting, our methodology is imperfect, and we are not even certain that the direction we have taken will turn out to be promising in the long run. Indeed, there are indications that other "mining techniques" may be more fruitful. (p. 398)

For more detail about the new Strupp system, consult the Strupp et al. (1966) report. Since the system is still quite tentative and untried, it will not be discussed further here. The following sections refer only to the original Strupp rating scales presented in Table 4.4.

3. Data Collection Context

Strupp's system has been applied primarily to various psychotherapy interviews selected from therapists of a wide range of orientations, experience, and disciplines. Also applications have been made to therapists' responses collected in Strupp's film analogue interview situations (Strupp, 1960; see also Chapter 7, below).

4. Data Form

The system has been applied to sound recordings, movies, videotapes, and written typescripts of the live therapy interaction, as well as to direct observations. To date Strupp has not studied the differential effect on his measures of rating interviews in their various data forms. He recommends (1966) that "if direct observation is not possible, a typescript plus a sound recording will probably yield optimum results; scoring can be done rather efficiently from the written record, and in doubtful instances the observer can resort to the sound recording." (p. 75)

5. Choice of Units

The basic "scoring unit" is "each and every therapist 'communication' as it occurs . . . the therapist communication occurring between two patient statements" (Strupp, 1966, p. 74), that is, the T of the P-T-P communication sequence. "Experience indicates that therapist communications are usually brief and concise. Moreover, even longer communications usually are devoted to the discussion of a single theme. In rare cases it may be necessary to subdivide a therapist communication into two or three units." (Strupp, 1960, p. 257)

In regard to the "contextual unit," Strupp presupposes that his raters have knowledge of the context in which a particular therapist communication occurs. The contextual unit is the entire therapy transaction up to the point of a particular therapist communication, but not beyond that point. In scoring a particular communication the observer is "guided by the history of the therapist-patient interaction as it has evolved up to that time. The background should be provided by studying the actual therapeutic proceedings rather than by reading a summary prepared by the therapist, which may be biased in unknown and unpredictable ways. Therapist communications should never be scored out of context." (p. 257)

Apparently, the same judges apply all five scales to the interview materials being rated. This procedure can easily contaminate ratings on the various scales, and can build in high intercorrelations among the five scales. Strupp does not discuss the alternate procedure of restricting a judge's task to only one scale by obtaining separate groups of judges for each of the five scales. He does not spell out the sequence in which the raters apply the five scales—whether they first rate all the data on one scale and then rate the other scales in turn; or whether they apply all five scales simultaneously to one protocol, and then to the other protocols in turn.

Typically the scores or ratings for therapist communications are summated over an entire therapy session, so that the session is the usual "summarizing unit." Strupp assumes that there is an additive or cumulative quality in therapeutic interventions, which are assigned unit weight.

> [The summarizing unit] consists of adding the frequencies obtained in each category and at each scale point. These totals may then be expressed as a proportion or as a percentage of the total number of interventions during an interview. In this way a profile of the therapist's activity for a given interview or series of interviews may be obtained. . . . With regard to two continua (depth-directedness and initiative), mean ratings may be obtained for each interview. . . . For some purposes it may be more useful to deal only with high-intensity (extreme) ratings, and to note their frequencies. This is advisable because the means tend to be heavily influenced by the low-level ratings, which are typically found to preponderate. With reference to therapeutic climate, it is almost indispensible to concentrate on nonzero scores which are usually very few in number. A mean in this case is almost totally devoid of meaning. (p. 259)

6. Participant-Context Restrictions

Since the contextual unit includes the entire therapy transaction up to the point of a particular therapist communication, ratings for

Strupp's system are made in the participant context, that is, with the patient's verbalizations present. Strupp has not considered or empirically assessed the effects on his system scores of judges' applying his scales with the patient's verbalizations omitted, in contrast to his usual participant-context procedure.

7. Type of Sampling Indicated

Since Strupp usually applies his system to entire therapy sessions, he has not considered whether samples of therapist communications extracted randomly or systematically from a total interview yield representative ratings, nor has he determined what the optimal size of the sampling units should be.

8. Sample Location Within the Interview

For the same reason, Strupp has not considered or empirically assessed whether it makes a difference regarding the scale scores obtained to sample from early, middle, or late portions of a particular interview hour.

9. Sample Location Over Therapy Interviews

Similarly, Strupp has not determined whether ratings of the therapist for a single interview are representative of the therapist's behavior over the entire case from initiation to termination. Furthermore, he has not considered where or how frequently along this interview continuum samples should be extracted to characterize accurately the therapist's behavior during a particular therapy interaction.

10. Clinical Sophistication of Judges

Strupp considers naive judges unsuitable for his rating tasks. The kind of judge required is a "trained observer," that is,

> [an observer who has become] sensitized to the important issues in this field (psychotherapy), who is keenly aware of the phenomena of psychodynamics, who has received thorough training in psychopathology, and who is fully familiar with the theoretical basis of psychoanalysis and its newer developments. He should preferably have undergone personal analysis for the purpose of having attained a deeper awareness of the dynamics he is called upon to assess and to have had experience as a psychotherapist as well. (Strupp, 1966, pp. 72-73)

> Above all, he must have a solid grasp of the major technical operations used in therapy and their respective rationales. (Strupp, 1960, p. 259)

These are clearly stringent criteria for rater selection, and limit the possibilities of applications of his system. To date Strupp has not empirically contrasted experienced therapists and clinically naive judges' ratings on his various scales; such a comparison would provide important evidence regarding the scales' construct validity.

Apparently, then, inference is built in as a necessary ingredient of Strupp's scales. On the other hand, he cautions that

> [the observer] must as far as possible divorce himself from his own theoretical predilections, and attempt to empathize with the therapeutic goals of the therapist whose procedures he is observing. Nevertheless, he can never abandon the general conceptions of psychotherapy which are basic to his understanding of the interactive process. He must be critical of the therapist's technical procedures, but not from the point of view of what he, the rater, would have done at a given juncture. This is a difficult assignment. (p. 258)

11. Training Required of Judges

A standardized training procedure is not presented in any detail by Strupp. He mentions only that

> It seems reasonable to expect judges to . . . [have] a fair amount of training in the use of the instrument they are using. . . . In general, a rater must have a thorough familiarity with the basic dimensions, and he must have a firm grasp of the general formulations underlying the scales, the definition of the scale points, the illustrative examples, and the special scoring rules. Following this he must score a number of protocols, and discuss his scorings with a more experienced observer. (Strupp, 1966, p. 73)
>
> Finally, it is necessary to conduct reliability studies to test intra- as well as inter-rater agreement. (Strupp, 1960, p. 259)

12. Training Manual

A scale manual (Strupp, 1966) in mimeographed form is available from the author; an abbreviated version of the manual was published previously (Strupp, 1960). Both sources provide theoretical rationales for development of the scales, and descriptions of each of the scales and scale stages. The 1966 manual provides rules for scoring and a scored sample interview to guide judges in training. To date, however, no standardized training procedure is available. "Since too few judges have been trained in this method, it is impossible at this time to outline a systematic training procedure." (Strupp, 1966, p. 73)

13. Interrater and Intrarater Reliabilities Reported

> An incisive analysis of rater agreement must deal with the ratings of independent judges on a unit-by-unit basis. . . . For the intensity scales which yield fairly large variances (depth-directedness and initiative), the product-moment coefficient of correlation appears adequate. . . . [For therapeutic climate] one solution is to deal with totals of all plus and minus scores per interview. With reference to the discrete categories (type and dynamic focus) a simple but useful index is provided by determining the over-all percent agreement. (Strupp, 1690, p. 260)

The system was independently applied by two judges to typescripts of a Wolberg interview and of filmed interviews. For Type of Therapeutic Activity and Dynamic Focus, overall percentage of agreement ranged from 80 to 85 percent regarding the number of units on which the two raters agreed. For Depth Directedness and Initiative, product-moment correlations were calculated between the two judges' ratings on a unit-by-unit basis. The resulting coefficients ranged from 0.86 to 0.90. An interpretable reliability index was not provided for Therapeutic Climate. This study suggests that high interrater agreement can be obtained by trained and clinically experienced judges for at least four of the five scales. Strupp cautions that "the verbal activity of some therapists can be rated much more reliably than that of others. Also, every record will typically include a residue of communications which defies quantification, either because it seems to be ambiguous or because it is 'atypical'. (Strupp, 1966, p. 131)

Strupp (1960) reports interjudge reliabilities for applications of his system to therapist responses in his experimental film interviews. For a random sample of twenty written answer sheets, independently rated by two judges, percentage of agreement on the five systems ranged from 77.9 percent to 96.0 percent. Agreement meant that both raters assigned therapist communications to the same category, or that they gave it an intensity score no more than one-half step apart.

14. Dimensionality Considerations

For Strupp's system, dimensionality issues are twofold. How many independent factors are present among the five category scales? To date Strupp has not clearly assessed the degree of relationship present among the five scales. The limited data regarding intercorrelations among the scales suggest that there may be some redundancy. Strupp concludes in the manual that "the degree of correlation among the scales and categories is presently an open question. It was demonstrated, however, that Scale I (Depth Directedness) and Scale VI (Initiative) are correlated approximately 0.85, which leaves little room for independence" (Strupp, 1966, p. 131). The second question is whether each of the five scales assesses a single (in contrast to multiple) factor. Strupp has not considered this latter dimensionality issue.

15. Validity Studies

Studies of therapists in Strupp's film-analogue situation are summarized in his 1960 volume. Studies of therapists in both naturalistic and analogue situations using the Strupp system are summarized in Strupp (1962a, 1962b). Studies reporting on the application and development of his new scoring system are presented in Strupp, Chassan, and Ewing (1966). All these studies have focused primarily on comparing the interview behavior of therapists differing in level of experience, theoretical orientation, and professional affiliation. Studies have shown that the system discriminates the therapist's activity within single hours and over a series of hours with reasonable sensitivity, and that it permits meaningful comparisons between the communications of therapists subscribing to different theoretical orientations, differing in terms of experience and similar variables.

RELATED SCALES OR CONSTRUCTS

Strupp spends some time in his manual comparing his scales with the Bales (1950) interaction process system. There are similarities as well as differences in the two systems. One of the reasons Strupp constructed his system was that he felt Bales' system was too general, not sufficiently analytical for an analysis of psychotherapy. He further felt that "the systems of Porter (1943) and Snyder (1945) are useful for categorizing the activities of the client-centered counselor, but they are unsuitable for the data of psychoanalytically oriented therapy" (Strupp, 1966, p. 11), since the systems were too narrow.

It seems likely that Strupp's Therapeutic Climate scale might correlate considerably with Truax's Nonpossessive Warmth or other conditions scales (see below) as well as with Barrett-Lennard's Relationship Inventory subscales (see Chapter 7). Strupp's Depth Directedness and Initiative scales show considerable similarity to Harway et al.'s Depth of Interpretation Scale (see above) as well as to Howe and Pope's Therapist Activity Level Scale (see above).

References

Auerbach, A. H. An application of Strupp's method of content analysis to psychotherapy. *Psychiatry*, 1963, 26, 137.

Bales, R. F. *Interaction process analysis*. Reading, Mass.: Addison-Wesley, 1950.

Bellak, L., and Smith, M. B. An experimental exploration of the psychoanalytic process. *Psychoanalytic Quarterly*, 1956, 25, 385-414.

Collier, R. M. A scale for rating responses of the psychotherapist. *Journal of Consulting Psychology*, 1953, 17, 321-26.

Porter, E. H., Jr. The development and evaluation of a measure of counseling interview procedures. *Educational and Psychological Measurement*, 1943, 3, 105-26; 215-38.

________. *An introduction to therapeutic counseling*. Boston: Houghton Mifflin, 1950.

Snyder, W. U. An investigation of the nature of nondirective psychotherapy, *Journal of Genetic Psychology*, 1945, 33, 193-223.

Strupp, H. H. A multidimensional system for analyzing psychotherapeutic techniques. *Psychiatry*, 1957, 20, 293-306. (a)

________. A multidimensional analysis of technique in brief psychotherapy. *Psychiatry*, 1957, 20, 387-97. (b)

________. A multidimensional analysis of therapist activity in analytic and client-centered therapy. *Journal of Consulting Psychology*, 1957, 21, 301-308. (c)

________. The psychotherapists' contribution to the treatment process. *Behavioral Science*, 1958, 3, 34-67. (a)

________. The performance of psychoanalytic and client-centered therapists in an initial interview. *Journal of Consulting Psychology*, 1958, 22, 265-74. (b)

________. The performance of psychiatrist and psychologists in a therapeutic interview. *Journal of Clinical Psychology*, 1958, 14, 219-26. (c)

________. *Psychotherapists in action: explorations of the therapist's contribution to the treatment process*. New York: Grune & Stratton, 1960.

________. The therapist's contribution to the treatment process: beginning and vagaries of a research program. In H. H. Strupp and L. Luborsky (Eds.), *Research in psychotherapy*. Vol. 2. Washington, D.C.: American Psychological Association, 1962, Pp. 25-40. (a)

________. Patient-doctor relationships: psychotherapists contribution to the treatment process. In A. J. Bahrach (Ed.), *Experimental foundations of clinical psychology*. New York: Basic Books, 1962. Pp. 576-615. (b)

________. *A multidimensional system for analyzing psychotherapeutic communications: manual*, 2d ed. Chapel Hill: University of North Carolina, 1966. (Mimeographed)

Strupp, H. H., Chassan, J. B., and Ewing, J. A. Toward the longitudinal study of the psychotherapeutic process. In L. A. Gottschalk and A. H. Auerbach (Eds.), *Methods of research in psychotherapy*. New York: Appleton-Century-Crofts, 1966. Pp. 361-400.

Strupp, H. H., and Williams, J. V. Some determinants of clinical evaluations of different psychiatrists. *AMA Archives of General Psychiatry*, 1960, 2, 434.
Wallach, M. S., and Strupp, H. H. Psychotherapists' clinical judgments and attitudes toward patients. *Journal of Consulting Psychology*, 1960, 24, 316.

Scales for Therapist Accurate Empathy, Nonpossessive Warmth, and Genuineness

Charles B. Truax

1. Rationale for Development of the Scales

Truax's considerable work on scale development was done within Roger's client-centered framework. Truax describes the basic assumption underlying his three therapist conditions' scales as follows:

> Despite the bewildering array of divergent theories and the difficulty in translating concepts from the language of one theory to that of another, several common threads weave their way through almost every major theory of psychotherapy and counseling, including the psychoanalytic, the client-centered, the behavioristic, and many of the more eclectic and derivative theories. In one way or another, all have emphasized the importance of the therapist's ability to be integrated, mature, genuine, authentic, or congruent in his relationship to the patient. They have all stressed also the importance of the therapist's ability to provide a nonthreatening, trusting, safe, or secure atmosphere by his acceptance, nonpossessive warmth, unconditional positive regard, or love. Finally, virtually all theories of psychotherapy emphasize that for the therapist to be helpful he must be accurately empathic, be "with" the client, be understanding, or grasp the patient's meaning. These three sets of characteristics can, for lack of better words, be termed *accurate empathy, nonpossessive warmth,* and *genuineness.* The discovery of the therapeutic effectiveness of these three interpersonal skills grew out of Freud's historic development of the "talking cure." They are, however, aspects of the therapist's behavior that cut across virtually all theories of psychotherapy and appear to be common elements in a wide variety of approaches to psychotherapy and counseling. Their occurrence and recurrence in theoretical orientations derived from different patient populations, from different periods in time, and from effective therapists who have widely differing personalities, suggest that they are indeed central ingredients in effective psychotherapy. In more recent years they have been given more specific attention and have

grown in their central importance. Thus, Rogers (1957) specifies that the therapist's ability to communicate empathic understanding and unconditional positive regard for the patient, and his being a congruent or genuine person in the relationship, are both "necessary and sufficient" conditions for patient therapeutic change.

> Rogers deserves enormous credit for his 1957 statement, since it served to bring client-centered theory into closer alignment with other positions. More important, it focused renewed interest on these interpersonal therapeutic skills and served as an impetus to further thought and research. Rogers' position was, of course, the basic impetus for the present authors' research and current thinking. While many other theorists had stressed these same factors at an earlier date, Rogers was one of the first leading theorists to give them a special preeminence as *the* effective ingredients for successful therapy. (Truax and Carkhuff, 1967, p. 25)
>
> These three therapeutic ingredients, as Shoben (1953) has noted, are not at all unique to psychotherapy or counseling. Instead, they are qualities of universal human experience that are present or absent in varying degrees in virtually all human relationship. (p. 32)
>
> Although [our research efforts] have also incorporated aspects of other schools of thought, the original efforts grew out of the client-centered orientation. This was due in part to Rogers' early advocacy of research as a means of more fully understanding the intricacies and complexities of the therapeutic transaction; in part to his pioneering in the use of the tape recorder as a means of objectively capturing significant aspects of the therapeutic process; in part to his own openness to new evidence in modifying his existing theoretic stance; but his major contribution was the theoretic specification (1957) of empathy, warmth, and genuineness (empathic understanding, unconditional positive regard, and congruence) as both *necessary and sufficient conditions* for therapeutic outcome. . . . While few researchers believed that any three therapist characteristics would in fact be either necessary or sufficient to account for the therapist's contribution to patient outcome, Rogers' recent theoretical formulation proved to be the major stimulus for research in this area. (p. 80)

2. *Description of the Scales*

When accurate empathy, nonpossessive warmth, and genuineness are thought of as dimensions of the psychotherapeutic process, then some attempt to specify degrees of these three factors is a necessary prior step to research and training. Building on the work of prior researchers, attempts were made in 1957 to specify rating scales measuring accurate empathy, nonpossessive warmth, and genuineness. These global scales made heavy use of the raters, who were asked to draw upon their own abundant experience of being undersood and misunderstood, warmly and coldly received, and met with an artificial and a genuine human being. At first the scales were quite closely tied to Rogers' statements and grew out of a seminar with him during the early part of 1957. Since that time the evidence has suggested that "empathy" is not so related to client improvement as "accurate empathy," which contains elements of the psychoanalytic view of moment-to-moment diagnostic accuracy. The evidence has also suggested that "unconditionality" of positive regard does not greatly contribute to outcome, and that what seems most related to outcome is the communication of a "nonpossessive" warmth in the sense specified by Alexander (1950). Also, what seemed most related to client improvement was not simply a congruence between the therapist's organismic self and his behavior or self-concept, but rather the absence of defensiveness or phoniness—his seeming genuineness. Thus the identifying labels for the three therapeutic interpersonal skills . . . have changed. (Truax and Carkhuff, 1967, p. 43)

The three rating scales [themselves] . . . have not changed since 1962. Most certainly they will be changed and greatly improved upon. It has been a constant temptation to modify the scales in the hope of improving them—a temptation resisted in order to allow more direct comparisons to be made between studies and training efforts based on them. Although the present measurement scales are highly inferential and crude in construction, they represent a beginning attempt to specify the operational meaning of the concepts. (p. 43)

Abbreviated forms of the three therapist conditions' scales are presented in Table 4.5.[1] For greater detail and examples of the various stages, the reader is referred to the Truax and Carkhuff volume (1967), pp. 46-72.

1. In a personal communication (February 1971), Truax states that the three scales now have been modified. "The empathy scale . . . has hardly been changed at all. It has been primarily a slight change in emphasis. On the other hand, there has been some change in the genuineness and warmth scales which have led to higher measured levels of reliability. Also, in . . . two recent studies, the revised scales have worked out better than the originals in terms of predicting outcome, so I finally decided to change them." Copies of the revised scales are available from Truax upon request.

A TENTATIVE SCALE FOR THE MEASUREMENT OF ACCURATE EMPATHY

The first of the three therapist scales is a nine-point annotated and anchored rating scale.

> Accurate empathy involves more than just the ability of the therapist to sense the client or patient's "private world" as if it were his own. It also involves more than just his ability to know what the patient means. Accurate empathy involves both the therapist's sensitivity to current feelings and his verbal facility to communicate this understanding in a language attuned to the client's current feelings. It is not necessary—indeed it would seem undesirable—for the therapist to *share* the client's feelings in any sense that would require him to feel the same emotions. It is instead an appreciation and a sensitive awareness of those feelings. At deeper levels of empathy, it also involves enough understanding of patterns of human feelings and experience to sense feelings that the client only partially reveals. With such experience and knowledge, the therapist can communicate what the client clearly knows as well as meanings in the client's experience of which he is scarcely aware. (Truax and Carkhuff, 1967, p. 46)

> The range of this nine-point scale extends from a low point where the therapist manifests a virtual lack of empathic understanding of the patient (stage 1) to a high point where he shows an unfalteringly accurate response to the patient's full range of expressed and implicity affect (stage nine). . . . At a high level of accurate empathy the message "I am with you" is unmistakably clear—the therapist's remarks fit compatibly with the patient's mood and content. At a low level of accurate empathy the therapist may be off on a tangent of his own, may have misinterpreted what the patient is feeling, or may be so preoccupied with his own intellectual interpretations that he is scarcely aware of the patient. (Rogers, Gendlin, Kiesler, and Truax, 1967, p. 139)

A TENTATIVE SCALE FOR THE MEASUREMENT OF NON-POSSESSIVE WARMTH

> The dimension of nonpossessive warmth or unconditional positive regard, ranges from a high level where the therapist warmly accepts the patient's experience as part of that person, without imposing conditions, to a low level where the therapist evaluates a patient or his feelings, expresses dislike or disapproval, or expresses warmth in a selective and evaluative way. Thus, a warm positive feeling toward the client may still rate quite low in this

> scale if it is given conditionally. Nonpossessive warmth . . . involves valuing the patient as a person, separate from any evaluation of his behavior or thoughts. Thus, a therapist can evaluate the patient's behavior or thoughts but still rate high on warmth if it is quite clear that his valuing of the individual is uncontaminated and unconditional. . . . It is not necessary—indeed, it would seem undesirable—for the therapist to be nonselective in reinforcing, or to sanction or approve thoughts and behaviors that are disapproved by society. Nonpossessive warmth is present when the therapist appreciates such feelings or behaviors and their meaning to the client, but shows a nonpossessive caring for the person and not for his behavior. The therapist's response to the patient's thoughts or behaviors is a search for their meaning or value within the patient rather than disapproval or approval. (Truax and Carkhuff, 1967, pp. 59-60)

This five-point annotated and anchored rating scale defines "five levels of unconditional positive regard, beginning with an almost complete lack of regard or acceptance (stage 1) and progressing to a high level where the therapist unerringly communicates to the patient a deep and genuine caring for him as a person with human potentialities . . . (stage five)" (Rogers et al., 1967, p. 140).

A TENTATIVE SCALE FOR THE MEASUREMENT OF THERAPIST GENUINENESS OR SELF-CONGRUENCE

This five-point annotated and anchored rating scale is

> an attempt to define five degrees of therapist genuineness, beginning at a very low level where the therapist presents a facade or defends and denies feelings; and continuing to a high level of self-congruence where the therapist is freely and deeply himself. A high level of self-congruence does not mean that the therapist must overtly express his feelings but only that he does not deny them. Thus, the therapist may be actively reflecting, interpreting, analyzing, or in other ways functioning as a therapist; but this functioning must be self-congruent, so that he is being himself in the moment, rather than presenting a professional facade. Thus the therapist's response must be sincere rather than phony; it must express his real feelings or being rather than defensiveness.
>
> "Being himself" simply means that at the moment the therapist is really whatever his response denotes. It does not mean that the therapist must disclose his total self, but only that whatever he

> does show is a real aspect of himself, not a response growing out of defensiveness or a merely "professional" response that has been learned and repeated. (Truax and Carkhuff, 1967, pp. 68-69)

More recently Truax has become interested in an additional therapist dimension, for the assessment of which he had previously developed a five-point scale. This is "A Tentative Scale for the Measurement of Intensity and Intimacy of Interpersonal Contact" (Truax, 1962; Truax and Carkhuff, 1967). Since the author presents little data regarding this scale, it will simply be described here and not referred to in later sections.

> The intensity and intimacy of the therapist's focus on the client is theoretically viewed as a separable aspect of the therapeutic process. . . . It seems quite significant that when accurate empathy, nonpossessive warmth, and genuineness are conceptually abstracted from the interpersonal transaction of therapy, the vital sense of intensity and personal intimacy that seems characteristic of successful therapy is somehow left out of the final abstraction. A tentative attempt at conceptualizing and measuring the intensity and intimacy of the therapist's relationship with the client seems to have borne some fruit. A tentative five-point scale has been developed attempting to specify stages along the dimension of therapist intensity and intimacy, ranging from a low point of aloof remoteness to a high point of intense absorption (Truax, 1962). At the lower end of the intensity and intimacy scale, the therapist is subdued and distinct in voice and manner; there is an aloofness from feelings and a formal, conventional, or reserved atmosphere, a remoteness or detachment which makes the therapist appear as an "outsider" or a stranger, an inattentiveness of indifference which makes him appear unconcerned. The total interaction gives a "cool" or intellectual flavor. By contrast, at the higher ranges of the intensity and intimacy scale, the therapist communicates an intensity in voice and manner which has a compellingly personal note; there is an accentuated feeling tone communicated by a voice and manner that are both deeply concerned and confidential; a heightened atmosphere is achieved by the therapist's close, almost suspended attentiveness; his voice combines both depth and solicitous closeness, communicating an accentuated feeling tone and a fervid concentration. (Truax and Carkhuff, 1967, pp. 289-90)

Finally, the author has also developed a scale of Depth of Self-Exploration to measure *patient* process in therapy. This scale is presented below (see Chapter 5). Most of the sections that follow are equally pertinent to the Depth of Self-Exploration Scale as well as to the three therapist conditions' measures being discussed here.

3. Data Collection Context

The author has extensively applied his therapist conditions scales to individual and group psychotherapy in a variety of settings, including hospitalized patients and inmates as well as outpatients of several diagnostic descriptions. The major studies by Truax and his colleagues have been of individual therapy with hospitalized schizophrenic patients (Truax and Carkhuff, 1967; also reported separately by Rogers et al., 1967), group therapy with hospitalized chronic patients (Truax, Carkhuff, and Kodman, 1965), group therapy with institutionalized juvenile delinquents (Truax and Wargo, 1966), and a study of diagnostic interviewing and subsequent individual psychotherapy of outpatients (Truax et al., 1966) as well as others. The author reports numerous other studies by other investigators relevant to the same therapist dimensions (Truax and Carkhuff, 1967, Chapter 3).

A program for applying the research instruments to the training of professional and lay persons is described by Truax, Carkhuff, and Douds (1964). It is also described, much more extensively, in the 1967 Truax and Carkhuff volume.

> One way of directly attacking the central question of causation would be to train prospective therapists specifically to provide high levels of accurate empathy, nonpossessive warmth, and genuineness, and then see if they were indeed effective in producing constructive change in patients or clients. (Truax and Carkhuff, 1967, p. 107)

> The currently available evidence . . . suggest that these ingredients . . . are teachable; and that even nonprofessional persons lacking expert knowledge of psychopathology and personality dynamics can, under supervision, produce positive changes in chronic hospitalized patient populations after specific training in the communication of accurate empathy, nonpossessive warmth, and therapist genuineness. (pp. 11-12)

4. Data Form

Truax does not explicitly discuss the differential effects on his scales' ratings of providing judges with typescripts, tape recordings, or audio-video presentations of psychotherapy interview data. He does state, however, that "the scales were designed primarily for use with live observations or tape recordings of counseling or therapy interviews. They have been used with only a slight loss in reliability on typescripts of therapeutic interaction" (Truax and Carkhuff, 1967, pp. 43-44). By far the majority of the scale applications have been to tape-recorded segments of individual and group psychotherapy sessions.

Truax cites Shapiro's (1965) study which showed that individuals differ in the degree of congruence between their linguistic and nonlinguistic behavior. He also cites a later study (Shapiro, 1966) which found that the degree of verbal communicated pleasantness (warmth) did not predict facially communicated pleasantness (warmth). Truax speculates from these findings that the "therapist who wishes to become more empathic must learn that he can be influenced by different channels of emotionality. He must choose a response at one or another level or one which is a response to cues from the whole person. Of course, the psychotherapist must remember that the client will be responding to the therapist's linguistic and nonlinguistic behavior as well" (Truax and Carkhuff, 1967, p. 289). This avowed emphasis on all the communication channels (for example, words, voice qualities, facial expressions) suggest that different therapist conditions scores might result from video, audio, or typescript presentations of the therapist's interview behavior. An empirical check of this possibility could produce quite informative results.

5. Choice of Units

The most frequent sample of psychotherapy used for conditions' ratings seems to be four- or five-minute tape-recorded segments, although the size has varied in different studies. "The authors and others have applied the scales to samples of psychotherapeutic interaction varying from as short as two minutes to as long as sixteen minutes of continuous therapy transactions" (Truax and Carkhuff, 1967, p. 44). To date the author has not explicitly discussed or empirically evaluated differential effects of his rating scales' scores of extracting different size samples from the same psychotherapy sessions.

The "scoring unit" for the Truax system, then, is an individual temporal unit, usally four or five minutes in length, randomly extracted from the total session. Although the "contextual unit" and "summarizing unit" are not specified, it is clear they are identical with the scoring unit. That is, in scoring a particular time segment the judge considers *only* the patient and therapist verbalizations present in that segment. Series of statements are usally rated in a standard random order. Similarly, the summarizing unit would be the average of the rating values independently assigned a particular time segment by a group of judges. In some studies the summarizing unit has been larger, for example, an average rating for a total session or an average for the entire case.

In the analysis of group psychotherapy sessions, Truax has apparently followed one of two procedures. For the first, "two kinds of samples (patient-therapist-patient and therapist-patient-therapist) were taken for each patient in [the] different groups throughout the course of group therapy" (p. 105). It is not clear whether this interactive unit was exhaustively sampled over the entire session for each subject or was scored for a subunit of each session. For the second, "*time* samples of therapeutic interaction were also taken from the same groups" (p. 105). The size of these time samples as well as their location is not specified in the 1967 volume.

6. Participant-Context Restrictions

Truax has empirically addressed the participant-context issue.

> [In one study] 50 samples of tape-recorded therapeutic transactions obtained throughout the course of therapy with five different patients and therapists provided the basic data for analysis. Using stereophonic recordings with tightly focused "gun" microphones and careful editing, it was possible to obtain only the therapist statement portion of the same 50 samples (the patient's statements had been completely edited out). Ratings were then made on both the set of complete samples (therapist and patient transactions) and separately on the edited samples (containing only the therapist statements). Analysis of those ratings indicated no significant differences between the measurements of accurate empathy and nonpossessive warmth, in the edited and unedited samples for the different therapy cases, for the different sessions from which the samples were drawn, or for different raters. Further, the correlation across the samples between the measures obtained from these conditions in the edited and unedited samples approximated quite closely the reliabilities of the scales themselves. Thus, the direct evidence from that study indicates that measurement of the therapist's levels of therapeutic conditions is in general not contaminated by the patient's responses. (Truax and Carkhuff, 1967, p. 104).

A recent critique of the Accurate Empathy Scale suggests that, rather than being a positive finding, it represents a challenge to the construct validity of the scale itself. Chinsky and Rappaport (1970) state that

> . . . examination of the nine defining points of the AE scale clearly indicates that ratings of therapist-only samples could not have been made in terms of AE–leastwise not as this construct is defined by the scale points. For example, Stage 1 is described as "Therapist seems completely unaware of even the most conspicuous of the client's feelings. . . . " Similar definitions, each contingent on the content and/or feeling of the patient's statements are given for all nine scale points. How can one assess the accuracy of a therapist's empathy unless these is someone to whom the therapist is responding? (p. 380)

The authors conclude that "the most parsimonious explanation for the high correlation between patient-therapist and therapist-only samples is that raters are responding to some quality of the therapist (perhaps voice quality, tone, inflection, or language style) not implied in the definition of AE. . . . [Similarly] the assumption that a more general therapist trait is being measured by AE would also explain the results" (p. 380). Apparently, this issue is conceptually crucial, and needs further theoretical and empirical consideration before precise interpretation of accurate empathy scores is possible.[2]

7. *Type of Sampling Indicated*

Apparently the typical procedure has been random time sampling from the psychotherapy sessions.

> [for the Wisconsin study] we decided on random sampling, not only because it was more practical than systematic sampling, but also because it was particularly compatible with our general theoretical orientation and assumptions. The conditions . . . variables in this study, as theoretically conceived, are content free. They represent attitudinal . . . components of the therapy relationship that are assumed to be omnipresent in the therapy interaction, being independent of specific topics or problems. Theoretically it is not the occurrence of any specific event at any special moment in therapy that is effective, but rather the general or cumulative operation of the attitudinal relationship (conditions) factors that leads to the therapeutic process and, in turn, to constructive personality change. (Rogers el al. 1967, pp. 136-37)

Truax has not empirically assessed differential effects on his rating scale scores of random versus various systematic sampling procedures.

2. Truax has in press, in the *Psychological Bulletin*, a reply to Chinsky and Rappaport's critique.

8. Sample Location Within the Interview

Truax has consistently used random time sampling of specific interview hours, although in most cases restrictions are added. For example, in the Wisconsin study

> each four-minute segment was extracted at random from the latter half of the therapy or sampling interview tape according to a standardized procedure. First, each tape was timed and the midpoint determined. Then the last half of the tape was entered at a randomly determined time point, and a segment consisting of the four subsequent minutes was transcribed onto a small reel. There was only one prerequisite—the segment taken had to contain a minimum of two patient statements and two therapist responses. If this criterion was not met by the first entry, the segmenter was instructed to use his best judgment to find a segment meeting this criterion, first in another portion of the latter half of the therapy hour or in the first half of the hour. (Rogers, et al. 1967, p. 138)

Truax has not assessed how representative of therapists' behavior in the total session are rating scale scores obtained from various time periods within the recorded hour.

9. Sample Location over Therapy Interviews

Truax's sampling procedures over the series of interviews from initiation to termination have been relatively exhaustive, varying in different studies from systematic time sampling—for example, every fifth interview throughout the course of treatment (Truax and Carkhuff, 1967, p. 85)—to exhaustive representation of the entire interaction—for example, consecutive five-minute samples taken throughout a series of twenty-eight interviews (p. 88). To date Truax has not explicitly discussed or empirically evaluated how representative of the entire therapy are samples extracted from various locations across the interview continuum.

Data from the Wisconsin study suggest that, at least for accurate empathy ratings, samples taken from early interviews might be unrepresentative of the total case. Ratings of fourteen schizophrenic patients for interviews two to fifteen were intercorrelated. Accurate empathy scores for the cases for the second interview were correlated with empathy scores for each successive interview, as well as with the average of interviews two to fifteen.

> Apparently there was little relative consistency in the level of accurate empathy offered by the therapist over the first few interviews. It was not until interviews seven and eight (then not

> consistently until the eleventh interview) that the level of AE in one hour could be predicted from that of the preceding hour. This suggested that the relative level of accurate empathy for the various cases reversed itself, before stabilizing gradually at about the seventh therapy interview. (Rogers et al., 1967, pp. 157-58)

10. Clinical Sophistication of Judges

Truax has generally used undergraduate judges for his scale ratings. Separate groups of from three to five judges each rate the data utilizing one of the three conditions scales. "In an effort to obtain 'objective' ratings uncontaminated by the theoretic bias of the rater, undergraduate students who were naive with respect to the theory and practice of psychotherapy were trained separately in the use of the three scales" (Truax and Carkhuff, 1967, p. 85). To date the author has not empirically contrasted ratings of clinically sophisticated judges with those obtained by his usual undergraduates.

11. Training Required of Judges

The author does not explicitly deal with this procedure in his 1967 volume except to note that "the raters themselves were trained on other data to a minimum rate-rerate and interrater reliability of 0.50" (Truax and Carkhuff, 1967, p. 85).[3] The usual training procedure is, however, spelled out in detail in the Rogers et al. (1967) volume:

> The (conditions) scale raters were trained in informally supervised practice sessions. The purpose of this procedure was to permit raters to develop a mutual scale conception and task set with a minimum of staff intervention. All training was done by a single staff member in individual and group sessions. Each rater was first given a copy of the relevant scale to study and was assigned to rate practice materials. Blocks of practice ratings (ten per block) for all trainees were then intercorrelated. When the interrater (Pearsonian) correlations reached 0.60 the raters were assigned to project data. In instances where the reliability did not rise quickly to this correlation value the raters were assembled and told that their

3. In a personal communication (February 1971), Truax refers to "an excellent study completed in 1970 by Donald Pare at the University of Florida. He did a rather exhaustive study on widely varying groups of raters who were given approximately one hour training in the use of the accurate empathy scale. He then had them rate some 18 samples which had been rated by experienced raters at Arkansas. It turned out that individuals regardless of the degree of authoritarianism, socioeconomic status, or level of educational attainment agreed quite closely with the much more extensively trained raters at the University of Arkansas ($r = 0.77$)."

> ratings were not in agreement. Disputed tapes were played and the raters were allowed to discuss and resolve their discrepancies without interference from the staff member. At no time did the staff member offer opinions regarding the rating of a specific segment. Thus the raters were permitted to develop a mutual set and manner of applying the scale to the therapy data. Periodically the staff members assessed their general conceptualization of the scale by requiring them to define scale stages, as well as to define issues not relevant to each scale stage. The major criterion for training, however, was the interrater reliability. (pp. 142-43)

12. Training Manual

No manual is available. However, it seems it would take little effort to provide a manual since the training procedure has been spelled out in some detail, the scale provides numerous examples of each scale stage, and a set of training tapes are available for training purposes. If a manual were available it would be quite helpful to other interested investigators.[4]

13. Interrater and Intrarater Reliabilities Reported

Truax reports data indicating that judges attain moderately high levels of interjudge agreement in applying the three scales. The coefficients reported were in the earlier studies Pearson intercorrelations among the judges, and more recently Ebel's intraclass coefficients, r_{11} being an estimate of the average intercorrelation among the judges, and r_{kk} representing the reliability of the average scores (of the group of judges) for the segment sample involved.

> The reliability of the scales is easy to assess. The question is simply, can you get repeated measures that are closely alike? A way of answering that question is to correlate different raters' ratings on the scales for the same samples of therapeutic transactions. Such correlations for twenty-eight studies involving a variety of therapist and patient populations [are presented]. (Truax and Carkhuff, 1967, p. 44)

The values show that r_{11} values, for the AE, NW, and G scales respectively, have ranges of 0.43-0.79, 0.48-0.84, and 0.40-0.62, while the r_{kk} values have ranges of 0.50-0.95, 0.52-0.95, and 0.25-0.95 respectively. The median r_{kk} values reported are 0.85 for

4. In a personal communication (February 1971), Truax states that the beginning of a training manual was published by Dr. Frank Lawlis as a discussion paper at the Arkansas Rehabilitation and Training Center (1968).

AE, 0.77 for NW, and 0.72 for G. Truax concludes that "the answer in general, then, seems to be that most often a moderate to high degree of reliability is obtained with the scales whether measurement is of counseling or therapy, group or individual" (p. 44).

14. Dimensionality Considerations

Dimensionality considerations cover two issues with the three conditions' scales. The first has to do with the degree of association among the three separate scales; the second with the issue of whether or not each scale is tapping a single dimension only, in contrast to several variously related subfactors.

The former question has proved interesting, both theoretically and empirically.

> As Rogers and Truax (1967) have suggested, the order in which these three therapeutic conditions are considered is especially significant because of their interlocking nature. To be facilitative toward another human being requires that we be deeply sensitive to his moment-to-moment experience, grasping both the core meaning and signifance and the content of his experience and feelings. Such deep empathic understanding requires first that we have at least a degree of warmth and respect for the other person. Thus, empathic understanding can scarcely exist without a prior or concomitant feeling of nonpossessive warmth. In turn, neither the empathy nor the warmth could be constructively meaningful in any human encounter unless it were "real." Unless the counselor or therapist is "genuine" in relating to the client, his warmth and empathy may even have a potentially threatening meaning. . . . In essence, then, the suggestion by Rogers and Truax was that the element of genuineness or authenticity is most basic to a relationship. Once this reality of the person of the therapist is established, the warmth and respect communicated to the patient becomes the second central ingredient in a effective relationship. Finally, given a relationship characterized by warmth and genuineness, the "work" of therapy or counseling proceeds through the therapist's moment-by-moment empathic grasp of the meaning and significance of the client's world. (Truax and Carkhuff, 1967, p. 32)

This quotation draws the picture theoretically, but what does the data say regarding the interrelationship among Truax's three conditions' scales? Truax replies:

> Since some of the early studies have obtained moderately high intercorrelations between the measures of accurate empathy, non-

> possessive warmth, and genuineness, it is natural to suspect that there may be one underlying dimension—a sort of "good therapy relationship" dimension. The evidence just reviewed . . . however, clearly indicates the functional independence of these three therapeutic conditions. In most of the studies cited there were strong positive intercorrelations, but in others there were no relationships; and in the one group therapy study and the John Hopkins study of individual therapy, substantial *negative* correlations between the three therapeutic ingredients were obtained. . . . There is an important lesson in this for psychotherapy research in general (indeed for much of psychological research): If we had looked only at the interrelationships obtained on a very large sample of therapists we would have easily concluded that we were dealing with one underlying factor (since they were on the average positively intercorrelated). If we were to factor analyze results from a large sample of therapists, we would most likely obtain one general factor. However, that would have completely obscured the facts that the three therapeutic ingredients are functionally independent, and that in particular therapists (or subsamples of therapists) these three ingredients sometimes vary independtly and sometimes are even characteristically negatively related! (pp. 132-33)

Truax has not to date explicitly considered the second intrascale dimensionality issue. The critique of Chinsky and Rappaport above implies that this issue also might be quite relevant regarding the construct validity of the three scales. Furthermore, Kiesler, Mathieu, and Klein (1967), based on the experience of the Wisconsin study, remark that

> A closer inspection of the conditions scale definitions . . . suggest rather strongly that the current conditions scales are multidimensional. The Accurate Empathy Scale, in the form used in this study, generally defines the overall impact of the therapist's response to the patient's phenomenological frame of reference, his implicit as well as expressed desire to understand the patient from this perspective, and his skill in communicating an empathic grasp of the materials presented by the client. The Unconditional Positive Regard Scale appears similarly complex, including not only the therapist's affective responses (that is, his expressed warmth and affection for the patient), but also the degree of conditionality shown in his reaction to specific components of the patient's personality and symptomatology. . . . Thus, not only are each of the conditions variables defined so that they are in some degree dependent on either the patient's stimulus value or the quality of

> the interaction, but each has been conceptualized in multidimensional terms for the specific rating scales. (p. 303)

To the extent that this scale analysis is correct, further dimensional unraveling similar to the precise work on the Depth of Interpretation and Level of Therapist Activity Scales (see Harway et al. and Howe and Pope, above for each of the scales) is necessary.

15. Validity Studies

Truax, in his volume with Carkhuff (1967, Chapter 3), summarizes his studies with the three conditions scales, and relates this evidence to that of other investigators.

> These studies taken together suggest that therapists or counselors who are accurately empathic, nonpossessively warm in attitude, and genuine are indeed effective: The greater the degree to which these elements were present in the therapeutic encounter, the greater was the resulting constructive personality change in the patient. These findings seem to hold for a wide variety of therapists and counselors, *regardless of their training or theoretic orientation*; and for a wide variety of clients or patients, including college underachievers, juvenile deliquents, hospitalized schizophrenics, college counselees, mild to severe outpatient neurotics, and the mixed variety of hospitalized patients. Further, the evidence suggests that these findings hold in a variety of therapeutic contexts and in both individual and group psychotherapy or counseling. (p. 100)

> The present research evidence, while in reality only a beginning step toward specifying the nature of the antecendents to constructive or deteriorative personality and behavior change, does represent a significant movement toward understanding, and thus toward predicting and influencing behavior or personality development and change. Research seems consistently to find empathy, warmth, and genuineness characteristic of human encounters that change people—for the better. Future research must be aimed not only at developing further evidence to define more solidly the contexts within which these three conditions are indeed ingredients in effective psychotherapy, learning, education, and human development, but also toward further specifying the exact behaviors and characteristics relevant to change. . . . The finding that most human encounters can indeed be for better or for worse suggests promising leads for research into the prevention rather than just the treatment of psychological disturbance and upset, of

> underachivement, and of the symptoms of psychological poverty. The implications hold not only for the training and functioning of psychotherapists, but also for the training of teachers and educators, marriage partners, employers and supervisors, and parents. (pp. 141-42)

The second half of Truax and Carkhuff (1967) is devoted to a description of a didactic and experiential training program "for learning the effective practice of counseling or psychotherapy," tied closely to the authors' research findings and theoretic view. Truax and Carkhuff first specify the ingredients of effective training for therapeutic practice. Next they present an overview of how this view is translated into actual training practice, focusing on the operational specifics and sequencing of training. Then they emphasize and provide transcripts of the structured experiential component of training, the quasi-group therapy sessions with trainees as participants. Finally, they present a detailed application of the training program and its evaluation.

RELATED SCALES OR CONSTRUCTS

Truax and Carkhuff (1967) report two slight modifications of the Accurate Empathy scale by other researchers. The first is a ten-point version used by A. E. Bergin and S. Solomon, which "was found useful by them in dealing with tapes taken from trainees in clinical psychology. . . . Their revision involved the addition of a new stage at the lower end of the scale, which allows for greater differentiation when rating tapes from relatively unempathic therapists" (p. 55). The second version is a schematic presentation of levels of accurate empathy, developed by R. A. Melloh, which has been "found useful for both research raters and therapist trainees. It provides a brief summary of the scale, and is intended to facilitate the training of raters in the use of the scale" (p. 59).

Kiesler (1967) has developed a five-point scale of therapist congruence or genuineness which was applied in the Wisconsin study.

> [The scale] ranges from a point where there is an obvious discrepancy between the therapist's feelings about the patient and his concurrent communication to the patient (stage 1) to a high point where the therapist communicates both his positive and negative feelings about the patient openly and freely, without traces of defensiveness or retreat into professionalism (stage 5). . . . [The ratings] were limited to instances where the patient questioned, explicitly or implicitly, the therapist's feelings or opinions about him. . . . The therapist's response was rated according to the de-

gree to which his feelings about the patient were freely and openly expressed. (Rogers et al., 1967, pp. 139-40)

Moderate levels of interjudge reliability have been obtained for the scale, but unfortunately the scale does not discriminate adequately among therapists. The ratings were "distributed bimodally with the majority of ratings falling at stage 5. In effect the therapists and the sampling interview in this sample were judged either highly congruent or neutral, with no therapist being judged as phony or defensive" (p. 152). The Kiesler congruence scale obviously, then, needs considerably more work before it can be meaningfully applied in process research. The detailed version of this congruence scale can be found in Rogers et al. (1967, pp. 581-84).

References

Alexander, F. Analysis of the therapeutic factors in psychoanalytic treatment. *Psychoanalytic Quarterly,* 1950, 19, 482-500.

Chinsky, J. M., and Rappaport, J. Brief critique of the meaning and reliability of "Accurate Empathy" ratings. *Psychological Bulletin,* 1970, 73, 379-82.

Kiesler, D. J. A scale for the rating of congruence. In C. R. Rogers, E. T. Gendlin, D. J. Kiesler, and C. B. Truax, *The therapeutic relationship and its impact: a study of psychotherapy with schizophrenics.* Madison: University of Wisconsin Press, 1967. Pp. 581-84.

Kiesler, D. J., Mathieu, P. L. and Klein, M. H. A summary of the issues and conclusions. In C. R. Rogers, E. T. Gendlin, D. J. Kiesler, and C. B. Truax, *The therapeutic relationship and its impact: a study of psychotherapy with schizophrenics.* Madison: University of Wisconsin Press, 1967. Pp. 295-311.

Pare, D. D. Accurate empathy scale: relative of absolute? Unpublished doctoral dissertation, University of Florida, 1970.

Rogers, C. R. The necessary and sufficient conditions of therapeutic personality change. *Journal of Consulting Psychology,* 1957, 21, 95-103.

Rogers, C. R., Gendlin, E. T., Kiesler, D. J., and Truax, C. B. *The therapeutic relationship and its impact: a study of psychotherapy with schizophrenics.* Madison: University of Wisconsin Press, 1967.

Rogers, C. R. and Truax, C. B. The therapeutic conditions antecedent to change: a theoretical view. In C. R. Rogers, E. T. Gendlin, D. J. Diesler, and C. B. Truax, *The therapeutic relationship and its impact: A study of psychotherapy with schizophrenics*. Madison: University of Wisconsin Press, 1967, Pp. 97-108.

Shapiro, J. G. Consistency in the expression of emotion. Unpublished doctoral dissertation, Pennsylvania State University, 1965.

Shoben, E. J. Some observations on psychotherapy and the learning process. In O. H. Mowrer (Ed.), *Psychotherapy: theory and research.* New York: Ronald Press, 1953.

Truax, C. B. A tentative approach to the conceptualization and measurement of intensity and intimacy of interpersonal contact as a variable in psychotherapy. *Discussion Papers,* Wisconsin Psychiatric Institute, University of Wisconsin, 1962, 25 (b).

Truax, C. B., and Carkhuff, R, R, *Toward effective counseling and psychotherapy: training and practice.* Chicago: Aldine, 1967.

Truax, C. B., Carkhuff, R. R., and Douds, J. Toward an integration of the didactic and experiential approaches to training in counseling and psychotherapy. *Journal of Counseling Psychology,* 1964, 11, 240-47.

Truax, C. B., Carkhuff, R. R., and Kodman, F. Relationships between therapist-offered conditions and patient change in group psychotherapy. *Journal of Clinical Psychology,* 1965, 21, 327-39.

Truax, C. B., and Mitchell, K. M. Research on certain therapist interpersonal skills in relation to process and outcome. In A. E. Bergin and S. L. Garfield (Eds.), *Handbook of psychotherapy and behavior change.* New York: Wiley, 1971. Pp. 299-344.

Truax, C. B., and Wargo, D. G. Psychotherapeutic encounters that change behavior: for better or for worse. *American Journal of Psychotherapy,* 1966, 22, 499-520.

Truax, C. B., Wargo, D. G., Frank, J. D., Imber, S. D., Battle, C. C., Hoehn-Saric, R., Nash, E. H., and Stone, A. R. The therapist's contribution to accurate empathy, nonpossessive warmth, and genuineness in psychotherapy. *Journal of Clinical Psychology,* 1966, 22, 331-34.

5

Major Process Systems for Analyzing Patient Interview Behaviors

The systems presented in this chapter focus on measuring one or more aspects of patient behavior in psychotherapy interviews. Three of the systems are multidimensional (Bordin; Gottschalk and Gleser; and Hall and Van De Castle), two focus on assessing unitary patient variables (Klein et al.; Truax). Four systems involve ordinal measurement in the form of one or more rating scales. The fifth (Hall and Van De Castle) is a category (nominal) system for content analysis of patient dreams.

Gottschalk and Gleser's scales are oldest, appearing in 1961; Hall and Van De Castle's system was published in 1966; Klein et al.'s and Truax's in 1967; Bordin's in 1968.

One of the systems (Hall and Van De Castle) was empirically derived within a psychoanalytic framework, two were quite directly derived from psychoanalytic theory (Bordin; Gottschalk and Gleser), and the remaining two directly from Rogerian theory (Klein et al.; Truax).

Before presenting these five major systems, it seems appropriate to describe several prominent forerunners that dominated content analysis of psychotherapy in the 1950s. These systems have since become much less influential, and appear to be becoming obsolete. A brief look at these early systems will provide some perspective for patient interview measurement.

By far the most influential of the early measures of patient interview behavior was the Discomfort-Relief Quotient (DRQ) of Dollard and Mowrer (1947). The measure was derived from a form of learning theory which states that responses are incited by drives and reinforced by drive reduction. Since the learning of new habits is accompanied by drive reduction, the new learning that occurs in successful therapy ought to be accompanied by a reduction in drive. The DRQ is an attempt to measure the momentary drive state of the patient in therapy. Each word is first classified as drive-discomfort (suffering, tension, pain, unhappiness), reward-relief (comfort, satisfaction, enjoyment), or neutral (neither discomfort nor relief). For a particular patient speech sample, the DRQ is calculated by dividing the number of patient words indicating discomfort or tension by the number of words indicating discomfort plus the number of words indicating relief or tension reduction. Since Dollard abandoned the measure before developing his 1959 process system (with Auld, see above, Chapter 3), the measure has gradually dropped out of sight in psychotherapy literature. For a time, however, the measure appeared quite promising.

Another popular measure was Raimy's (1948) Positive-Negative-Ambivalent Quotient (PNAvQ). Raimy's measure, independently developed, was similar in structure to the DRQ. Whereas the DRQ included all statements of the patient, Raimy's quotient was restricted to statements of the patient about himself, and was considered an index of his positive and negative emotional reactions. The quotient is calculated from classifications of patient sentences as representative of positive, negative, or ambivalent feelings about himself. According to the rationale, successful patients should show, over therapy, an increase in positive statements about himself and a decrease in negative statements. PNAvQ apparently has also disappeared from the literature.

Finally, Mahl (1956) developed a method of investigating momentary anxiety in patients by measuring various paralinguistic aspects of patient speech. He was originally interested in two general aspects of patient speech: hesitancies and silences, and disturbances in speech. Because of complications with the silence measure, Mahl has since discontinued its use. He has retained his interest in the speech-disturbance ratio, for which he identified eight types of speech disruption in interview protocols, among them the "ah" sound, repetitions, stuttering, tongue slips, and omissions. By assessing these eight categories for two-minute samples of patient speech, Mahl calculates a Speech-Disturbance Ratio (later referred to as the Non-Ah ratio). The ratio represents the number of speech disturbances divided by the number of words spoken by the patient. Mahl (1959; 1959b) summarized investigations to that date providing evidence for the validity of the Non-Ah ratio as a measure of anxiety.

Currently, the DRQ, PNAvQ, and Non-Ah quotients seem to be of historical interest only. Construct validity evidence for each has been equivocal, and investigators seem to have lost interest in pursuing the measures further. Each generated much interest and excitement in its time, and they deserve a place as the "granddads" of patient process measurement in psychotherapy.

References

Dollard J., and Mowrer, O. H. A method for measuring tension in written documents. *Journal of Abnormal and Social Psychology*, 1947, 42, 3-32.

Mahl, G. F. Disturbances and silences in the patient's speech in psychotherapy. *Journal of Abnormal and Social Psychology*, 1956, 53, 1-15.

________. Exploring emotional states by content analysis. In I. Pool (Ed.), *Trends in content analysis*. Urbana: University of Illinois Press, 1959. Chap. 3. (a)

________. Measuring the patient's anxiety during interviews from "expressive" aspects of his speech. *Transactions of the New York Academy of Sciences*, 1959, 21, 149-57. (b)

Raimy, V. C. Self-reference in counseling interviews. *Journal of Consulting Psychology*, 1948, 12, 153-63.

The Free Association Scales

Edward S. Bordin

1. Rationale for Development of the Scales

With the development of the Free Association Scale, Bordin continues his long-term interest in investigating the psychoanalytic interview (see his Depth of Interpretation Scale, Chapter 4). He became increasingly interested in the role of therapist ambiguity in psychotherapy, and this interest led him into a further examination of the psychic processes involved in free association.

Bordin's working assumption is that observations of the capacity to free associate will prove highly indicative of the person's mental health.

> The psychotherapist (the psychoanalytic one, at any rate) sets a task for his patient, which if he were able to perform it fully adequately, would demonstrate that he was not in need of psychotherapy. . . . [This would represent] a state in which the person is able to experience a free flow of ideas accompanied by rich affect all of which are available for expression. In short, he associates freely. (Bordin, 1963, p. 5)

In other words, to the extent that the patient can follow the Basic Rule of psychoanalysis, to free associate, to that extent the patient's functioning moves toward normal. "Were it possible to calibrate differences in adequacy of response to the task of free association, we will have established an important foundation for the accumulation of a network of evidence on which the study of personality changes in psychotherapy must be based." (p. 5)

Bordin's conceptualization leans heavily on Bellak's (1961) description of the free-associative process. Bellak emphasizes that

> . . . the person be given the maximim opportunity to experience himself, to hear the inner messages emitted in response to his relaxed posture, and the echoes of remote of immediate past experience. All these in turn act as stimuli for new experiences. This chaining of experiences amounts to the analysand's filling the external void with his internal environment. . . . The instruction to say whatever comes to mind without selection or concern for its meaning or appropriateness is an invitation to relax these functions–perceiving, reasoning, etc., that we exercise in adapting to reality. This is an invitation to regress to that earlier mode of experiencing that Freud termed primary process. . . . The best working analytic patient is able to oscilate between regression and increased adaptive functions while exercising the synthetic functioning, and thereby producing new insights, working through and reintegrating previous appreceptive distortions. (p. 14)

In short, the analysand regresses "in the service of the ego." (Bordin, 1963, pp. 6-7)

Bordin's basic goal, then, was to develop a scale that would measure individual differences in a psychoanalytic patient's ability to perform the basic task of psychoanalytic therapy, that is, to free associate.

2. *Description of the Scales*

Bordin's first scaling attempt involved a single six-point scale tapping the ability to free associate. Table 5.1 presents this and subsequent subscales developed. This original scale ranged from a low point of severely blocked association, through uninvolved listing, little-involved light conversation, relaxed-animated conversation, and mixed conversation, to the high point of loose-free association. However, application of the scale revealed that it was not unidimensional. Bordin (1963) attempted to evolve purer dimensions that were embedded in the descriptions of his original scale. "The three part characteristics of free association we identified are involvement, spontaneity, and freedom. Each was differentiated into a five-point rating scale." (p.8)

Bordin's current free-association scale consists of three five-point subscales shown in Table 5.1.

> *Involvement* is evaluated in terms of the person's attitudes toward what he is saying. It includes the range of feelings, sorrow to joy, but excludes anxiety and tension. It is intended to reflect that aspect of acting and experiencing in which drive expression plays an important part. It differentiates those who can permit and achieve an integration between ideation and affect from those who maintain a separation between the two, often, as in the case of the intellectualizer, giving the superficial impression of being able to plumb the depth of their experience. (pp. 8-9)
>
> *Spontaneity* attempts to capture that aspect of expression that deals with the chaining of memories. Formal communications, whether written or spoken, are the products of a great deal of planning and reorganization of the person's original experience of the ideas and affects expressed. They are amplified and ordered to fit the context of the audience and the requirements of syntax. The requirements of free association call for communication of ideas as they are initially experienced rather than in this reworked form. (p. 9)
>
> *Freedom* concerns itself with "an aspect of tension and anxiety as it is displayed in the opposite to freedom, namely, guardedness and inhibition." (p. 9)

Besides the overall six-point scale and the three subscales, the author provides a system for rating six content categories. Each interview is given a primary rating (what category the predominant portion of the interview fits in), as well as secondary ratings when applicable. The six categories include the following groups: inability to talk-silence, communications primarily about the task, communications primarily about discrete immediate environmental stimuli, communications about interpersonal experience, and communications primarily about abstract ideas.

3. Data Collection Context

Bordin (1963) decided to study the free-associative process in an experimental interview situation "to avoid the necessity, even were the opportunity made available, of intruding into the highly charged personal nature of an ongoing psychoanalysis." (p. 7) The analogue situation further permits him to investigate the parameters of therapist ambiguity as they affect free association, which was his original interest. Male college students were the subjects of these studies involving thirty-minute experimental sessions. The study is structured to the subjects as one "of different methods of measuring personality" in which will be included "an interview such as is often conducted in psychotherapy." (p. 7)

The instructions given to the subjects were: "What we are going to do here is conduct a session similar to those sometimes used in psychotherapy. It will be about thirty-minutes long, and what you are to do is say whatever comes into your mind, even if it seems trivial, irrelevant, unpleasant, or not the kind of thing you would customarily say in polite society. Lie back and begin." (Bordin, 1966, p. 196)

4. Data Form

Data to which the scale is applied take the form of tape recordings of these thirty-minute experimental interviews as well as typescripts made from the recordings. Judges made their assessments while simultaneously listening to the tape recordings and reading the transcripts before them.

5. Choice of Units

The unit scored is apparently the total thirty-minute session. Raters are instructed to "listen to at least ten minutes of the tape, four at the beginning and end and two in the middle, while following along with the transcripts. They are encouraged to listen more when in doubt or to sense more fully some significant passages." (Bordin, 1966, p. 201) The subject receives an overall score for the six-point scale as well as for each of the three subscales. The general rating is done first, then the three part scores, while ratings of content can be made at any point.

Apparently, then, the "scoring," "contextual," and "summarizing" units are identical. The scoring unit is the patient's verbalizations during the total thirty-minute session; the context in which the ratings are made is the contents of the total thirty-minute session; and the score used in data analysis is the average of judges' independent FA ratings for the total thirty-minute session.

6. Participant-Context Restrictions

In Bordin's experimental interview, the therapist is mostly silent; if he speaks, he is restricted to repeating the task structure for the subject to say whatever comes into his mind. The problem of the effect of the therapist's verbalizations on the subject's communications is of little relevance in that situation. However, if the scale were to be applied to live psychotherapy interviews, whether the therapist's communications should be deleted or left intact becomes more crucial, and would have to be empirically assessed.

7. Type of Sampling Indicated

One can conclude that there is no sampling of the basic raw data since raters are permitted to audit the entire thirty minutes. However, the instructions to listen to at least ten minutes at clearly prescribed points within the experimental interview put whatever sampling this entails under the stratified rubric. It might be useful if Bordin considered the effects on his ratings of alternate stratified procedures (for example, including larger chunks from the middle of the session) as well as of a random sampling approach. These issues would be increasingly important if the scale is later applied to recorded psychoanalytic therapy sessions.

8. Sample Location Within the Interview

The comments above refer primarily to Bordin's experimental interview. If the scale is subsequently applied to psychotherapy sessions, the problem of sample size and location within the hour will become quite important. It will likely be impossible, and certainly uneconomical, to rate every minute of every psychotherapy session. Some kind of sampling will become necessary, and it will become crucial to compare random versus stratified sampling as well as differential effects of sampling from various time points (early, middle, late) within a particular session.

9. Sample Location over Therapy Interviews

Again, if the scale is to be applied to a series of psychotherapy interviews from initiation of therapy to termination, it will be necessary to assess the problem of differential effects of sampling from various time points over the sequence of interviews (early, middle, or near termination) on the scale scores obtained.

10. Clinical Sophistication of Judges

The judges who have applied the scale have been advanced students in clinical psychology "all of whom have had diagnostic and psychotherapeutic experience." (Bordin, 1966, p. 202) The differential effects on the ratings obtained of using clinically naive or even more clinically sophisticated judges has not been assessed.

11. Training Required of Judges

The training procedure has not been described in detail, but it seems to involve the judges' practicing with the scale on six to twelve trial interviews. When the judges reach a "satisfactory" level of agreement, they are ready to begin rating experimental tapes. "In the latter (six) trials we have obtained average percentage of agreement of 0.75." (Bordin, 1966, p. 202)

12. Training Manual

A training manual outlining standardized procedures for training judges to learn and apply the free-association scales is not available. The beginnings of a manual are currently in the form of a dittoed sheet of instructions for rating interviews and rating conventions. Copies of this sheet containing the instructions and the rating scales themselves are available from Bordin.

13. Interrater and Intrarater Reliabilities Reported

Each experimental session receives a score for the six-point scale and a score for each of the three subscales. The score used in each instance has been either a consensus rating of the judges or the sum of the individual judges' ratings. The interrater reliabilities obtained have ranged from moderate to high. "Using Horst's (1949) method of analysis with five raters we have obtained reliabilities ranging from 0.68 to 0.93." (Bordin, 1963, p. 9) An alternate method of assessing reliability was to "compute the percentage of agreement for the raters by finding the ratio of agreements, taking two (raters) at time, to the total possible number of agreements. Knowing the number of scoring categories for each scale, one can compute the agreement expected by chance and, using the expected distribution for number of interviews on which all three agree, two out of three, and none, a chi-square can be computed." (Bordin, 1966, p. 202) Using this procedure in another study, Bordin obtained interrater agreements ranging from 53 to 85 percent. In most of the studies reported, each interview has been rated by at least three judges.

14. Dimensionality Considerations

Bordin consistently has been concerned with the dimensionality problem in the rating scales he has developed. His concern regarding the FA scale led to his development of three separate subscales. By attempting to pull out unidimensional components of the original FA scale, he hoped to identify independent attributes. If this extraction were successful, the subscale intercorrelations should approach zero. However, the obtained coefficients ranged from 0.42 to 0.68 among the subscales, and the three subscales correlate 0.62 to 0.88 with the original scale. "We were not very successful [in achieving independence]. At the same time, there is sufficient gap, especially in the case of spontaneity, between the common variance and the variance reflected in reliability to leave some room for a variance specific to each part characteristic." (Bordin, 1966, p. 203) He concludes: "Our three part attributes intercorrelate much more than is desirable to avoid unnecessary redundance, but not so greatly as to preclude any independent variance in each attribute. It does seem probable that the functional relationships among involvement, spontaneity, and freedom preclude the development of measures that vary with complete independence of one another." (Bordin, 1963, p. 9)

15. Validity Studies

Bordin has focused on scale development, unidimensionality analysis, scale revision, and assessment of interjudge reliability. He has embarked on a program of research focusing on the links between personality differences and free association, dissection of the psychic components of the free-associative process, and the influence of interventions on free-association. The rationale and plans for these studies are presented in his 1966 article. (pp. 204-207)

RELATED SCALES OR CONSTRUCTS

The major task for the psychoanalytic patient is to free associate. The nature of this task is spelled out further by analytic and neoanalytic writers who utilized the constructs of "insight," "working through," and absence of "resistances." To the extent, therefore, that Bordin's Scale is successful in assessing free association, particularly as defined by Bellak, it should be related to measures of these other therapy constructs. However, it is not possible to check this out; no major systematically developed scales are available for these other psychoanalytic constructs.

Furthermore, Bellak's definition of free association, which Bordin adopts, is conceptually similar to Rogers' (1958, 1959; Rogers et al., 1967) and Gendlin's (1962) constructs of Experiencing and its operational statement the Experiencing Scale (Klein et al., 1970). The two scales should show similar results. The same inference would apply also to Truax's Depth of Exploration Scale (Truax and Carkhuff, 1967) and to the Superficiality Ratio used by Pope and Siegman (1962).

References

Bellak, L. Free association: conceptual and clinical aspects. *International Journal of Psychoanalysis*, 196l, 62, 9-20.

Bordin, E. S. Response to the task of free association as a reflection of personality. Paper read at Seventh Internation Congress for Scientific Psychology, Washington, D. C., August 1963.

________. Free association: an experimental analogue of the psychoanalytic situation. In L. A. Gottschalk and A. H. Auerbach (Eds.), *Methods of research in psychotherapy*. New York: Appleton-Century-Crofts, 1966. pp. 189-208.

Gendlin, E. T. *Experiencing and the creation of meaning*. New York: Free Press of Glencoe, 1962.

Horst, P. A generalized expression for the reliability of measures. *Psychometrika*, 1949, 14, 21-31.

Klein, M. H., Mathieu, P. L., Kiesler, D. J., and Gendlin, E. T. *The experiencing scale: a research and training manual*. Madison: Wisconsin Psychiatric Institute, Bureau of Audio Visual Instruction, 1970.

Pope, B., and Siegman, A. W. The effect of therapist verbal activity level and specificity on patient productivity and speech disturbance in the initial interview. *Journal of Consulting Psychology*, 1962, 26, 489.

Rogers, C. R. A process conception of psychotherapy. *American Psychologist*, 1958, 13, 142-49.

________. A tentative scale for the measurement of process in psychotherapy. In E. A. Rubinstein and M. B. Parloff (Eds.), *Research in psychotherapy*. Vol. 1. Washington, D. C.: American Psychological Association, 1959. pp. 96-107.

Rogers, C. R., Gendlin, E. T., Kielser, D. J., and Truax, C. B. *The therapeutic relationship and its impact: a study of psychotherapy with schizophrenics*. Madison: University of Wisconsin Press, 1967.

Truax, C. B. and Carkhuff, R. R. *Toward effective counseling and psychotherapy*. Chicago: Aldine, 1967.

Gottschalk-Gleser Content Analysis Scales: Anxiety, Hostility, and Social Alienation-Personal Disorganization

Louis A. Gottschalk and Goldine C. Gleser

1. Rationale for Development of the Scales

The central rationale guiding the development of Gottschalk and Gleser's scales is relevant primarily to the first two of their scales, anxiety and hostility, both measures of patient affect states; it is of less relevance to their schizophrenic scale (social alienation-personal disorganization).

The authors had two goals in developing their scales. First, their intent was to develop measurement instruments of patient affect, conceptualized as state (momentary, transitory) rather than trait (relatively enduring and stable) conditions. Their working definition of affect follows:

> Affects are feeling states that have the attributes of quality and quantity. Affects and emotions have subjective, purely psychological components as well as physiological, biochemical, and behavioral concomitants. Continual mixtures of affects of relatively long duration occur and these constitute what is ordinarily designated as mood. Upon the background of mood, feeling states of relatively high intensity and variability may play, and these are generally referred to as emotions. Relatively smaller fluctuations of feeling states which occur irregularly are sometimes referred to, in a narrower sense, as affects. Since we are attempting to develop an instrument to measure immediate affect rather than the more prolonged feeling states usually referred to as mood, we do want to point out that we are not here equating affect with mood. (Gottschalk and Gleser, 1969, p. 14)

Their second aim was to develop objective measures of affects based on the content of patients' language.

> [Our aim] is to develop content categories which are as clearly defined as possible, so that scoring might be objective rather than intuitive and idiosyncratic, and might be based on literal rather than figurative assessment of content. (Gottschalk, Winget, and Gleser, 1969, p. 17)
>
> It is very important that those using the scales rely as much as possible on the literal or objective content of the language used by the subject. (Gottschalk, Winget and Gleser, 1969, p.28)

Thus, Gottschalk and Gleser's system focuses on the lexical, in contrast to formal or paralanguage, aspects of verbal communication. It provides "verbal behavior measures of transient affects . . . at the level of thematic content" (Gottschalk and Gleser, 1969, p. xii).

> This content analysis procedure is concerned with verbal communication of symbols or signs and, therefore, falls within the linguistic branch called semiotics. . . . Also, [it] is not limited to manifest content, that is, to the surface meaning of the content. It aims also to analyze the latent content, that is, the deeper layers of meaning embedded in the content. (Gottschalk, Winget, and Gleser, 1969, p. 1)

The authors take considerable pains to spell out the working assumptions for development of their affect scales.

> [1] The relative magnitude of an affect can be validly estimated from the typescript of the speech of an individual, using solely content variables and not including any paralanguage variables. (Gottschalk and Gleser, 1969, p. 15)
>
> [2] On the basis of verbal content alone, the magnitude of any one affect at any one period of time, is directly proportional to three primary factors: (*a*) the frequency of occurrence of categories of thematic statements; (*b*) the degree to which the verbal expression directly represents . . . the psychological activation of the specific affect; . . . (*c*) the degree of personal involvement attributed by the speaker to the emotionally relevant idea, feeling, action, or event. (pp. 15-16)
>
> [3] The degree of direct representation . . . of the specific affect in the verbal expression and the degree of personal involvement attributed by the speaker can be represented mathematically by a weighting factor. . . . Completely unconscious or repressed affect of any kind is considered, by our method of weighting, not to signify affect of high magnitude, but rather to amount to zero or no affect. (p. 16)
>
> [4] The occurrence of suppressed and repressed affects may be inferred from the content of verbal behavior by noting the appearance of a variety of defensive and adaptive mechanisms. . . . (*a*) affect or its associated ideation or behavior attributed to other human beings, (*b*) affect or its ideation or behavior occurring in subhuman animals or in inanimate objects, (*c*) affect and its equivalents repudiated or denied, and (*d*) affect and its equivalents acknowledged but reported to be present in attenuated form. (pp. 16-17)

[5] The immediate magnitude of an affect is considered to be approximately the same, whether the affectively toned verbal thematic reference is expressed in the past tense, present tense, or the future tense, as an intention, as a conditional probability, or as a wish. (p. 16)

[6] The product of the frequency of use of relevant categories or verbal statements and the numerical weights assigned to each thematic category provides an ordinal measure of the magnitude of the affect. . . .

[7] Individuals differ considerably in rate of speech, and the same individual may vary in rate of speech from one unit of time to another. (p. 17)

[8] Categories are assumed to be alternative ways of expressing the same psychological state at different times and in different situations, but they are not necessarily all used by a particular subject, regardless of the intensity of his affect. (p. 12)

Different persons have different preferred modes of expression. Certainly, in any one five-minute verbal sample, the subject is likely to utilize only a limited number of categories. (p. 11)

[9] Our approach to the problem of quantification has been to include both frequency and nonfrequency aspects of specific types of statements to assess *intensity*. This is accomplished by differentially weighting the specific content categories of a scale in proportion to the assumed intensity represented by statements classifiable in these content categories. The weights are initially assigned on the basis of clinical psychoanalytic theory and experience. They are later revised on the basis of further empirical studies where either comparisons of scores with other criteria or the results of predictive studies warrant a modification of the weights assigned to a content item within a category. Furthermore, linguistic lexical factors (such as comparative adverbs—"very," "much") are included as indicators of the magnitude of the psychological state and are given additional weight. (p. 10)

2. *Description of the Scales*

Gottschalk and Gleser's three scales, Anxiety, Hostility, and Social Alienation-Personal Disorganization, are presented in Table 5.2.

Their *Anxiety Scale* scans for indications of anxiety in six areas: death, mutilation, separation, guilt, shame, and diffuse or nonspecific anxiety.

> The type of anxiety this scale has been designed to measure might be termed "free" anxiety (in contrast to "bound" anxiety), which may manifest itself in the psychological mechanisms of conversion and hypochondriacal symptoms, in compulsions, in doing and undoing, in withdrawal from human relationships, and so forth. It is unlikely, however, that some aspects of bound anxiety are registered by our scale, particularly by means of those content items in the scale which involve the psychological mechanisms of displacement and denial. . . . There is evidence that our anxiety scores reflect not only the subjective awareness of anxiety from the conscious and preconscious level, but also the level of relevant autonomic arousal and the level of relevant postural and kinesic activity. (Gottschalk, Winget, and Gleser, 1969, p. 29)

The authors assume that "the subtypes of anxiety are of equivalent importance and relevance to the magnitude of overall anxiety of the subject and that they are therefore additive" (p. 30). Furthermore, since the scale is designed to tap immediate anxiety, the scores of an individual may fluctuate considerably from day to day, or hour to hour.

Gottschalk and Gleser have devised three separate *Hostility Scales*. As with anxiety, these scales were designed to assess the relative magnitude of transient rather that sustained affect.

> We have not thought of our approach as a direct measure of aggressive behavior. Since we have been primarily interested in assessing immediate and changing levels of affect, it is the anger component of the hostility concept which has invited our attention. In particular we have focused our interest on the direction of hostility, distinguishing between hostility directed away from the self, hostility directed toward the self, and ambivalently directed hostility. (Gottschalk and Gleser, 1969, p. 31)

For the *Hostility Directed Outward Scale*, the scoring categories

> are arranged on a continuum that varies from a denial of hostility, through references to anger without an object, to hostility toward a situation or infrahuman objects, and finally to varying degrees of hostility toward human beings. The latter subcategories range from expressions of mild dislike or criticism of an individual to stronger expressions of verbal aggression and physical violence. . . . In addition to the intensity continuum, ranging in weights from one to three, the scale includes levels of awareness of hostility. Statements that refer to the aggressive or hostile feelings

as having emanated from the speaker are classified as "overt" hostility directed outward. Aggression or hostility attributed to others as either active agents or passive recipients and the denial of hostile feelings, are classified as "covert." Statements in which the speaker alone is the recipient of the aggressive act are not scored on this scale. (Gottschalk, Winget, and Gleser, 1969, p. 62)

Our *Hostility Directed Inward Scale* is designed to measure transient and immediate thoughts, actions, and feelings that are self-critical, self-destructive, or self-punishing. (p. 93)

The thematic categories of the HDI Scale range in weight from one to four. A weight of one is given to statements about being painfully driven or obliged to meet one's standards or expectations, denials of hostility toward the self, or feelings of disappointment. A weight of two is assigned to verbal content in which the subject expresses a somewhat stronger feeling of deprivation, disappointment, lonesomeness, self-criticism or self-punishing attitude. A weight of three is given to references indicating a greater degree of depression or more intense criticism of the self or references to self-injury. The strongest weight, that of four, is given to all references indicative of the speaker's desire to die or attempts (with or without conscious intent) to kill himself. (pp. 93-94)

Verbal statements scored on the *Ambivalent Hostility Scale* are all themes about destructive, injurious, critical thoughts and actions of others (including situations and objects) toward the self. Our construct of ambivalent hostility pertains to statements by the speaker concerning hostility directed to him from sources outside himself. It . . . overlaps to some extent the constructs of both hostility directed inward and hostility directed outward, particularly the overt portion of the hostility outward scale. . . . The weights assigned to the content categories range from a numerical value of one (given either to denial of blame or to subhuman or inanimate agents acting hostilely toward the self) to a value of three (given to the four subcategories at the upper end of the scale which culminate in some other human attempting or threatening to kill the self. (p. 114)

The Social Alienation-Personal Disorganization (Schizophrenic) *Scale* can discriminate the relative severity of the schizophrenic syndrome and can also be used to discriminate schizophrenic from nonschizophrenic individuals. (p. 128)

The common denominations of the schizophrenic syndrome have

> been considered to be disturbances in the coherence and logicality of thinking processes and disturbance in human relationships, especially in the form of withdrawal, avoidance, and antagonism. Another principal characteristic of our working concept of the schizophrenic syndrome has been that it is a phenomenon quantitatively describable, that is, that there are relative degrees of severity of schizophrenia and that, in some schizophrenic individuals the severity can fluctuate considerably from day to day . . . [and] that the principal and characteristic features of schizophrenia—social alienation and personal disorganization—are present to varying extents in nonschizophrenic individuals, but not in such a continuous and/or extreme fashion. (Gottschalk and Gleser, 1969, pp. 40-41)

The scale contains five major groupings of categories: Interpersonal references, intrapersonal references, references to disorganization and repetition, questions or other references directed to the interviewer, and references to religious or biblical topics. This scale "was designed to measure a somewhat more enduring psychological state than those measured by our affect scales." (p. 84)

The authors are in the process of developing six additional content-analysis scales, all of which are in a relatively early stage of development. These include scales for measuring human relations, cognitive and intellectual impairment, achievement strivings, dependency and dependency frustration, health-sickness, and hope. They present the scales and their rationales in their scale manual (pp. 230-49). Because of their preliminary status, these six scales will not be considered further here.

3. Data Collection Context

The authors have primarily used a standardized, projective-type experimental interview to collect speech samples on which their scale ratings have been obtained.

> The principal method we have used to evoke speech has been to ask subjects to talk for five minutes, in response to purposely ambiguous instructions, about any interesting or dramatic personal life experience. This method of eliciting speech has been used in order to maximize the projective aspects of the human communication relationship, so that the speaker will be more likely to present evidence of his internal state rather than a reaction to cues from the interviewer. (Gottschalk and Gleser, 1969, p. 9)

The "Standardized Instructions for Obtaining Verbal Samples" are read aloud to the subject by the interviewer prior to turning on the tape recorder:

> This is a study of speaking and conversational habits. Upon a signal from me I would like you to speak for five minutes about any interesting or dramatic personal life experiences you have had. Once you have started I will be here listening to you but I would prefer not to reply to any questions you may feel like asking me, until the five-minute period is over. Do you have any questions you would like to ask me before we start? Well then, you may begin. (Gottschalk, Winget, and Gleser, 1969, p. 50)

During the client's task the therapist assumes an attitude of unresponsiveness, and makes a conscious attempt to keep any nonverbal cues at a minimum.

The authors, in using this standardized procedure, assume that "what the subject talks about during any one verbal sample depends in part on what psychological conflicts and feelings are being most prominently experienced at that time, that is, what feelings and conflicts are most highly aroused and focal at the moment" (p. 5).

The authors state further that "it is not necessary that a professionally trained person read the standardized instructions and operate the tape recorder. . . . The introduction of a technician in obtaining the speech samples . . . does not interfere in any discernible way with the validity and reliability of the scores obtained from the verbal samples, provided that the verbal samples in a particular study are all taken by the same person" (p. 6).

Finally, the authors have considered other data applications, and conclude that their content-analysis procedures can be applied to "interview material, psychotherapeutic, disgnostic, or otherwise"; to "dreams" (report of dreams, not to dreamer's associations to dream content); to "projective test data" (tape recordings of TAT responses); and to "written verbal samples" (at least ten minutes in length) (p. 15ff.).

4. Data Form

Typescripts made from the five-minute tape-recorded samples have been the primary form of raw data from which ratings are obtained. The authors present in their manual (Gottschalk, Winget, and Gleser, 1969, pp. 10ff.) extensive rules for preparing typescript verbal samples for coding. They report one study comparing differential effects on ratings of using various data forms: when the scorer only read a typescript of speech compared to when he read the typescript and listened to a tape-recording. The study suggests that "the reliability of a rater's judgments regarding anxiety made from small verbal samples is somewhat better when he listens to sound tapes of the speech while typescripts are read, than when he only reads the typescripts" (Gottschalk and Gleser, 1969, p. 254). However, the anxiety ratings made from the two different data forms intercorrelated 0.84. The authors conclude that these findings "tend to support a theory of the redundancy of lexical and vocal factors in speech, rather than an additive theory, on the expression and communication of the intensity of affects" (p. 256). Another study indicated that "affect scores obtained from ten-minute *written* verbal samples of 103 male college students . . . did not appear to be appreciably different (means and standard deviations) than comparable affect scores from spoken samples of a group of male college students" (p. 258).

5. Choice of Units

The basic typescript unit to be coded is "the clause, whether independent or dependent. . . . Instances where either the subject or predicate is omitted but is understood are considered as scorable clauses" (Gottschalk, Winget, and Gleser, 1969, p. 23). A sorter brackets off these clause units with diagonal marks on the transcript before the final transcript is reproduced and submitted to raters. Also a count is made of the number of words in the five-minute sample, which is used to obtain a correction factor. The authors provide rules for counting words in their manual (p. 12ff.). The basic "scoring unit," then, for Gottschalk and Gleser's system is the grammatical clause.

Often "a wider context than the clause to be scored must be considered" in the process of scoring particular clauses. "It may be necessary to take into account the clause immediately preceding and the one immediately following. . . . In still other subjects, the entire verbal sample needs to be considered, or relevant material will be omitted in the scoring" (p. 25). Evidently, then, the "contextual unit" for their ratings can include the contents of the entire five-minute sample, but seems to be more typically restricted to the clauses immediately preceding and following the scoring unit.

The authors do not specify their "summarizing unit." Apparently, the affect score typically used in data analysis is the average score for the total five-minute sample, calculated from judges' independent ratings of each of the clause units. They do caution that they "recommend using only verbal samples of at least 70 or more words. . . . The reliability of a language sample begins to decrease rapidly as the number of words drops under 100"(pp. 20, 26). Also, for particular studies, the authors recommend that the typed data either be broken down into equal temporal units (for example, two- or five-minute segments), or the units be based on the number of words spoken by one or both participants (for example, consecutive 500- word sequences).

6. Participant-Context Restrictions

Since only the subject's verbalizations are present on the five-minute verbal samples, one cannot directly assess the effect of the presence of the therapist on the affect ratings obtained. However, should the scales be applied to psychotherapy interviews, this issue would become important and would need to be empirically assessed. This seems particularly crucial in view of some of the authors' findings. "We do not know whether the content of verbal samples obtained without the presence of an observer differ in any significant way from those obtained by a trained technician. We suspect there may well be some subtle differences." (Gottschalk, Winget, and Gleser, 1969, p. 9) In one study, the findings tended to support the hypothesis "that the sexes behave differently with interviewers of different sexes or personalities, even when the interviews are extremely brief." (Gottschalk & Gleser, 1969, p. 267) "We have evidence that the personality and sex of the interviewer vis-a-vis the subject can have an effect on the overall level of affect scores obtained. . . . but it is difficult to distinguish between the effects of sex differences and other personality differences" (Gottschalk, Winget, and Gleser, 1969, p. 6).

7. Type of Sampling

Since the authors' raters assess the entire five-minute experimental sample, the issue of whether to sample randomly or systematically in psychotherapy does not arise. However, if the scales were to be used for rating psychotherapy interviews, sampling issues would be paramount.

8. Sample Location Within the Interview

The authors have not considered this issue. If the scales were to be applied to psychotherapy interviews, it would become important to determine what size sample is necessary and where in the interview the sample could be extracted in order to obtain affect ratings that would be representative of patient affect during a particular interview.

9. Sample Location over Therapy Interviews

The authors have not considered this issue. If the scales were to be applied to psychotherapy cases from initiation to termination, it would become important to determine the ranges of time points over the therapy interaction where one should sample in order to capture the trend of particular patients' affect over the therapy sequence.

10. Clinical Sophistication of Judges

The authors suggest that although clinically unsophisticated judges can perform the rating tasks, some caution is necessary in rater selection.

> While it is not necessary for a content analyst using these scales to be a psychiatrist, psychologist, social scientist, or even necessarily to be psychologically oriented, it is essential that persons trained to code verbal samples have adequate education, intelligence, and motivation to understand and use the assumptions and instructions. . . . In addition, some healthy degree of compulsiveness and the capacity to tolerate ambiguity are important attributes. (Gottschalk, Winget, and Gleser, 1969, p. 17)

The authors have not empirically assessed whether different degrees of clinical sophistication differentially influence the affect ratings obtained.

11. Training Required of Judges

In their manual the authors outline a relatively standardized procedure for judges to follow in order to learn to apply the scales. This involves studying the manual, becoming familiar with examples provided, studying the tabulation of the scoring of an experienced coder, studying previously scored verbal samples, scoring new samples and checking their scoring against others' to determine discrepancies, and attending coding conferences with other judges in which each verbal sample is reviewed clause by clause and all differences are thoroughly discussed (Gottschalk, Winget, and Gleser, 1969, pp. 17-18). "Training is considered adequate if the scores obtained on a sample of 30 or more cases correlate at least 0.80 with an experienced coder and if the average scores for the sample are comparable, indicating no bias in the overall application of the scale" (p. 18).

12. Training Manual

A manual is available. The authors provide a two-volume research and training manual (Gottschalk and Gleser, 1969; Gottschalk, Winget, and Gleser, 1969), which contains sections on theoretical background of the scales, detailed description of the various scales, rules for scoring the scales, instructions and standardized procedures for raters to follow, and various methodological and validity studies on the various scales.

13. Interrater and Intrarater Reliabilities Reported

The authors state, "we have adopted the routine of using the average of two independent (judges') scores for all our data." (Gottschalk, Winget, and Gleser, p. 20) Likewise, a correction factor is routinely applied to all scores: "Since our numerical indices of magnitude of emotion tend to vary with the number of words spoken per unit of time, it is deemed advisable to correct for this verbal-fluency factor . . . by adding 0.5 to the raw score obtained on an affect scale, multiplying by one hundred, and dividing by the number of words spoken." (p. 21) The authors present a formula for calculating this corrected score. Finally, "to reduce skewness the square root of this ratio is used as the final corrected score." (p. 22)

The authors typically use Cronbach et al.'s (1963) procedures for getting two reliability estimates: The reliability of scores using any one scorer (p^{2}_{xm}), and the reliability of average scores for any two independent raters ($p^{2}_{\bar{x}m}$). They state further that "there are no units such as items or other discrete stimuli that might be used to obtain an estimate of internal consistency within the 'test' itself" (Gottschalk and Gleser, 1969, p. 60).

> From time to time we have obtained estimates of the error variance attributable to coders and to occasions of scoring for each of our scales in order to determine whether any shift has occurred with the passage of time in the way the categories are interpreted. In this way we have attempted to maintain a "quality control" of the final scores used in our substantative research. (p. 51)

For the Anxiety Scale, on three separate samples of psychiatric outpatients, inpatients, and medical patients, on the six subscales, the p^{2}_{xm} coefficients ranged from 0.50 to 0.88, while the $p^{2}_{\bar{x}m}$ coefficients ranged from 0.67 to 0.94. For the total anxiety scores, the p^{2}_{xm} coefficients ranged from 0.73 to 0.86, while the $p^{2}_{\bar{x}m}$ values ranged from 0.84 to 0.93. The authors observe that the least reliable subscales are those for separation and shame anxiety (p. 53).

The same patient samples were used to obtain reliability estimates for the hostility scales. For the hostility outward scales, the p^{2}_{xm} coefficients ranged from 0.78 to 0.87, the $p^{2}_{\bar{x}m}$ values ranged from 0.88 to 0.94. For the ambivalent hostility scale, the corresponding values ranged from 0.76 to 0.92, and from 0.87 to 0.96; for the hostility inward scale, the coefficients ranged from 0.78 to 0.89, and from 0.88 to 0.94. The authors conclude that "the scoring reliability of the hostility scales is generally satisfactory. The scoring reliability of the overt hostility outward subscale is, however, sometimes a little low" (p. 56).

In discussing the Social Alienation-Personal Disorganization scale, the authors observe that only one coder has been used for most of the studies undertaken with the scale. However, in one study in which "logitudinal data were obtained over a nine-week period on 35 male and 39 female chronic hospitalized schizophrenics, two coders were employed. For the preliminary baseline data the two sets of scores were compared, and correlations of about 0.90 were found between coders." (p. 57)

14. Dimensionality Considerations

The authors have considered how the various affect scales are interrelated, as well as how the subcomponents of each scale are associated. In regard to the Anxiety Scale, in three separate samples, the six subscales "tend to be uncorrelated, and hence may be assumed to measure independent psychological components of anxiety." (Gottschalk and Gleser, 1969, p. 77) Intercorrelations obtained among the three hostility scales (outward, inward, ambivalent) indicate that "only the ambivalent hostility scale and the outward hostility scale are substantially correlated in a normative sample of individuals (0.41). There is, however, a small positive correlation (0.23) between scores on hostility inward and scores on overt hostility outward." (p. 88)

Another study looked at the intercorrelation of the various hostility scales with the total anxiety scale, on samples of employed personnel as well as psychiatric outpatients. The hostility inward scale correlated 0.35 and 0.64 with the total anxiety score; hostility outward, 0.39 and 0.35; and ambivalent hostility, 0.34 and 0.55. The authors conclude that "total anxiety is only moderately correlated with total hostility outward, hostility inward, and ambivalent hostility in the sample of employed personnel. . . . The total anxiety score is somewhat more highly correlated with hostility inward and with ambivalent hostility in the sample of psychiatric outpatients." (p. 93)

15. Validity Studies

The manuals summarize the authors' research. The methods have been used to investigate such psychophysiological processes as the relationship of anxiety, hostility, or other psychological states to pulse rate and blood pressure, galvanic skin response, oropharyngeal bacterial flora, skin temperature, phases of menstrual cycle, penile erections during dreams, plasma hydrosycorticosteroids, and plasma-free fatty acids in subjects who are awake or those who are asleep or dreaming. The relative levels of various psychological states have been explored in patients suffering coronary heart disease, essential hypertension, dermatologic inpatients, patients with neoplastic diseases of the chest, inpatients suffering progressive phases of terminal cancer, general medical patients as compared to general psychiatric inpatients or outpatients, patients with acute or chronic impairment of brain function. In addition, the scale has been used in psychopharmacological studies, and has been applied to psychotherapy interviews.

RELATED SCALES OR CONSTRUCTS

> Validity studies indicate that the measure of hostility directed inward correlates with the psychological constructs of "depression" and "fatigue" as assessed by adjective checklists; the depression and acute anxiety scores derived from the Wittenborn rating scales; the scores obtained from the Beck depression inventory, and a clinical depression scale devised by Gottschalk. It measures a psychological construct dissimilar to that measured by the Oken hostility scale and other assessment procedures designed to measure anger or outwardly directed hostility. (Gottschalk, Winget, and Gleser, 1969, p. 93)
>
> Witkin et al. (1966, 1968) have used our scales, particularly the shame and guilt subscales of our Anxiety Scale, to explore the relationship of these affects to certain cognitive and perceptual styles, namely, the field-dependent and field-independent classifications.

Anxiety Scale state ratings correlate positively, and to a low-moderate degree, with various measures of trait anxiety (such as MMPI Pt scale, Cattell's IPAT, etc.).

If it is presumed that more stable individual differences in anxiety also exist among persons, so that some persons react with more anxiety than others under a great variety of circumstances, then the scores on immediate anxiety would contain some variance attributable to the specific response in the particular situation. Only by combining scores from speech samples obtained under different conditions over a period of time could one expect to obtain an average score having considerable congruence with trait measures. (Gottschalk and Gleser, 1969, p. 103)

References

Cronbach, L. J., Rajaratnam, N.,and Gleser, G. C. Theory of generalizability: a liberalization of reliability theory. *British Journal of Statistical Psychology,* 1963, 16, 137-63.

Gottschalk, L. A., and Gleser, G. C. *The measurement of psychological states through the content analysis of verbal behavior.* Berkeley: University of California Press, 1969.

Gottschalk, L. A., Winget, C. N., & Gleser, G. C. *Manual of instructions for using the Gottschalk-Gleser content analysis scales: anxiety, hostility, and social alienation-personal disorganiation.* Berkeley: University of California Press, 1969.

Witkin, H. A., Lewis, H. B., and Weil, E. Shame and guilt reactions of more differentiated and less differentiated patients early in therapy. Paper read at the Annual Meeting of the American Psychological Association, New York City, 1966.

———. Affective reactions and patient-therapist interactions among more differentiated and less differentiated patients early in therapy. *Journal of Nervous and Mental Disease,* 1968, 146, 193-208.

The Content Analysis of Dreams

Calvin S. Hall and Robert L. Van De Castle

1. Rationale for Development of the System

Hall and Van De Castle were perplexed at the dearth of quantitative approaches to the study of dreams, particularly since dreaming took a central position in psychoanalytic psychotherapy theory. They noted that Freud and others "have advanced different theoretical interpretations of what constitutes the hidden message within dreams, but the methodology of investigating dreams has remained fixated at a qualitative stage of development." (Hall and Van De Castle, 1966, p. ix)

The giant informational strides forward in the physiological domain have greatly outpaced the contributions forthcoming from psychological studies. (p. 26)

Since the discovery of the objective indicators of dreaming by Aserinsky and Kleitman (1953) . . . it is now known that every individual dreams; he actually spends approximately twenty percent of his sleeping time engaged in dreaming. The pattern of dreaming is cyclical one throughout sleep. Dream periods occur with surprising regularity, their timing being such that approximately ninety minutes elapse between the onset of each successive dream period. Their duration may range from a few minutes to as long as an hour, and they tend to increase in length as sleep progresses. (p. 25)

Research efforts on the psychological aspects of dreaming have been hobbled because of a dearth of suitable measurement devices for dealing with the material of the dream in any objective or quantitative fashion. There have been only a few scattered attempts by others to construct scales for scoring dreams and these have, for the most part, dealt with isolated dimensions. . . . What is needed is a comprehensive scoring system which will encompass within its purview all the main features of the dream. It has been our intent to provide such a system. (p. 26)

The hypothesis might be offered that no radically new approaches were possible as long as attention was focused exclusively on the latent content of dreams. . . . We feel that the time for a new approach, a quantitative one based upon analysis of the manifest content, has arrived. (p. ix)

The main contribution of this book is . . . a methodological one. For the first time, a comprehensive system of classifying and scoring the contents of reported dreams has been described and made available to the dream investigator. (p. x)

We fully anticipate in the years to come that objective dream analysis will verify many current hypotheses regarding personality as well as reveal new dimensions of man. We are committed to the belief that dream analysis is one of the most powerful tools for comprehending the dynamics of human behavior. (p. 238)

2. Description of the Scoring System

For Hall and Van De Castle (1966), a dream "may be operationally defined as that which a person reports when he is asked to relate a dream, excluding statements which are comments upon or interpretations of the dream." (p. 18) Again, a dream is "anything that a subject said following 'I dreamed. . . .' " (p. 11)

> The classification system that we are presenting . . . is primarily an empirical one, although we will also describe several theoretical scales. It has been our intention to make the system a comprehensive one so that it would be possible to score virtually all aspects of a dream. We wanted it to be empirical and comprehensive so that it could accommodate itself to many different kinds of research on dreams. (p. 28)

Their final scoring system consists of sixteen different empirical scales and three theoretical scales. It is presented in Table 5.3. With the empirical categories, the authors score "the physical surroundings in which the dream takes place, the characters in the dream, the various activities they engage in, what environmental events befall the characters, and how they felt about what happened to them" (p. 115). "The broad empirical classes are settings and objects; characters; their activities and interactions with each other and with the environment; their emotions; and the qualities and attributes which are used to describe people, things, and events." (p. 28)

The three theoretical scales attempt to measure the psychoanalytic constructs of castration anxiety, castration wish and penis envy; oral incorporation and oral emphasis; and regression.

> The formulation of classes was guided by the following considerations. (1) We did not begin to formulate any class within the broad headings until we were thoroughly conversant with dreams from having read and studied a large number of dream reports. (2) No class of items which was represented fairly frequently in dreams was omitted. . . . (3) We tried to choose classes that would reflect dimensions or aspects of personality that would appear in almost any theoretical position and which we thought would be considered relevant by any theorist. . . . (4) The classes should have a high degree of interscorer agreement. (p. 29)

3. Data Collection Context

In order to standardize their procedure, the authors decided on a very specific form of data collection, that of collecting dream reports. They did not want to collect a single dream from each subject since this often yields unusual or dramatic reports; not did they wish to analyze dream records from clinicians' files, which are likely to be biased. They rejected the procedure of continually awakening subjects throughout the night and tape-recording their dream reports following each REM awakening. They were looking for a procedure that would have much more general research applicability. They decided to focus their content-analysis system on "written dream reports recalled (by the subject) in the morning after arising" (Hall and Van De Castle, 1966, p. 31), and have used this context in all later studies.

Chapter 14 of the authors' manual presents normative data on the frequency of occurrence of the various dream elements obtained from samples of one hundred males and one hundred females between the ages of 19 and 25, all undergraduates at either Western Reserve University or Baldwin Wallace College between 1947 and 1950. These subjects wrote their dreams on the standard form, and turned them in (each folder containing a series of twelve to sixteen dream reports) as part of an optional class assignment. The authors selected a restricted random sample of five of the dreams of each subject which met the criterion of being between 50 and 300 words in length. The resulting one thousand dream reports were then analyzed by means of the various content scales. "These norms should be appropriate for dream series collected in a similar fashion from college students. They may not be appropriate for single dreams because when a person is asked to report just one dream, he usually relates one that has some unusual or outstanding quality, or one that possesses strong emotional intensity." (pp. 158-59) Also, in a separate publication, Hall (1963a) presents a listing of 868 of the dream reports collected on his normative sample. The actual dream reports given by the subjects are printed *in toto* and made available for inspection and use by other investigators.

4. Data Form

The basic data to which the scoring system is applied is the report of the dream by the subject, written by the subject on a standard form. The subject's report is subsequently typed on 5 x 8 cards, with his explanatory comments in parentheses. Judges applying the scoring system rate the typewritten cards, and record their scores on a scoring card.

Hall reports (1963a) that the following instructions were used:

> "On the inside page, you are asked to write down your dream in as complete detail as you are able to. Do not abbreviate the dream. Report it as fully as you recall it. After you have recorded the dream, you are then asked to interpret it. Think about its meaning and write down your explanation of the content in the space

> provided. Then answer the questions on the back page. Record only one dream on a page." On the back page, the student was asked (1) to identify each person in the dream as to sex, approximate age, and relationship to the dreamer, (2) to describe his feelings and emotions during the dream, (3) to say whether he was a participant or observer, (4) to tell whether the dream, on the whole, was pleasant, unpleasant, neither, or both, (5) to describe the setting of the dream, (6) to say whether he had the same dream before, and (7) to specify any colors that appeared in the dream. (p. i)

In the 1966 volume, Hall and Van De Castle modified these instructions:

> After having experimented with several types of forms used for recording dreams, we have come to prefer a 5x8 card, for this purpose. An advantage of having dreams recorded on this size card is the great ease of storing and filing them. They are also a convenient size to work with when scoring. The following instructions are printed at the top of the card: (Name, Date of Dream, Place, Date of this Report, Age, Sex), and then: "Please describe the dream exactly and as fully as you can remember it. Your report should contain, whenever possible, a description of the setting of the dream, whether it was familiar to you or not, a description of the people, their sex, age, and relationship to you, and of any animals that appeared in the dream. If possible, describe your feelings during the dream and whether it was pleasant or unpleasant. Be sure to tell exactly what happened during the dream to you and the other characters. Continue your report on the other side and on additional cards if necessary." (p. 313)

The authors have not considered the differential effects on dream scores of coding subjects' written reports and audio or videotaped reports. The nature of their scoring categories probably restricts the system to typescript data. In terms of wider applicability of the system to psychotherapy interview dream reports, it would seem useful to examine the limits of applicability of the system to audio and videotaped formats, and/or to consider possibilities of modifying the system for these purposes.

Hall et al. (1966) have empirically assessed the differential effects on dream scores of collecting dreams from subjects in the sleep laboratory in contrast to subjects recalling the dream at home upon awakening. Their study found that

> dreams reported at home differed in content from dreams report-

> ed after REM period awakenings in the laboratory. The major difference was that of dramatic quality. Home dreams tended to be more dramatic, laboratory dreams more prosaic. . . . Few overt sex dreams with or without accompanying emissions are reported in the laboratory. . . . [However,] home dreams were no more bizarre than laboratory dreams; [and] the proportion of laboratory dreams and home dreams with color in them was the same. (pp. 46-49)
>
> [On] the basis of studies of NREM dream reports . . . it appears that they are even more prosaic than reports from REM periods. Therefore, had we sampled NREM stages of sleep, the differences between home and laboratory dreams should have been even more pronounced. . . . The most that can be said for the present is that there are three different samples of dreams—home dreams, REM dreams, and NREM dreams. A closer examination of dreams obtained from various NREM stages, as well as from sleep onset and from sleep termination, might disclose several other samples in addition to the three enumerated above. (p. 45)
>
> [In conclusion] we do not know whether the sample of home dreams and the sample of laboratory dreams are drawn from the same or from different populations of dreams. We do not have much confidence that the question is even methodologically answerable. Sampling dreams throughout the night, whether at home or in the laboratory, requires awakening a person, and this condition may affect the contents of one's dream life. There seems to be no way out of this dilemma. Fortunately, failure to solve this problem . . . should not be a handicap to research on dreams as long as the investigator uses the same procedure for collecting dreams from all of his subjects. (p. 47)

5. *Choice of Units*

Hall asserts there is no best way to unitize dream protocols; rather the choice of unit depends upon the objectives of the investigator. He discusses in some detail alternative approaches to unitizing dream protocols in his 1966 paper (pp. 153-55). For Hall's system, the unit scored is the total dream report of the subject recorded on a 5x8 index card. The authors do not discuss or report data regarding individual dream productivity for subjects; that is, regarding individual differences in length of written dream reports, and the possible differential effects this productivity factor has on obtained dream scores.

The "contextual" and "summarizing" units are apparently identical to the scoring unit. The context for scoring each particular category of the system is the entire written dream report, since the judges consider the total report in making each category judgment. Similarly, the scores used in data analysis (summarizing units) are frequencies of occurrence of the various scoring categories for a given subject's dream report.

Regarding the serial scoring of a sample of dream reports, Hall and Van De Castle (1966) state that

> we generally prefer to score a unit of 50 dreams on each scale . . . [we feel it is] better to score across all 50 dreams for a particular scale, than it is to score across all scales for a single dream. . . . We would advocate that the sequence of (category) scoring follow the same sequence of scale presentation found [in our manual]. (p. 33)

> All of the scoring symbols consist of capital letters or marks that are found on a regular typewriter. Although over one hundred scoring symbols exist, . . . no duplication of a scoring symbol appears within or between any scale. Due to these features, it is possible to have the entire classification system punched on IBM cards and thereby take advantage of mechanical data processing procedures. (p. 35)

6. Participant-Context Restrictions

Since only the subject's written verbalizations are present on the cards which are scored, the problem of the effect of the therapist or experimenter's presence does not arise. If the system or some modification were applied to psychotherapy interviews (Hall, 1968), however, this issue would become crucial and would need to be empirically evaluated.

7. Type of Sampling Indicated

Since the scoring system is applied to the total written report of a single dream of each subject, problems of sampling do not arise. Moreover, it seems unlikely that sampling would ever be appropriate for a dream report since a veridical representation of a dream would seem to require the entire recalled content of the dream.

8. Sample Location Within the Interview

If the system can be applied in its present or modified form to dream reports spontaneously occurring in psychotherapy interviews (Hall,

1963; 1968), it seems apparent that one cannot randomly sample within a particular interview and expect to have a representative sample of dream reports occurring. Instead the researcher would be forced to audit the entire interview and extract the tape-recorded sections in which dream reports occur. It further seems unlikely that more than one dream report would occur in a single session.

9. Sample Location over Therapy Interviews

It would seem necessary in analyzing dreams in psychotherapy that the entirety of every interview session be edited and the sections recording patients' dream reports be extracted. The series of dream reports extracted from the entire series of interviews could then either be scored in its entirety, or sampled in some random or systematic manner. Of course, the differential effects of these various sampling procedures would have to be empirically established.

10. Clinical Sophistication of Judges

The authors do not explicitly discuss judge sophistication, but they seem to imply that the system can be applied by either clinically naive or sophisticated judges. They report no data on the comparative effects of using different judge samples.

11. Training Required of Judges

Hall and Van De Castle (1966) outline a relatively standardized procedure for judges to follow in order to learn and apply their scoring system.

> Before beginning to score for a particular scale, the description of the scale, the illustrative examples, and special rules for that scale should be thoroughly studied. After some familiarity with the scale has been developed in this fashion, the scorer should next attempt to score the dreams (ten dream reports).... By doing so, he can compare his scores with that listed for the dreams.... It may also be helpful to survey the normative figures contained in Chapter 14 so that an approximate idea of the frequency with which different subclasses appear can be gained.... Following these various "warmup exercises," the investigator should now be in a position to proceed with the actual scoring of his dream sample. After scoring a unit of 50 dreams, the careful researcher will rescore the first ten or so dreams of the unit to insure that the scoring set he evolved toward the completion of the unit did not differ from the one he had when he started the unit. (p. 34)

12. Training Manual

There is a manual. The authors' book provides the theoretical and methodological rationales for development of their scoring system, a detailed presentation of the scoring system with examples and rules for scoring, some recommendations for scorer training, data from reliability and validity studies, normative data for the various scoring categories, a review of dream-content analysis systems devised by others, and examples of scored dream series.

13. Interrater and Intrarater Reliabilities

In assessing interjudge reliability for their scoring system. Hall and Van De Castle (1966) consider two different perspectives:

> [We have to] be concerned with assessing how closely two judges can agree on the total number of scorable elements in a large sample. For each of the scoring classifications, we will report the total number of elements scored by each judge for a sample of either 50 or 100 dreams. Whenever possible we shall also try to report a correlation coefficient based upon ten pairs of judges' scores for the number of elements contained within units of five or ten dreams. These two figures, the total number of scores per judge and the correlation coefficient between the number of their scores, should provide an indication of how similar the frequency counts listed in the norms would have been if a different judge had scored them. (p. 148)

The data collected showed that the "correlation coefficients indicating agreement on the total number of elements present as well as the number of elements within separate classes were generally in the nineties. With coefficients of this magnitude it would have been possible to substitute one judge for another, as they obtained approximately equivalent scores" (p. 156).

The authors provide a second reliability perspective. "In order to demonstrate how similarly the judges score each individual dream, a percentage-of-perfect-agreement figure will be reported for each scoring classification. . . . The numerator will contain the number of scoring agreements, and the denominator will consist of the number of agreements plus the number of scoring disagreements" (pp. 148-49). The figures presented by the authors on perfect agreement "range from about 60 percent to 90 percent, depending on the complexity of the scale being scored" (p. 157).

The authors conclude that "the reliability figures described in this chapter for the various dream scales are generally higher than those reported for most projective techniques, and the authors feel that they are substantial enough to warrant their use in a broad spectrum of research studies" (p. 157).

14. Dimensionality Considerations

The authors do not discuss nor do they provide data regarding either the intercorrelations among their various scoring categories, or whether the particular scoring categories are assessing unitary constructs.

15. Validity Studies

Hall and Van De Castle (1966) suggest several research strategies for applying their system to research problems.

> These quantitative measures may . . . be employed in a variety of scientific enterprises. We will mention only a few. (1) The dreams of people differing in age, sex, ethnic group, pathology, or any other discriminable attribute may be compared for content classes and the significance of the obtained differences statistically evaluated. (2) The influence of natural or experimental variables upon dreams can be determined. For example, the investigator may wish to know whether the temperature of the sleeping quarters affects dreams. . . . Or if he wants to know whether some experience during the day can influence dreams that night. . . . (3) What changes in dreams take place over a period of time or during the course of psychotherapy? . . . (4) In what respects do dreams give the same, and in what respects do they give different, information from other devices used to assess personality? . . . (5) Does the behavior of the dreamer in his dreams correspond to his behavior in waking life? Does an aggressive person have aggressive dreams, and a depressed person depressed dreams? . . . (6) In order to test hypotheses derived from a particular personality theory, theoretical scales for analyzing dreams must be constructed which will measure the variables under investigation. (7) Finally, we would mention the tremendous scientific usefulness of appropriate norms for dreams expressed in numerical terms. Norms are almost a scientific *sine qua non* for any type of behavior research. (pp. 24-25)

The authors, and others, are continuing a systematic analysis of dream reports with their content-analysis system, investigating hypotheses derived from psychoanalytic theory as well as continuities between dreams and waking behavior and personality (Lind and Hall,

1970; Bell and Hall, 1971). A few of their findings will be presented as representative of the kinds of investigations being pursued. Apparently, the literature has not yet been summarized in a single source.

Hall (1963a) studied the Oedipus Complex as reflected in the dreams of 951 male and 966 female subjects ranging in age from two to twenty-six years. For the study he assumed that the earliest conception of the father as a resented and feared stranger is represented in dreams by male characters who are not known to the dreamer; and that the sleeping person dreams about people who are connected, directly or indirectly, with conflicts, frustrations, insecurities, anxieties, or other emotions which have their inception in early childhood. He formulated five hypotheses, four of which were confirmed by the content-analysis results:

> (1) More strangers in dreams are males than females. (2) There is a higher proportion of male strangers in male dreams than in female dreams. (3) There is a higher proportion of aggressive encounters by the dreamer with male strangers than with any of the following classes of dream characters: (*a*) female strangers, (*b*) familiar males, and (*c*) familiar females. (4) The proportion of aggressive encounters with male strangers is greater for male dreamers than for female dreamers. (5) When subjects are asked to free associate to male strangers who appear in their dreams, they will give more father and male authority figure associations than any other class of association (unconfirmed). (pp. 337-38)

The results supported Oedipal theory, and Hall concludes that "the male stranger in dreams often represents the young child's fantasy of the father as a hostile stranger."

Hall (1964) tested Freud's notion that the female superego is not as fully internalized as that of the male. He predicted that in their dreams, women would be more often the victim of aggression, and that men would more often suffer a misfortune. Content analysis of 3,049 dreams seemed to confirm the hypothesis.

Hall (1966) compared the dreams of four groups of male hospitalized mental patients (five patients both alcoholic and schizophrenic, fifteen alcoholic, twenty schizophrenic, and ten patients neither alcoholic nor schizophrenic) with each other, and with his male college normals' normative scores. Only three significant differences were found among the four patient groups: the dream reports of schizophrenics were shorter than those of nonschizophrenics; and alcoholics both had more dreams in which an oral incorporation occurred, and also had fewer sex dreams. The primary difference emerging between the patient and college samples was the smaller number of friendly interactions between the dreamer and female characters in patient dreams, suggesting that developmentally mental patients are deficient in establishing friendly relations with females. The patient group also exhibited a lower incidence of male characters in their dreams, suggesting that "mental patients may be more 'feminine' than normal males."

Hall and Van De Castle (1965) investigated whether sex differences would be found in incidence of manifestations of castration complex (CA), castration wish (CW), and penis envy (PE) in dreams. It was hypothesized that male dreamers will report more dreams expressive of CA than they will dreams involving CW and PE, whereas the pattern would be reversed for females. The hypothesis was supported for three different groups of college students (total $n = 120$) evenly divided as to sex. Additional data were also presented to show that many more women than men dream about babies and weddings, and that the relative incidence of the various castration components remains quite stable throughout a long dream series spanning seventeen years.

Hall and Domhoff (1968) studied whether their content-analysis system would reveal differences between Freud and Jung's reported dreams that would be congruent with differences reported in their biographies. Each of Freud's twenty-eight and Jung's thirty-one reported dreams were scored by their system, and the scores compared with each other as well as with the normative group reported in their manual. Among other things, the authors found that Freud's dreams had more characters and fewer animals, and Freud dreamed more about friends and acquaintances while Jung's dreams focused more on members of his family. The authors speculate these findings are consistent with the known facts that Freud was a more sociable person, with a social life centered more outside the family, while Jung was more solitary and socialized primarily with his immediate family. Some other findings were that Jung's dreams contain no references to money, whereas Freud dreamed of money about as often as the norm group; that every time Jung, in his dream, was involved in a friendly interaction, he initiated the friendliness; while Freud was more often the recipient of friendliness; and in regard to agressive and friendly encounters, Jung's with both men and women were fairly typical, whereas Freud had many more aggressive encounters with females (almost none with males) and had many more friendly encounters with men than with women.

Finally, Smith and Hall (1964) analyzed 649 dreams collected by a woman from 1912 to 1963 for regressive elements. They found that the incidence of regression in her dreams did not change significantly during this period of fifty years.

RELATED SCALES OR CONSTRUCTS

In Chapter 15 of their book, Hall and Van De Camp spend considerable time comparing their system to those of other investigators studying dream reports. They list and describe in detail the various scales developed.

References

Aserinsky, E., and Kleitman, N. Regularly occurring periods of eye motility and concomitant phenomena during sleep. *Science*, 1953, 188, 273-74.

Bell, A. P., and Hall, C. S. *The personality of a child molester: an analysis of dreams*. Chicago: Aldine, 1971.

Hall, C. S. *Dreams of American College students*. Lawrence: University of Kansas Publications, 1963. (a)

________. Strangers in dreams: an empirical confirmation of the Oedipus complex. *Journal of Personality*, 1963, 31, 336-45. (b)

________. A modest confirmation of Freud's theory of a distinction between the superego of men and women. *Journal of Abnormal and Social Psychology*, 1964, 69, 440-42.

________. A comparison of the dreams of four groups of hospitalized mental patients with each other and with a normal population. *Journal of Nervous and Mental Disease*, 1966, 143, 135-39.

________. Review of May-Caligor volume, "Dreams and Symbols." *Psychiatry and Social Science Review*, 1968, 2, 19-22.

Hall, C. S., et al. Studies of dreams reported in the laboratory and at home. *Monograph Series No. 1*, Santa Cruz, Cal.: Institute of Dream Research, 1966.

Hall, C. S. and Domhoff, W. The dreams of Freud and Jung. *Psychology Today*, June, 1968, 42ff.

Hall, C. S., and Van De Castle, R. L. An empirical investigation of the castration complex in dreams. *Journal of Personality*, 1965, 33, 20-29.

________. *The content analysis of dreams*. New York: Appleton-Century-Crofts, 1966.

Lind, A., and Hall, C. S. *Dreams, life, and literature: a study of Franz Kafka*. Chapel Hill: University of North Carolina Press, 1970.

Smith, M. E., and Hall, C. S. An investigation of regression in a long dream series. *Journal of Gerontology*, 1964, 19, 66-71.

The Experiencing Scale

Marjorie H. Klein, Philippa L. Mathieu,
Eugene T. Gendlin, and Donald J. Kiesler

1. Rationale for Development of the Scale

The authors' major goal in constructing the Experiencing Scale was to present a technique, derived from the client-centered framework "for evaluating the quality of a patient's self-involvment in psychotherapy directly from tape recordings or typescripts of the therapy session" (Klein, Mathieu, Gendlin, and Kiesler, 1970, p. 1). The continuum of experiencing involved is presumably "important for all forms of therapy where change in the patient's level of expressiveness, self-awareness, or self-understanding is a goal, or where self-attitudes are in any way manipulated as a part of the treatment procedure" (p. 1)–in other words for the various experiential-insight oriented therapies.

Rogers (1958, 1959; see also Walker, Rablen, and Rogers, 1960; Rogers, Gendlin, Kiesler, and Truax, 1967) spelled out in some detail the patient process behavior indicative of the changes in functioning that characterize a successful therapeutic relationship. In giving the experiencing construct a central role in his thinking, Rogers drew heavily on the earlier theoretical and research work of Gendlin (Gendlin and Zimring, 1955; Gendlin, Jenney, and Schlein, 1960). Although couched in phenemonological language consistent with their basic theoretical stance, the Rogers and Gendlin descriptions bear some similarities to the neo-analytical (Fenichel, 1945; Sullivan, 1965; Fromm-Reichmann, 1950; Alexander and French, 1942; Singer, 1965) constructs of "insight," "lack of resistance," and "working through." The upshot is that the ideal in-therapy behavior desired of a psychotherapy patient seems to encompass his ability to focus on and express freely the feeling, attitudinal, and meaning correlates of his behaviors and experiences; to compare, contrast, and integrate the affective and rational components of this complex; and to use this differentiated but integrated composite as an immediate referent for present and subsequent behavior, particularly in the interpersonal sphere. All this, of course, implies growth and change (Rogers, 1958; Gendlin and Zimring, 1955; Gendlin, 1962, 1964).

> Noting that most approaches tend to reify and slice the frozen moment of the interaction in therapy, Rogers tried to capture the dynamics of the processes occurring when a patient moves from remoteness, rigidity, and stasis to live fully and meaningfully in a changing flow of feelings. At the same time that he defined the steps of therapeutic progress and the sequence of personality change, he implied a view of optimal personality functioning which is the logical endpoint of the continuum.
>
> Rogers discussed seven closely related strands or aspects of process that characterized the patient's subjective state, internal organization, and readiness for change, with special emphasis on the way these are manifested in patient communication. *Communication of self* considers the patient's willingness to talk about

> himself and expose the full range of experiences and feelings that made up his self-conception. The *personal construct* strand deals with the rigidity of the patient's ideas about himself and the degree to which he feels responsible for shaping and changing them. *Relationship to problems* deals with the manner in which problems are defined and experienced, and *manner or relating* measures the patient's acceptance of interpersonal relationships, especially with the therapist, and the extent of his openness to his feelings in the interpersonal context. The dimension of *incongruence* is concerned with the completeness, integration, or degree of correspondence between the patient's experiences as apparent to an outside observer and his representation of them. The remaining two strands, *relationship to feelings* and personal meanings, and *manner of experiencing* deal with the quality of the patient's awareness, his acceptance of his feelings and his inner life, and the extent to which his inner awareness is used as the referent for thought and action. . . . Putting these process strands together to describe the course of change and growth that is possible in the open, accepting atmosphere of good psychotherapy, Rogers ascribed a central role to experiencing. The other process strands, while distinct at low process levels, are thought to merge or flow into the experiencing strand at high levels. (Klein et al., 1970, pp. 2-3)

The correlated changes outlined for the seven process strands specify the changes in internal functioning essential for personality change, and establish their sequence apart from the specific problems and content areas involved—in effect, define the optimally healthy person. Although different patients may start psychotherapy at different points on the continua, work over different ranges of the scale, work at different rates, or recycle through the various stages many times, perhaps taking up and resolving different problems and aspects of their lives, progressively more advanced levels of focusing are essential for progress in any area.

> The lowest stages of process are marked by the blockage of internal communication and an avoidance of feelings or conflicts that prevents growth and change. Moving along the continuum, the patient progresses through stages where feelings are partially communicated, at first reluctantly and indirectly as remote, externalized, or intrusive events, later more immediately and fully, to a point where the growing and sometimes distressing awareness of feelings and personal meanings culminates in the discovery of the self as an experiencing being providing a valid and distinct perspective. . . . Thus, at the very highest stages, the patient is

> living authentically as a fully functioning person. . . . Feelings and personal meanings are experienced accurately, with immediacy, and are steadily available as referents for thought and action. (pp. 3-4)

Rogers' main purpose in developing the process conception was to clarify his theory regarding the phenemonon of incongruence between awareness and experience, and to define the process of change from incongruence to congruence that was basic to his thinking about personality change. To do this the term "experience" had to be redefined as a dynamic process, rather than as a storehouse of events. This conceptual problem was in large measure solved by his use of Gendlin's definition of experiencing.

The Experiencing construct is a phenomonological statement of this ideal in therapy patient behavior. The Experiencing (EXP) Scale, its operational statement, evolved from Gendlin's formulation of experiencing (Gendlin and Zimring, 1955; Gendlin, 1962), from Rogers' global process scale (1958; 1959), and from the early form of the EXP Scale developed by Gendlin and Tomlinson (1961). The current EXP Scale (Klein et al., 1970) is a modification of the Gendlin and Tomlinson version, designed to reflect Gendlin's conception.

2. Description of the Scale

Experiencing refers to "the quality of an individual's experiencing of himself, the extent to which his ongoing, bodily, felt flow of experiencing is the basic datum of his awareness and communications about himself, and the extent to which this inner datum is integral to action and thought" (Klein et al., 1970, p. 1). The scale is a seven-point annotated and anchored rating device. Table 5.4 presents an abbreviated version of the scale and its stages (for the complete detailed form consult the training manual, Klein et al., 1970, pp. 56-64).

> At a low level on the contiuum of experiencing, discourse is markedly impersonal or superficial. Moving up the scale, there is a progression from simple, limited, or externalized self-references to inwardly elaborated descriptions of feelings. At higher experiencing levels, feelings are explored and emergent levels of experiencing serve as the basic referents for problem-resolution and self-understanding. Independent of specific pathology or problem content, and apart from details of therapists' technique, this scale attempts to assess the degree to which the patient communicates

> his personal, phenomenological perspective and employs it productively in the therapy session. (Klein et al., 1970, p. 1)

In developing the present EXP Scale, the authors attempted to preserve the integrity of Gendlin's conception, and tried not to deviate from the original scale developed by Gendlin and Tomlinson. However, the desire to standardize training altered the scale somewhat.

> Most changes are intended to direct the rater's attention to the patient's manifest verbalizations and reduce the need for rater inferences about the patient's motives, intended communication, internal state, health, or capacity for self-awareness. . . . The inference that the EXP Scale taps [Gendlin's experiencing] process . . . can be based on two assumptions: that the patient's manner of talking about his feelings and experiencing is a valid index of the quality of his experiencing; and that in the therapy relationship the patient must talk openly about his feelings and experiencing if the process of self-exploration is to be meaningful. (pp. 29-30)

3. Data Collection Context

The EXP Scale was designed for direct application to tape recordings or typescripts of psychotherapy interviews, and to date has been used primarily for this purpose. Available research suggests that the scale can serve a variety of needs.

> It is sensitive to shifts in patient involvement, even within a single interview session, making it useful for microscopic process studies, for example, to evaluate the effectiveness of therapist interventions, to assess the productivity of different topics, to appraise different patterns of interaction between patients and therapists, or to establish a profile of patient performance within the therapy hour. Sampling segments over a broader span of time could characterize trends of involvement during treatment or pinpoint special moments or phases in therapy (for example, when work was very good or resistance was high). Averaging discrete ratings over therapy as a whole or in part yields a gross estimate of the quality of the patient's work, making the scale suitable for comparing different groups or measuring change. To the extent that experiencing is relevant in nontherapeutic settings, the scale may also be used to evaluate other kinds of research interviews. (Klein et al., 1970, pp. 1-2)

4. Data Form

The EXP Scale was designed for direct application to audiotape-recorded segments (samples) of the therapy interview. Studies to date have primarily used tape recordings. Studies are currently under way by several of the authors to evaluate the differential effect of typescript, video, or audio-visual presentations as well on EXP ratings.

5. Choice of Units

Typically for the EXP Scale, the "scoring," "contextual," and "summarizing" units are identical, although in some studies the summarizing units used in data analyses are larger. The unit scored by judges is typically a four- to eight-minute tape-recorded segment extracted from therapy sessions and presented on three-inch tape spools. The contextual unit is the same time segment—judges are cognizant only of the content present on the four- to eight-minute sample, and have no other information about the case. Segments are edited for names and other identifying material before being presented to judges, and are presented to judges in a standard random order. In most studies, the basic summarizing unit has been the same four- to eight-minute sample, which provides an estimate of the trend of experiencing, either over a particular therapy hour or over the total therapy sessions. In other studies ratings of multiple four- to eight-minute segments are averaged over particular therapy hours or over the entire therapy case to provide estimates of overall level of patient experiencing.

As mentioned, the majority of studies using the Exp Scale have used segments of four- to eight-minute size, sampled from particular interviews. To determine the ideal segment length, in one study EXP ratings were compared for two-, four-, eight-, and sixteen-minute samples drawn from each of two therapy hours with eight normal, eight schizophrenic, and eight neurotic subjects.

> Only the absolute level of EXP rating was influenced by segment length. Longer segments received higher ratings presumably because they had more information value. The reliabilities, the range, and the discriminatory power of the ratings were independent of the length of the segment. Thus, while it would obviously be unwise to mix segment lengths in a given study, EXP ratings from short or from long segments are likely to differentiate among patients equally reliably. Our experience using the scale and working with raters suggests in general that segments of five to eight minutes

> provide enough material to identify high levels of EXP without becoming unmanageably complex or tedious. (Klein et al., 1970, p. 34)

6. Participant-Context Restrictions

EXP ratings made with and without therapist statements present on tape recordings have been compared and show virtually no difference between ratings made under the two conditions. This finding "suggests that EXP can be rated reliably from the patient's speech alone, but that similar ratings can be obtained when the therapist's speech is present, eliminating the need to edit. Of course, deleting the therapist's speech may be advisable in studies where the therapist's remarks are of special research interest or where there is reason to believe that they may seriously bias the EXP ratings" (Klein, et al., 1970, pp. 34-35).

To evaluate whether EXP ratings are confounded by temporal speech patterns of the therapist or patient, one study compared EXP ratings with Matarazzo and Saslow Interaction Chronograph (IC) measures taken from the same eight-minute segments of therapy for twenty-four cases.

> There was no evidence that the EXP ratings were systematically influenced by the amount or tempo of the patient's speech, by the amount or tempo of the therapist's speech, or by any other temporal characteristics of the interaction that were measured. . . . These findings were consistent with our intention that EXP ratings assess the quality of the patient's verbal expression independent of the rate of speech or formal characteristic of the therapy interaction. (p. 34)

7. Type of Sampling Indicated

The primary approach to sampling interview segments in EXP scale studies has been that of random sampling. A table of random numbers has been used to determine the time point in the interview where the various size segment transcriptions are to begin (for example, if the number from the table is 20, a four-minute sample extracted would begin twenty minutes into the interview hour and continue through the twenty-third minute). This random sampling approach was dictated from Rogers' theory which emphasizes the pervasive and cumulative nature of patient and therapist factors operating in psychotherapy. However, some studies suggest that alternate procedures of sampling should also be considered.

8. Sample Location Within the Interview

Several studies addressed themselves to the issue of where within the therapy hour one should extract segments of EXP ratings. In one study, EXP process ratings of four-minute segments were highly correlated with ratings of the hour as a whole, indicating the adequacy of a brief sample. Another study suggested that the issue may be complex. It considered differential effects on EXP ratings of sampling from various locations within particular interviews, as well as random versus systematic sampling, for samples of schizophrenic, neurotic, and normal cases. Twenty-four therapy hours, chosen from both early and late case interviews, were each divided into five successive eight-minute segments. EXP scores obtained for the three diagnostic groups were significantly different. Neurotic patients showed a consistently upward linear trend, so that they were talking most meaningfully about themselves near the end of the hour. Schizophrenics showed a sawtooth pattern, and normals an inverted U shaped curve. Next, two random samples were drawn from the same data and the results compared with that obtained from the five systematically obtained time blocks. Different profiles of significance were obtained: one random sample and the later time blocks reflected differences between groups; the other random sample and earlier time blocks did not.

> [In conclusion] random sampling may be superior in providing data more representative of the range of process in a given group and may afford more equitable coverage to several groups, provided that the number of observations is sufficiently large that the bias from unequal representation of certain interview points is minimized. Sampling of standard time periods may have more precision and offer better control of the time factor in small samples, but it may not always yield representative data, or data that can be readily interpreted without supporting information regarding the specific nature of intra-interview process trends. Thus, it is important to bear in mind that the precision of any systematic sampling is strictly contingent upon the amount of reliable information available to the researcher regarding trends in the population as a whole. (Klein et al., 1970, p. 33)

9. Sample Location over Therapy Interviews

Some EXP Scale studies have sampled only a few interviews over the total therapy (for example, one early, one middle, and one near termination), while others have sampled quite extensively by taking a sample from every therapy interview.

> As a general rule it is important to sample from at least two time periods in therapy, especially if EXP is to be considered in relation to criteria of outcome. Some of the past studies suggest that it is even more desirable to include samples from the midpoint or working phase of therapy. Sampling only initial and terminal hours risks missing the patient's actual work and progress, getting instead early routine arrangements, goal-setting, or self-descriptions or terminating material involving future plans, external details, a review of progress, or a period when defenses are deliberately reinstituted. Also, some studies have shown that we cannot expect a strictly linear trend for EXP, so the more samples taken from each case, the greater is the likelihood of getting reliable estimates of the variability, range, and trend of EXP. (Klein et al., 1970, p. 32)

10. Clinical Sophistication of Judges

The majority of EXP studies have used clinically unsophisticated, liberal arts undergraduate judges for EXP ratings. One study looked at this issue by comparing EXP ratings of the same tapes made by a group of clinical and counseling psychologists with ratings done by a group of undergraduate judges. "Correlations between the two groups of raters approach their reliabilities and the means were almost identical, indicating either that the sophisticated raters were not hampered in their use of the scale by theoretical reservations or personal biases, or that naive raters can be trained to professional competence in this skill" (Klein et al., 1970, p. 39). Apparently clinical sophistication is unnecessary for reliable and equivalent EXP Scale applications, and of course the economical savings from using naive raters are considerable.

11. Training Required of Judges

Detailed training instructions and procedures for the EXP Scale are presented in a standardized form in the authors' Research and Training Manual (Klein et al., 1970). Training involves eight two-hour sessions in which the judges study the scale, independently apply it to blocks of ten training tape segments, and compare their ratings to the criterion ratings for each segment, and respective rationales, presented in the manual. Comparison of each trainee's ratings with the criterion ratings can be done alone or in group discussion. Of the ninety tape training segments involved, the first seventy are used by the trainee to learn the scale, while trainees' independent ratings on the last twenty samples are used to assess whether adequate interrater reliabilities are occurring as well as to determine the degree of correlation of each judge's ratings with the criterion ratings for these twenty segments.

Availability of a standardized training manual together with the feasibility of using naive raters permits wide and easy application of EXP ratings by other investigators.

12. Training Manual

The authors have published a two-volume research and training manual which provides the theoretical derivation of the scale, methodological and validity studies, the rater training manual, ninety tape-recorded training segments on seven-inch reels, transcripts of these ninety segments, and criterion ratings and rationale for each of the ninety tape segments. The manual and training tapes are available from the Bureau of Audio Visual Instruction of the University of Wisconsin to any qualified mental health professional or researchers.

13. Interrater and Intrarater Reliabilities Reported

The EXP score given for each experimental segment is typically the average rating across all judges for a particular segment. In most studies at least three judges have independently rated each of the experimental segments, so that the score for a particular segment would be the average of the three EXP scores given for that segment. An alternative is to use the modal (most frequently occurring) rating of the three judges for the particular segment.

Judges make two EXP ratings for each experimental segment. A *modal* rating is the rating that characterizes the overall, general, or average scale level of the segment or unit. A *peak* rating is given to the highest EXP scale level reached in the segment or unit being rated. "We strongly suggest that mode and peak ratings be analyzed separately as they have given slightly different results in some studies." (Klein et al., 1970, p. 44)

Interrater reliabilities obtained in EXP Scale studies have generally been high. The statistical approach primarily has been Ebel's (1951) intraclass estimate which yields an estimate of the reliability of the means of the judges ratings (r_{kk}) and an estimate of the average intercorrelation of all possible judge pairs (r_{11}). The r_{11} values obtained in the various studies have ranged from 0.44 to 0.67, while the crucial r_{kk} coefficients vary from 0.76 to 0.91 (see Klein et al., 1970, p. 45).

14. Dimensionality Considerations

The authors have not empirically considered whether their scale is measuring a single dimension or whether several relatively independent subdimensions are operative.

15. Validity Studies

Detailed summaries of studies applying the EXP Scale can be found in the Research and Training Manual (Klein et al., 1970) as well as in Rogers et al. (1967). Various studies have examined the relationship of Experiencing in therapy to subsequent patient outcome measures, to level of therapist "conditions" (accurate empathy, positive regard, and congruence), and to diagnostic category as well as other personality and demographic factors.

Representative examples of findings with the scale are: (1) Experiencing clearly differentiates gross diagnostic groups' functioning in psychotherapy, with psychoneurotics attaining deeper (higher) levels than schizophrenics. This finding has consistently emerged both from exhaustive samplings *within* particular interview hours and *across* the therapy interview series. (2) *Level* of experiencing of patients in psychotherapy is related to outcome as measured by various independent criteria, with more successful cases showing higher levels of Experiencing at all stages of therapy. This finding has emerged for both psychoneurotic and schizophrenic cases. (3) Patients in therapy show reliable but non-monotonic (tends to be U-shaped) Experiencing *change* across therapy interviews, although to date no correlates of this change have been demonstrated. The evidence is against Experiencing change being an important component of successful therapy, although alternate sampling procedures might be considered before this conclusion is accepted as final. (4) Level of patient Experiencing is related to level of therapist "conditions" (particularly rated empathy and perceived congruence), in that patients of highly empathic and congruent therapists manifest higher levels of Experiencing in therapy. The direction of causality in this relationship is unclear at present. Interpretation is further clouded by the fact that these patient and therapist process measures both seem to be related to a constellation of patient trait variables (for example, verbal facility and productivity, sex and socioeconomic background) present before therapy is initiated, and to more successful outcome.

RELATED SCALES OR CONSTRUCTS

The construct of Experiencing is rather closely related to other therapy constructs such as insight, working through, absence of resistances, and high-quality free association. A scale quite similar in format and theoretical derivation is Truax's Depth of Self-Exploration Scale (see below, this chapter). The Superficiality Ratio used by Siegman and Pope (see above, Chapter 4) appears to be a gross estimate of patient experiencing. Bordin's Free Association Scale (see above, this chapter) contains elements quite similar to Experiencing, and is derived from Bellak's conceptualization which shows similarity to Gendlin's. The various resistance scales listed in Chapter 6 could be considered negative measures of insight or experiencing. Butler et al.'s and Rice's (see above, Chapter 3) patient categories are also conceptually and empirically close to experiencing.

More recently, Gendlin expanded the Experiencing construct and devised an experimental, instructional procedure to facilitate client "focusing," a construct very similar to Experiencing. His research program has concentrated on the physiological and personality correlates of focusing ability, primarily among nonpsychiatric patients. (Gendlin, 1969; Gendlin et al., 1968)

Investigators at Ohio State University have modified the Experiencing Scale to make the instrument more applicable to nonpatient undergraduates participating in various analogue studies. Suchman (1965) observed that the EXP Scale gave constricted ranges of scores when used for recordings of pseudo-clinical interviews with university students. He decided to construct a rating scale for measuring self-disclosure based on subjects' voice quality and language style as well as on the content of their disclosure, representing subjects' willingness to communicate feelings. The result was Suchman's six-point Revealingness Scale, which extended the EXP Scale to lower levels of experiencing or revealingness. The Revealingness Scale should provide a more discriminating measure when personal communication is not very deep. The scale has been used in two studies: Haggerty (1964) and Mellers (1965). Keller (1965) is developing a scale for measuring revealingness in children.

At Emory University, Doster (1968, 1969) developed a seven-point scale similar to Suchman's and serving a similar purpose. His Disclosure Rating Scale assesses the extent to which the subject focuses on various aspects of himself. The subject's treatment of a particular topic can range from a nonpersonal or superficial approach to an entirely personal approach. The scale ranges from Stage 0 (complete absence of any personal involvement) to Stage 6 where the subject focuses entirely on himself, providing an intimate picture of various aspects of himself as they relate to the topic. Doster's Disclosure Scale has been applied in experimental interview studies where subjects are requested to talk about various public and private topics, such as "guilt," "anger," and "self-control". (Doster, 1968, 1969; Hays, 1970; McAllister, 1970)

Finally, Jourard's Self-Disclosure Questionnaire and, more recently, Greene's Self-Disclosure Sentence Completion Blank (see Chapter 6) are self-report measures of constructs apparently close to that underlying the Experiencing Scale. However, no empirical relationships among these measures and Experiencing have been established.

References

Alexander, F., and French, T. M. *Psychoanalytic therapy*. New York: Norton, 1942.

Doster, J. A. Need for social approval and information about the recipient in the disclosure of information about the "public" and "private" self. Unpublished master's thesis, Emory University, 1968.

________. Effects of instructions, modeling and role rehersal on verbal behavior in an interview situation. Unpublished doctoral dissertation, Emory University, 1969.

Ebel, R. L. Estimation of the reliability of ratings. *Psychometrika*, 1951, 16, 407-24.

Fenichel, O. *The psychoanalytic theory of the neuroses*. New York: Norton, 1945.

Fromm-Reichmann, F. *Principles of intensive psychotherapy*. Chicago: University of Chicago Press, 1950.

Gendlin, E. T. *Experiencing and the creation of meaning*. New York: Free Press of Glencoe, 1962.

________. A theory of personality change. In P. Worchel and D. Byrne (Eds.), *Personality change*. New York: Wiley, 1964.

________. Focusing. *Psychotherapy: Theory, Research and Practice*, 1969, 6, 4-15.

Gendlin, E. T., Beebe, J., Cassens, J., Klein, M. H., and Oberlander, M. Focusing ability in psychotherapy, personality, and creativity. In J. M. Schlien (Ed.), *Research in psychotherapy*. Vol. 3. Washington, D. C.: American Psychological Association, 1968. Pp. 217-41.

Gendlin, E. T., Jenney, R., and Schlein, J. M. Counselor ratings of process and outcome in client-centered therapy. *Journal of Clinical Psychology*, 1960, 16, 210-13.

Gendlin, E. T., and Tomlinson, T. M. Psychotherapy process rating scale: Experiencing (EXP) Scale. Unpublished manuscript. Wisconsin Psychiatric Institute, 1961.

________. The process conception and its measurement. In C. R. Rogers, E. T. Gendlin, D. J. Kiesler, and C. B. Traux, *The therapeutic relationship and its impact: a study of psychotherapy with schizophrenics*. Madison: University of Wisconsin Press, 1967.

Gendlin, E. T., and Zimring, F. M. The qualities or dimension of experiencing and their change. University of Chicago Library, *Counseling Center Discussion Papers*, 1955, 1 (3).

Haggerty, P. A. The concept of self-disclosure. Unpublished master's thesis, The Ohio State University, 1964.

Hays, C. The effects of interviewer disclosure upon subjects' disclosure level during the interview. Unpublished doctoral dissertation, Emory University, 1970.

Keller, J. Revealingness and creativity in children. Unpublished master's thesis, The Ohio State University, 1965.

Klein, M. H., Mathieu, P. L., Gendlin, E. T., and Kiesler, D. J. *The Experiencing Scale: a research and training manual*. Madison: Wisconsin Psychiatric Institute, Bureau of Audio Visual Instruction, 1970. 2 vols.

McAllister, A. D. An exploration of certain parameters of the interview situation. Unpublished master's thesis, Emory University, 1970.

Mellers, D. E. Self-disclosure and perception of childhood. Unpublished master's thesis, The Ohio State University, 1965.

Rogers, C. R. A process conception of psychotherapy. *American Psychologist*, 1958, 13, 142-49.

________. A tentative scale for the measurement of process in psychotherapy. In E. A. Rubinstein and M. B. Parloff (Eds.), *Research in psychotherapy*. Vol. 1. Washington, D. C.: American Psychological Association, 1959. Pp. 96-107.

Rogers, C. R., Gendlin, E. T., Kiesler, D. J., and Truax, C. B. *The therapeutic relationship and its impact: a study of psychotherapy with schizophrenics*. Madison: University of Wisconsin Press, 1967.

Singer, E. *Key concepts in psychotherapy*. New York: Random House, 1965.

Suchman, D. I. A scale for the measurement of Revealingness in spoken behavior. Unpublished master's thesis, The Ohio State University, 1965.

Sullivan, H. S. *Collected works*. New York: Basic Books, 1965.

Walker, A. M., Rablen, R. A., and Rogers, C. R. Development of a scale to measure process changes in psychotherapy. *Journal of Clincial Psychology*, 1960, 16, 79-85.

A Tentative Scale for the Measurement of Depth of Self-Exploration

Charles B. Truax

1. Rationale for Development of the Scale

Truax's scale measuring the level of self-exploration the patient manifests in his interview behavior derived directly from Rogers' (1957) theory, as did his previous scales for measuring therapist "conditions" (described in Chapter 4). Truax (Truax and Carkhuff, 1967) presents the rationale underlying the Depth of Self-Exploration (DX) Scale as follows:

> For the practice of psychotherapy, perhaps the most crucial question to ask about the patient is "What do successful patients do *in* psychotherapy that is different from unsuccessful patients?" In the moment-to-moment encounter with the client, the therapist takes some clues from the patient's moment-by-moment behavior as guidelines for evaluating his own effectiveness. Perhaps the most useful guideline would be an increase in the kind of client behavior

that is typical of successful cases and untypical of failure cases.

In successful psychotherapy, both individual and group, the patient spends much of his time in self-exploration . . . attempting to understand and define his own beliefs, values, motives, and actions . . . .while the therapist, by reason of his training and knowledge, is attempting to facilitate this process. This is the essence of the "talking cure" pioneered by Freud and his associates. In the terminology of psychoanalytic theory, this process of self-exploration is described as the patient's becoming aware of and exploring unconscious material and distortion effects of that unconscious material upon perception of reality (Munroe, 1955) . . . . In what can be termed the "ego psychology" tradition, therapeutic change is viewed as occurring through the client's ability to solve his problems himself as he sees more deeply into them as a result of the facilitative interaction with the therapist. This central role of the client's self-exploration and verbal revelation, although more structured, is seen in virtually all forms of psychotherapy, including behavior therapy.

Rogers in particular has stressed the role of patient self-exploration. In attempting to describe this in the client, Rogers (1955) describes in a different language the basic phenomena dealt with by Freud: "Optimal therapy has meant an exploration of increasingly strange and unknown and dangerous feelings in himself. . . . Thus he becomes acquainted with elements of his experiences which have in the past been denied to awareness as too threatening, too damaging to the structure of the self."

Regardless of one's theoretic viewpoint about the significance of different areas of content and different manners of relating, the "talking cure" of counseling, or psychotherapy, obviously relies upon some degree of verbal interchange. A mass of research evidence has been accumulated which in broad form tends to verify the significance for outcome of the client's degree of self-exploration. Much of this research has been stimulated by the work of Rogers (1951). (Truax and Carkhuff, 1967) pp. 189-90

Taken together, the available research evidence tends to confirm clinical and theoretic writings that point to the significance for outcome of the client's engagement in the process of self-exploration. However, there is far from a one-to-one relationship between the various measures of self-exploration and therapeutic outcome. This, in turn, suggests that a large part of psychotherapeutic outcome is not mediated by the patient's verbal or even emotional self-exploration throughout the course of counseling or psychotherapy. It may be that our current and crude measurement of the client's behavior is insensitive to many of the significant emotional and cognitive happenings. It may also be that much of the change in the patient comes about *between* therapy sessions as he is trying out new modes of living in a tentative fashion and risking himself in new ways of relating to the world. We suspect that both these possibilities are true. (p. 193)

2. Description of the Scale

DX is a nine-point annotated and anchored rating scale based upon the theoretic and clinical conception of self-exploration as an antecedent to psychotherapeutic outcome. Aspects of the present scale were derived from the original Process Scale developed by Rogers, Walker, and Rablen (1960) and the specific subscales developed by Gendlin and Tomlinson, (1962). It is an attempt to measure the extent of patient self-exploration, with additional weightings or correlations given for "personally private" and "personally damning" material. An earlier version of the present scale included factors of relationship quality, personal constructs, relationship to problem elements of the self, immediacy of feeling, and defensiveness. Research using that scale, however, indicated that those additional factors showed no relationship to outcome; and for that reason they are omitted in the current version. (Truax and Carkhuff, 1967, p. 194)

Truax's Depth of Self-Exploration Scale is presented in Table 5.5. The scale "attempts to define the extent to which patients engage in self-exploration, ranging from no demonstrable intrapersonal exploration to a very high level of self-probing and exploration. Although the basic scale is intended to be a continuum, corrections should be added to determine the final assigned scale value." (p. 195)

As several of the sections usually included for each scale would duplicate the information provided for Truax's three therapist scales of accurate empathy, nonpossessive warmth, and genuineness elsewhere in this volume (above, Chapter 4), Sections 3, 4, 5, 7, 10, and 11 are omitted here.

6. Participant-Context Restrictions

Judges making the DX ratings usually listen to segments containing both the patient's and the therapist's verbalizations. Truax has not considered the issue of participant context for his DX scale. It remains to be determined whether edited (therapist's speech removed) and unedited (both participants present) segments yield equally reliable scale ratings.

8. Sample Location Within the Interview

Truax's usual sampling procedure for DX ratings has been to randomly extract segments (four or five minutes in length) from particular therapy sessions along the time continuum. He has not explicitly discussed or empirically evaluated the effect on DX ratings of what size and from where in the hour samples can be taken that will be representative of the patient's self-exploratory behavior for the entire session.

9. Sample Location Over Therapy Interviews

The sampling procedure has ranged from selecting interviews representative of the different stages of the case interaction (for example, every fifth interview) to rating segments covering every minute of the total therapy interaction. Truax has not examined the effects of various sampling procedures on yielding DX scores differentially representative of the patient's behavior over the entire therapy sequence from initiation to termination.

12. Training Manual

There is no manual as yet. However, training tapes are available, and the training procedure (identical to that for the therapist conditions scales) is spelled out in some detail.

13. Interrater and Intrarater Reliabilities Reported

In the 1967 volume, Truax summarizes the reliability figures obtained from Depth of Self-Exploration ratings in various studies. The values reported are Ebel's intraclass coefficients, with r_{11} representing the estimated average correlation among a group of raters, and r_{kk} indicating the reliability of the average of the judges' ratings for particular segments. The reported r_{11} values range from 0.59 to 0.68, with a median coefficient of 0.68; the r_{kk} values from 0.68 to 0.88, with a median of 0.78.

Truax concludes that "in general, then, the scale can be considered to be reasonably reliable, particularly in view of the inherent ambiguity of tape-recorded samples of the therapeutic process." (Truax and Carkhuff, 1967, p. 194)

14. Dimensionality Considerations

Although Truax intended that his scale represent a continuum of patient behavior, he has not yet assessed whether the scale measures a unitary factor or more complex multiple variables.

15. Validity Studies

Findings relating Depth of Self-Exploration ratings to more successful outcome and measures of therapist conditions are summarized in Truax and Carkhuff. (1967, 189-93) "Taken together, the available research evidence tends to confirm clinical and theoretic writings that point to the significance for outcome to the client's engagement in the process of self-exploration." (p. 193)

RELATED SCALES OR CONSTRUCTS

The Depth of Self-Exploration Scale is similar both in theoretical derivation and definitions of the scale stages to the Experiencing Scale presented above. It is likely that it correlates highly with the Experiencing Scale and is associated with the other scales related to Experiencing. (see number 16 in the Experiencing Scale section above, this chapter)

References

Gendlin, E. T., and Tomlinson, T. M. Experiencing scale. Mimeographed paper, Wisconsin Psychiatric Institute, University of Wisconsin, 1962.

Munroe, R. L. *Schools of psychoanalytic thought*. New York: Dryden Press, 1955.

Rogers, C. R. *Client-centered therapy*. Boston: Houghton Mifflin, 1951.

_______. The concept of a fully functioning person. Unpublished manuscript, Chicago Counseling Center, University of Chicago, 1955.

_______. The necessary and sufficient conditions of therapeutic personality change. *Journal of Consulting Psychology,* 1957, 21, 95-103.

Rogers, C. R., Walker, A., and Rablen, R. Development of a scale to measure process changes in psychotherapy. *Journal of Clinical Psychology,* 1960, 16, 79-85.

Truax, C. B. A tentative scale for the measurement of depth of intrepersonal exploration (DX). *Discussion Papers,* Wisconsin Psychiatric Institute, University of Wisconsin, 1962, 29.

Truax, C. B., and Carkhuff, R. R. *Towards effective counseling and psychotherapy.* Chicago: Aldine, 1967.

6

Minor Process Systems for Analyzing Psychotherapy Interviews

It is my judgment that most of the systems presented in this chapter have had little heuristic impact on the area of psychotherapy theory and research. Most measures included have not been pursued by subsequent and coordinated research effort on the part of their authors or others. The few exceptions followed up extensively were later abandoned because of equivocal or contradictory findings. In short, the process systems of this chapter have tended to be one-shot research attempts.

This fact is unfortunate, since many of these attempts show ingenuity and promise, and should clearly have a fate better than an unobtrusive burial in the literature. By resuscitating them here, they may have a greater future impact. Perhaps creative investigators can integrate aspects of these previous operational attempts into new and better systems, within the framework of a serious and long-range program of methodological and substantative research. At the very least, future process investigators, before embarking on development of new measures, should consult this chapter as well as the rest of the volume. We can no longer afford the redundancy and disjointedness previously characteristic of the field.

The first section presents briefly the multivariate or omnibus-like published systems which were not included as major systems in Chapters 3 through 5. These content-analysis procedures attempt to measure multiple factors, either of therapist behavior, of patient behavior, or both. The second section summarizes, in tabular form, the over one hundred minor measures developed for measuring unitary process factors, either of therapist or of patient behaviors occurring in psychotherapy interviews.

Eight Multivariate Systems

Four of the eight content-analysis systems were designed to measure aspects of both therapist and patient behavior in the interview, two were designed for therapist behavior only, and two for patient behavior only. Two of the four omnibus systems are basically atheoretical in origin, emphasizing primarily formal or interactional characteristics of the patient and therapist interview participants (Eldred et al.; Holzman and Forman); the third (Lasswell) assumes a psychoanalytic framework; while the fourth (Leary et al.) derives from an interpersonal theory of personality. Both therapist systems (Porter and Berdie) have origins in Rogerian theory. Finally, of the two patient systems, one is derived directly from psychoanalytic theory (Bellak and Smith), while the other (Saper and Anderson) is atheoretical. These eight systems will be summarized briefly, in chronological order of their publication date, under the three subsections below.

Four Omnibus Systems

Lasswell's General Purpose System

Lasswell not only pioneered in tape recording of psychotherapy interviews (see Chapter 2), but he also developed one of the earliest content-analysis systems for coding therapist and patient behaviors in psychotherapy (Lasswell, 1935, 1937, 1938). His 1938 classification system scores who makes a statement (patient, therapist, or other), to whom the statement refers (patient, therapist, or other), and what attitude is expressed (favorable, unfavorable). A previous report (1935) indicates that he classified patient responses further, according to whether their statement referred to the therapist or not. He hypothesized that reference to the therapist was a sign of "conscious affect," while "unconscious tension" was indicated by instances of slow speech and the occurrence of pauses. He developed a rationale linking the latter language indicators to the two constructs by showing their relevance to psychoanalytic theory.

Lasswell's 1935 and 1937 studies tested these hypotheses and found that: (*a*) slow speech is indeed correlated with unconscious tension (defined by high skin conductivity), while reference to the therapist correlated highly with conscious affect (defined by heart rate); (*b*) both slow speech and high skin conductivity are negatively correlated to both references to the therapist and increased heart rate; and (*c*) unconscious affect (slow speech and high skin conductivity) decreased over the course of the interview, while conscious affect increased.

Apparently, neither Lasswell nor others followed up these early findings with continued application and development of the system and constructs proposed.

Eldred and Associates

Eldred, Hamburg, Inwood, Salzman, Meyersburg, and Goodrich (1954) introduced a novel and clever observer technique which led to development of a quite circumscribed but productive (in their sample) procedure for studying psychotherapy process. The group originally sought to study communication in the psychotherapy interview. They were looking for methods "which would permit a more thorough, systematic analysis of interview material, less vulnerable to distortion unconsciously introduced by the observer's bias. One way to minimize this difficulty is to have more than one psychiatric observer. Another is to make sound recordings of the interviews. The present study has combined these two approaches in an effort to explore certain aspects of verbal communication during psychotherapeutic interviews."

Six psychiatrists met as a group weekly for a period of two or more hours to analyze the cases of three patient-therapist pairs who met three to five hours per week for therapy sessions. At their weekly meetings the psychiatrist group would listen to the recorded interviews and discuss them. Over time a methodology emerged as a fruitful direction of inquiry.

> A number of specific segments of communication were suggested by the data—for example, periods of silence, patient's total productions versus therapist's total productions, and level of abstraction for adjectives and verbs. In this context it was noticed that there frequently occurred drastic changes of subject in the verbal content of the interchange. Several questions about this specific phenomenon arose, such as: How often do such changes occur? What is their effect upon communication between doctor and patient? Under what conditions do they occur? . . . The group . . . decided to center their attention upon drastic changes of subject and the prominent features of a series of such exchanges.

The group found that the instances of "abrupt transition" (in Sullivan's terms) on which they agreed could be operationally defined as "a sudden shift in the literal content of the verbal communication which introduced at least two of the following: (*a*) a different kind of experience, (*b*) a different person, and (*c*) a different time reference. . . . Only those instances of change of subject which met this definition were included in this study. . . . The group identified in 18 interviews (5, 6, and 7 respectively for three patient-therapist pairs) a total of 58 changes of subject."

Eldred et al. then devised a coding system for scoring these change-of-subject events. They do not describe explicitly their exact "scoring" or "contextual" units, which apparently were defined differently for each of the five major categories developed. The contextual unit included at least more than a particular interview, in some cases clearly involving information "gleaned from previous interviews" as well as the discussion and biases of the other members of the psychiatrist group, since the judgments were not made independently.

The five categories developed by Eldred et al. are: (1) *Direction of Change of Subject* (having resulted in more direct communication, less direct communication, no determinable effect upon communication). Direct communication is defined as "verbal communication which is in the direction of more nearly accurate, more nearly complete and comprehensive expression of one's feelings." (2) *Awareness of Change of Subject* (conscious, unconscious, or undetermined). A given change of subject is considered conscious "when it is apparent from the verbal content that the person changing the subject has a definite goal of communication toward which he is moving in changing the subject." (3) *Initiator of Change of Subject* (either therapist or patient). (4) *Techniques of Change of Subject* (a shift in time reference, by introducing emotionally laden material about matter other than that under discussion, by a prolonged period of silence, by shifting from a topic of unknown communicability to one of previously established communicability, by introduction of self-recriminatory material, by shifting from conversational pleasantries to the work of analysis and vice versa, by the therapist's communicating disapproval or disinterest in the preceding subject, by the therapist's making a too rigid interpretation of unconscious material, and by reintroduction of a subject occurring previously in the interview). (5) *Causes of the Change of Subject* (one of the participants becomes anxious about the subject under discussion, for purpose of introducing material more relevant to the patient's emotional problems, by insight on the part of either party, by free association, by a poorly worded communication heard as a change of subject by the other participant, because the existing subject seemed to have been exhausted, because either participant needs to communicate about a subject of greater immediacy to the patient's feelings, and because one of the participants becomes anxious about his relationship with the other).

The 1954 report presents provocative findings using the system. For example, (*a*) there is an average of three drastic changes of subject per interview in the overall figures; (*b*) of the fifty-eight changes of subject, thirty-one tended to make for more direct communication and forty-two were found to be conscious: (*c*) the patients changed the subject forty-two times while the therapists changed the subject sixteen times, giving a ratio of 2.6:1; (*d*) conscious changes of subject led to more direct communication five times more frequently than they led to less direct communication; and (*e*) when the patient changed the subject, communication was made more directly 3.5 times (25:7) as frequently as it was made less direct.

The authors conclude:

> It has been suggested that the clinical evaluation of the psychotherapeutic interview can be supplemented by the detailed study of specific, circumscribed segments of the verbal transactions of the interviews. The results of studying one such segment are sufficiently illuminating to indicate the need for the delineation and methodological study of other naturally occurring, circumscribed phenomena. It is further suggested that from such studies a number of related criteria for evaluating the psychotherapeutic process might be evolved. These indices would supplement the more intuitive, subjective methods of evaluation, insofar as they permit a higher degree of explicitness and precision of observation.

The subsequent literature does not reveal any follow-up by Eldred et al. or by others of this interesting process analysis approach.

Leary et al.'s Interpersonal System

Besides the highly complex process system he developed with Gill (see Chapter 3), Leary was involved in a long-term project studying personality from an interpersonal framework (Freedman, Leary, Ossorio, and Coffey, 1950; LaForge, 1963; LaForge, Freedman, Leary, Naboisek, and Coffey, 1954; LaForge and Suczek, 1955; Leary, 1955, 1957; Leary and Coffey, 1955a, 1955b; Leary and

Harvey 1956). This project culminated in a book published by Leary (1957) presenting a theoretical and empirical system for the study of human personality.

Leary proposes a two-dimensional model for classifying interpersonal behavior along orthogonal axes of dominance-submission and hostility-affect. These two dimensions incorporate, on an Interpersonal Circle, a set of sixteen interpersonal variables. Leary's system deals with interpersonal behavior at five levels. Level I (Public Communication) concerns the interpersonal impact of the subject on others, his social stimulus value (measured by ratings of social behavior, sociometric ratings, MMPI indexes, and scores from standard situation tests). Level II (Conscious Descriptions) concerns the subject's view of himself and the world obtained from interviews, an autobiography, checklist, and questionnaire (measured by ratings of diagnostic and therapy interviews, Interpersonal Adjective Check List scores, or ratings of autobiographies). Level III (Preconscious Symbolization) taps the subject's autistic, projective fantasy productions (measured from projective tests, dream productions, waking fantasies, and certain MMPI indexes). Level IV (Unexpressed Unconscious) is defined by two criteria: the interpersonal themes significantly omitted at the top three levels and significantly avoided on tests of subliminal preceptions, selective forgetting, and the like (methods of measuring not yet developed). Level V (Ego Ideal) comprises the subjects statements about his interpersonal ideas, standards, conceptions of good and evil as obtained in an interview, autobiography, questionnaire, or checklist (measured by scores from the Interpersonal Adjective Check List, and ratings of diagnostic and therapy interviews).

Behavior at each level is coded according to a circular continuum of the sixteen interpersonal variables. Each variable is defined along an intensity dimension so that there is an adaptive and maladaptive aspect to each of the sixteen interpersonal security operations.

The level most directly relevant for psychotherapy process research is Level II, dealing with interpersonal traits.

> There is only one criterion for determining Level II data: conscious verbal report of the subject. We are interested in what the subject says, the content of his verbal expressions. From there we focus on the interpersonal themes which he attributes to himself and to others. (Leary, 1957, p. 132)

The patient's statements about himself and others are coded according to the matrix of 16 variables. The themes of categories employed are derived from the circular continuum of interper-

> sonal variables. . . . The interpersonal traits were developed by simply replacing the verbs of Level I with the coordinate or appropriate adjective. (p. 136)

In practice, the data of Level II are obtained from judges ("two or more trained technicians") rating diagnostic or therapy (individual or group) interviews (apparently typescripts) or from the patient's self-ratings on the Interpersonal Check List. The patient can also fill out the ICI on the therapist, and the therapist can rate the patient. Leary (1957) reported a few examples of applications of his Level II process system to typescripts of group psychotherapy interactions. A previous report (Leary and Coffey, 1955) was devoted to group psychotherapy analysis.

Leary (1957) concluded:

> The Kaiser foundation research project has undertaken extensive studies of process in psychotherapy. The aim of these studies is to apply the interpersonal system to the therapeutic interactions and to the perceptions of the patient and therapist. The working principle employed in these studies is: the patient and therapist comprise a basic interacting unit. We do not study the patient in therapy, but both the patient and therapist as they interacted. (p. 143)

To my knowledge, Leary and his colleagues have not subsequently published reports of these studies utilizing the Interpersonal Circle.

Cutler (1958) used the Interpersonal Circle in a quite ingenious way to study therapist countertransference. As part of his study he selected sixteen adjectives that would correspond to the sixteen traits on the Interpersonal Circle. The adjectives, with the letters denoting the respective code categories on Leary's Circle, are as follows: (*A*) dominating, (*B*) boastful, (*C*) rejecting, (*D*) punitive, (*E*) critical, (*F*) complaining, (*G*) suspicious, (*H*) apologetic, (*I*) submissive, (*J*) respectful, (*K*) dependent, (*L*) agreeable, (*M*) affiliative, (*N*) supportive, (*O*) generous, and (*P*) advising.

Using these sixteen adjectives, independent judges then coded therapy interviews on the Circle. By summing across all the interviews of a given therapist, Cutler determined the total number of actual manifestations by the therapist and by the patient of each of the sixteen interpersonal behavior categories. For coding a given statement or response, exact agreement by two judges ranged from 62 to 71 percent, partial agreement from 24 to 33 percent, and disagreement from 5 to 10 percent. The total number of ratings of each trait by the two judges correlated from 0.75 to 0.84. These are respectable levels of interjudge agreements.

Cutler's findings will not be discussed here, nor will other aspects of his design, although both are quite innovative. The point is that Leary et al.'s Interpersonal Circle apparently holds considerable promise for therapy process research. Unfortunately, the system has not been applied further to interview data, with the one exception of Mueller and Dilling. (1969)

Holzman and Forman's System

Holzman and Forman (1966) have developed a multivariate system for measuring both therapist and patient interview behaviors. Although their content-analysis procedure was developed for a long-term study of the process of psychotherapy of schizophrenics, the system will be briefly presented here since it can be applied to psychoneurotic patients (and their therapists) as well. The authors state that application of their system

> is not limited to the study of process in psychotherapy. It is applicable to the study of any verbal material which deals naturalistically rather than technically with social and psychological aspects of human life and interrelationships. . . . Our goal has been to devise a content-analysis system of sufficient generality that, to cite two examples: (*a*) psychotherapeutic dialogues can be compared to other dialogues with postulated similarities to psychotherapy, and (*b*) schizophrenic verbal behavior can be compared to other categories of verbal behavior.

The data form for their system is the typescript. "With two minor exceptions our data are confined to verbalizations. Nonverbal aspects of the patient-therapist interactions are not included as data. . . . As long as the correlation between verbal and nonverbal aspects of the therapeutic interaction is not negative, even though our method is less sensitive than one which takes account of nonverbal aspects, it will not violate the reality of the interaction."

The "scoring unit" for the system is the meaning unit, defined as "either a simple sentence, a complex sentence, or a simple or complex sentence fragment. Thus the sentence as defined by English grammar is the typical meaning unit, except that compound sentences are broken into simple sentences, and incomplete sentences are recognized as meaning units." The authors do not explicitly discuss the "contextual" unit for their system. For the sample studied in the 1966 report, the "summarizing" unit consists of blocks of "four interviews for each therapist-patient pair from the first, third, fifth, and tenth 4-week period of the therapies."

Holzman and Forman developed a five-dimensional content analysis for categorizing the verbal behavior of patients and of therapists at various times during the course of therapy. The five separate dimensions are: (1) *Form or Grammatical Structure* of the meaning unit included fifteen category-items (questions, contentless interjections, reflections, instructions, demands, agreements, disagreements, statements having as subject neither patient nor therapist, statements having patient as subject, answers, nonanswers, statements having therapist as subject, solicitous remarks, inexact statements, and impersonal questions). (2) *Manifest Content* of the meaning unit includes eight subcategories (therapist's ideas and behavior, patient's behavior, patient's feelings, patient's cognitive processes, patient's ideas of behavior of others, patient's symptoms, therapist's feelings, and patient's fantasies). (3) Coding of *Patient Objects* is done if one is manifestly contained in the meaning unit, and consists of twelve subcategories (mother, father, therapist, patient's self, patient's body parts, member of patient's family, member of hospital ward community, available persons, unavailable persons, unreal persons, cathected inanimate objects and animals, and indefinite persons). (4) *Locus of Patient's Difficulties* contains five items (statement that difficulty does not exist, denial of knowing or failure to communicate knowing whether a difficulty does exist, patient's difficulty lies in the feelings and/or behavior of another, in his physical symptoms, or in his own feelings and behavior). (5) *Approval-Disapproval of the "Other" in Therapy* is tripartite (neither manifest and direct approval nor disapproval, manifest and direct approval, and manifest and direct disapproval).

> The only coding . . . which every meaning unit must receive is a form coding (category 1). A unit need not receive other codings because the content dimension (category 2) has a limited group of categories, which does not cover all content; not all units contain patient objects (category 3); most units are neither manifestly and directly approving or disapproving (category 5); and not all units assign a locus to the patient's difficulties (category 4). . . . All coding is done on the basis of manifest rather than latent characteristics of units.

To date all coding is done by two judges (unidentified and level of experience and training unspecified). For three of the major categories (form, patient content, and patient object) for four periods of therapy, the percentage of exact agreement between two judges on a scoring unit by scoring unit basis ranged from 74 to 88 percent. No figures are presented for the remaining two categories.

In a preliminary study applying their system, interviews by Rogers and by Felder with a schizophrenic girl were compared with the author's sample of eleven psychoanalytically oriented therapists on the three major categories for which reliability figures were presented. The authors found that "if we were to characterize Rogers' system as it was manifest in this interview, we would call it nonquestioning, rather than nondirective, because the two question categories were his two least frequent; and statements having content, the second most directive category, his most frequent. However, Rogers is less directive than 7 of the 8 psychoanalytically oriented therapists with whom he was compared." In another instance, Felder's second highest category was F, therapist's feelings. The psychoanalytically oriented therapists have F as second lowest category. "This difference is consistent with Whitaker and Malone's description of the difference in therapist role betwen the two schools. . . . For Felder, verbally sharing his own feelings with his patient is a high-ranking category, while for the psychoanalytically oriented therapist it is low."

The authors have not yet used their patient data in any systematic way. However, they state that

> because our content-analysis system is symmetrical, the same analysis we have conducted concerning therapist verbal contribution to the therapy can be made for the patients. We are interested in the same questions: What characteristics of patient verbal behavior display consistency? Are there variables which systematically (rather than randomly) differentiate the patients? Will the findings regarding patients be consistent with these findings regarding therapists so that we are able to build up a coherent empirical description of the therapeutic process?

Two Therapist Systems

Porter's System

Porter (1943) was the earliest nondirective researcher to develop a content-analysis system for studying psychotherapy. His system, measuring therapist behavior only, was apparently quickly superseded by the introduction of Snyder's nondirective system in 1945 (see Chapter 3) which built on Porter's therapist categories and added categories for scoring patient behaviors as well.

Porter's system was developed

> to compare the counseling procedures used by therapists of different points of view. Nowhere in the literature available at that time

> were there any clear-cut descriptions of how therapists proceeded within any point of view. All that was available consisted in a description of goals and subgoals of the therapeutic sequence. The counselor was informed that he was to establish rapport, but he was not told how to do it. . . . He was informed that warmth and understanding were desirable, but again he was not told how to implement these concepts. In brief, each point of view had definite notions of what was to be accomplished, but no instructions were available as to procedure. . . . Since there were no clear-cut criteria available in the literature as to just what constituted guidance interview procedures, directive procedures, nondirective procedures, or analytic procedures, the writer turned to phonographic recordings of interviews. By studying the individual counselor responses, certain relationships began to suggest themselves. Through the process of grouping and regrouping responses which seemed to be implementations of the same procedures, a series of categories were finally settled upon. (Porter, 1950, pp. 177-78)

The resulting therapist coding system consisted of four major category headings. (Porter, 1950, pp. 178-79) (1) *Defining the Interview Situation*: (*a*) defines in terms of diagnostic/remedial purposes, procedures, etc.; (*b*) defines in terms of client responsibility for directing the interview/reaching decisions, etc.; (*c*) unclassifiable. (2) *Bringing Out and Developing the Problem Situation*: Therapist uses lead which: (*a*) forces choosing and developing of topic upon client; (*b*) indicates topic but leaves development to client; (*c*) indicates topic and delimits development to confirmation, negation, or the supplying of specific items of information; (*d*) unclassifiable. (3) *Developing the Client's Insight and Understanding*: Therapist responds in such a way as to indicate: (*a*) recognition of subject content or implied subject content; (*b*) recognition of expression of feeling or attitude in immediately preceding verbal response(s); (*c*) interpretation or recognition of feeling of attitude not expressed in immediately preceding verbal response(s); (*d*) identifies a problem, source of difficulty, condition needing correction, etc., through test interpretations, evaluative remarks, etc.; (*e*) interprets test results but not as indicating a problem, source of difficulty, etc.; (*f*) expresses approval, disapproval, shock, or other personal reaction in regard to the client (but not to identify a problem); (*g*) explains, discusses, or gives information related to the problem or treatment; (*h*) unclassifiable. (4) *Sponsoring Client Activity Fostering Decision Making*: Proposes client activity: (*a*) directly or through questioning technique; (*b*) in response to question of what to do. Influences the making of a decision by: (*c*) marshalling and evaluating evidence, expressing personal opinion, persuading pro or con; (*d*) indicating decision is up to the client; (*e*) indicating acceptance or approval of decision; (*f*) reassuring; (*g*) irrelevant response; (*h*) otherwise unclassifiable.

The data form used by Porter (1950) was typescripts of recorded therapy interviews. Each therapist response was coded using the above categories.

> The checklist . . . represents an effort not to impose concepts external to the data upon the data. Every effort was made to describe each procedure as a procedure, without reference to whether it might be considered good, bad, or indifferent from anyone's point of view, whether it might be considered directive, nondirective, analytic, or any other external categorization. In other words, the checklist was designed to determine what the data would show about themselves. (p. 179)

Porter felt the category system developed by Snyder did not anchor itself in the data only, but rather introduced concepts external to the data. Neither Porter nor other investigators (with the exception of Berdie, discussed next) have followed up the 1943 empirical efforts.

Berdie's System

In 1958, Berdie reported on a long-range program of research on the counseling interview conducted at the Student Counseling Service of the University of Minnesota. The project started in 1940 and continued to the time of the 1958 report.

The earliest phase of the project, which continued until 1948, consisted of an intensive analysis of forty-eight counseling interviews, with each of three counselors having sixteen interviews, leading to an eventual coding of 17,538 therapist statements. A modification of Porter's (1943) content-analysis system was used in this first phase of the project, with an additional scale of directiveness being added. Intercorrelations among eight judges applying the modified system ranged from 0.63 to 0.87 for Porter's major categories. No findings were reported for the therapist categories, and no consistent relationship was found between rated therapist directedness and students' reactions to counseling.

At the beginning of the next phase of the project in 1948, the research staff developed a different process system,

> [a] more meaningful method of analyzing and describing counselor behavior in the interview. After testing several methods, we

> decided to use a bi-dimensional system for categorizing counselor statements. Each [therapist] response was to be classified, first, according to purpose, and second, according to technique. The counselor response was defined as a statement made by a counselor and extending from the termination of the counselor's previous comment to the initiation of the counselee's succeeding statement.

The system that evolved consists of two major categories, with categories according to purpose having four subcategories and twenty-one techniques. The system is reproduced below in outline form; Berdie's (1958) article contains examples of each subcategory. (1) *Categories According to Purpose*: (*a*) use by therapist of various techniques to elicit client's expression of feelings, attitudes, and information; (*b*) introduction by the therapist of information, or the therapist's feelings or attitudes, to give the client additional information; (*c*) use by the therapist of various techniques, the aim of which is to facilitate the client's perception of relationships between ideas, feelings, or attitudes expressed in the immediately preceding client response; (*d*) use by the therapist of various techniques to establish an interpersonal relationship between therapist and client. (2) *Techniques*: (*a*) nondirective leads: a request to the client to express himself, without the therapist specifying the topic; (*b*) questions: asking for information, attitudes, and feelings; (*c*) requested repetition; (*d*) citing experimental findings or opinion if acknowledgement is given to a specific source; (*e*) interpretation: therapist responses that either indicate relationship (one aspect must be inherent in the client's preceding statement) or respond to feelings that have not been expressed by the client; (*f*) restatement of content or feeling: repetition of the idea expressed by the client which does not reorganize the statement in such a manner as to reveal more clearly the client's feeling or idea; (*g*) clarification of feeling or content: therapist responses to reorganize or synthesize the feelings of content expressed by the client (not merely changing the client's wording); (*h*) summarizing: therapist stating outcomes of the counseling contact; (*i*) advice: recommending following a course of action; (*j*) statement of alternatives; (*k*) referral for services elsewhere; (*l*) description of persons (including client), programs, services, regulations, or procedures of the agency or other agencies; (*m*) challenging; (*n*) disapproval; (*o*) reassurance: assurance, reinforcement, approval, praise, or agreement; (*p*) sympathy; (*q*) anecdotes and illustrations; (*r*) simple participation (uh-hm); (*s*) description, discussion, and selection of tests; (*t*) social amenities; (*u*) unclassifiable.

This new system was applied to typescripts of four counselors each having fifty interviews at the rate of two per week. Two teams of judges independently scored the therapist responses, three judges using only typescripts and three separate judges using typescripts while listening to tape recordings. On a sample of thirty-two interviews, the agreement for the typescript team was 62 percent; for the other group of judges, 68 percent, while the two teams agreed with each other 72 percent. These figures were based on a very stringent standard of agreement; not only did judges have to agree as to which of the four purposes applied, but also which of the twenty-one techniques best described a particular therapist statement.

Berdie concluded from these studies that reliable observation can be made of counseling interviews; that observations based on both typescript and recordings were somewhat preferable to those based on typescript alone; and characteristic patterns of counseling for different counselors could be identified with the system.

His 1958 report described a third phase of the project investigating the outcome of counseling. The data for the scoring system on this phase were not available at that time. Apparently, the findings have not been reported, and the system has not been utilized elsewhere.

Two Patient Systems

The Saper and Anderson System

Saper (1951) presented a content-analysis system that analyzed patient communications in four general areas: topical orientation, time reference, direction of verbally expressed affect, and intensity of verbally expressed affect. Anderson (1954), following up on Saper's work, devised a complete set of instructions for scoring the four categories.

The "scoring unit" used by Anderson was the "thought unit," defined as a consecutive series of words expressing a thought or idea that would stand alone. The unit rarely extended more than one sentence. He did not discuss or define the "contextual" or "summarizing" units for his system.

Each patient thought unit was scored in four categories. (1) The *Topical Scale* was used to characterize the focus or referent of the patient's verbalization. The six subcategories included: (*a*) self; (*b*) primary personal relationship; (*c*) secondary personal relationship; (*d*) therapist; (*e*) experiment; (*f*) generalized others. (2) The *Time Category* consisted of the following five subcategories: (*a*) now; (*b*) current; (*c*) progressive or universal time; (*d*) past; (*e*) future. (3) The *Affect Categories* described the emotion or feeling which the patient expressed toward a topical referent. The four subcategories are: (*a*) positive affect; (*b*) negative affect; (*c*) ambivalent affect; (*d*) descriptive or indeterminate affect. (4) The *Intensity Categories* referred to the degree of conviction or strength of feeling in the verbal unit as it was spoken by the patient. The three subcategories are: (*a*) maximal affect; (*b*) moderate affect; (*c*) minimal affect.

After an interval of ten months, one judge reclassified 526 units from the interviews. The intrajudge reliability expressed in terms of percentage of agreement was: overall, 85 percent; topic, 85 percent; affect, 82 percent; and intensity, 88 percent. The same judge's percentage of agreement for determining thought units for one interview was also quite high, 90 percent. To determine interjudge reliability, a second judge scored a sample of units from the interviews. The resulting agreement percentages were comparable to those found for rerate stability: topic, 82 percent; time, 75 percent; affect, 73 percent; and intensity, 82 percent.

In his 1954 intensive study of a single client-centered psychotherapy case, Anderson found that changes in the level of patient physiological behavior (heart rate) were positively related to predictable modifications in the pattern of the patient's verbal communication. This confirmed his expectation that there are positive and significant relationships between a patient's emotional (heart rate) and cognitive (verbal behavior) behavior during client-centered psychotherapy.

Bellak and Smith's System

In 1956 Bellak and Smith published a report on "An Experimental Exploration of the Psychoanalytic Process," using blocks of therapy sessions (fifty and sixty sessions respectively) from two cases. One of the major purposes of their study was to make the events of psychoanalysis public and observable, so that other investigators could replicate the findings obtained. Apparently no one has followed up their measurement procedure or the system of process variables they developed, with the single exception of Strupp et al. (see Chapter 4).

The authors' data form involved typescripts of analytic sessions as well as comments dictated by the treating analyst after each hour. Their process system exclusively scores patient interview behaviors. The "scoring unit" employed was the total-session typescripts for a week's analytic sessions. "On the basis of each week's records, two [analyst judges] made predictions of what would happen in this analysis in the next session, in the next week, and in the next month." Starting one week later than the predictor judges, two separate analysts judged what in fact happened in the succeeding (that week's) analytic sessions. The treating analyst also made predictions that were not communicated to the other analyst participants.

After a four-week period, a meeting was held for the five analyst-participants to discuss the statistical results obtained, and the predicting and assessing roles were switched for the next four-week period. It is unclear what their "contextual unit" was for scoring patient responses, except that it was larger than the scoring unit, since the judges had a memory of each preceding week's experience in their cumulative and successive rating task, and had unknown amounts of discussion information from the other judges.

The patient variables measured by Bellak and Smith's system included fourteen behaviors and eleven defensive processes. The fourteen behaviors included: transference (positive and negative), acting out, insight, resistance, anxiety, aggression (extra and in-therapy), passivity, guilt, depression, elation, oral striving, anal striving, phallic strivings, oedipal strivings, genital strivings, homosexuality, and scoptophilia. The eleven defense mechanisms were: repression, projection, rationalization, isolation, denial, intellectualization, displacement, reaction formation, regression, reversal, and identification with aggressor. The predictor and assessor judges rated each category as present or absent, and additionally assessed each behavior as consciously or unconsciously present.

Surprisingly, Bellak and Smith report moderate interjudge reliability figures for assessment of most of these variables for both sets of judges. Reliabilities for the two assessor judges ranged from 0.11 to 0.78 for the fourteen patient behavior categories (ratings of defenses were omitted). For the two predictor judges corresponding coefficients ranged from 0.07 to 0.95.

The authors summarize their findings as follows: "There is no doubt that the participating analysts were able, quantatively, to agree on the structure of a case. While they were able to predict the absolute status of the patient on the several variables with considerable success, they were unsuccessful in predicting the variables in which positive or negative change would occur in a given period in this part of the experiment."

It seems unlikely that this type of process system will offer much to psychotherapy research unless it is further modified in more operational directions. The authors' reliability figures cover only some of the variables, and only those instances where two judges agreed that a variable was present. Keeping in mind the common training, orientation, and experiential background of the analysts involved, the interjudges reliabilities are far from impressive. The authors themselves conclude that "there was great divergence in the conception and definition of variables among the participants. Though clinically each seemed to know what he was doing and talking about, it became strikingly clear that analytic concepts are poorly defined and not so useful for communication as they might be. . . . We suggest that a team of psychoanalysts and social scientists be formed for attempts at definition of the basic vocabulary." Not too surprisingly, this interdisciplinary effort remains to be done. The subsequent sterile history of their process system seems to challenge the authors' final statement: "The method seems valuable for furthering the statement of psychoanalytic hypotheses in scientifically acceptable forms and definitions."

Univariate Minor Process Instruments

The more than one hundred separate measures summarized in this section represent various attempts at definition of single therapist or patient interview variables. With very few exceptions, these measures were applied in one-shot research attempts. As with the preceding minor systems, however, there is evidence of innovation and creativity in some of these operational attempts.

Table 6.1 summarizes these therapist and patient measures. It is hoped that this format will permit future investigators to trace quickly previous measurement attempts on a particular process variable of interest. This table, together with Table 2.1 and the preceding section of this chapter, should provide a skeletal view of all the instruments available in the literature to date for directly investigating the process of psychotherapy.

The table's grouping labels are somewhat arbitrary, and a few of the authors cited are listed under several headings. Included in the table are some analogue studies which defined a particular construct either in terms of experimental manipulations or as a dependent variable measure. In regard to the therapist variables, most measurement attempts have been directed to the constructs of liking for client (9 citations), ambiguity (6), countertransference (5), interpretation (4), and acceptance (4). These frequencies, of course, do not include the relevant major systems presented in Chapters 3 through 5. Among the patient variables, the most frequently studied are anxiety (frustration, tension; 13 citations), resistance (defensiveness, transference; 11), self (9), self-disclosure (13), and speech and silence (10). Finally, the majority of the efforts have been directed at measuring patient in contrast to therapist interview behaviors.

References

Abeles, N. Liking for clients—its relationship to therapist's personality: unexpected findings. *Psychotherapy: Theory Research and Practice*, 1967, 4, 19-21.

Aidman, T. An objective study of the changing relationship between the present self and wanted self pictures as expressed by the client in client-centered therapy. Unpublished doctoral dissertation, University of Chicago, 1951.

Anderson, R. P. An investigation of the relationship between physiological and verbal behavior during client-centered psychotherapy. Unpublished doctoral dissertation, University of Chicago, 1954.

———. Physiological and verbal behavior during client-centered counseling. *Journal of Counseling Psychology*, 1956, 3, 174-84.

Aronson, H. and Weintraub, W. Verbal productivity as a measure of change in affective status. *Psychological Reports*, 1967, 20, 483-87.

Ashby, J. D., Ford, D. H., Guerney, B. G., Jr., and Guerney, L. F. Effects on clients of a reflective and leading type of psychotherapy. *Psychological Monographs*, 1957, 71.

Bellak, L., and Smith, M. B. An experimental exploration of the psychoanalytic process. *Psychoanalytic Quarterly*, 1956, 25, 385-414.

Berdie, R. F. A program of counseling interview research. *Educational and Psychological Measurement*, 1958, 18, 255-74.

Berg, I. A. Word choice in the interview and personal adjustment. *Journal of Counseling Psychology*, 1958, 5, 130-35.

Blau, B. A. A comparison of more improved with less improved clients treated by client-centered methods. In W. U. Snyder (Ed.), *Group report of a program of research in psychotherapy*. University Park: Pennsylvania State College, 1953, pp. 120-26. (Mimeographed)

Block, W. E. A preliminary study of achievement motive theory as a basis of patient expectations in psychotherapy. *Journal of Clinical Psychology*, 1964, 20, 268-71.

Boder, D. P. The adjective-verb quotient: a contribution to the psychology of language. *Psychological Records*, 1940, 22, 310-43.

Boomer, D. S., and Goodrich, D. W. Speech disturbance and judged anxiety. *Journal of Consulting Psychology*, 1961, 25, 160-64.

Bordin, E. S. Ambiguity as a therapeutic variable. *Journal of Consulting Psychology*, 1955, 19, 9-15.

Bowman, P. H. A study of the consistency of current, wish, and proper self concepts as a measure of therapeutic progress. Unpublished doctoral dissertation, University of Chicago, 1951.

Braaten, L. J. The movement from nonself to self in client-centered psychotherapy. *Journal of Counseling Psychology*, 1961, 8, 20-24.

Bugental, J. F. T. A method for assessing self and not-self attitudes during the therapeutic series. *Journal of Consulting Psychology*, 1952, 16, 435-39.

Campbell, R. E. Counselor personality and background and his interview subrole behavior. *Journal of Counseling Psychology*, 1962, 9, 329-34.

Caracena, P. F. Elicitation of dependency expressions in the initial stage of psychotherapy. *Journal of Counseling Psychology*, 1965, 12, 268-74.

Carkhuff, R. R., Berenson, B. B., and Southworth, A. J. Empathic understanding in interpersonal processes: a scale for measurement. Unpublished research scale, University of Massachusetts, 1964. (a)

———. Respect or positive regard in interpersonal processes: a scale for measurement. Unpublished research scale, University of Massachusetts, 1964. (b)

———. Congruence or genuineness in interpersonal processes: a scale for measurement. Unpublished research scale, University of Massachusetts, 1964. (c)

Carnes, E. F. Counselor flexibility: its extent and its relationship to other factors in the interview. *Abstracts of Doctoral Dissertations: 1949-1950*, Ohio State University, 1951, 61, 67-72.

Carnes, E. F., and Robinson, F. P. The role of client talk in the counseling interview. *Educational and Psychological Measurement*, 1948, 8, 635-44.

Colby, K. M. Experiment on the effects of an observer's presence on the imago system during psychoanalytic free-association. *Behavioral Science*, 1960, 5, 216-32.

Collier, R. M. A scale for rating responses of the psychotherapist. *Journal of Consulting Psychology*, 1953, 17, 321-26.

Cook, J. J. Silence in psychotherapy. *Journal of Counseling Psychology* 1964, 11, 42-46.

Crisp, A. H. An attempt to measure an aspect of "transference." *British Journal of Medical Psychology*, 1964, 37, 17-30. (a)

________. Development and application of a measure of "transference." *Journal of Psychosomatic Research*, 1964, 8, 327-35. (b)

Curran, C. A. *Personality Factors in Counseling*. New York: Grune & Stratton, 1945.

Cutler, R. L. Countertransference effects in psychotherapy. *Journal of Consulting Psychology*, 1958, 22, 349-56.

Danskin, D. G. Roles played by counselors in their interviews. *Journal of Counseling Psychology*, 1955, 2, 22-27.

Danskin, D. G., and Robinson, F. P. Differences in "degree of lead" among experienced counselors. *Journal of Counseling Psychology*, 1954, 1, 78-83.

Daulton, M. J. A study of factors relating to resistance in the interview. Unpublished master's thesis, Ohio State University, 1947.

Dibner, A. S. The relationship of ambiguity and anxiety in a clinical interview. Unpublished doctoral dissertation, University of Michigan, 1953.

________. Cue-counting: a measure of anxiety in interviews. *Journal of Consulting Psychology*, 1956, 20, 475-78.

________. Ambiguity and anxiety. *Journal of Abnormal and Social Psychology*, 1958, 56, 165-74.

DiMascio, A. A., Boyd, R. W., and Greenblatt, M. Physiological correlates of tension and antagonism during psychotherapy: a study of interpersonal physiology. *Psychosomatic Medicine*, 1957, 19, 99-104.

Dipboye, W. J. Analysis of counselor style by discussion units. *Journal of Counseling Psychology*, 1954, 1, 21-26.

Dittes, J. E. Galvanic skin response as a measure of patient's reaction to therapist permissiveness. *Journal of Abnormal and Social Psychology*, 1957, 55, 295-303.

Dittmann, A. T. The interpersonal process in psychotherapy: development of a research method. *Journal of Abnormal and Social Psychology*, 1952, 47, 236-44.

Dollard, J., and Mowrer, O. H. A method of measuring tension in written documents. *Journal of Abnormal and Social Psychology*, 1947, 42, 3-32.

Doster, J. A. Need for social approval and information about the "public" and "private" self. Unpublished master's thesis, Emory University, 1968.

Ehrlich, D., and Wiener, D. N. The measurement of values on psychotherapeutic settings. *Journal of General Psychology*, 1961, 64, 358-72.

Eldred, S. H., Hamburg, D. A., Inwood, E. R., Salzman, L. Meyersburg, H. A., and Goodrich, G. A procedure for the systematic analysis of psychotherapeutic interviews. *Psychiatry*, 1954, 17, 337-45.

Elton, C. F. A study of client responsibility: counselor technique or interview outcome? *Educational and Psychological Measurement*, 1950, 10, 728-37.

Fiedler, F. E. A method of objective quantification of certain countertransference attitudes. *Journal of Clinical Psychology*, 1951, 7, 101-107.

Fisher, S. Plausibility and depth of interpretation. *Journal of Consulting Psychology*, 1956, 20, 249-56.

Fitzgerald, E. Measurement of openness to experience: a study of regression in the service of the ego. *Journal of Personality and Social Psychology*, 1966, 4, 63.

Freedman, M., Leary T., Ossorio, A., and Coffey, H. The interpersonal dimensions of personality. *Journal of Personality*, 1950, 20, 143-62.

Garfield, S. L., and Affleck, D. C. Therapists' judgments concerning patients considered for psychotherapy. *Journal of Consulting Psychology*, 1961, 25, 505-509.

Gendlin, E. T. A scale for rating the manner of relating. In C. R. Rogers, E. T. Gendlin, D. J. Kiesler, and C. B. Truax. *The therapeutic relationship and its impact: a study of psychotherapy with schizophrenics*. Madison: University of Wisconsin Press, 1967. Pp. 603-11.

Gendlin, E. T., Beebe, J., Cassens, J., Klein, M. H., and Oberlander, M. Focusing ability in psychotherapy, personality, and creativity. In J. M. Shlien, et al. (Eds.), *Research in psychotherapy*. Vol. 3. Washington, D.C.: American Psychological Association, 1968. Pp. 217-41.

Gillespie, J. R., Jr. Verbal signs of resistance in client-centered therapy. In W. V. Snyder (Ed.), *Group report of a program of research in psychotherapy*. State College: Pennsylvania State University, 1953. Pp. 105-19.

Goldenberg, G. M., and Auld, F., Jr. Equivalance of silence to resistance. *Journal of Consulting Psychology*, 1964, 28, 476.

Goldman-Eisler, F. Individual differences between interviewers and their effect on interviewee's conversational behavior. *Journal of Mental Science*, 1952, 98, 660-71.

_______. Speech-breathing activity: a measure of tension and affect during interviews. *British Journal of Psychology*, 1955, 46, 53-63.

Gottschalk, L. A., Mayerson, P, and Gottlieb, A. A. Prediction and evaluation of outcome in an emergency brief psychotherapy clinic. *Journal of Nervous and Mental Disease*, 1967, 144, 77-96.

Haigh, G. Defensive behavior in client-centered therapy. *Journal of Consulting Psychology*, 1949, 13, 181-89.

Halkides, G. An experimental study of four conditions necessary for therapeutic change. Unpublished doctoral dissertation, University of Chicago, 1958.

Heller, K. Dependency changes in psychotherapy as a function of the discrepancy between conscious self-description and projective test performance. Unpublished doctoral dissertation, Pennsylvania State University, 1959.

_______. Ambiguity in the interview interaction. In J. M. Shlien et al. (Eds.), *Research in Psychotherapy*. Vol. 3. Washington, D.C.: American Psychological Association, 1968. Pp. 242-59.

Hoffman, A. E. A study of reported behavior changes in counseling. *Journal of Consulting Psychology*, 1949, 13, 190-95.

_______. An analysis of counselor sub-roles. *Journal of Counseling Psychology*, 1959, 6, 61-67.

Hogan, R. A. A measure of client defensiveness. In W. Wolff and J. A. Precker (Eds.), *Success in Psychotherapy*. New York: Grune & Stratton, 1952. Pp. 112-42.

Holzman, M. S., and Forman, V. P. A multidimensional content-analysis system applied to the analysis of therapeutic technique in psychotherapy with schizophrenic patients. *Psychological Bulletin*, 1966, 66, 263-81.

Isaacs, K. S. Relatability, a proposed construct and an approach to its validation. Unpublished doctoral dissertation, University of Chicago, 1956.

Isaacs, K. S., and Haggard, K. S. Some methods used in the study of affect in psychotherapy. In L. A. Gottschalk, and A. H. Auerbach (Eds.), *Methods of research in psychotherapy*. New York: Appleton-Century-Crofts, 1966. Pp. 226-39.

Jaffe, J. Language of the dyad: a method of interaction analysis in psychiatric interviews. *Psychiatry*, 1958, 21, 249-58.

Jarrett, F. Silence in psychiatric interviews. *British Journal of Medical Psychology*, 1966, 39, 357-62.

Kanfer, F. H. Verbal rate, eyeblink, and content in structured psychiatric interviews. *Journal of Abnormal and Social Psychology*, 1960, 61, 341-47.

Kiesler, D. J. A scale for the rating of congruence. In C. R. Rogers el al., *The therapeutic relationship and its impact: a study of psychotherapy with schizophrenics*. Madison: University of Wisconsin Press, 1967. Pp. 581-84.

Klien, M. H., and Mathieu, P. L. A scale of therapist experiencing. Madison: Wisconsin Psychiatric Institute, 1970.

Krause, M. S. Anxiety in verbal behavior: an intercorrelational study. *Journal of Consulting Psychology*, 1961, 25, 272.

Krause, M. S., and Pilisuk, M. Anxiety in verbal behavior: a validation study. *Journal of Consulting Psychology*, 1961, 25, 414-19.

LaForge, R. Research use of the ICL (Technical Report 3, No. 4), Eugene: Oregon Research Institute, 1963.

LaForge, R., Freedman, M., Leary, T., Naboisek, H., and Coffey, H. The interpersonal dimension of personality: II. An objective study of repression. *Journal of Personality*, 1954, 23, 129-53.

LaForge, R. and Suczek, R. The interpersonal dimension of personality: III. An interpersonal checklist. *Journal of Personality*, 1955, 24, 94-112.

Lasswell, H. D. Verbal references and physiological changes during the psychoanalytic interview: a preliminary communication. *Psychoanalytic Review*, 1935, 22, 10-24.

———. Veraenderungen an einer Versuchsperson waehrend einer Kurzen Folge von psychoanalytischen Interviews. *Imago*, 1937, 23, 375-80.

———. A provisional classification of symbol data. *Psychiatry*, 1938, 1, 197-204.

Leary, T. Theory and measurement methodology in interpersonal communication. *Psychiatry*, 1955, 18, 147-61.

———. *Interpersonal diagnosis of personality*. New York: Ronald Press, 1957.

Leary, T., and Coffey, H. Interpersonal diagnosis: some problems of methodology and validation. *Journal of Abnormal and Social Psychology*, 1955, 50, 110-25. (a)

———. The prediction of interpersonal behavior in group psychotherapy. *Psychodrama and Group Psychotherapy Monographs*, 1955 (28). (b)

Leary, T., and Harvey, J. S. A methodology for measurement of personality changes in psychotherapy. *Journal of Clinical Psychology*, 1956, 12, 123-32.

Lowinger, P., and Dobie, S. Attitudes and emotions of the psychiatrist in the initial interview. *American Journal of Psychotherapy*, 1966, 20, 17-34.

Mahl, G. F. Disturbances and silences in the patient's speech in psychotherapy. *Journal of Abnormal and Social Psychology*, 1956, 53, 1-15.

Meerloo, J. A. M. Psychoanalysis as an experiment in communication. *Psychoanalysis and Psychoanalytic Review*, 1959, 46, 75-89.

Mich, R. M. A study of resistance during psychotherapy. Unpublished doctoral dissertation, University of Colorado. Ann Arbor, Mich.: University Microfilms, 1956, No. 13,766.

Miller, H. E. "Acceptance" and related attitudes as demonstrated in psychotherapeutic interviews. *Journal of Clinical Psychology*, 1949, 5, 83-87.

Mueller, W. J., and Dilling, C. A. Studying interpersonal themes in psychotherapy research. *Journal of Counseling Psychology*, 1969, 16, 50-58.

Osburn, H. G. An investigation of the ambiguity dimension of counselor behavior. Unpublished doctoral dissertation, University of Michigan, 1951.

Page, H. A. An assessment of the predictive value of certain language measures in psychotherapeutic counseling. In W. U. Snyder (Ed.), *Group report of a program of research in psychotherapy*. State College: Pennsylvania State College, 1953. Pp. 88-93.

Parloff, M. B., Goldstein, N., and Iflund, B. Communication of values and therapeutic change. *Archives of General Psychiatry*, 1960, 2, 300-304.

Pope, B., Blass, T., Siegman, A. W., and Raher, J. Anxiety and depression in speech. *Journal of Consulting and Clinical Psychology*, 1970,35, 128-33.

Pope, B., and Siegman, A. W. Interviewer specificity and topical focus in relation to interviewee productivity. *Journal of Verbal Learning and Verbal Behavior*, 1965, 4, 188-92.

Porter, E. H., Jr. The development and evaluation of a measure of counseling interview procedures. *Education and Psychological Measurement*, 1943, 3, 105-26; 215-38.

________. *An introduction to therapeutic counseling.* Boston: Houghton Mifflin, 1950.

Raimy, V. C. Self reference in counseling interviews. *Journal of Consulting Psychology*, 1948, 12, 153-63.

Rank, R. Counseling competence and perceptions. *Personnel Guidance Journal*, 1966, 45, 359-65.

Raskin, A. Observable signs of anxiety or distress during psychotherapy. *Journal of Consulting Psychology*, 1962, 26, 389.

Raskin, N. J. An objective study of the locus-of-evaluation factor in psychotherapy. In W. Wolff and J. A. Precker (Eds.), *Success in psychotherapy*. New York: Grune & Stratton, 1952.

Raush, H. L., and Bordin, E. S. Warmth in personality development and in psychotherapy. *Psychiatry*, 1957, 20, 351-63.

Rawn, M. L. An experimental study of transference and resistance phenomena in psychoanalytically oriented psychotherapy. *Journal of Clinical Psychology*, 1958, 14, 418-25.

Redlich, F. C., Hollingshead, A. B., and Bellis, E. Social class differences in attitudes toward psychiatry. *American Journal of Orthopsychiatry*, 1955, 25, 60-70.

Reid, J. R., and Finesinger, J. E. The role of insight in psychotherapy. American Journal of Psychiatry, 1952, 108, 726-34.

Ringler, D. Some determinants of therapist behavior. Unpublished doctoral dissertation, University of Michigan, 1957.

Rogers, C. R. The development of insight in a counseling relationship. *Journal of Consulting Psychology*, 1944, 8, 331-41.

Rosenman, S. Changes in the representations of self, other, and interrelationship in client-centered therapy. *Journal of Counseling Psychology*, 1955, 2, 271-77.

Roshal, J. V. G. The type-token ratio as a measure of changes in behavior variability during psychotherapy. In W. U. Snyder (Ed.), *Group report of a program for research in psychotherapy*. University Park: Pennsylvania State College, 1953, Pp. 94-104.

Rottschafer, R. H., and Renzaglia, G. A. The relationship of dependent-like verbal behaviors to counselor style and induced set. *Journal of Consulting Psychology*, 1962, 26, 172-77.

Russell, P. D., and Snyder, W. U. Counselor anxiety in relation to amount of clinical experience and quality of affect demonstrated by clients. *Journal of Consulting Psychology*, 1963, 27, 358-63.

Saper, B. A multidimensional analysis for the study of the psychotherapeutic interview. Unpublished doctoral dissertation, University of California, 1951.

Sheerer, E. T. An analysis of the relationship between acceptance of and respect for self and acceptance of and respect for others in ten counseling cases. *Journal of Consulting Psychology*, 1949, 13, 169-75.

Sklansky, M. A., Isaacs, K. S., and Haggard, E. A. A method for the study of verbal interactions and levels of meaning in psychotherapy. In J. S. Gottlieb and G. Tourney (Eds.), *Scientific papers and discussions, divisional meeting, Mid-West area district branches*. Detroit: American Psychiatric Association, 1960. Pp 133-48.

Sommer, G. R., and Killian, L. M. Areas of value differences: I. A method of investigation. *Journal of Social Psychology*, 1954, 39, 227-35.

Sommer, G. R., Mazo, B., and Lehner, G. F. J. An empirical investigation of therapeutic "listening." *Journal of Clinical Psychology*, 1955, 11, 132-36.

Speisman, J. C. The relationship between depth of interpretation and verbal expressions of resistance in psychotherapy. Unpublished doctoral dissertation, University of Michigan, 1956.

Stock, D. An investigation into the interrelationships between the self-concept and feelings directed toward other persons and groups. *Journal of Consulting Psychology*, 1949, 13, 176-80.

Stoler, N. Client likeability: a variable in the study of psychotherapy. *Journal of Consulting Psychology*, 1963, 27, 175-78.

Strietfeld, J. W. Expressed acceptance of self and others by psychotherapists. *Journal of Consulting Psychology*, 1959, 23, 435-41.

Strupp, H. H., Wallach, M. S., Wogan, M. and Jenkins, J. W. Psychotherapists' assessment of former patient. *Journal of Nervous and Mental Disease*, 1963, 137, 222-30.

Suchman, D. I. A scale for the measurement of Revealingness in spoken behavior. Unpublished master's thesis, Ohio State University, 1965.

Temerlin, M. K. One determinant of the capacity to free-associate in psychotherapy. *Journal of Abnormal and Social Psychology*, 1956, 53, 16-18.

Thetford, W. N. An objective measurement of frustration tolerance in evaluating psychotherapy. In N. W. Wolff and V. A. Precker (Eds.), *Success in psychotherapy*. New York: Grune & Stratton, 1952.

Tindall, R. H., and Robinson, F. P. The use of silence as a technique in counseling. *Journal of Clinical Psychology*, 1947, 3, 136-41.

Todd, W. B., and Ewing, T. N. Changes in self-reference during counseling. *Journal of Counseling Psychology*, 1961, 8, 112-15.

Tolor, A., and Reznikoff, M. A new approach to insight: a preliminary report. *Journal of Nervous and Mental Disease*, 1960, 130, 286-96.

Toman, W. Pause analysis as a short interviewing technique. *Journal of Consulting Psychology*, 1953, 17, 1-7.

Tomlinson, T. M. A scale for the rating of personal constructs. In C. R. Rogers,

(Ed.), *The therapeutic relationship and its impact: a study of psychotherapy with schizophrenics.* Madison: University of Wisconsin Press, 1967. Pp. 593-97.

Tomlinson, T. M., and Stoler, N. The relationship between affective evaluation and ratings of therapy process and outcome with schizophrenics. *Psychotherapy: Theory Research and Practice,* 1967, 4, 14-18.

Townsend, A. H. An empirical measurement of ambiguity in the context of psychotherapy. *Michigan Academy of Science, Arts and Letters,* 1956, 41, 349-55.

Truax, C. B., and Carkhuff, R. R. Concreteness: a neglected variable in research in psychotherapy. *Journal of Clinical Psychology,* 1964, 20, 264-67.

Van der Veen, F., and Tomlinson, T. A scale for rating the manner of problem expression. In C. R. Rogers et al. (Eds.), *The therapeutic relationship and its impact: a study of psychotherapy with schizophrenics.* Madison: University of Wisconsin Press, 1967. Pp. 599-601.

Vargas, M. J. Changes in self-awareness during client-centered therapy. In C. R. Rogers and R. F. Dymond (Eds.), *Psychotherapy and personality change.* Chicago: University of Chicago Press, 1954. Pp. 145-65.

Walker, A. M., Rablen, R. A., and Rogers, C. R. Development of a scale to measure process changes in psychotherapy. *Journal of Clinical Psychology,* 1960, 16, 79-85.

White, A. M., Fichtenbaum, L., and Dollard, J. Evaluation of silence in initial interviews with psychiatric clinic patients. *Journal of Nervous and Mental disease,* 1964, 139, 550-57.

White, R. K. Black boy: a value analysis. *Journal of Abnormal and Social Psychology,* 1947, 42, 440-61.

________. *Value-analysis, the nature and use of the method.* Glen Gardner, N. J.: Libertarian Press, 1951.

Winder, C. C., Ahmad, F. Z., Bandura, A., and Rau, L. C. Dependency of patients, psychotherapists' responses, and aspects of psychotherapy. *Journal of Consulting Psychology,* 1962, 26, 129-34.

Yulis, S., and Kiesler, D. J. Contertransference response as a function of therapist anxiety and content of patient talk. *Journal of Consulting and Clinical Psychology,* 1968, 32, 413-19.

Zavalloni, R. The process of choice in therapeutic counseling. *Antonianum,* 1954, 29, 157-324.

III

Systems of Indirect Psychotherapy Process Analysis

7

Indirect Assessment of Therapist and Patient Interview Behaviors

Previous chapters have reviewed measures that are applied directly to the psychotherapy participants' verbalizations. The instruments presented here focus on *indirect* assessment of therapist and patient process behaviors. None of the latter measures are typically applied by judges to tape-recorded or other transcriptions of therapist-patient interview communications, although a minority of them can be adapted to that purpose.

Of the twenty-eight measures, two involve TAT-like projective measures, two involve experimental manipulation of the interview procedure itself, and two involve standardized analogue presentation. The remaining twenty-two measures consist of questionnaires filled in by the patient, the therapist, or both.

The questionnaires are, first, inventories designed to measure the participants' relationship perceptions as they occur during a particular psychotherapy transaction. The procedure involves administration during the treatment sequence, usually immediately after a designated session or block of sessions, to tap relationship perceptions that occurred within that particular interview or block of interviews. For example the patient may be asked to report how he perceived the therapist's understanding during that session, or the therapist may report how well he felt he communicated understanding in that interview. Some of the measures are designed exclusively for patients' perceptions, some for therapists' perceptions, and some are responded to by both participants.

The second type of questionnaire is designed to measure more general attitudes about psychotherapy, about the therapeutic relationship, or about therapist technique behaviors, independent of any particular dyadic transaction. These self-reports are obtained from either therapists or patients (or the public). They assess either patients' or therapists' general conceptions of, or preferences for, various aspects of the therapeutic relationship and technique. The questions asked are of the tenor: "How would you like one of the therapy participants to act?" "How would you act if you were in therapy?" "What do you consider the ideal therapeutic relationship?"

The devices presented in this chapter, therefore, represent a somewhat unique assessment domain. They require either patient or therapist self-reports about their particular therapy interaction or about therapy transactions more generally, and thereby tend to assess either momentary expectancies and interpersonal perceptions, or general attitudes about therapeutic relationships or ideal or desired therapist behaviors. This domain is relatively distinct from that focusing on more traditional personality or interest traits. To the limited extent that it taps therapist or patient trait systems, it falls more appropriately in the domain of interpersonal traits and interpersonal theories of personality.

Measures of Participant Perceptions During Specific Psychotherapy Transactions

Each of the instruments presented in this section is designed to tap the participants' perceptions of a particular therapist–patient relationship-in-progress. They come closest to being direct process measures, and some can be easily adapted to that purpose. Rather than having judges assess the quality of the patient–therapist interview relationship directly from tape-recorded verbalization, these measures require that the participants, usually outside the interview situation, report their feelings about the relationship.

The devices tend to have theoretical anchoring in either Rogerian or psychoanalytic theory. The relevant Rogerian constructs are those of therapist "conditions," more specifically the therapist's relationship attitudes of empathic understanding, positive regard, and congruence. The corresponding psychoanalytic concepts are patient "transference," and (in more recent analytic theory) the positive and negative aspects of therapist "countertransference."

Various questionnaire devices will be presented first. The relationship inventories included are those of Barrett-Lennard; Snyder and Snyder; Anderson and Anderson; and Lorr. Barrett-Lennard's inventory measures both patient and therapist perceptions of the relationship; Snyder and Snyder developed separate measures of patient and therapist perceptions or affect; Anderson and Anderson's questionnaire is designed to be applied by judges to verbalizations of both therapist and patient; Lorr's instrument assesses only patient perceptions. Mendelsohn and Geller, as well as Strupp, Fox, and Lessler developed questionnaires to be administered to patients after therapy termination, to assess their evaluational attitudes toward their therapy experience. Libo developed a projective measure of the patient's attraction to his therapist. The second part of this section will describe experimental modifications of the traditional interview situation by Kagan, Kratwhol, and Miller and by Nathan and his colleagues. Both groups utilize videotape procedures to tap participants' relationship perception.

QUESTIONNAIRE PROCEDURES

The Relationship Inventory

Barrett-Lennard (1959b)

The Relationship Inventory was developed to measure Rogers' therapists conditions of empathic understanding, positive regard, unconditionality of regard, and congruence. A fifth therapist dimension, "willingness to be known," had been introduced in the original scale version, but was dropped from the final version of the inventory.

> Two of the variables, the concepts of empathic understanding and congruence of the therapist, correspond in essence with the meanings given by Rogers (1957, 1959), although reformulated. . . . Two others, level of regard and unconditionality of regard, represent a division of the concept of unconditionality of regard, originally formulated by Standal (1954), into what are considered by the investigator to be two separate components. They are, therefore, newly defined. (Barrett-Lennard, 1962)

> In developing and applying this new technique I assumed that a client is most directly influenced, in the relationship with his therapist, by what he experiences and perceives his therapist's response to him to be. From this point of view it appeared most meaningful to employ client perceptions as the basic data from which to assess the effective therapeutic quality of a relationship. (Barrett-Lennard, 1959b, p. 1)

The items were constructed by Barrett-Lennard. He revised early forms from feedback of other counselors regarding their adequacy for representing the constructs involved. A formal content-validation procedure was also carried out to eliminate any items not consistently classified by a group of five qualified judges as either "positive" or "negative" expressions of the variable they were designed to represent. The subtests were derived using a combination of item analysis and rational-theoretical considerations. A careful attempt was made, within the bounds of Rogerian theory, to make the items within each subtest consistent both with theory and with each other.

The scale items have gone through several revisions since the original form (1962). The currently final form (1964 Revision) was based

> (*a*) on item-analysis results from several samples of data obtained with earlier versions of the instrument, (*b*) on other technical considerations, such as achieving a numerical balance of positively and negatively stated items in each of the four scales, (*c*) on minor theoretical refinements, particularly in respect to the unconditionality of regard scale, and (*d*) on the concern to alter or replace items of a relatively abstract or verbally difficult kind. (Barrett-Lennard, 1966, p. 1)

The 1964 revision contains sixty-four items, sixteen each for the four scales, eight positively and eight negatively expressed. The respondent replies by choosing one of six levels of agreement for each item, ranging numerically from +3 to -3: "I feel it is probably true," +1 ("probably not true," -1); "I feel it is true," +2 ("is not true," -2); "I strongly feel that it is true," +3 ("not true," -3). In studies of the therapy relationship the scale is administered to the patient and/or the therapist immediately following a therapy hour. There are four forms of the inventory, with only the pronouns changed to meet all the possible sex combinations of the patient-therapist pair.

The four variables measured by the Relationship Inventory are:

(1) *Empathic Understanding* refers to "the extent to which one person is conscious of the immediate awareness of another . . . an active process of desiring to know the full present and changing awareness of another person, of reaching out to receive his communication and meaning, and of translating his words and signs into experienced meaning that matches at least those aspects of his awareness that are most important to him at the moment." (Barrett-Lennard, 1959b. p. 2) Examples of items tapping this factor (from the 1964 revision) are: "He nearly always knows exactly what I mean" (+). "He understands me" (+). "He appreciates exactly how the things I experience feel to me" (+). "His response to me is usually so fixed and automatic that I don't really get through to him" (-). "His own attitudes toward some of the things I do or say prevent him from understanding me" (-).

(2) *Level of Regard* is defined as "the overall level or tendency of one person's affective response to another. Or to use a factorial analogy, it is the composite 'loading' of all the distinguishable feeling reactions of one person toward another, both positive and negative, in a single abstract dimension." (p. 2.) Item examples are: "He respects me as a person"(+). "I feel appreciated by him" (+). "He is friendly and warm with me" (+). "I feel that he disapproves of me" (-). "He finds me rather dull and uninteresting" (-). "He is impatient with me" (-). "At times he feels contempt for me" (-).

(3) *Unconditionality of Regard* originally referred to "the aspect of constancy or variability of affective response, regardless of its general level. The less that A's immediate regard for B varies in response to changes in B's feelings toward himself, or toward A, or to the kinds of experiences or attitudes that B is communicating to A, or to any other varying condition, the more unconditional it is". (p. 3) In the 1964 revision this definition was refined.

> In order for variation (in warmth, interest, liking, etc.) in A's response to B to imply conditionality, this variation needs to be linked in the perceiver's experience with some quality or behavior of B. For example, if A reports, in reference to B, that "Sometimes I feel more warmly toward him than I do at other times," this certainly implies variation in A's affective response or attitude, but it may or may not mean that this variation is conditional (or contingent) on discriminated attributes of B's behavior, attitudes, or feelings, etc. It could be that A experiences his varying warmth-interest in B as resulting essentially from factors extraneous to their relationship, such as variation in mood. (Barrett-Lennard, 1970, pp. 5-6)

Items exemplifying unconditionality are: "Whether I am feeling happy or unhappy with myself makes no real difference to the way he feels about me" (+). "I can [or could] be openly critical or appreciative of him without really making him feel any differently about me" (+). "Depending on my behavior he has a better opinion of me sometimes than he has at other times" (-). "Sometimes I am more worthwhile in his eyes than I am at other times" (-).

(4) *Therapist Congruence* refers to

> the degree to which a person is functionally integrated in the context of his relationship with another, such that there is absence of conflict or inconsistency between his primary experience, his conscious awareness, and his overt communication. . . . Direct evidence of lack of congruence includes, for example, inconsistency between what the individual says and what he implies by expres-

> sion, gestures, or tone of voice. Indications of psychological discomfort or anxiety (implying threat and defense) are also important evidence of lack of congruence. (Barrett-Lennard, 1959b, p. 4)

Item examples are: "He is comfortable and at ease in our relationship" (+). "I feel that he is real and genuine with me" (+). "Sometimes he is not at all comfortable but we go on, outwardly ignoring it" (-). "He wants me to think that he likes me or understands me more than he really does" (-). "I believe that he has feelings he does not tell me about that are causing difficulty in our relationship" (-).

Barrett-Lennard reports good test-retest reliability for the 1964 revision, with coefficients ranging for the subtests from 0.79 to 0.91 in one sample, and from 0.86 to 0.92 in another. Mills and Zytowski (1967) report test-retest coefficients of 0.80 to 0.87 for Form MO, and 0.74 to 0.90 for Form OS. Two separate factor analyses of the intercorrelations among the four subtests both yielded three factors, but drew separate conclusions. Mills and Zytowski (1967) extracted three components, the first of which accounted for two-thirds of the variance. They conclude that the presence of this general component "seriously questions the presence of multiple (and independent) characteristics of a relationship as measured by the Relationship Inventory. There appears to be a single dominant characteristic across all the relationships measured to which all four subtests contribute strongly. . . . [These findings] strongly suggest that the multiple characteristics of a helping relationship used in these earlier studies may well be only differential manifestations of a single overriding characteristic for such a relationship." Walker and Little (1969), however, extracted three factors which they labeled as nonevaluative, psychological insight (or empathy), and likeability (or regard). They conclude that the "unconditionality dimensions and regard dimensions define separate factors, and that the empathy and congruence dimensions are explained by a single factor." Apparently, the dimensionality characteristics of the Relationship Inventory remain to be established unequivocally, although the evidence suggests there are no more than three factors being measured by the four subtests.

Barrett-Lennard has not summarized the many studies which have applied his inventory, although he currently has a manual in preparation. As of 1969, more than sixty studies had been reported (Barrett-Lennard and Elliott, 1969). The RI has been found to be useful in a variety of situations. Its initial value in assessing the effects of psychotherapy (Barrett-Lennard, 1962) has been extended to other areas of human interaction such as parent-child, mother-daughter, teacher-pupil, and marital relationships. The instrument has been used in these studies with very diverse samples of subjects (for example, chronic schizophrenic patients, college students, and juvenile delinquents) and in the context of a wide variety of specific research problems. Barrett-Lennard (1966) states:

> It can be used to tap interpersonal perceptions in a variety of levels: how I perceive the other responding to me; how I respond to the other; how I think the other perceives my response to him; how I think the other sees his response to me; how I would like the other to respond to me; etc. In each case corresponding data can be gathered from both participants in a relationship, from the standpoint of an external observer, in reference to a generalized relationship with a group of persons . . . as well as with an individual person and, of course, at different points in time for the same relationship. In such ways as these the qualities of relationship may themselves be zeroed in on from many angles, in addition to studying the association between the relationship factors and other classes of personality and behavioral variables. (p. 5)

Patient Affect and Therapist Affect Scales

Snyder and Snyder (1961)

In constructing their relationship questionnaires, the authors drew considerably from W. U. Snyder's doctoral students, (Ashby, Ford, Guerney and Guerney, 1957) scales, "the Client Personal Reaction Questionnaire" and "The Therapist Personal Reaction Questionnaire," as well as from Bown (1954). In their 1961 volume, Snyder and Snyder state:

> About five years ago we became very much convinced that the relationship that develops between therapist and client is the essential core of the therapy. We felt that if there were an adequate way of measuring this relationship, much progress would be made possible in improving psychotherapy. It appeared desirable to develop some method of measuring those fairly subtle attitudes toward each other of which both client and therapist are aware as therapy progresses. It should be possible to measure them after each interview, so that a "running account" of the trends in the relationship would be available. (p. 1)
>
> Although we have focused on the relationship, we wish to make it clear that this is only one of the facets of psychotherapy. It seems to us that therapeutic techniques are probably equally important in determining the degree of success that is achieved. However, our

> research cannot effectively cope with all important aspects of therapy, and . . . we have limited ourselves to consideration of that part of therapy, and have discussed techniques only when they are concerned with, or contribute to, the therapy relationship. (p. 3)
>
> The term relationship, or interpersonal relationship, is a psychological unknown. It is used loosely by many persons, and meanings are often quite idiosyncratic. . . . As we see it, the therapy relationship is best described as the reciprocity of various sets of affective attitudes which two or more persons hold toward each other in psychotherapy. The form of behavior we wish to include in the concept of relationship is limited to attitudes, which of course, include affect. Thus, the therapeutic relationship must consist, by our definition, of some sort of mathematical relation between transference and countertransference attitudes. This could be a summation, equation, or in most cases perhaps a ratio. (p. 270)
>
> In our effort to throw light on the relationship we have focused on the feelings of the therapist and client toward each other as expressed in scales filled out shortly after each interview. . . . It was necessary to construct and initiate validation of two a priori scales, the Therapist's Affect Scale and the Client's Affect Scale. We used these scales to study the therapist's and the client's overall interactions to each other, and also their interview-by-interview changes in affect. We also wished to examine how accurately the therapist was able to judge the client's affect toward himself after each interview. (p. 13)

The criteria that guided construction of their questionnaires were that the scales had to be short enough to be administered after each interview, and that items had to relate to affect occurring during that interview only, and not to affect developed over a longer period of time. They selected some of the Ashby et al. items and constructed some new ones. The original Client Affect Scale contained 200 items; the original Therapist Affect Scale, 196 items. The client scale contained ten a priori subscales of items believed to measure needs or motives such as "affiliation" or "fear of exposure." The therapist scale contained a priori scales designed to measure "understanding," "feeling of success," "derogatory feelings," and the like.

These original scales were applied in the study of psychotherapy reported in Snyder and Snyder's 1961 volume. The resulting item scores were factor-analyzed at several representative interview points across therapy, and further item analyses were performed. From their findings "it became apparent that only the positive and negative aspects of the factors were incontrovertible. We were forced to the conclusion that most of our priori scales were not independent of each other except insofar as they were positive or negative." (p. 27) Subsequent item analyses led to the final versions of the two scales. The Client's Affect Scale now contained a set of 108 positive and 158 negative items—Positive Attitudes of the Client (PAC) and Negative Attitudes of the Client (NAC) respectively. The final Therapist's Affect Scale consisted of 84 positive and 182 negative items—Positive Attitudes of the Therapist (PAT) and Negative Attitudes of the Therapist (NAT) respectively.

"In similar situations it is usually considered cumbersome to have both negative and positive scales, or at least a combined score is usually desired. For this purpose we found that a simple algebraic summation of the positive and negative scores was entirely satisfactory, and produced the following final scales: Client's Affect Scale (PAC-NAC), Therapist's Affect Scale (PAT-NAT)." (Snyder and Snyder, 1961, p. 39) Hence, for the final versions of the scales, only one overall score is obtained, which represents for the client and therapist respectively the algebraic summation of his positive and negative feelings toward the other participant.

Items and a scoring key for the final Client's Affect Scale are presented in the authors' 1961 volume (pp. 387-96). Examples of the client items are: "Today many of the things my counselor said just seemed to hit the nail on the head." "My counselor is intellectual and analytical without much real feeling for my problems." "Today I was pleased with my counselor's interest and attention." "Today my counselor treated me as a client, not as a person." "Today I felt my counselor diaspproved of me." "Today I felt I could count on my counselor to assume the responsibility for solving my problems." "Today I had some fantasies that were pretty hurtful to the counselor."

Items and a scoring key of the final Therapist's Affect Scale are presented in Snyder and Snyder's 1961 volume (pp. 377-86). Examples of items in the therapist questionnaire are: "Today I felt that we had a pretty relaxed, understanding kind of relationship." "Today I feel that I'll miss having these interviews a little when the client decides to terminate." "The hour seemed to be dragging with this client today." "Today this client hits me where it hurts." "Today the client was afraid of the therapist." "Today the client was hostile." "Today the client showed excessive dependency and inability to proceed without undue assistance." "The client feels he is unworthy because he has to ask for help."

The authors provide no reliability information in their 1961 volume. Internal consistency reliability is the only concern, since the instrument was designed as a momentary-state measure, and since there are no equivalent forms available.

Snyder and Snyder's 1961 volume presents the only evidence regarding the validity of the Client's and the Therapist's Affect Scales. Samples of the findings from their 1961 study are: (1) The clients' positive attitudes tended to increase throughout the therapy process, and negative attitudes tended to rise toward a high point at the middle of therapy, and then to decline. (2) Positive transference for nine "better" cases drops markedly toward the middle of therapy but then during the last third of therapy rises to a considerably higher level than at any previous time. In the case of eleven "poorer" clients, the transference tends to fluctuate at a much lower level than for the better cases; at the end of the first third of therapy it rises to approximately the same level as the better clients' lowest level, and thereafter tends to drop off, with a slight upturn near termination. (3) For the authors, the most central measure of the relationship between transference and countertransference lay in the association between the Client Affect Scale and Therapist Affect Scale scores. The obtained overall correlation between the PAC-NAC and PAT-NAT scores was 0.70. The authors conclude from this and other findings that there was a tendency for transference and countertransference to covary with each other throughout the therapy process. "To us it seems that relationship is a basic component of therapy. Without it, techniques are of little value. When client and therapist are properly matched, they can develop an effective interpersonal and therapeutic relationship which is quite reciprocal in character, and which grows increasingly positive, making an effective therapeutic outcome probable." (p. 367)

Rapport Rating Scale or Interview Rating Scale

Anderson and Anderson (1962)

Anderson and Anderson (1962) attempted to measure aspects of the therapy relationship by providing "an explicit, operational definition of the counseling relationship characterized by ideal rapport. . . . The operational definition was made in terms of attitudes and behaviors of clients and counselors. Assumptions regarding the study were that rapport is of importance early in counseling; it is relevant to communication; it is observable behavior perceived by both participants in the relationship; and it can be assessed by an observer." (p. 18)

The authors collected a series of 163 items dealing with counselor and client attitudes and behaviors from transcribed case material, clients, counselors, and the Q-universes of Fiedler (1950a) and Bown (1954). Seven psychologists and one psychiatrist coded the items into three categories: good-poor rapport, ambiguous or unrelated to rapport, and those defying classification. Of the 163 items, 99 were judged as relevant in describing rapport, and these 99 formed the "Rapport Rating Scale." One hundred counseling psychologists then rated each of the 99 items on a nine-point scale ranging from "good rapport" to "bad rapport." The sample of psychologists included American Psychological Association members of Division 12 and/or Division 17 who were "known to be authors and as being actually engaged in counseling activity." In rating the 99 items, each judge used his own conception of ideal rapport. The items were rated also by a client sample, consisting of sixty-two clients from the University of Texas Testing and Guidance Bureau (fifteen males and fifteen females with more than five hours of counseling, and sixteen males and sixteen females with less than five interviews). The majority of these clients were still in group counseling at the time they received the scales in the mail.

Of the two samples, sixty-nine of one hundred counselors (69%) and thirty-four of sixty-two clients (53 percent) returned the scale. After eliminating each item checked by a least 10 percent of the therapists as "unclassifiable," seventy-seven items remained. Of these seventy-seven items, they selected fifty that had Q values of 1.0 or less (that is, the fifty showing the least disagreement among the judges); these formed the final "Interview Rating Scale." Items in the final scale are evenly divided between items representing good and poor rapport; eighteen items refer to client behaviors and attitudes while the remaining refer to counselor behavior.

The fifty items are separated into the following logical categories. (1) *Positive Client*. Item examples are: "The client has confidence in the counselor." "The client feels the counselor has a genuine desire to be of service." "The client feels accepted as an individual." "The client can talk freely about his innermost feelings." (2) *Negative Client*. "The client distrusts the counselor." "The client feels frustration with the counselor." "The client feels more like a 'case' than an individual." "The client feels blocked and frustrated in his attempt to relate to the counselor." (3) *Positive Counselor*. "The counselor creates a feeling of 'warmth' in the relationship." "The counselor's tone of voice conveys the ability to share the client's feelings." "The counselor is very patient." (4) *Negative Counselor*. "The counselor has a condescending attitude." "The counselor insists on being always 'right'." "The counselor is uncertain of himself." "The counselor acts cold and distant."

Anderson and Anderson were interested in obtaining those items that both judge groups (counselors and clients) agreed represented good or poor rapport. To determine the extent to which this occurred, the medians of the fifty items selected from the counselors' ratings were correlated with these same item medians from the client's ratings. The obtained Pearson r was 0.98, indicating that "we had a series of items on which both clients and counselors agreed as representing the extremes of rapport. . . . [This result] supports the findings of Fiedler and Bown; that is, when described in terms of specific behaviors and attitudes, there is a core of agreement among clients and counselors concerning the nature of ideal rapport or the ideal relationship."

Finally, the authors briefly report the findings of two studies (Correll, 1955; Brams, 1961) that applied their "Interview Rating Scale." They conclude that "both of these studies support the original purpose of the scale, that is to rate interviews in terms of the effectiveness of communication or, as we termed it, rapport; moreover, further judicious exploration of the scale as a research instrument and as a tool in counselor training is justified by these results." However, little further exploration has occurred.

The Client's Perceptions Inventory

Lorr (1965)

Lorr (1965) describes the rationale for development of his inventory as follows.

> The patient's feeling and attitudes toward the therapist have long been recognized as important features of the therapeutic relationship. This aspect of the relationship has become identified with Freud's term *transference*. . . . The view taken here is similar to that expressed by Schutz (1958), although the latter did not express his hypothesis in terms of transference relationships. The basic notion is that when a patient perceives his adult position in an interpersonal situation to be similar to his own childhood relation, the adult behavior evoked will be similar to his childhood behavior toward significant others. . . . In brief, knowledge of how a patient *perceives* his therapist at any given stage of therapy is likely to be a good predictor of his way of *relating* to him. It is the neurotic ways of relating to others interpersonally, and the conflicts that ensue, that represent a large share of a patient's problems. The patient's perceptions of his therapist are thus of value in understanding and modifying the former's behavior. (p. 577)

Lorr felt, consequently, that it would be of considerable value to determine the major ways in which clients view their therapists, and designed an inventory to measure these dimensions. The eight dimensions postulated (1965) "were in part based on conceptualizations proposed by Fiedler (1950) of what constitutes a good therapeutic relationship and the interpersonal categories developed by Leary and his colleagues (Leary, 1957)." (p. 577) The constructs selected were: directiveness, nurturance, understanding, acceptance, equalitarianism, independence-encouraging, critical detachment, and hostile rejection. An inventory of sixty-five statements was constructed in which each of the constructs was defined by four to ten statements to be rated by the client on a scale of frequency of occurrence.

The inventory was administered to 523 male patients in individual psychotherapy at forty-three Veterans Administration outpatient clinics throughout the United States. Approximately half of the sample were neurotic, one-third psychotics, and the remainder personality disorders and psychosomatic cases. The item responses were intercorrelated and factor analyzed.

The five factors extracted, with exemplary items and respective factor loadings, were:

(1) *Understanding* is defined "by behaviors that indicate the therapist understands what the patient is communicating and what he is feeling." Items examples are: "Seems to know exactly what I mean." (0.66) "Seems to understand how I feel." (0.6l) "Understands me even when I don't express myself well." (0.59) "Misses the point I'm trying to get accross." (-0.48) "Has a hard time seeing things as I do." (-0.47)

(2) *Accepting* is the broadest of the five factors. "Interest, nurturance, and equalitarianism appear to play equal roles in definition of this factor." Items are: "Shows a real interest in me and my problems." (0.66) "Is easy to talk to." (0.58) "Makes me feel he is one person I can really trust." (0.52) "Is quick to praise and commend me when I am doing well." (0.50) "Understands my problems and worries." (0.49) "Shows a real liking and affection for me." (0.47) "Seems to have a very real respect for me." (0.45) "Relates to me as though I were a companion." (0.43)

(3) *Authoritarian* refers to those "behaviors of the therapist relating to control. The client perceives the therapist as offering advice, direction, and assistance in reaching decisions." Item examples are: "Is full of advice about everything I do." (0.6l) "Seems to try to get me to accept his standards." (0.52) "Expects me to accept his ideas and opinions." (0.50) "Makes me feel that I don't have to agree with him." (-0.29) "Tells me what I should talk about." (0.28)

(4) *Independence-Encouraging* is a "relatively small but sharply

defined" factor. The pattern "describes the postulated Independence-Encouraging construct." Items loading on the factor are: "Expects an individual to shoulder his own responsibilities." (0.71) "Thinks people should be able to help themselves." (0.67) "Encourages me to work on my problems in my own way." (0.51) "Tries to get me to make my own decisions." (0.47)

(5) *Critical-Hostile* is defined by the client perceiving his therapist "as critical, cold, impatient, and even competitive and disapproving." Examples of items are: "Becomes impatient when I make mistakes." (0.46) "Acts smug and superior as though he knew all the answers." (0.45) "Gives me the impression he doesn't like me." (0.37) "Talks down to me as if I were a child." (0.35) "Acts as though I were dull and uninteresting." (0.29) "Seems glad to have the interview finished." (0.28)

Lorr obtained factor scores for his sample of patients and intercorrelated the five extracted factors. "The correlations among the factors indicated that on the whole the five factors are relatively independent. The small positive intercorrelations among . . . understanding, accepting, and authoritarian imply that a higher order factor common to the three could be demonstrated. (Lorr, 1965)

Lorr further found that patient ratings of overall improvement and therapist judgments of patient satisfaction (both obtained at therapy termination) were significantly correlated with each of the five factors, with the coefficients ranging in absolute value from 0.13 to 0.31. The more the client perceived his therapist as understanding, accepting, and fostering independence, and the less he saw him as authoritarian and critical-hostile, the better the client rated his improvement at termination, and the more his therapist judged him as satisfied with treatment.

Finally, Lorr compares his extracted factors with those hypothesized by Fiedler (1950), and Apfelbaum (1958), as well as to the components of "warmth" that Raush and Bordin (1957) identified. Fiedler's first factor,

> the therapist's ability to communicate with and understand the patient, appears to be confirmed in the Understanding factor. The emotional distance which the therapist assumes toward the patient (close versus far), Fiedler's second dimension, appears to be represented both by Critical-Hostile and Accepting. The third Fiedler variable, therapist status in relation to the patient (equal, superior, or subordinate), appears to be a composite. The attitude of superiority is reflected in the Authoritarian factor. The equalitarian tendencies are absorbed in the Accepting factor. Raush and Bordin (1957) analyzed the concept of therapist warmth and found it

> divisible into commitment, understanding, and spontaneity. The first two correspond well with the constructs of Accepting and Understanding measured by the Inventory. (Lorr, 1966, p. 579)

Finally, Apfelbaum (1958) extracted two factors, warmth-nurturance versus coldness-indifference, and directiveness versus nondirectiveness. Apfelbaum's former factor would be a composite of Lorr's Accepting and Critical-Hostile, while the directiveness-nondirectiveness is a composite of Authoritarian and Independency-Encouraging.

A Scale of Client Attitudes Toward Counseling

Mendelsohn and Geller (1965)

Mendelsohn and Geller (1965) note that "the client has not often been asked about his view of the counseling experience and the effect of that experience on his subsequent behavior." The authors rationally derived a set of twenty-one items to assess client's post-counseling assessments of their therapy and therapists. Their first sample consisted of forty-one females and thirty-one males who were mailed the questionnaire three to twelve months after termination of the interview series; forty-five of the seventy-two previous clients returned the questionnaires. Their second sample involved 178 undergraduate and graduate students. The original twenty-one-item version was administered to the first sample, and was revised to twenty-seven items based on the four clusters isolated.

The revised twenty-seven-item questionnaire was administered to the second sample, who responded to each item on a seven-point Likert scale. The item responses were intercorrelated, and a cluster analysis revealed four clusters. (1) *Evaluation,* exemplified by the following items: "To the extent possible, my objective in coming to the Counseling Center was accomplished." "I am well satisfied with my counseling experience." "As a result of counseling there has been a change in what I am doing or planning to do." "I received benefit from counseling through starting on a plan for my future." (2) *Comfort-Rapport* (Willingness to Return). "I felt comfortable with the counselor." "If things get rough, I would like to return to my counselor or to the Counseling Center." (3) *Judged Competence* (aspects of the counselor's behavior, his skill in conducting the counseling interviews). "At times the counselor dominated the discussion too much." "Of the problems we worked on, the counselor dealt insufficiently with those that were most important to me." "The counselor spent too much time giving me concrete information like test scores, school requirements, etc." "The counselor tended to jump to conclusions."

> To summarize these findings, three major clusters emerged in both studies: Evaluation, Comfort-Rapport, and Judged Competence. Likewise, in both analyses, the clusters show a pattern of unexpectedly low positive correlations with each other, a finding which suggests that clients did not respond in terms of a generally favorable or unfavorable set determined by a particular aspect of their experience. . . . [Furthermore,] the effect of [patient-therapist] similarity on outcome clearly varies with the criterion used—it is linear with duration, curvilinear with Evaluation, unrelated to Judged Competence, and depending on the sample, both linear and curvilinear with Comfort-Rapport. (Mendelsohn and Geller, 1965)

Patients' Evaluation of the Psychotherapy Experience

Strupp, Fox, and Lessler (1969)

Strupp, Fox, and Lessler (1969) set for themselves

> the task of studying what former psychotherapy patients said about the nature of their emotional problems and what seemed to have helped them. More specifically, we were interested in exploring the reasons they gave for seeking the help of a psychotherapist, the steps they took to become patients, the experiences they underwent during therapy, and their reactions to the experience. We asked the patients to speak for themselves and to assess the overall value of their experience. (p. xv)

The authors present two studies in their 1969 volume. They summarize briefly the methodology and findings of an original study of a sample of private patients seen over extended periods of time by highly experienced therapists. (Strupp, Wallach, and Wogan, 1964) The authors devised a questionnaire and mailed it to seventy-six former patients, of whom forty-four (58 percent) responded. For the second study, "it seemed important to broaden our study to a larger sample of clinic patients who, we hoped, would make the survey representative of all individuals seen in outpatient psychotherapy in this country today." Of 244 questionnaires mailed to former patients of the Adult Psychiatric Outpatient Clinic at North Carolina Memorial Hospital, 131 (64 percent) were eventually returned. All patients in this sample had at least twenty-five therapy interviews, and had left therapy at least one year prior to the beginning of the study.

The entire questionnaire sent out consisted of various free response items inquiring into demographic characteristics, reasons for leaving therapy, whether in treatment since leaving, and so on. Embedded in the total questionnaire was a series of forty-one items (Items 25-65) which dealt specifically with the patients' attitudes toward the therapists' behavior and their relationships. Each of these forty-one items was scored on a five-point scale (+2, strongly agree; 0, undecided; -2, strongly disagree). The authors "included a sizeable number of items (41) dealing with the patient's attitudes toward the therapist and the degree to which he (patient) felt respected and accepted by him. Each item represented a hypothetical relationship between the patient's attitude and therapeutic outcome."

The entire questionnaire, of which the forty-one attitude items were only a part, was subjected to a cluster analysis. In this procedure the "members of the project staff" independently and jointly inspected the table of item intercorrelations, in order to find item pairs where the correlation was quite high (usually at 0.70 and 0.80). Once such a pair was found, items that were highly correlated with both of the items in the pair were added, until the staff began to disagree on placement of particular items (usually r values around 0.50). Besides the intercorrelation pattern, the staff judges took into account the "meaning of the items, whether they seem to belong in a given cluster. The aim was to develop clusters that were internally consistent while being highly differentiated from each other." Hence the cluster analysis procedure was partly an empirical and partly a judgmental task.

By this procedure twelve clusters were isolated in the first study, of which eight were replicated in the second. Of the eight replicated factors, only four involved the forty-one attitude items inserted in the overall questionnaire. The four relationship clusters emerging from the patient-perception questionnaire data were:

(1) *Therapist's Warmth* (five items), a broad estimate of the therapist's attitudes during therapy, with the major dimensions being the warmth versus coldness and closeness (informality) versus distance (formality). Items defining this cluster are: "The therapist tended to be rather stiff and formal" (-). "His general attitude was rather cold and distant" (-). "I felt there usually was a good deal of warmth in the way he talked to me" (+). "The tone of his statements tended to be rather cold" (-). "The therapist's manner of speaking seemed rather formal" (-).

(2) *Therapist's Interest, Integrity, and Respect* (six items), representing the patient's perception of the therapist interest, respect, and

acceptance, as well as his trust in the therapist's integrity. "I am convinced the therapist respected me as a person" (+). "I feel the therapist was genuinely interested in helping me" (+). "I was never sure whether the therapist thought I was a worthwhile person" (-). "I had a feeling of absolute trust in the therapist's integrity as a person" (+). "I usually felt I was fully accepted by the therapist" (+). "I never had the slightest doubt about the therapist's interest in helping me" (+).

(3) *Intensity of Emotional Experience* (two items), the extent to which the patient experienced psychotherapy as an intensely emotional experience in which painful experiences were mobilized. "My therapy was an intensely emotional experience" (+). "My therapy was often a rather painful experience" (+).

(4) *Therapist's Experience/Anxiety Level* (two items), the extent to which the therapist was perceived as active in therapy. The first item is: "I feel the therapist was rather active most of the time" (+). The second item was not one of the forty-one attitude items: "What impression did you have of his level of experience as a therapist?" (The answer correlated 0.55 with the first attitude item).

Some of the findings reported by Strupp, Fox, and Lessler (1969) are: (*a*) Approximately three-fourths of the patients considered their psychotherapy a worthwhile experience. "The complaints or symptoms which brought them to the clinic had not completely disappeared, but there was little question in their minds that there had been marked improvement." The reported improvements were primarily in the areas of better interpersonal relations, increase in self-esteem, greater interest in living, greater energy and satisfaction, and a greater sense of mastery of their problem. (*b*) "The amount of improvement noted by a patient in psychotherapy is highly correlated with his attitudes toward the therapist. . . . The therapist's warmth, his respect and interest, and his perceived competence and activity emerged as important ingredients in the amount of change reported by the patient." (*c*) By correlating the patients' evaluations with therapist's terminal assessments of the patient's therapy, "we were able to demonstrate substantial areas of agreement between patients and therapists concerning the essential aspects and results of the therapeutic experience."

The Picture Impressions Test

Libo (1965)

Libo's TAT-like projective device (Libo, 1956, 1957, 1969) was designed "to measure the *attraction* of a patient toward his therapist (and toward the clinical setting which the therapist represents). Attraction is defined as the resultant of all forces acting on the patient to maintain his relationship with the therapist. This is commonly called 'the strength of the patient-therapist relationship." (Libo, 1969, p. 1) The Picture Impressions Test consists of four cards depicting therapy-like situations to which the client is requested to respond in a manner analogous to TAT administrations. The task usually requires from twenty to thirty minutes, and is typically administered after the first treatment interview. A crucial aspect is that the test be administered by the therapist and that he remain with the patient throughout the entire story-writing session.

> [This] method of administering the Picture Impressions Test derives . . . from the oft-noted sensitivity of projective techniques to the interpersonal situation in which they are administered. . . . Since attraction is a contemporaneous (here and now) rather than a genetic (central need) concept, both the content of the four pictures and the method of administration (that is, by the therapist) are designed to capitalize on, rather than minimize, the interpersonal, situational influence on projective expression. The technique is therefore designed to elicit stories that would reflect some immediate, situationally determined themes, rather than only those which would reflect generalized, stable traits or attitudes toward all doctors or all treatment situations. (Libo, 1969, pp. 1-2)

Apparently, this restriction has not been observed by studies which have used the PIT. Libo (1969) cites and does not criticize at least two studies (Heller and Goldstein, 1961; Miller and Abeles, 1967) in which the PIT was not administered by the client's subsequent therapist, and was administered before therapy began.

To score the written stories of the client, Libo (1969) developed a coding system centered around the construct of "Locomotion, which is defined as actual or attempted movement, physical or psychological, of the patient toward the therapist."

> The way in which the patient depicts patient-therapist relationships in the stories is treated as a direct reflection of his own attraction to his therapist (that is, the patient projects his present need to "belong with" his particular therapist). Thus, an individual who is strongly attracted to his doctor would write stories depicting a patient's actual or desired movement toward a therapist, and actual or expected benefit received through contact with him. On the other hand, an individual who is minimally attracted to, or is repelled by, his doctor should write stories describing a patient's

actual or desired movement away from a therapist and actual or expected dissatisfaction with him.

The coding system consists of five categories, each of which is scored as positive or negative. Intrajudge and interjudge reliability reported in several studies indicate percentages of agreement ranging from the mid-80s to the mid-90s. The five categories are: (1) *Locomotion, Actual or Attempted (Al)*: + is defined as "actual or attempted movement, physical or psychological, of the patient toward the therapist." (2) *Barriers to Desired Locomotion* (BL): + refers to barriers, physical or psychological, personal or situational, to the occurrence of AL+, but not caused by the doctor or characteristics of the relationship. (3) *Desired Locomotion* (DL): + means desire of the individual for AL+. (4) *Barriers to Desired Locomotion Overcome* (BLO): + refers to barriers being overcome by the individual, doctor, or other factors. (5) *Satisfaction* (S): + means that a gain in satisfaction or benefit occurs, actual or expected, caused by the doctor, the setting he represents, or the doctor-patient relationship.

Two scores are derived for each protocol. The Total Score is the algebraic sum of all the + and - scores occurring for the five categories. The second is the number of the four stories receiving a score (only stories containing four essential ingredients are scored by the categories), which is interpreted as the subject's degree of involvement in the story-writing task, "often itself an indication of attraction."

Libo's manual (1969) cites five previous studies which have used the Picture Impression Test: Heller and Goldstein (1961), Libo (1957), Miller and Abeles (1967), Pope and Siegman (1966, 1968). To date findings with the instrument generally have been positive.

Basic Dimensions of Interpersonal Behavior

Postscript

It seems appropriate to note that converging evidence suggests that much of social interpersonal behavior can be represented by two major interpersonal dimensions. Bierman (1969) most recently makes this point, and cites previous investigators who suggested the same thesis. "Evidence from developmental, personality, abnormal, and small-group process perspectives has been converging on the saliency of two basic dimensions of interpersonal behavior. The accumulating research indicates that much of social behavior can be represented by combinations of the two orthogonal dimensions of active expressiveness versus passive restrictedness and of acceptance versus rejection." (p. 338) The thesis of Biermen's report is that "the active-passive and accepting-rejecting dimensions provide a useful framework for studying the interpersonal functioning of counselors and psychotherapists with their clients." He proceeds to summarize the relevant psychotherapy process and analogue research, reinterpreting findings within this two-dimensional framework. He concludes:

> The survey of studies on the consequences of these relational dimensions for child-rearing, for educational, and for psychotherapeutic outcomes suggests that conditions of active engagement in the context of positive regard and accurate empathic understanding are optimal for personal development and well-being. The consistency of effects of therapist-offered conditions with the effects of parent- and teacher-offered conditions lends support to the generality of the two-dimensional model, in which psychotherapy can be seen as a special case of dyadic interaction and by which helpee as well as helper can be assessed on the same interpersonal dimensions." (pp. 348-49)

Future studies of the psychotherapy relationship, such as those presented in this section, should begin their conceptualization within this two-dimensional framework or some similar one. This evidence, furthermore, suggests that psychotherapy investigators might reap unusual benefits by serious attempts to apply interpersonal theories of personality and their measurement methodologies (for example, Leary, 1957; Schutz, 1958) to the interpersonal events of psychotherapy.

EXPERIMENTAL PROCEDURES

Interpersonal Process Recall

Kagan, Krathwohl, and Miller (1963)

Kagan, Krathwohl, and Miller (1963) have developed a very interesting indirect technique for studying the psychotherapy process and dynamics occurring during actual psychotherapy. They developed their procedure while investigating the dynamics of the therapy relationship, and therapist empathy in particular. The technique, called Interpersonal Process Recall, involves filming psychotherapy interviews on videotape and, immediately after the session, playing it back for the patient and therapist who are seated in separate rooms.

> Although variations are contemplated, our experimentation thus far has been structured in the following manner. A counselor and client conduct a counseling interview within the studio of our closed circuit television installation. . . . The studio is curtained, the cameras are pre-set and unmanned so that a minimum of distraction exists. The interview is enacted and the two participants are video-tape recorded on a split screen with head and torso head-on views enlarged as much as the screen permits. Immediately after the interview is concluded, the counselor and client proceed to separate, darkened viewing rooms to witness a playback of their interview, each in the presence of another trained counselor (referred to as interrogator). Thus, two people in each room observe and react to the recently concluded interview.
>
> The interrogators encourage the subjects to describe their feelings, interpret statements, and translate body movement at various times during the replayed interview. Any interrogator or subject may stop the playback and discuss his recalled feelings and elaborate on meanings. Whenever one subject or interrogator stops the replay, it is automatically stopped for the other team. Thus, it is possible to examine the recalled interpersonal communication at precisely the same time for both parties. The interrogation sessions are recorded on audio tape. (pp. 237-38)

Although the authors are involved in a long-range research project, apparently the only publication in the general literature has been the 1963 report. In that report the authors presented excerpts from a single case demonstrating the potential utility of their procedure. At that time only three cases had been completed using the IPR procedure.

Kagan, Krathwohl, and Miller (1963) concluded:

> Examination of protocols leads us to believe that IPR permits a breakdown of the usual defenses in interpersonal communication; introspection by all parties involved in a given communication at critical points of the interaction process; and a permanent and complete record of a given interaction with relevant interpretations by the interacting parties. These properties suggest its use to examine certain components of empathy using IPR protocols. It may be possible to validate specific aspects of counseling theory by examining the relation of IPR responses to the course of therapy. New insight may be gained into various interpersonal

situations such as teacher-pupil, foreman-worker, and parent-child. It may be possible to examine group structure and interaction. We hope to explore its usefulness as a device for counselor training and screening. (pp. 242-43)

Kagan and his colleagues recently reported their findings with the IPR technique (Greenberg, Kagan, and Bowes, 1969; Kagan and Krathwohl, 1967). More recently these investigators have introduced a new procedure for interview analysis to offset some of the limitations of IPR (Danish and Kagan, 1969; Kagan and Schauble, 1969; Resnikoff, Kagan and Schauble, 1970). In the new procedure, called Video Tape Recall of Affect Simulation (VRAS), clients are confronted with films which encourage them to engage in simulated interpersonal relationships. Professional actors were trained to portray four basic types of affect (hostility, affection, fear of hostility, fear of affection) with varying degrees of intensity. Each actor was instructed to direct the emotion at an imaginary individual directly behind the video camera lens so that the viewer would see the resultant image as if the actor were talking directly to him. The films are shown to individual clients who are instructed to imagine that the person they see is talking directly and privately to them. As the client views the vignettes, he is videotaped. At the conclusion of the simulation experience, a counselor enters the room, the videotape of the client's reaction is replayed, and the client's recall of his thoughts and feelings during the simulation experience serves as the basis for the counseling session.

To date Kagan and his colleagues have focused on the potential of the IPR and VRAS techniques for counselor screening and training, as well as for facilitating client progress during psychotherapy.

TRACCOM

Nathan and Colleagues (1964)

Nathan and his colleagues (Nathan, Schneller, and Lindsley, 1964; Nathan, Marland, and Lindsley, 1965; Nathan, Bull, and Rossi, 1968) have developed a promising new laboratory methodology for measuring changes in interpersonal affect which occur during two-person relationships. Their TRACCOM procedure (Televised Reciprocal Analysis of Conjugate Communication) permits study of the effect of naturally occurring events in continuous dyadic relationships on a nonverbal communication variable, that is, the rate at which a person will push a switch to see and hear his communication partner.

> Therapist and patient sat in separate, sound-attenuated rooms. Each room had a loudspeaker and a television monitor which were connected through separate conjugate programmers to a microphone and television camera in the other room. Each subject had a single handswitch which he pushed continuously to see and hear his partner. The conjugate programmers converted each subject's rate of responding to brightness of the television picture and intensity of the loudspeaker sound. A single press of the handswitch briefly illuminated the subject's television screen and raised the sound intensity of his loudspeaker to barely liminal levels. Moderate rates of responding increased image and voice to moderate brightness and intensity, while responding at high ("required") rates (at or beyond 120 responses per minute) caused image and voice to achieve maximum brightness and intensity. (Nathan, Bull, and Rossi, 1968, p. 42)

Each subject's rate of responding is recorded automatically and continuously on a separate cumulative recorder. Since most subjects respond well above the "required" response rate once response acquisition has occurred, the method's maximum sensitivity to events of psychotherapy occur in periods of "overresponding." The authors record two TRACCOM indexes: single and multiple session response rates, and single session response-rate range and variability (range = highest session rate minus the lowest session rate; variability = the standard deviation of the session's response rates).

The authors assume that TRACCOM behavior can serve as an accurate measure of the affective component of process change in continuing "two-person relationships." Some representative findings for the measure are: (1) "The responding behavior of sixteen psychiatric patients varied with changes in verbal content during the course of single psychiatric admission interviews. Topics judged emotionally laden for patients often were accompanied by altered rates of pushing." (2) Operant responding over a series of ten supervisory sessions by three student nurses and their supervisors "paralleled the supervisor's judgment of the significance and value of each relationship to its members." (3) In a study of two patients (one depressive, the other a character disorder) with the same psychiatric resident therapist, the therapist rated each patient after each session and provided a summary report after termination, while the patients completed a Barrett-Lennard Relationship Inventory on the therapist at the end of each session and after termination. The findings showed that the character disorder patient increased his rate of responding (7,870 to 9,500 responses per hour) and raised his RI evaluations of the therapists during his eleven therapy sessions; the depressive patient decreased his responding from 9,800 and 8,130 responses per hour and reduced his RI evaluations of the therapist across his therapy interviews. Although the character disorder dramatically increased his operant rate to see and hear his therapist, the therapist increased his responding only very moderately; with the depressive, who markedly decreased his response rate to see and hear the therapist, the therapist showed an increased responding "more than twice the rate he had shown with [the character disorder]."

> [In conclusion, the data] suggest that the range and variability of a single S's operant communication responses are more restricted with a "favorite" communication partner than with another partner, and that a S's highest and lowest rate of responding in a session occur when he is discussing material very distressing to him. . . . These results, tentative as they are now, lend support to hopes that this technique, whose sensitivity to important communication and psychotherapy events has been established, can now be extended to detailed analysis of more discrete and subtle events in two-person relationship, to permit study of therapy "whys" in addition to therapy "whens." (Nathan, Bull, and Rossi, 1968, p. 48)

General Conceptions of the Therapeutic Relationship and Therapist Technique

The questionnaire instruments of this section do not assess particular therapist-patient interactions, but are designed to assess more general attitudes about psychotherapy, the therapeutic relationship, or therapist technique behaviors, independent of any particular psychotherapy transaction. Some of these studies were reviewed previously by Gardner (1964), who also summarized findings on the association between relationship factors and therapeutic outcome, as well as with other patient and therapist variables. These self-report instruments are filled out by either groups of therapists or groups of patients (or normal subjects), but not in the context of a particular ongoing case. Most of these inventories were developed to tap either patients' or therapists' general conceptions of, or preferences for, various aspects of the therapeutic relationship and therapeutic technique. The general questions asked are: "How would you like a particular therapy participant to act?" "How do you (therapist) typically act?" "What do you consider the ideal therapeutic relationship?" A smaller number of inventories attempt to assess patients' dispositional attitudes toward therapy, particularly the favorableness of their expectancies of psychotherapy.

Although the constructs developed in these inventories are quite similar to those found in the preceding section of this chapter, the two groups of inventories are clearly distinct. The major difference is that the questionnaires in the preceding section were filled out on a particular ongoing relationship, on a specific patient-therapist dyad in interaction. Although the inventories presented below are filled out by groups of therapists or groups of patients (or normals), in no case is the respondent rating a particular ongoing relationship, or the other participant in a psychotherapy dyad; instead, he is expressing his attitudes toward aspects of psychotherapy "in general."

MEASURES OF THERAPISTS' CONCEPTIONS AND PREFERENCES

Attitudes Toward General Counseling

Chase (1946), McClelland and Sinaiko (1950)

Chase (1946) attempted, in a military separation counseling setting, to identify "good" in contrast to "harmful" counselor responses in a "general counseling situation." He derived a seventy-four-item scale to characterize good and harmful counselor interview behaviors from statements endorsed by a majority of "expert" counselors. The items included: permitting the counselee to express himself freely, reprimanding the counselee for displaying aggressiveness, advising the counselee to stay on the safe side and not to take chances, pointing out a problem or condition needing correction, helping or aiding the counselee to verbalize his thoughts, sharing warmth and feeling, glossing over excessive worries, and assuming a superior attitude.

McClelland and Sinaiko (1950), attempting to modify the questionnaire so that it might be useful in counseling situations more generally, dropped ten of the original Chase items because they were specific to military separation counseling. A group of expert counselors was identified, all having at least ten years counseling experience and all from the University of Minnesota. The group of thirteen counselors included four academic instructors of counseling courses, four full-time counselors, and five who divided their time between administration and counseling. The judges were given the shortened form (with sixty-four items) of the Chase questionnaire, and asked to endorse the items in terms of what they would do in a "general counseling situation." They assumed (as did Chase) that "judges are capable of making responses to the Chase questionnaire items in terms of a general counseling situation. If a meaningful key could be devised, the use of a questionnaire of this type might be of considerable value in the selection and training of counselors."

A "Minnesota" key for scoring the revised questionnaire was obtained. Means and SDs were computed for each of the sixty-four items (responses were weighted on a five-point Likert scale), and all items having an SD of 0.8 or larger were eliminated. This left the final scale consisting of 40 items. The forty-item version was administered to undergraduates and to graduate student counseling interns and counselors at Minnesota. There were 106 students taking either the guidance techniques or counseling practices course, and 53 graduate students in Psychology or Educational Psychology. The questionnaires were scored both by the Minnesota and the Chase keys.

From the findings, the authors conclude:

> Although it was possible to obtain considerable agreement among a carefully selected group of judges on the desirability of certain counseling practices, two obvious limitations of the questionnaire approach must be mentioned. First, most of the judges spoke about the artificiality of rating practices in a "general counseling situation." They reported that specification of the type of client problem, as well as the nature of the agency function, seemed important in keying "correct" responses. Second, the low reliability of the scale (as filled in by the student sample) makes the current approach suspect. . . . The reservations attendant to the use of the Chase items about counselor ideas are such to indicate that they should not be used in their present form. (McClelland and Sinaiko, 1950)

Others have apparently heeded McClelland and Sinaiko's advice, since the instrument seems to have disappeared from the literature.

A Simple Measure of Counselors' Attitudes

Porter (1949)

One of the earliest approaches to objective measurement of counselor attitudes was suggested by Porter (1949, 1950). The quantitative test developed by Porter as an exercise in counselor training consists of a series of counseling situations with five alternative responses to each of the situations.

Porter developed two instruments, The Counseling Procedures Pre-Test and the Counseling Procedures Post-Test. The latter is not scored quantitatively and will not be discussed here. The Pre-Test consists of four parts. Part 1 presents a series of twenty-five excerpts from counseling interviews. Following each client statement is a series of five possible counselor responses, from which the respondent selects "the response which best approximates the response you would like to see." Part 2 presents ten examples of possible interchanges between counselors and students. Here the counselor starts each exchange, the student replies, and the counselor's subsequent response to the client is presented as a multiple-choice problem. Part 3 presents the first ten consecutive responses in an interview with one U. S. veteran client. Following each response are five alternative formulations of aims or purposes which the counselor might wish to follow, from which the respondent picks the one "which you feel indicates the best aim or purpose which the counselor might try to effect at this particular point in the interview." (Porter, 1950) Part 4 consists of ten consecutive statements made by a 35-year-old man who sought help because of inability to hold a job for any length of time. Here each statement is followed by four counselor responses from which the respondent selects the one "which you feel most accurately reflects the client's attitude, the situation as it appears to the client; the alternative which if spoken to the client you feel would be most likely to evoke an immediate reply of, 'That's right!" Part 5 presents twenty consecutive responses made by a 21-year-old veteran who had been referred by an academic advisor. The respondent's task was "to write on a separate sheet the response which you feel you would most likely use or which would be most helpful to the client."

The total pretest contains seventy-five items. Parts 1 to 3 are designed to measure the same fundamental characteristics of the counselor, "the attitudes which he implements when confronted by different client attitudes in different situations." In the alternatives following items 1 to 45 (Parts 1 to 3), each alternative exemplifies one of five basically different counselor attitudes. (1) *Evaluative*: "a response which indicates the counselor has made a judgment of relative goodness, appropriateness, effectiveness, rightness. He has in some way implied what the client might or ought to do, grossly or subtly." (2) *Interpretive*: "a response which indicates the counselor's intent is to teach, to impart meaning to the client, to show him. He has in some way implied what the client might or ought to think, grossly or subtly." (3) *Supportive*: "a response which indicates the counselor's intent is to reassure, to reduce the client's intensity of feeling, to pacify. He has in some way implied that the client need not feel as he does." (4) *Probing*: "a response which indicates the counselor's intent is to seek further information, provoke further discussion along a certain line, to query. He has in some way implied that the client ought or might profitably develop or discuss a point further." (5) *Understanding*: "a response which indicates the counselor's intent is to so respond as in effect to ask the client whether the counselor understands correctly what the client is saying, how the client feels about it, how it strikes the client, how the client sees it."

In Part 4 (ten items), all of the alternatives following the test item are phrased as attempts to effect an understanding attitude, with the alternatives differing and scored in the following ways. (1) *Content*: "a response in which the attempt at understanding is implemented in large part by a simple repetition of the same words used by the client." (2) *Shallow or Partial*: "a response in which the attempt at understanding is implemented in a limited way by involving only a portion of what the client expressed or by undercutting or watering-down the feeling tone expressed." (3) *Reflection*: "a response in which the attempt at understanding is implemented by a rephrasing in fresh words the gist of the client's expression without changing either the meaning or feeling tone." (4) *Interpretive*: "a response in which the attempt to understand actually goes beyond the meaning of the client and adds meaning not expressed by the client." For Part 5 (twenty items), no numerical score is directly obtainable.

The items of Porter's Counseling Procedures Pre-Test as well as the scoring key are provided in his 1950 volume. He reports no norms or quantitative results using the study in that volume.

Hopke (1955) applied a modified version of the Porter pretest in a study of both students and counselors. Instead of using Porter's multiple-choice format, he required his respondents to rank the alternatives to each item, from 1 (most appropriate) to 5 (least appropriate). From his results he concluded: (*a*) Porter's "test of counselor attitudes can be used in the comparison of groups with an acceptable degree of reliability." (*b*) "The rank order method of scoring the test is found to be superior in reliability to the first choice total procedure for two of the five attitudes measured on the test." (*c*) The "study indicates there is a substantial relationship between test performance and the types of responses employed by ten counselors in actual counseling situations."

The Ideal Therapeutic Relationship Q-Sort

Fiedler (1950)

Fiedler (1950a, 1950b, 1951) published a series of studies on therapists' conceptions of the ideal therapeutic relationship which had a considerable impact at that time. Fielder introduced his questionnaire instrument as follows.

> There has been little, if any disagreement among psychotherapists as to the paramount importance of a good therapeutic relationship to eventual cure. . . . Yet, the differences of opinion as to what constitutes a good therapeutic relationship are quite marked. Rogers favors a relationship which permits the patient most scope, and in which the therapist intervenes as little as possible, while Horney and Thorne advocate greater intervention and activity on the part of the therapist. One question we wish to answer here is, Are these differences in theory semantic, or do they represent actual divergencies in the goal therapists set for themselves? If the theory and training of therapists are of greater importance than therapeutic skill, we will expect therapists of different schools to differ more from those of other schools than from therapists within their own school. If, on the other hand, experience and skill are of greater importance (that is, if the concept of what a therapeutic relationship ideally should be is derived from personal experience and skill) we will expect the more expert to agree among themselves irrespective of school, rather than with the less expert within their own school. . . . If there are any real differences in schools as to the relationship which they attempt to achieve, we will expect a factor analysis to yield as many factors as there are points of view. If, on the other hand, these differences are present in theory only, and only one type of relationship is actually considered maximally effective, we will expect to find only one general factor among therapists of different schools. (Fiedler, 1950a, p. 239)

Fielder had therapists from various schools describe their conceptions of an ideal therapeutic relationship by means of a specially devised Q-sort, consisting of seventy-five statements describing various aspects of a therapeutic relationship. He found a high degree of congruence among the various schools represented, and observed that the agreement increased with experience. The therapists in his sample, despite differences in theoretical orientation, were in essential agreement as to what constitutes a good therapeutic relationship.

In a subsequent analysis (1950b) using the same Q-sort as a basis for coding recorded therapy interviews, Fiedler found that therapist agreement was also reflected in interview behavior. Expert therapists from all schools represented in this sample functioned very close to the way experts in the previous study said they should. Furthermore, the assortment of experts functioned in the interview more like each other than like less experienced therapists within their own school. Fiedler concluded that despite theoretical differences, therapists of all schools strive to achieve very similar kinds of relationships, and the extent to which they succeed in this is related to experience as a therapist.

A series of factor analyses carried out by Fiedler in his various studies agreed in confirming the presence of one general factor among the seventy-five relationship items of his Q-sort deck. Although not labeled by Fiedler, the item content indicates an overall factor of focus on and accuracy of empathic understanding on the part of the therapist. Examples of Fiedler items loading highly on this factor are: "Is able to participate completely in the patient's communication." "Comments are always right in line with what the patient is trying to convey." "Really tried to understand the patient's feelings." "Sees the patient as a co-worker in a common problem." "Usually maintains rapport with the patient." "Is interested but emotionally uninvolved." "Acts neither superior nor submissive to the patient." Examples of items loading least or negatively on the general factor are: "Shows no comprehension of the feeling the patient is trying to communicate." "Acts in a very superior manner toward the patient." "Is hostile towards the patient." "Feels disgusted by the patient." "His own needs completely interfere with his understanding of the patient."

Subsequent studies using Fiedler's measure suggest caution in generalizing Fiedler's findings and conclusions (Thomas, Polansky, and Kounin, 1955; Sonne and Goldman, 1957; Apfelbaum, 1958; Streitfeld, 1959; Lesser, 1961; Parloff, 1961; Soper and Combs, 1962; Mueller, Gatsch, and Ralston, 1963; Gonyea, 1963). For example, findings by Parloff (1961) were interpreted to provide "limited support" for the hypothesis that therapy outcome is related to quality of the therapeutic relationship in group psychotherapy. Lesser (1961) found counseling progress unrelated to a measure of empathic understanding based on Fiedler's Q-sort items. Streitfeld (1959) found no correlation between therapists' expressed acceptance of others, which he regarded as an important aspect of Fiedler's measure, and supervisors' ratings of therapeutic competence. Gonyea (1963) concluded that "our results did not support the assumption of a positive correlation between (Fiedler's measure of the) Ideal Therapeutic Relationship and counseling outcome. The slight tendency toward an inverse relation between ITR and outcome can probably be discounted as insignificant. Quality of the therapeutic relationship, as defined by Fiedler's Q-sort, is apparently irrelevant to counseling outcome (as measured in our study)."

Personal Characteristics of Counselors

Cottle, Lewis, and Penney (1954)

Cottle (1953) reviewed the literature dealing with characteristics of counselors. Cottle and Lewis (1954) described the derivation of a pool of items which would differentiate between male counselors in college counseling bureaus and a miscellaneous college student group. Cottle, Lewis, and Penney (1954) demonstrated that the same battery not only differentiates intern counselors from students, but also from intern teachers.

The authors drew 150 items from the Guilford-Zimmerman Temperament Survey, the MMPI, and the counseling psychologist scale of the Strong Vocational Interest Inventory. They found on an original sample and on cross-validation that 55 of the 150 items differentiated the intern counselors from the intern teachers and other groups. They concluded that "it seems evident from this pilot study that the answers of counselors to the items of this experimental scale can be differentiated from those of teachers." Apparently neither the authors not others have followed up this potential selection device for counseling psychology interns.

A Questionnaire Survey of British Psychoanalysts

Glover (1955)

Glover (1955) was among the first to attempt to study actual operations of psychotherapists. He restricted his survey to British psychoanalysts, all of whom had quite similar training in orthodox analysis, and who subscribed to the technical rules and procedures they had been taught. Glover's concern was the manner in which the psychotherapists carried out these analytic rules in actual practice.

His questionnaire items ranged in content from major technical operations (such as free association, interpretations, handling of transference problems) to minor aspects (the patient's or the analyst's smoking, telephone conversations, etc.). The questions related to the analysts practices in general, or on the average, in dealing with their patients.

Glover's data supported his original expectation that the practices of even a relatively homogeneous group of psychotherapists diverged considerably. He found general agreement that analysis of the transference is the major therapeutic device, but also that there was wide variation in the technique of interpretation and in many other aspects covered by his questionnaire. On general questions there was greater agreement among the analysts; as the questions became more specific, disagreement increased. Assuming that the questionnaire responses correlate positively with what the analysts actually did in practice, Glover's findings showed rather dramatically that wide differences of therapist attitudes and behaviors exist even among psychotherapists subscribing to the same theoretical orientation.

Film Analogues for Measuring Therapist Technique and Attitudes

Strupp (1960)

Strupp, beginning with a series of studies reported in 1955 (which are summarized in his 1960 volume as well as in his 1962 article), developed an analogue procedure for studying the interview behavior and relationship attitudes of a wide range of psychotherapists in practice during that period. He set out to devise an experimental situation "resembling the therapeutic setting, to keep the stimulus invariant, and to study the responses of a group of therapists under these conditions. Whatever differences are observed must necessarily then be attributable to the therapist variable. Using such a technique, one might succeed in establishing systematic relationships between the therapists' responses and such variables as: level of experience, theoretical orientation, professional affiliation, attitudes, and the like." (Strupp, 1962, p. 26)

> The performance of any two therapists, even in clearly defined and highly specific situation, will reveal differences. It is the antecedents of such differences that constitute the focus of our inquiry. By the same token, there will be many similarities which will be equally important. . . . [Our] investigation attempts to explore how the therapist structures the therapeutic problems (perceptions and evaluations), how these conceptualizations are related to what he proposes to do (treatment plans, goals, proposed procedures), and what he actually does (technique). Our aim is to investigate these interrelationships as well as to explain possible differences among therapists in terms of systematic effects produced by their training, experience, and personalities. (Strupp, 1959, p. 35)

Strupp's experimental analogue procedure was developed in three distinct stages. For the original phase, the stimulus materials consisted of a series of twenty-seven short paragraphs of patient statements typed on individual cards. The statements were culled from published therapy interviews thought to represent a fair cross section of neurotic patients in early interviews. The card series was presented to therapists individually, and they were free to formulate a comment to the patient in their own words, or to remain silent. The therapists were instructed to assume that the patient statement occurred early in therapy, that the problem had come up for the first time, and that none of the patients was hospitalized. The series contained a variety of complaints, statements by a borderline patient, suicide threats, and communications illustrating blocking, requests for direct advice, hostility, and negativism.

In the second phase, a sound film presentation of a single patient-therapist interaction was employed (Strupp, 1960). "Adaptations were made in an existing film which had originally been produced by the Veterans Administration for training purposes—designed to illustrate phobic mechanisms—which was an unrehearsed interview between a middle-aged neurotic man and a young resident in psychiatry." The film was adapted by interrupting the interview sequence at twenty-eight predetermined points which usually occurred immediately before an intervention by the film therapist (never after), or at natural breaks in the patient's recital, or at points immediately preceding a change of topic introduced by the film therapist. Uniform titles, "What would you do?" were inserted at the twenty-eight points in the thirty-minute interview sequence and remained projected for a fixed period of thirty seconds ("a predetermined optimum to allow the respondent a reasonable amount of time, sufficient for most therapists, to consider and write down his comments"). The standard film was shown to groups of therapists ranging in size from less than ten to well over one hundred, not individually as previously.

Still unsatisfied with his experimental precedure, Strupp modified it again into its present form. "In order to diversify the stimulus material and in order to cross check results obtained by means of the initial film, six motion picture sequences, each lasting approximately 15 minutes, have been produced. . . . These films show different patients and therapists. All roles are portrayed by actors. The scripts, however, were derived from actual psychiatric interviews. In all films the focus is almost exclusively on the patient, with the interviewer contributing only minimally." (Strupp, 1962, p. 28) The final version of the experimental procedure consists in showing a film to a psychotherapist in a private setting without other persons being present. The titles "What would you do?" each lasting about thirty seconds have been retained and occur six to eight times in each film sequence. The therapist responds by talking out loud into a tape recorder. If he wishes to give no response, he either remains silent or says "no response."

Throughout the various phases of development the therapist was asked to respond to a comprehensive questionnaire and a biographical information blank after completing the film analogue procedure. The questionnaire items assessed diagnostic impressions, treatment plans and goals, formulations of the patient's dynamics, problems in treatment, estimates of the patient's anxiety, emotional maturity, social adjustment, prognosis with and without therapy, the respondent's attitudes toward the film patient and therapist, and an evaluation of the film therapist's performance. The biographical data blank contained twenty-four questions concerning the therapist's training, theoretical orientation, and current therapeutic activity. Studies using this procedure, then, collect two kinds of data: the tape-recorded responses of the viewing therapist to the film patient at the interruption points, and responses to the questionnaire and data form.

Examples of some of Strupp's findings using this procedure are: (1) Clearcut technique and attitude differentiations were found between therapists subscribing to diametrically opposed theoretical positions, such as client-centered and analytically-oriented therapists. (2) There are clear-cut qualitative differences between experienced and inexperienced therapists regarding their skills in empathizing and responding to patients' communications. (3) Analysis of therapists' formulations about the course of the transference revealed that more experienced therapists tended to give statements in terms of interpersonal dynamics rather than statistically descriptive ones. (4) Ratings of therapists' film responses showed that therapists with a history of personal analysis responded more empathically to the film patients than did unanalyzed therapists. (5) High levels of intercorrelation were found among therapists' judgments of the patient's insight, lack of defensiveness, motivation for therapy, favorableness of prognosis, and the therapist's liking for the patient.

Strupp (1959) cautions that his analogue procedure "rests on the assumption that the (respondent) therapist's simulated interview behavior bears a relationship to his performance as a therapist in similar real-life therapy situations, and that valid inferences can be drawn from this sample of his behavior. It is not maintained that the interview between the film patient and any audience therapist would have proceeded exactly as indicated by the therapist's hypothetical responses." (p. 35) After reviewing the evidence he had collected before his 1962 report, Strupp drew the conclusion that

> clinical impression and therapeutic planning are influenced by

> attitudinal variables with the therapist. Group I therapists appear to be more tolerant, more humane, more permissive, more "democratic," and more "therapeutic." Group II therapists emerge as more directive, disciplinarian, moralistic, and harsh. This contrast suggests the hypothesis that Group I therapists are "warmer" in their communications to the patient, and that "cold" rejecting comments will be less frequent. (1959, p. 65)

Strupp (1962) outlined the direction in which he was moving in further research with the analogue procedure. "We are directing our attention increasingly to research concerned with (*a*) greater systematization of observations of the naturally occurring events in psychotherapy, (*b*) basic process in psychotherapy, and (*c*) patients' perceptions of psychotherapy and the therapist's personality. We are continuing research, albeit with somewhat less emphasis, on the personality of the psychotherapist." (p. 39) The most recent application of the film analogues is a study by Strupp and Wallach (1965).

A Standardized Interview Survey of Psychotherapists

Wolff (1956)

Wolff (1956) set out to study the status of psychotherapy as viewed by adherents of various schools of therapy, "an inquiry into basic concepts of modern psychotherapy."

> Areas in which investigation could contribute to a clarification of psychiatric issues were mapped out. They were as follows. (1) To what extent does modern psychotherapy have a common terminology? Do psychotherapists of different schools mean the same thing if they use the same term? (2) What are the main areas of criticism of various psychotherapeutic systems? (3) What are the basic controversies concerning the use of different techniques? (4) What is the proportion of success and failure with different types of patients? What are the claims of effectiveness for the various schools of psychotherapy? (5) What are the personality factors involved in the techniques and effectiveness of the various schools. (pp. vii-viii)

To answer these questions, Wolff, with the help of "discussions with psychotherapists," constructed a series of twenty-eight questions which served "as a guide in the spontaneous living situation of a personal interview," that is, in standardized interviews he conducted with a sample of psychotherapists.

> For our purposes . . . the sample did not necessarily need to be large since characteristic opinions rather than fact were wanted. . . . Psychotherapists of various schools of thought, such as Freudian, Adlerian, Jungian, followers of Sullivan and of Horney, advocates of brief therapy and of group therapy, child therapists and therapists in hospitals were approached. The sample was limited to the area of New York City and narrowed further by selecting a predetermined number of representatives of different schools. After the sample was defined, I queried fifty psychotherapists of whom forty-three granted me a guided interview (usually lasting about one hour). My wife assisted me in writing down the answers. (pp. ix-x)

Among the forty-three therapists interviewed were many of national reputation. During the interviews Wolff did not adhere rigidly to the wording of the twenty-eight questions; rather they "were freely formulated, with slight deviations designed to integrate them into the general discussion."

The bulk of Wolff's volume is an abbreviated transcript of the dialogue between him and twenty-two of the therapists (two samples from each of eleven schools). One brief chapter summarizes his quantitative handling of the free responses of the sample of therapists. Samples of his findings for some of the questions asked are as follows. (1) "Which type of psychotherapy do you think is best and why?" Seventy percent of the interviewees mentioned their own approach, while 30 percent stated their choice of therapy depended on the individual case. (2) "Are you completely satisfied with the theoretical framework of the therapy you use or does it have shortcomings? In which area?" Seventy-five percent of the therapists were dissatisfied with the theoretical framework they endorsed; the 25 percent who were satisfied were primarily from the Adlerian and Jungian schools. (3) "To what extent is your therapy directive or nondirective?" Twenty-seven percent used a strictly nondirective approach, 23 percent a strictly directive approach, and 50 percent varied their approach according to the patient. (4) "Do you consider it important to make a diagnosis?" The importance of diagnosis was denied by 15 percent, diagnosis was used as a tentative working hypothesis by 35 percent, while 50 percent considered diagnosis essential. (5) "Do you use dreams? If so, to what extent?" Dreams were always used by 45 percent, and to a limited degree by 55 percent. (6) "How important do you consider transference?" Seventy percent followed the Freudian concept of transference as a phenomenon based upon the patient's projections, while 30 percent interpreted transference as the interpersonal relationship between the patient and therapist. (7) "Do you make conditions concerning the patient's environment, his habits?" Fourteen percent never make any conditions nor give suggestions to the patient, 40 percent give advice, and 46 percent impose conditions if necessary. (8) "Do you feel that the patient-therapist relationship should be completely detached or may it carry over to social relationships?" Social relationships were rejected entirely by 45 percent, 25 percent allowed it in exceptional cases, 16 percent found it admissable during therapy, and 14 percent after therapy had ended. (9) "What is the average length of your therapy; how many hours weekly?" With the average neurotic patient, the average length reported was less than one year for 24 percent, one to two years for 44 percent, and about two years for 32 percent.

Wolff described the study reported in his volume as "a pilot study, later to be enlarged and to include therapists in other countries as well." The follow-up study has not yet appeared.

A Questionnaire Measuring Common Issues in the Conduct of Psychotherapy

Fey (1958)

Fey (1958) constructed a questionnaire focusing on issues commonly arising in the conduct of psychotherapy. For the first twenty-seven of thirty items on the inventory, the item answers ranged from one (yes, always, routinely) through five (no, never). The final three items assess the respondent's tendencies in marking the questionnaire items themselves.

The inventory was mailed to each professional in a midwestern university city who was known to be conducting "consecutive interview treatment." Of thirty-six therapists contacted (twenty-nine psychiatrists, five psychologists, two social workers), thirty-four responded. From data supplied by the therapists, Fey classified his sample into four groups: Rogerians (seven), Analysts (five), Young Eclectics (eight), and Older Eclectics (14).

Analysis of replies to the questionnaire revealed that (*a*) Rogerians were most homogeneous in their responses, Analysts least; (*b*) Analysts and Young Eclectics were most similar as groups, while Older Eclectics and Rogerians were least similar; (*c*) analysis of variance showed significant differences among the questionnaire responses for the four groups.

All thirty items of the questionnaire were intercorrelated and factor-analyzed. Four factors emerged. *Factor one* "seems to represent a dimension involving a distinct, perhaps rigid, separation of professional and social roles in the therapists." Item examples are: "Do you contact a patient who fails to appear or to notify you on two consecutive appointments?" (No: -); "Would you ever go to the patient's home to do psychotherapy?" (Yes: +); "Would you deliberately avoid being in a social situation with your patient?" (No: -). *Factor two* is described as emphasis upon getting and giving information and help; seems associated with the traditional, rational, flexible approach to health problems. Items are: "Do you obtain from the patient a detailed case history before beginning psychotherapy?" (Yes: +); "Would you accept a small gift from a patient in psychotherapy?" (Yes: +); "Ordinarily, do you answer general questions of fact such as, are psychiatrists always doctors?" (Yes: +); "Do you deliberately assume different therapeutic roles with different patients?" (Yes: +). *Factor three* is "thought to reflect the broad spectrum, resourceful, somewhat supportive approach to patients." Representative items are:"Do you interview the relatives or friends of a patient . . . for the purpose of obtaining more complete knowledge about the patient?" (Yes: +); "Do you make any attempts to ease the environmental stress upon your patient by contacting significant others in his life?" (Yes: +); "Do you attempt to maintain a definite and consistent length of interviews?" (No: +). *Factor four* "focuses on the activity of the therapist, stresses his artful, almost expedient virtuosity in dealing with his patients from moment to moment." Items are: "As therapist, do you ask your patient questions?" (Yes: +); "Do you try to maintain the same therapeutic role throughout the entire course of therapy with a given patient?" (No: +); The number of middle or "three" answers to the items (Many: +).

Fey observes that "it would have been convenient if one of Fiedler's major dimensions could be shown to coincide with certain of the factors isolated by this work; in the writer's judgment, none convincingly does." He concluded that the brief scales for the four factor clusters are differentially sensitive to both the factors of therapist doctrine and therapist experience. Apparently, neither Fey or others have subsequently applied his common-conduct-issues questionnaire.

A Survey of Psychotherapists' Technique Conceptions

Meehl and Glueck

Meehl (1960) described an unpublished study by Meehl and Glueck where they studied responses from 168 psychotherapists to a questionnaire dealing with 132 aspects of therapeutic technique. The therapist sample included both medical and nonmedical practioners, and represented a wide spectrum of orientations including, among others, Freudians, neo-Freudians, Radovians, Sullivanians, eclectics, and "mixed."

Meehl does not report the results or the questionnaire items systematically since his paper was focusing on other issues. He parenthetically included a sample of results, which will be reproduced here. Apparently the questionnaire responses were not factor-analyzed, nor were any other aspects of the study followed up.

> One of our items reads: "It greatly speeds therapy if the therapist has prior knowledge of the client's dynamics and content from such devices as the Rorschach and TAT." While the self-styled groups differ significantly in their response to this item (ranging from a unanimous negative among Rogerians to a two-thirds affirmative among George Kelly disciples), all groups except the last tend to respond negatively. The overall percentage who believe that such prior knowledge of the client's personality greatly speeds therapy is only 17 percent. (Meehl, 1960, p. 19)

> We have some other interesting results which suggest considerable skepticism among therapists as to the significance of causal understanding itself in the treatment process. For example, 43 percent state that "Warmth and real sympathy are much more important than an accurate causal understanding of the client's difficulty." Over one-third believe that "Literary, dramatic, esthetic, or mystical people are likely to be better therapists than people of a primarily scientific, logical, or mathematical bent." Four out of five believe that "The personality of the therapist is more important than the theory of personality he holds." About half believe that "Interpretation as a tool is greatly overrated at present." Two out of five go as far to say that "Under proper conditions an incorrect interpretation, not even near to the actual facts, can have a real and long-lasting therapeutic effect." Time does not permit us to read other examples of items which, in the aggregate, suggest minimization of the importance of the therapist's forming a "correct" picture of the client's psyche. (pp. 19-20)

A Goal Statement Inventory

Michaux, Lorr, and McNair

Michaux and Lorr (1961) and McNair and Lorr (1964b) set out to evaluate therapist treatment goals and their relation to therapeutic outcome. The initial study focused on identification and quantitative measurement of major therapist goals. A sample of goals was obtained by asking therapists to provide free response descriptions of their specific goals in treating 282 VA outpatient clinic cases. The question asked was: "Specifically, what do you aim to accomplish with this patient within the next four months by way of helping him handle or solve (his problems)? In other words, what are your treatment goals in relation to the problems as you see them now?" Michaux and Lorr developed and reported a three-category qualitative schema for classifying the goal statements. The three categories were: (1) *Reconstructive* goals, where the major aims are personality changes or modification with insight (for example, work through pathological patterns, help the patient understand his self-defeating behavior, enable the patient to assert more active tendencies in his relations with others). (2) *Supportive* goals, where the aims are stabilizing current adjustment patterns (for example, stabilize present adjustment, forestall relapse or psychotic break, help patient weather a current crisis, strengthen defenses). (3) *Relationship* goals, where the aims are to improve the patient's adjustment by fostering his relationship with the therapist (for example, develop patient's motivation for treatment, enable patient to trust the therapist, improve patient's ability to communicate with the therapist, let patient identify with the therapist).

The later report (McNair and Lorr, 1964b) described the authors' attempt to quantify goals and to determine by factor analysis whether the qualitative categories accurately reflected the principal kinds of goals. The items for the Goal Statement Inventory (GSI) were selected to sample the kinds of goals classified into Michaux and Lorr's three categories. The GSI was administered to the 259 therapists who indicated whether each goal on the GSI was or was not one of their specific goals for the next six months in treating 523 VA outpatients.

The responses were factor-analyzed, yielding three factors which differed somewhat from the original three coding categories. The three factors extracted from the GSI are: (1) *Reconstructive* goals ("the conventional goals of psychotherapy with neurotics . . . have in common the therapeutic aims of shaping personality change and developing insights"). Item examples are: Relate past experiences to present problems; relate emotions to life situation; work through a pathological pattern; awareness of reactions to significant others; increase self-esteem. (2) *Stabilization* goals ("have in common the aims of maintaining the patient's current adjustment pattern and preventing worsening"). Representative items are: Remain out of NP hospital; prevent worsening; accept present limitations; strengthen defenses; help patient accept and trust therapist. (3) *Situational*

Adjustment goals "defined by aims which emphasize adjustment to the current life situation"). Examples are: Improve job adjustment; achieve specific reality goals (for example, change residence); relate to others with less friction; handle a current crisis.

Lorr and McNair (1966) conclude: Results of the work with the GSI indicate that there are at least three distinct kinds of aims in psychotherapy which may be measured objectively. While there may be still other kinds of aims, the GSI probably samples rather well the more common goals of outpatient psychotherapy." (p. 589)

The Therapist Orientation Questionnaire

Sundland and Barker (1962)

Sundland and Barker (1962) report a carefully conceived and executed study of the orientations of psychotherapists. They state that

> a major difficulty with the recent experiments and studies on psychotherapy is that the therapist is incompletely described by such data as his age, sex, and number of years experience, i.e. a major experimental condition is inadequately described. The availability of a measure of the therapist variable should lead to greater comparability between studies and should encourage research on the differential effects of therapists. Presently available categories are based on crude stereotypes ("Freudian") rather than reported attitudes or behavior. . . . The present study attempts to provide a measure of explicit differences between therapists. (p. 201)
>
> There have been several studies of the attitudes of psychotherapists done by Fiedler (1950a, 1950b), Glover (1955), Wolff (1956), Fey (1958), and Meehl and Glueck (referred to in Meehl, 1960). However, all these studies lacked breadth either in sampling of attitudes or the sampling of therapists. Typically, they studied a limited number of therapy relevant attitudes of a small and unrepresentative sample of therapists. None of the studies has resulted in a comprehensive measure of the therapist variable in the therapy situation. (p. 201)

The authors reviewed the literature on psychotherapy, and identified 252 issues which had been points of controversy among therapeutic schools. A preliminary questionnaire was devised to sample these issues, and given to sixteen psychotherapists of various orientations. Items that effected no division whatsoever among these therapists were discarded. The remaining items were grouped according to issues, and careful descriptions of 16 scales were written. Items were then constructed for each of these subtests, taking care to have a balance of positive and negative items for each subtest.

The resulting Therapist Orientation Questionnaire (TOQ) was initially composed of 133 items designed to reflect evenly both poles of sixteen scales of therapist attitudes and methods, scored on five-point Likert scales. Item analysis procedures reduced the number of items; the final form is composed of ninety-four items distributed across sixteen scales.

The sixteen subtests were as follows. (1) *Frequency of Activity* (six items): whether the therapist believes that a talkative, active role is desirable or undesirable. (2) *Type of Activity* (seven items): refers to degree of lead and depth of interpretation; whether the therapist believed it was desirable to go beyond, or beneath, what the patient was consciously aware of. (3) *Emotional Tenor of the Relationship* (fourteen items): the degree of emotional involvement of the therapist, whether an impersonal approach is felt to be better than a warm, personal approach. (4) *Spontaneity in the Therapeutic Relationship* (five items): does the therapist believe his actions are spontaneous and unreasoned? (5) *Planning of the Therapeutic Relationship* (nine items): does the therapist look upon his behavior as planned and does he believe in an overall treatment plan? (6) *Conceptualization of the Therapeutic Relationship* (three items): whether the therapist tries to figure out the nature of the patient's relationship with him. (7) *Goals of Therapy* (ten items): whether or not the therapist reports having particular goals for the patient. (8) *Therapist's Security* (five items): positive regard, unconditionality, empathic understanding, security in the situation, and willingness to make himself known. (9) *Theory of Personal Growth* (six items): whether therapy is seen as removing something that is barring the patient's own growth; whether or not the therapist believed in a "life force" within people which urged them to physical and mental health. (10) *Cognitive Therapeutic Gains* (four items): whether the therapist thought that "understanding" was an important result of therapy. (11) *Learning Process in Therapy* (three items): whether the nature of the therapeutic learning process is a verbal and conceptual one, or an affective, nonverbal and nonconceptual one. (12) *Topics Important to Therapy* (three items): whether the therapist believes it is important that the patient discuss his childhood. (13) *Theory of Neurosis* (two items): whether neurosis is caused by an ineffectual conscience rather than a too strong one. (14) *Criteria for Success* (four items): whether therapists thought that it was important for the patient to adjust to the goals of society. (15) *Theory of Motiva-*

tion (six items): the importance that therapists ascribed to the concept of unconscious processes. (16) *Curative Aspect of the Therapist* (four items): whether the training or the personality of the therapist is more important.

Therapist Orientation Questionnaires were mailed to randomly selected members of the American Psychological Association who listed psychotherapy as a first or second interest in the 1959 Directory. Of 400 TOQs mailed, 45 were undeliverable, and 244 were returned. Initial results were based on replies of 139 therapists that were received before an arbitrary closing date.

The questionnaire item responses were factor-analyzed, and six first-order factors were extracted, with the first three factors "appearing to be variants of the second order general factor."

> One of the most interesting and surprising findings of the analysis was that there is a general factor which cuts across the majority of the scales. In terms of these items this general factor must be considered the most significant single continuum upon which to compare therapists. For convenience, one pole of the general factor will be labeled the "analytic" pole—using analytic in its broad sense as a mode of attending and responding, not as an abbreviation for "psychoanalytic." The other pole of the general factor will be labeled the "experiential" pole, congruent with its emphasis upon nonrational, nonverbal experiencing. In terms of the subtests with higher loadings, the analytic pole stresses conceptualizing, the training of the therapist, planning of therapy, unconscious processes, and a restriction of therapist spontaneity. The experiential pole deemphasizes conceptualizing, stresses the personality of the therapist, an unplanned approach to therapy, deemphasizes unconscious processes, and accepts therapist spontaneity.

Sundland and Barker composed three groups (80 percent of their sample) according to stated orientation: Freudian (60), Sullivanian (40) and Rogerian (31). The three schools were found to differ on nine of sixteen scales. For eight of the nine significant differences, the Sullivanian group occupied the midpoint on the scales. The greatest differences were between Freudians and Rogerians. An important finding in terms of previous studies was that the obtained differences on the sixteen subtests were almost entirely between orientation, rather than between levels of experience.

> The results of the present research indicate that there is a limit to the generalizability of Fiedler's conclusion (that experts are more

> like other experts than like neophytes of their own orientation). In terms of the attitudes measured here, the differences between therapists are clearly better accounted for by their theoretical orientation than by their amount of experience. . . . The items used by Fiedler appear to be very similar to the items dropped from the TOQ early in its construction . . . items which did not discriminate any therapists in the pilot study were dropped from the TOQ. Inspection of these items revealed that they were largely expressing that empathy was important and that the therapist would empathically relate to his patient. This kind of item made up the bulk of Fiedler's Q-sort.

Sundland and Barker's 1962 report stated that "currently a broader study is in progress using a revised and larger form of the TOQ composed of 24 attitudinal scales. The broader sample contains national samples of therapists from psychology, psychiatry, and psychiatric social work." Apparently the authors have not reported on this later study to date.

The Usual Therapeutic Practices Scale

Wallach and Strupp (1964)

Wallach and Strupp (1964) outlined the rationale for development of their instrument as follows:

> The present investigation represents a preliminary attempt to study therapist's preferences for and attitudes towards therapeutic practices which are hypothesized to be fairly basic. We were not concerned with highly specific aspects of the therapist's operations, such as particular ways of handling therapeutic problems, methods of interpretation, and the like. Our concern was with more general attitudinal variations. In a number of respects this research is related to earlier studies by Glover (1955), Meehl (1960), Fey (1968), and to the comprehensive work of Sundland and Barker (1962). (Wallach and Strupp, 1964, p. 120)
>
> There may be true (demonstrable) differences in the operations of therapists which may cut across theoretical orientations and personality differences. . . . We might say that therapists of different theoretical persuasions may be more similar in their procedures than they realize or are willing to admit; however, they may also be more different, and both similarities and differences may be along heretofore unsuspected lines. Relying on our own experi-

> ence, the results of previous investigations by members of our group, and our general knowledge of the field, we constructed a 17-item scale dealing with what we considered to be major instances of the therapist's usual therapeutic practices. The respondent's task was simply one of stating on a six-point scale his agreement or disagreement with a given proposition. (p. 120)

The Usual Therapeutic Practices Scale (UTP) was administered to two samples, one consisting of 59 medical psychotherapists, the other of 248 psychiatrists and psychologist psychotherapists throughout the United States. The questionnaire item scores were intercorrelated, and factor analysis revealed six factors, although "only four factors appeared worthy of serious consideration." The extracted factors are: (1) *Maintenance of Personal Distance* refers to the extent to which the therapist allows himself to get personally involved in the treatment. Examples of items loading on this factor are: "Rarely answer personal questions" (+). "Keep all aspects of my private life out of therapy" (+). "Almost never answer personal questions of opinion" (+). "Rarely express own feelings in treatment" (+). "Therapist should be more like a blank screen than a person in therapy" (+). (2) *Preference for Intensive (Psychoanalytic, Uncovering) Psychotherapy*. Representative items are: "Prefer to conduct intensive rather than goal-limited therapy" (+). "Almost never let silences build up during the therapy hour" (-). "Prefer patients not to develop intense feelings about me" (-). (3) *Preference for Keeping Verbal Interventions to a Minimum* refers to the emphasis that therapist communications should be restricted to those which are clearly in the patient's interest. Items are: "Verbal interventions are usually sparing and concise" (+). "Rarely express own feelings in treatment" (+). "Generally tend to be active" (-). (4) *View of Psychotherapy as an Artistic and Artful Activity*, which includes an emphasis on flexibility as opposed to rigidly controlled procedures. Item examples are: "Usually willing to grant extra interviews" (+). "Consider psychotherapy much more an art than a science" (+).

Regarding the factor structure, Wallach and Strupp (1964) note that

> one is on safe grounds only regarding Factor one which is the only factor which emerged with sufficient strength and clarity to enable one to be sure about its meaning. The remaining factors account for relatively small amounts of the total variance; nevertheless, the fact that it was possible to replicate them lends support to our belief that we are dealing with meaningful constructs. . . . [This first factor] emphasizes the importance of the therapist's person (his direct personal involvement) in the interpersonal relationship

> with the patient. The factor shows marked congruence with Sundland and Barker's (1962) general factor, which was found to cut across a number of scales. . . . Somewhat in contrast to their conclusion, we tend to believe that "analytic" does refer to "psychoanalytic" in the sense of the therapists studied and deliberate restriction of his free-and-easy participation in the therapeutic interaction. This restraint is viewed as a function of his training in psychoanalytic principles with its emphasis on analysis of the transference situation, as opposed to a theoretical position which stresses the curative aspects of a good interpersonal relationship in and of itself. (p. 124)

A relatively consistent finding was that of no relationship between any of the factors and therapist experience. "In the present study, as in the report by Sundland and Barker (1962), therapists' levels of experience seem unrelated to reported therapeutic activity. Theoretical orientation, on the other hand, once again was related significantly to a number of the factors isolated. Usually the psychoanalytic groups appear as most dissimilar from the client-centered group" (Wallach and Strupp, 1964, p. 124). Orthodox Freudians were highest in maintaining personal distance, preference for intensive therapy, and lowest in considering therapy an artistic activity, and highest in keeping verbal interventions at a minimum. Client-centered therapists were distinct in considering psychotherapy an art, and in their lack of preference for intensive psychotherapy.

The AID Technique Scales

McNair and Lorr (1964)

McNair and Lorr (1964a) postulated three independent factors of therapist technique. The three postulated technique factors were: (1) psychoanalytically oriented techniques (A), consisting of seventeen scales; (2) impersonal versus personal affective approaches to patients (I), subsuming twenty-one scales; and (3) directive, active therapeutic interventions (D), including nineteen scales. The original form of AID consisted of fifty-seven scales. "A majority of the statements represented modifications of those used by Sundland and Barker, but some were suggested in an earlier article by Fey (1958); the remainder were original." (McNair and Lorr, 1966, p. 585) All AID scales were written as descriptions of how therapists should conduct therapy or behave during interviews. Respondents indicated degree of agreement or disagreement on eight-point scales.

AID was administered to 192 male and 73 female psychotherapists practicing at 43 VA Mental Hygiene Clinics, including 67 psychiatrists, 103 clinical psychologists, and 95 social workers. The AID item responses were intercorrelated and factor-analyzed, confirming the presence of the three hypothesized factors. The resulting three factors are:

(1) *Psychoanalytic Techniques* appears "to represent the extent of use of traditional analytic techniques." Item examples are: analyzes resistance; discusses childhood events; uses free association; interprets dreams; interprets mannerisms and slips of tongue; interprets unconscious motives; believes learning causes of behavior is the major result.

(2) *Impersonal versus Personal Techniques* represents a continuum of expression versus control of affect toward patients; high scores endorse an aloof, detached impersonal approach in contrast to low scores indicating spontaneous action and practice of a relationship-type therapy. Items are: keeps office free of personal photos, mementos, etc.; takes a detached, impersonal approach; uses patient's first name (-); spontaneously expresses feelings (-); feelings are unchanged if patient is critical or appreciative; acts reserved and uninvolved; never shows anger at patient; considers walking about therapy room acceptable (-); sometimes discusses news, movies, sports, etc. (-); considers therapist personality more important than technique (-).

(3) *Directive Techniques* appears to tap the extent to which therapists assume active control of the treatment task, defined by techniques for planning therapy, for actively implementing those plans, and for shaping the therapeutic interaction and a therapist-determined direction. Representative items are: sets long-range treatment goals; aims at social adjustment of patient; considers treatment plan unnecessary (-); accepts patients' own goals (-); assumes different roles with different patients; considers case history and diagnosis essential to treatment; takes fairly passive, silent role (-).

After the three technique factors were identified, therapists in the sample were classified into one of eight technique patterns on the basis of whether their factor scores were above or below the median on each factor. The authors summarize their findings as follows:

> The resulting patterns of technique were clearly related to other therapist characteristics. Each professional group (psychiatrists, psychologists, social workers) exhibited distinct preferences for one or two of the patterns, suggesting a strong relationship between therapeutic approach and training of the therapist. Male and female therapists preferred different approaches, with women

more often endorsing patterns with high scores on the Impersonal factor. As expected, therapists who had some personal analysis were more likely to endorse the four patterns characterized by high scores on the analytic factor. Experience of therapists was unrelated to the techniques they endorsed. (McNair and Lorr, 1966, p. 587)

MEASURES OF PATIENTS' CONCEPTIONS AND PREFERENCES

A Scale on Attitudes Toward Counseling

Form (1955)

Form (1955) set out to develop a measure of students' attitudes toward the Counseling Center on a particular midwestern university campus. He argues that "one of the factors related to the effectiveness of counseling programs is the prevailing climate of opinion toward them. This was the research premise of a study designed to explore the relationship between student attitudes toward counselors on a college campus and different factors in their personal and social background. Student attitudes toward counseling services were measured by a specially constructed Counseling Attitudes Scale."

The author constructed 120 items expressing counseling attitudes, and gave them to eighty judges to be sorted according to Thurstone's method of equal appearing intervals. The author used the interquartile range values of these judgments on each of the items as an index of the degree of ambiguity of the item, so that all scale items having Q values of more than 1.71 (median Q value of the 120 items) were rejected. Sixty-two items survived this procedure, to which the author added fifteen additional items. These seventy-seven items were to be answered on five-point Likert scales of agreement-disagreement.

This version of the scale was administered to a sample of 200 undergraduate students, and a total score on all seventy-seven items was obtained for each subject. An item analysis reduced the item pool to twenty-two items which constitute the final version of the "Counseling Attitude Scale."

Examples of statements about the counseling center to which students indicated their degree of agreement are: "I think the Counseling Center is a great asset to X College." "I feel the Counseling Center is highly inadequate to solve any kind of problem." "Talks with counselors at the Center are tension releasing if nothing else." "I feel that I cannot trust anyone at the Counseling Center to help me." "I believe the Counseling Center does not adequately interpret test results." "The Counseling Center is a poor excuse for a clinic where students may take their problems." "I recommend the services of the Counseling Center to all who need help."

The twenty-two-item final version of the Scale was mailed, along with other instruments, to 605 undergraduate students selected by a stratified random sampling technique; 544 were returned. The split-half reliability of the Scale was 0.94 and the coefficient of reproducability was 0.87 indicating that "the scale tends to be unidimensional." When the respondents were grouped into "strongly favorable attitudes" (total score of 15 or more), "low favorable attitudes" (scores between 8 and 14), and "unfavorable attitudes" (below 8), only 21 of the 544 students had "unfavorable" attitudes. In terms of the other measures obtained, the findings indicated that younger students, underclassmen, nonveterans, and unmarried students indicated more favorable attitudes. The author concludes that "the scale needs further refinement. Much would be gained by retesting it with another population." Apparently no further work with the instrument has been done since Form's (1955) report.

The Psychiatric Attitudes Battery

Reznikoff, Brady, and Zeller (1959)

Reznikoff, Brady, and Zeller (1959) developed an instrument for hospitalized psychiatric patients, focusing on their attitudes toward the broad social matrix of the institutional setting. The measures were designed to elicit attitudes in three interrelated areas: toward the psychiatric hospital, toward the psychiatrist, and towards psychiatric treatment. The purpose was "to develop reliable procedures for getting a kind of attitudinal profile of the psychiatric patient which, by virtue of its objective and quantitative nature, will permit a more systematic study of the influence of attitudes on the patient's behavior and the clinical course of the illness. The procedures are so constituded that they can be used to assess attitudes on non-patient populations as well."

The battery requires from thirty to ninety minutes to complete. It consists of four procedures: (1) The *Picture Attitudes Test* is a TAT-like projective device aimed at assessing the patient's least conscious attitudes toward psychiatry. It is designed after Libo's (1956) procedures, and consists of a male patient-therapist picture, a female patient-therapist card, and a card depicting a hospital scene. (2) The *Sentence Completion Attitudes Test* consists of twenty-one incomplete sentences, seven in each of the three attitudinal areas (psychiatric hospital, psychiatrist, and psychiatric treatment). Examples of the items are: Coming to a psychiatric hospital .... Psychiatrists are .... The worst thing about psychiatric treatment .... Patients in psychiatric hospitals seldom .... Seeing a psychiatrist .... After psychiatric treatment a person .... (3) *Multiple-Choice Attitudes Questionnaire* consists of twelve items, four in each of three attitude areas. For each item there are three foils, designed to reflect attitudes that are favorable or optimistic, neutral, or unfavorable and pessimistic. Item examples are: The conditions in psychiatric hospitals are (*a*) better than in other types of hospitals, (*b*) about the same as in other types of hospitals, (*c*) worse than in other types of hospitals. Seeing a psychiatrist would be helpful to (*a*) some people, (*b*) few people (*c*) many people. Psychiatric treatment is (*a*) rarely successful, (*b*) usually successful, (*c*) sometimes successful. (4) The *Souelen Attitude Scale* consists of two equivalent forms of thirty-six items each. Each item is a statement about some aspect of mental hospital life with which a subject is asked to express agreement or disagreement.

The authors' 1959 report was a preliminary one indicating that "methods of scoring the procedures have been developed, and reliability was found to be adequate." Apparently neither the authors not others have published subsequent reports regarding the psychiatric attitudes battery.

Mental Health Conceptions of the General Public and of Experts

Nunnally (1961)

Nunnally (1961) reports a carefully conducted and extensive survey of current attitudes toward mental health problems and professionals.

> We decided to study public reactions to mental illness—psychoses, neuroses, and lesser disturbances. The plan was to study popular conceptions of mental illness and how these conceptions develop and change, both naturally and as a function of outside influences. Our research did not specifically deal with the nature of mental health itself, but rather with what people think and feel about mental health phenomena—popular ideas about the causes, symptoms, treatment, and social effects of mental disorders. . . . The research was intended to provide some partial answers to two very large questions: (1) What are the existing conceptions of mental health? (2) How can the existing conceptions be changed

for the better? The first question involves "descriptive" or measurement and survey studies; the second experimental studies. (pp. 2-3)

Nunnally and his colleagues measured the attitudes and information held by three sources: the general public, experts (psychologists and psychiatrists), and the mass media. Information was measured by a questionnaire constructed for this purpose and administered to samples of the general public and experts. Attitudes were measured by an adaptation of Osgood's semantic differential procedure, for the general public and the experts; attitudes of the mass media were assessed through content-analysis procedures applied to samples of mental-health relevant communications. Samples of the general public were drawn from several geographic areas (Illinois, Tennessee, and Oregon) and were carefully selected as "approximate miniatures of the United States population in terms of education, sex ratio, income, religious affiliation, and age." The expert samples consisted of 150 psychologists (APA members and diplomates involved in clinical, counseling, or guidance work) and 150 psychiatrists (drawn from the Group for the Advancement of Psychiatry).

The instrument of primary interest here is the information questionnaire developed by the research group. A preliminary search of the three sources (what was currently being said by members of the public, by experts, and in the mass media) was made "to determine the content coverage needed in our measures of information." Over 3,000 opinion statements were gathered which related to causes, symptoms, prognosis, treatment, incidence, and social significance of mental-health problems. This set was reduced to 240 items by removing apparent duplicate statements. In an initial administration of the 240-item version to a sample of the public, 60 more items were eliminated (those with which everyone either agreed strongly or disagreed strongly), leaving 180. Responses to these 180 items were then factor-analyzed, yielding ten information factors. (1) *Look and Act Different* (the mentally ill are recognizably different in manner and appearance from normal persons). (2) *Will Power* (once adjustment is lost, the psychiatrist exercises his own will power to bolster the patient's failing will. Persons who remain mentally ill do not "try" to get better). (3) *Avoidance of Morbid Thoughts* (mental disturbances can be avoided by keeping busy, reading books on "peace of mind" and not discussing troublesome topics). (4) *Sex Distinction* (women are more prone to mental disorder than men). (5) *Guidance and Support* (mental health can be maintained by depending on strong persons in the environment). (6) *Hoplelessness* (there is little that can be done to cure a mental disorder). (7) *Imme-*

diate External Environment Versus Personality Dynamics (mental troubles are caused by pressures in the immediate environment: physical exhaustion, financial and social problems). (8) *Nonseriousness* (emotional difficulties are relatively unimportant problems that cause little damage to the individual). (9) *Age Function* (persons become more susceptible to emotional disorders as they grow older), and (10) *Organic Causes* (mental disorder is brought on by organic factors like poor diet and diseases of the nervous system).

From the factor-analytic results, the researchers derived a revised and final form of the questionnaire containing only fifty items that loaded highly on the factors. The final questionnaire form was then administered to samples of the public in Tennessee and Oregon. The same questionnaire was also administered to the 300 psychologist and psychiatrist experts. In their case, instead of asking the respondent what he personally believed, he was asked "to indicate what he thought the public should be told." That is, he was asked to rate the extent to which each opinion statement "should be repudiated or suggested in public information programs" on a seven-point "repudiate-support scale."

Some of the findings found for the information questionnaire are: (1) Public information is not highly structured. "Correlations among the items were generally low. . . . The factors which were derived were not statistically strong. Few of the loadings were above 0.40 and the first ten centroid factors explained less than 25 percent of the total item variance. These facts indicate that the information statements do not fall into neat groups." (2) The responses to the items by the public are not markedly different in most cases from expert responses. Experts were more in agreement on the questionnaire items than members of the general public—the item variances of the experts "were in all cases lower than those of the lay public and generally tended to be less than one-half as large." (3) "Whereas on the average the members of the public generally agree with the experts, there are two groups in the population whose knowledge is apparently inaccurate. These are people with less than a high-school education, and people over 50 years of age."

Finally, the experts' questionnaire responses as well as their orientation and profession data were factor-analyzed, yielding five centroid factors, only three of which were interpretable, and only two considered to be major dimensions. The three interpretable information factors emerging for the psychotherapists' conceptions of what the public should be told about mental-health problems are: (1) *Psychiatrist or Psychotherapist's Role* (the best methods of therapy; the degree of directiveness that characterizes the effective therapist; the effective therapist as teaching, correcting, and explaining).

Item examples are: Psychiatrists try to show the mental patient where his ideas are incorrect (0.60). The main job of the psychiatrist is to explain to the patient the origin of his troubles (0.57). The good psychiatrist acts like a father to his patients (0.43). Psychiatrists have to have a good sense of humor in order to help their patients. (2) *Causes of Mental Disorders* (the influences that make for better or worse emotional adjustment; seem to explain mental disorders in terms of the individual's childhood and the history of his personal experience). Items are: Physical rest will not prevent a mental disorder (0.48). A change of climate seldom helps an emotional disorder (0.46). Adult problems are less important in causing emotional disorders than the individual's childhood experience (0.37). Helping the mentally ill person with his financial and social problems will not cure his disorder (.35). (3) *Professional Affiliation* (an array of items that psychologists tend to endorse more strongly than do psychiatrists; more skeptical of organic, physical explanations of mental disorder). Item examples are: Professional affiliation–psychologist (0.42). A poor diet does not lead to feeblemindedness (0.38). Physical exhaustion does not lead to a nervous breakdown (0.35). In regard to this last factor, however, the author states that "on the average psychologists and psychiatrists are in good agreement. What the factor analysis shows is that there are at least two dimensions of disagreement within both professions."

Finally, both the general public and experts rated the following three concepts on seventeen bipolar semantic differential scales: Psychiatrist, Mental Patient, and Mental Hospital. Some of the findings regarding the general public's attitudes toward the psychiatrist and mental treatments were as follows. (1) All the professions studied were held in high esteem by the public, the mental-health professions included. "The mental professions are rated as sincere, effective, dependable, etc." (2) The medical doctor or physician is rated higher than any professional whose profession starts with the syllable "psych." (3) No significant differences are found among public attitudes toward the various subprofessions in the mental-health field. (4) The public does not trust mental treatment methods and institutions as much as physical treatment methods and institutions.

Attitudes Toward Seeking Professional Psychological Help Scale

Fischer and Turner (1970)

Fischer and Turner (1970) set out to develop a continuously scored scale that would reflect a subject's attitude toward seeking professional counseling for psychological disturbances, "in contrast to psychiatric treatment and mental hospitals (Reznikoff, Brady, and Zeller, 1959; Nunnally, 1961)."

> [We attempted] to clarify an attitude and personality domain which applies to one's tendency to seek or to resist professional aid during a personal crisis or following prolonged psychological discomfort. . . . One person may view the decision to get professional help as a sign of personal weakness, indicative of failure; for him the move to get professional help represents a last-ditch desperate action spurred by a psychologically intolerable situation. Another individual may approach a clinical psychologist or psychiatrist willingly and openly, for a relatively minor problem, and with a genuine expectation of appreciable changes resulting from therapy. The authors assume that such attitudinal differences underlie actual help seeking. . . . [Undoubtedly] there are numerous personality, interpersonal, and social components which can affect an individual's decision to accept or seek professional counseling for psychological problems: his own preconceptions and beliefs about psychiatric treatment, the support he gets from family and friends, the stigma surrounding psychiatric care, his ability to introspect and disclose feelings and experiences, the immediacy or press of the psychological or interpersonal difficulty, etc. A primary goal of the present study was to construct a scale which samples an attitude domain corresponding to many of the pertinent factors. (Fischer and Turner, 1970, pp. 79-80)

The preliminary attitude statements were written by a pool of clinical psychologists from numerous mental-health settings, including state and federal hospitals, clinics, private practice, and school settings. Forty-seven statements were selected as representative of the general orientation toward seeking professional help for psychological problems. These forty-seven preliminary statements were then judged by a panel of fourteen clinical and counseling psychologists and psychiatrists as to their relevance to the hypothetical attitude domain and according to whether they reflected a positive or negative attitude. Thirty-one items were judged highly relevant and were unanimously rated as either positive or negative.

The thirty-one items were administered to seventy-eight high school and nineteen nursing students who responded to each item on a four-point Likert scale of agreement-disagreement. Item analysis indicated that all thirty-one items correlated significantly with the total score, and that none correlated more than 0.25 with Marlowe-

Crowne social desirability. The scale was administered again to a second sample, and two items were eliminated by item analysis.

The remaining twenty-nine items (eleven positive, eighteen negative) constituted the final version of the Attitudes Toward Seeking Professional Psychological Help Scale. The questionnaires of the 212 subjects tested thus far were rescored for the twenty-nine items, with the following results. Internal consistency reliability was 0.86, compared to 0.83 on a later sample. Test-retest reliability (from five days to eight weeks) coefficients ranged from 0.73 to 0.89, with most in the 0.80s. On all samples, females tended to endorse all items in the positive direction, with the sex difference being significant for sixteen of the twenty-nine items. All students tended to express positive attitudes toward help seeking, with subjects who had previous professional contact scoring significantly higher on the scale than those who had not.

Responses of 424 college and nursing students were intercorrelated and factor-analyzed with four factors emerging as "clearly definable and interpretable" (1) *Recognition of Personal Need for Professional Psychological Help* (eight items). Item examples are: "A person with a strong character can get over mental conflicts by himself, and would have little need of a psychiatrist" (-). "At some future time I might want to have psychological counseling" (+). "Emotional difficulties, like many things, tend to work out by themselves" (-). (2) *Tolerance of the Stigma Associated with Psychiatric Help* (five items). Examples are: "Having been a psychiatric patient is a blot on a person's life" (-). "If I thought I needed psychiatric help, I would get it no matter who knew about it" (+). (3) *Interpersonal Openness Regarding One's Problems* (seven items). Representative items are: "I would willingly confide intimate matters to an appropriate person if I thought it might help me or a member of my family" (+). "There are experiences in my life I would not discuss with anyone" (-). "It is probably best not to know everything about oneself" (-). (4) *Confidence in the Mental-Health Professional* (nine items). Items are: "If I were experiencing a serious emotional crisis at this point in my life, I would be confident that I could find relief in psychotherapy" (+). "I would rather be advised by a close friend than by a psychologist, even for an emotional problem" (-). "If a good friend asked my advice about a mental problem, I might recommend that he see a psychiatrist" (+).

The factor analysis was replicated on samples of 180 males and 201 females, and "essentially the same four factors emerged in the new samples." The scale subtests were intercorrelated with other personality data available: Marlowe-Crowne social desirability, California F scale, Rotter's interpersonal trust and internal-external control scales, and a masculinity scale. Among other things, the authors found that high authoritarians and high external controls tended to express negative attitudes, while for females only high SD and high interpersonal trust subjects tended to express positive attitudes.

Fischer and Turner conclude:

> Because of its explicit referents, the scale may have some effectiveness in predicting length of stay and outcome in psychotherapy. But, as with most attitude scales, these items should not be used to screen individual applicants. . . . In future studies, the four factors should be interpreted with reference to the overall scale, rather than used as separate measures. . . . Currently the authors are gathering data to examine the correspondence of help-seeking orientation to developmental and sociological variables such as birth order, educational level, occupational goals, socioeconomic class of origin, and religious values. We would also like to test which items and factors best predict who will seek help in settings where access to a clinical psychologist is fairly easy and involves no great time or financial committment.

References

Anderson, R. P., and Anderson, G. V. Development of an instrument for measuring rapport. *Personnel Guidance Journal*, 1962, 41, 18-24.

Anthony, N. A longitudinal analysis of the effect of experience on the therapeutic approach. *Journal of Clinical Psychology*, 1967, 23, 512-16.

Apfelbaum, B. *Dimensions of Transference in Psychotherapy*, Berkeley: University of California Publications, 1958.

Ashby, J. D., Ford, D. H., Guerney, B. G., and Guerney, L. F. Effects on clients of a reflective and leading type of psychotherapy. *Psychological Monographs*, 1957, 71, (24, Whole No. 453).

Barrett-Lennard, G. T. Dimensions of perceived therapist response related to therapeutic change. Unpublished doctoral dissertation, University of Chicago, 1959. (a)

________. The Relationship Inventory: a technique for measuring therapeutic dimensions of an interpersonal relationship. Paper read at the annual conferences of the Southeastern Psychological Association, St. Augustine, Fla., April 24, 1959. (b)

________. Dimensions of therapist response as causal factors in therapeutic change. *Psychological Monographs*, 1962, 76 (43, Whole No. 562).

________. Technical note on the 64-item revision of the Relationship Inventory. University of Waterloo, Canada, 1966. (Mimeographed.) (a)

________. Studies in progress, using the Relationship Inventory. Annotated list for private circulation, University of Waterloo, Ontario, Canada, September 1966 (b)

________. Supplement: The 1964 revision of the Relationship Inventory. University of Waterloo, Ontario, Canada, July 1968. (Mimeographed.)

———. Technical note on the 64-item revision of the Relationship Inventory. University of Waterloo, Ontario, Canada, December 1969. (Mimeographed.)

———. The relationship Inventory: revision process (draft form). University of Waterloo, Canada, 1970.

Barrett-Lennard, G. T., and Elliott, G. A. Partial list of reported studies using the Relationship Inventory (revised). University of Waterloo, Ontario, Canada, December 1969. (Mimeographed list.)

Barrett-Lennard, G. T., and Jewell, L. N. A selection of reported studies using the Relationship Inventory, University of Waterloo, Ontario, Canada, May, 1966. (Mimeographed annotated list.)

Bierman, R. Dimensions of interpersonal facilitation in psychotherapy and child development. *Psychological Bulletin*, 1969, 72, 338-52.

Cannon, H. J. Personality variables and counselor-client affect. *Journal of Counseling Psychology*, 1964, 11, 35-41.

Chase, W. P. Measurement of attitudes toward counseling. Educational and Psychological Measurement, 1946, 6, 467-73.

Cottle, W. C. Personal characteristics of counselors: I. A review of the literature. *Personnel and Guidance Journal*, 1953, 31, 445-50.

Cottle, W. C., Lewis, W. W., Jr., and Penney, M. M. Personal characteristics of counselors: III. Experimental scale. *Journal of Counseling Psychology*, 1954, 1, 74-77.

Currier, C. B. Patient-therapist relationship and the process of psychotherapy. Doctoral dissertation, University of Florida. Ann Arbor, Mich.: University Microfilms, 1964, No. 5600.

Danish, S. J., and Kagan, N. Emotional simulation in counseling and psychotherapy. *Psychotherapy: Theory, Research and Practice*, 1969, 6, 261-63.

Fey, N. F. Doctrine and experience: their influence upon the psychotherapist. *Journal of Consulting Psychology*, 1958, 22, 403-409.

Fiedler, F. E. The concept of an ideal therapeutic relationship. *Journal of Consulting Psychology*, 1950, 14, 239-45. (a)

———. A comparison of therapeutic relationships in psychoanalytic, nondirective, and Adlerian therapy. *Journal of Consulting Psychology*, 1950, 14, 435-36. (b)

———. Factor analyses of psychoanalytic, nondirective, and Adlerian therapeutic relationship. *Journal of Consulting Psychology*, 1951, 15, 32-38.

Fiefel, H., and Eels, J. Patients and therapists assess the same psychotherapy. Paper read at the American Psychological Association, St. Louis, Mo., September 1962.

Fischer, E. H., and Turner, J. L. Orientations to seeking professional help: development and research utility of an attitude scale. *Journal of Consulting and Clinical Psychology*, 1970, 35, 79-90.

Form, A. L. The Construction of a scale on attitudes toward counseling. *Journal of Counseling Psychology*, 1955, 2, 96-102.

Gardner, G. The psychotherapeutic relationship. *Psychological Bulletin*, 1964, 61, 426-37.

Glover, E. *The techniques of psychoanalysis.* New York: International Universities Press, 1955.

Gonyea, G. C. The "ideal therapeutic relationship" and counseling outcome. *Journal of Clinical Psychology*, 1963, 19, 481-87.

Greenberg, B. S., Kagan, N., and Bowes, J. Dimensions of empathic judgment of clients by counselors. *Journal of Counseling Psychology*, 1969, 16, 303-308.

Grigg, A. E., and Goodstein, L. D. The use of clients as judges of the counselor's performance. *Journal of Counseling Psychology*, 1957, 4, 31-36.

Heller, K., and Goldstein, A. P. Client dependency and therapist expectancy as relationship maintaining variables in psychotherapy. *Journal of Consulting Psychology*, 1961, 25, 371-75.

Hopke, W. E. The measurement of counselor attitudes. *Journal of Counseling Psychology*, 1955, 2, 212-16.

Kagan, N., and Krathwohl, D. R. Studies in human interaction: interpersonal process recall stimulated by videotape. *Final Report*, U.S. Office of Education, Project No. 5-0800. East Lansing: Michigan State University Educational Publication Series, 1967.

Kagan, N., Krathwohl, D. R., and Miller, R. Stimulated recall in therapy using video tapes: a case study. *Journal of Counseling Psychology*, 1963, 10, 237-43.

Kagan, N., and Schauble, P. G.i14, Affect simulation in interpersonal process recall. *Journal of Counseling Psychology*, 1969, 16, 309-13.

Leary, T. *Interpersonal diagnosis of personality*. New York: Ronald Press, 1957.

Lesser, W. M. The relationship between counseling proper and empathic understanding. *Journal of Counseling Psychology*, 1961, 8, 330-36.

Libo, L. M. *Picture-Impression Test*. Baltimore: University of Maryland Psychiatric Institute, 1956.

———. The projective expression of patient-therapist attraction. *Journal of Clinical Psychology*, 1957, 13, 33-36.

———. *Manual for the Picture Impressions Test*. Palo Alto, Calif.: Consulting Psychologists Press, 1969.

Lorr, M. Client perceptions of therapists: a study of the therapeutic relationship. *Journal of Consulting Psychology*, 1965, 29, 146-49.

Lorr, M., and McNair, D. M. An interpersonal behavior circle. *Journal of Abnormal and Social Psychology*, 1963, 67, 68-75.

———. The interview relationship in therapy. *Journal of Nervous and Mental Disease*, 1964, 139, 328-31.

———. Methods relating to evaluation of therapeutic outcome. In L. A. Gottschalk and A. H. Auerbach (Eds.), *Methods of research in psychotherapy*. New York: Appleton-Century-Crofts, 1966. Pp. 573-94.

McClelland, W. A., and Sinaiko, H. W. An investigation of a counselor attitude questionnaire. *Educational and Psychological Measurement*, 1950, 10, 128-33.

McNair, D. M., and Lorr, M. An analysis of professed psychotherapeutic techniques. *Journal of Clinical Psychology*, 1964, 28, 265-71. (a)

———. Three kinds of psychotherapy goals. *Journal of Clinical Psychology*, 1964, 20, 390-93.

Meehl, P. E. The cognitive activity of the clinician. *American Psychologist*, 1960, 15, 19-27.

Mendelsohn, G. A., and Geller, M. H. Structure of client attitudes toward counseling and their relation to client-counselor similarity. *Journal of Consulting Psychology*, 1965, 29, 63-72.

Michaux, W. W., and Lorr, M. Psychotherapists' treatment goals. *Journal of Counseling Psychology*, 1961, 8, 250-54.

Mills, D. H., and Mencke, R. Characteristics of effective counselors: a reevaluation. *Counselor Education and Supervision*, 1967, 6, 332-34.

Mills, D. H., and Zytowski, D. G. Helping relationship: a structural analysis. *Journal of Counseling Psychology*, 1967, 14, 193-97.

Moss, C. S., Ourth, L., Aurenshine, C., and Shallenberger, P. Attitudes of experienced psychologist-therapists. *American Psychologist*, 1960, 15, 414. (Abstract.)

Mueller, W. J., Gatsch, C., and Ralston, J. K. The prediction of counselor interview behavior. *Personnel Guidance Journal*, 1963, 41, 513-17.

Mullen, J. A., and Abeles, N. The projective expression of college students' expectations with regard to psychotherapy. *Journal of Clinical Psychology*, 1967, 23, 393-96.

Nathan, P. E., Bull, T. A., and Rossi, A. M. Operant range and variability during psychotherapy: description of possible communication signatures. *Journal of Nervous and Mental Diseases*, 1968, 146, 41-49.

Nunnally, J. C., Jr. *Popular conceptions of mental health*. New York: Holt, Rinehart and Winston, 1961.

Parloff, M. B. Therapist-patient relationship and outcome of psychotherapy. *Journal of Consulting Psychology*, 1961, 25, 29-38.

Pope, B., and Siegman, A. W. Interviewee-interviewer relationship and verbal behavior of interviewee in the initial interview. *Psychotherapy*, 1966, 3, 149-52.

________. Interviewer warmth and interviewee verbal behavior. *Journal of Clinical and Consulting Psychology*, 1968, 32, 588-95.

Porter, E. H., Jr. A simple measure of counselor attitudes. In E. G. Williamson (Ed.), *Trends in student personnel work*. Minneapolis: University of Minnesota Press, 1949. Pp. 129-35.

________. *An introduction to therapeutic counseling*. Boston: Houghton Mifflin, 1950.

Rausch, H. L., and Bordin, E. S. Warmth in personality development and in psychotherapy. *Psychiatry*, 1957, 20, 351-63.

Resnikoff, A., Kagan, N., and Schauble, P. G. Acceleration of psychotherapy through stimulated videotape recall. *American Journal of Psychotherapy*, 1970, 24, 102-11.

Reznikoff, M., Brady, J. P., and Zeller, W. W. The psychiatric attitudes battery: a procedure for assessing attitudes toward psychiatric treatment and hospitals. *Journal of Clinical Psychology*, 1959, 15, 260-65.

Rogers, C. R. The necessary and sufficient conditions of therapeutic personality change. *Journal of Consulting Psychology*, 1957, 21, 95-103.

________. A theory of therapy, personality and interpersonal relationships as developed in the client-centered framework. In S. Koch (Ed.) *Psychology: a study of a science*. Vol. 3. New York: McGraw-Hill, 1959. Pp. 184-256.

Schutz, W. C. *FIRO: A three-dimensional theory of interpersonal behavior*. New York: Rinehart, 1958.

Snyder, W. J., and Snyder, B. J. *The psychotherapy relationship*. New York: Macmillan, 1961.

Sonne, T. R. and Goldman, L. Preferences of authoritarian and equalitarian personalities for client-centered and eclectic counseling. *Journal of Counseling Psychology*, 1957, 4, 129-35.

Soper, D. W., and Combs, A. W. The helping relationship as seen by teachers and therapists. *Journal of Consulting Psychology*, 1962, 26, 288.

Streitfeld, J. W. Expressed acceptance of self and others by psychotherapists. *Journal of Consulting Psychology*, 1959, 23, 435-41.

Strupp, H. H. *Psychotherapists in action*. New York: Grune & Stratton, 1960.

________. The therapist's contribution to the treatment process: beginnings and vagaries of a research program. In H. H. Strupp and L. Luborsky (Eds.),

Research in psychotherapy. Vol. 2. Washington, D. C.: American Psychological Association, 1962. Pp. 25-40.

Strupp, H. H., Fox, R. E., and Lessler, K. *Patients view their psychotherapy*. Baltimore: The Johns Hopkins Press, 1969.

Strupp, H. H., and Wallach, M. S. A further study of psychotherapists' responses in quasi-therapy situations. *Behavioral Science*, 1965, 10, 113-34.

Strupp, H. H., Wallach, M. S., and Wogan, M. Psychotherapy experience in retrospect: questionnaire survey of former patients and their therapists. *Psychological Monographs*, 1964, No. 78.

Sundland, D. M., and Barker, E. N. The orientations of psychotherapists. *Journal of Consulting Psychology*, 1962, 26, 201-12.

Thomas, E., Polansky N., and Kounin, J. The expected behavior of a potentially helpful person. *Human Relations*, 1955, 8, 165-74.

Walker, B. S., and Little, D. F. Factor analysis of the Barrett-Lennard Relationship Inventory. *Journal of Counseling Psychology*, 1969, 16, 516-21.

Wallach, M. S., and Strupp, H. H. Dimensions of psychotherapists' activities. *Journal of Counsulting Psychology*, 1964, 28, 120-25.

Wolff, W. *Contemporary psychotherapists examine themselves*. Springfield, Ill.: Charles C. Thomas, 1956.

Appendix: Tables

Table 2.1

*A summary of the therapist and patient variables measured by the seventeen major process systems presented in chapters 3, 4, and 5**

System		*Therapist Measures*		*Patient Measures*
A. Butler, Rice and Wagstaff (see Table 3.1)	A1.	*Freshness of words and combinations* (five categories: e.g., vivid metaphors; fresh colorful words of a sensory character; punchy, stimulating character; commonplace expressions)	A1.	*Level of expression* (analysis of action, analysis of feeling, responsiveness)
	A2.	*Voice quality* (eight categories: e.g., lively feeling tone; vigor, confidence, and warmth; exploring quality; tone of newness; high energy present; wispy and breathless)	A2.	*Voice qualities and manner of speaking* (emotional, focused, externalizing, limited)
	A3.	*Functional level of response* (seven categories: e.g., focuses within frame of reference of client; feelings are labeled rather than explored; explores the stimulus for a feeling; explores the edges of P's feelings)	A3.	*Quality of participation* (participating, observing)
B. Rice (see Table 3.2)	B1.	*Freshness of words and combinations* (fresh connotative language, ordinary language)	B1.	*Voice quality* (emotional, focused, externalizing, limited)
	B2.	*Voice quality* (expressive, usual, distorted)	B2.	*Expressive stance* (objective analysis and description, subjective reation, static feeling description, differentiated exploration)

System	Therapist Measure		Patient Measures	
	B3.	*Functional level* (inner exploring, observing, outside focus, unscorable)		
C. Dollard and Auld (see Table 3.3)	C1.	*D* (drive or demand eliciting statements)	C1.	*A* (anxiety and/or fear)
	C2.	*Interp* (interpretative statements)	C2.	*Conf* (confirmation of a therapist's statement)
	C3.	*M* (mm-hmm)	C3.	*Dep* (dependency needs)
	C4.	*Pretni* (a serious error by the therapist)	C4.	*Dream* (text of dream as reported)
	C5.	*R* (tension reduction statements)	C5.	*H* (hostile act or motive)
	C6.	*Unsc* (unscorable utterances of the therapist)	C6.	*H/Self* (hostility toward self)
			C7.	*L* (love)
			C8.	*LF* (laughter)
			C9.	*Mob* (social mobility)
			C10.	*N* (negation of a therapist's statement)
			C11.	*Obs* (obsessional thoughts or acts)
			C12.	*PSS* (psychosomatic symptom)
			C13.	*r* (reward or reduction in drive)
			C14.	*Reas* (reasoning or insight)
			C15.	*Res* (resistance)
			C16.	*S* (sexual feelings or motives)
			C17.	*Sigh* (a sigh)
			C18.	*W* (weeping)
			C19.	*Y* (affirmative statement not expanded)

D. Lennard and Bernstein (see Table 3.5)	D1.	*Grammatical form of propositions* (declarative, imperative, interrogratory)	D1.	*Grammatical form of propostions* (declarative, imperative, interrogatory)
	D2.	*Affective content of propostions* (affective, nonaffective, indeterminable)	D2.	*Affective content of propositions* (affective, nonaffective, indeterminable)
	D3.	*Interactive Process Categories* (descriptive, evaluative, and prescriptive propositions)	D3.	*Interaction process categories* (descriptive, evaluative, and prescriptive propositions)
	D4.	*Role system reference categories* (primary system, secondary system, tertiary systems, the self)	D4.	*Role system reference categories* (primary system, secondary system, tertiary system, the self)
	D5.	*Categories of therapist informational specificity* (eight categories scaling the amount of structure or information contained in each therapist message)		
E. Matarazzo (see Table 3.6)		*Original Chapple Interaction Chronograph measures:* 1. T Units 2. T Actions 3. T Silence 4. T Initiative 5. T Interruptions		*Original Chapple Interaction Chronograph measures:* 1. P Units 2. P Actions 3. P Silence 4. P Initiative 5. P Interruptions
		Measures currently used:		*Measures currently used:*
	E1.	*T mean speech duration* (the total amount of time the therapist speaks divided by his total number of speech units)	E1.	*P mean speech duration* (the total amount of time the patient speaks divided by his total number of speech units)

System		Therapist Measures		Patient Measures
	E2.	*T mean speech latency* (the total latency time divided by the number of units of therapist latency)	E2.	*P mean speech latency* (the total latency time divided by the number of units of patient latency)
	E3.	*T percentage interruption* (total number of times the therapist spoke divided into the number of these same speech units which were interruptions of the patient)	E3.	*P percentage interruption* (total number of times the patient spoke divided into the number of these same speech units which were interruptions of the therapist)
F. Murray (see Table 3.7)	F1.	*Instruction to free-associate*	F1.	*Drive categories* (14)—sex approval, sex anxiety, sex frustration, affection approval, affection anxiety, affection frustration, dependence approval, dependence anxiety, dependence frustration, approval, independence and self-assertion independence anxiety, independence frustration, unspecified anxiety, unspecified frustration)
	F2.	*Labels*	F2.	*Special categories* (5)—disturbances of free association, agreement with therapist remarks, intellectual discussion, generalized anxiety)
	F3.	*Discrimination*		
	F4.	*Similarities*		
	F5.	*Strong Approvals*		
	F6.	*Disapprovals*		
	F7.	*Demands*		
	F8.	*Directions*		
	F9.	*Mild probes*		
	F10.	*Mild approvals*		
	F11.	*Mm-hmm*		
	F12.	*Irrelevant*		

G. Snyder (see Table 3.8)	*1945 system:*	*1945 system:*
	1. *Lead-taking categories* (structuring, forcing client to choose and develop topic, directive, specific questions, non-directive leads and questions)	1. *Problem category*
	2. *Nondirective response-to-feeling categories* (simple acceptance, restatement of content or problem, clarification or recognition of feeling)	2. *Simple response categories* (asking for advice or information, answer to a question, simple acceptance, reflection of a clarification or interpretation)
	3. *Semi-directive response-to-feeling category: Interpretation*	3. *Understanding or action-taking categories* (understanding or insight, discussion of plans)
	4. *Directive counseling categories* (approval and encouragement, giving information or explanation, proposing client activity, persuasion, disapproval and criticism)	4. *Minor categories* (ending the contact, ending the series, not related to the problem, friendly discussion, unclassifiable)
	5. *Minor categories* (ending the contact, ending the series, friendly discussion, unclassifiable)	5. *Client feeling categories* (positive, negative, and ambivalent attitudes)
	1963 system:	*1963 system:*
	G1. *Lead-taking responses* (structuring, nondirective lead, directive lead, question)	G1. *Client need-responses* (15—anxiety hostility need, hostility pressure, dependency need, ego need nurturance need, sex need, sex pressure, dominance need, dominance pressure, affiliation need, affiliation pressure, vocational concern, mobility concern, physical concern)

System		Therapist Measures		Patient Measures
	G2.	*Reflective or Reeductative responses* (restatement, clarification interpretation, attenuation, advice, information)	G2.	*Client's in-therapy behavior categories* (8—shows insight, makes plans, shows resistance, confirms an interpretation deals with the relationship, asks a question, reports a dream, recalls unconscious material)
	G3.	*Relationship response*	G3.	*Categories of major and minor sources (or objects) of client affect* (11 Major Categories—the client, client's parents, father, authority figure (other), mother, sister, brother, client's wife, associates, the therapist, heterosexual love object, homosexual love object)
	G4.	*Supportive responses* (reassurance, offer of help, approval)		
	G5.	*Redirecting responses* (calling attention, challenging, withholding support, persuasion, disapproval)		
	G6.	*Type of therapist interpretations* (six-point scale)		
H. Howe and Pope (see Table 4.1)	H1.	*Therapist verbal activity level scale* (Form A and Form B, both 10-point empirical scales). Therapist verbal activity level is high when his verbal responses are relatively unambiguous, leading, and carry high inference.	M1.	*Involvement in free association* (five-point intensity scale). Evaluated in terms of P's attitudes toward what he is saying. It includes the range of feelings, from sorrow to joy, but excludes anxiety and tension. It differentiates those who can permit and achieve
M. Bordin (see Table 5.1)				

				an integration between ideation and effect from those who maintain a separation between the two.
			M2.	*Spontaneity of free assocation* (five-point intensity scale). Attempts to capture the aspect of expression dealing with the chaining of memories—at one end planned, at the other spontaneous. It is evaluated in terms of the degree to which the associative production is prepared, deliberate, formally structured and ordered, and polished.
			M3.	*Freedom of free association* (five-point intensity scale). Freedom versus inhibition. Inhibition is evaluated in terms of the degree of blocking, caution and circumlocution, censorship, and stiffness-constriction.
I. Harway et al. (see Table 4.2)	I1.	*Depth of interpretation scale* (nine-point empirical scale). An interpretation is the therapist's expression of his view of the patient's emotions and motivations. The greater the disparity between the view expressed by the therapist and the patient's own awareness of these emotions and motivations, the deeper the interpretation.	N1.	*Anxiety scale*. Scans for indications of anxiety in six areas: death, mutilation, separation, guilt, shame, and diffuse or nonspecific anxiety. Designed to measure "free" in contrast to "bound" anxiety, and to measure momentary (state) in contrast to trait anxiety.
N. Gottschalk and Gleser (see Table 5.2)			N2.	*Hostility directed outward scale*. The scoring categories are arranged on a continuum that

System	Therapist Measures	Patient Measures
		varies from denial of hostility, through references to anger without an object, to hostility toward a situation or infrahuman objects, and finally to varying degrees of hostility toward human beings. The latter categories range from expressions of mild dislike or criticism of an individual to stronger expressions of verbal aggression and physical violence. In addition, to the intensity continuum, ranging in weights from 1 to 3, the scale includes levels of awareness of hostility.
		N3. *Hostility directed inward scale.* Disigned to measure transient and immediate thoughts, actions, and feelings that are self-critical, self-destructive, or self-punishing. The thematic categories of the scale range in weight from 1 to 4.
		N4. *Ambivalent hostility scale.* Scores statements about destructive, injurious, critical thoughts and actions of others (including situations and objects) toward the self. Pertains to statements by P concerning hostility directed to him from sources outside himself.
		N5. *Social alienation-personal disorganization (schizophrenic) scale.* Designed to discriminate

		the relative severity of the schizophrenic syndrome and can also be used to discriminate schizophrenic from nonschizophrenic individuals. Scale contains five major groupings or categories: interpersonal references, intrapersonal references, references to disorganization and repetition, question or other references directed to the interviewer, and references to religious or biblical topics.
J. Siegman and Pope (see Table 4.3)	J1.	*Level of therapist specificity* (11-point empirical scale). Specificity is defined in terms of the limits a therapist's remark sets on the patient's response alternatives. A therapist remark has a high specificity level if it limits the patient to a specific matter or proposition thus limiting the range of possible alternatives from which the patient can select his reply.
O. Hall and Van De Castle (see Table 5.3)		*Empirical scales:*
	O1.	*Locale of dream*
	O2.	*Degree of familarity of setting*
	O3.	*Objects*
	O4.	*Aggressive interactions*
	O5.	*Friendly interactions*
	O6.	*Sexual interactions*
	O7.	*Activities*
	O8.	*Achievement outcomes*
	O9.	*Environmental press*
	O10.	*Anger*
	O11.	*Apprehension*
	O12.	*Happiness*
	O13.	*Sadness*
	O14.	*Confusion*
	O15.	*Modifiers*
	O16.	*Temporal scale*
	O17.	*Negative scale*

System	Therapist Measures	Patient Measures
		Theoretical scales: O18. *Castration anxiety, castration wish, and penis envy* O19. *Oral activities and oral references* (oral incorporation and oral emphasis) O20. *Regression scale*
K. Strupp (see Table 4.4) P. Klein et al. (see Table 5.4)	K1. *Type of therapeutic activity* (facilitating communication, exploratory operations, clarification, interpretive operations, structuring, direct guidance, activity not clearly relevant to the task of therapy, unclassifiable)	P1. *The experiencing scale* (seven-point annotated, and anchored rating scale). Refers to the extent to which the patient's ongoing, bodily, felt flow of experiencing is the basic datum of his awareness and communications about himself, and the extent to which it is integral to action and thought. At a low level the patient's discourse is markedly impersonal or superficial. At higher levels feelings are explored, and emergent levels of experiencing serve as basic referents for self-understanding and problem resolution.
	K2. *Depth-directedness* (five-point, graphic, intensity scale). A therapist's comment which operates on the manifest meaning of the patient's communication is at the "surface," one that propounds a hypothesis, inference, conjecture, or interpretation is "deep." K3. *Dynamic focus*. Therapist accepts P's formulation as it is presented; or therapist introduces a new frame of reference directing P's communications into a different channel.	

	K4.	*Initiative* (four-point, graphic, intensity scale). The extent to which the therapist assumes the initiative and steers the patient in the direction of a more or less specific goal.		
	K5.	*Therapeutic climate* (five-point, graphic intensity scale). A bipolar scale. The positive end includes all communications by which the therapist indicates acceptance, warmth, understanding, positive interest, tolerance, empathy, respect. The negative pole is defined by signs of rejection, coldness, sarcasm, lack of sympathy, cynicism, hostility, brutality, derision, mockery, taunting, teasing, belittling, etc.		
L. Truax (see Table 4.5)	L1.	*Accurate empathy scale* (nine-point, annotated, and anchored rating scale). Involves both the therapist's sensitivity to current feelings and his verbal facility to communicate this understanding in a language attuned to the patient's current feelings.	Q1.	*Depth of self-exploration scale* (nine-point, annotated, and anchored rating scale). Refers to the extent to which the patient engages in self-exploration, ranging from no demonstrable intrapersonal exploration to a very high level of self-probing and exploration. Additional weights or corrections are given for "personally private" and "personally damning" material.
Q. Truax (see Table 5.5)				

System	Therapist Measures	Patient Measures
	L2. *Nonpossessive warmth scale* (five-point, annotated, and anchored rating scale). Also called unconditional positive regard. Ranges from a high level where the therapist warmly accepts P's experience as part of that person, without imposing conditions; to a low level where the therapist evaluates P or his feelings, expresses dislike or disapproval, or expresses warmth in a selective and evaluative way.	
	L3. *Genuineness or self-congruence scale* (five-point, annotated and anchored rating scale). At a very low level the therapist presents a facade or defends and denies his feelings; at a high level the therapist is freely and deeply himself. A high level does not mean that the therapist must overtly express his feelings, but only that he does not deny them.	

*Leary and Gill's system is not summarized here, since the author found it impossible to do so within the format of the table. The reader should see Chapter 3 for a summary of Leary and Gill's patient and therapist measures.

For a tabular summary of all other psychotherapy process systems (minor systems, Chap. 6) which have been published, see Table 6.1.

Table 2.2
Comparison of the "scoring" and "contextual" units used by the seventeen major process systems

System	*Scoring Unit*	*Contextual Unit*
1. Butler, Rice, and Wagstaff; Rice	The "total response." For T: everything said between two client responses. For P: everything said between two therapist responses.	Judges may listen to preceding P (or T) response when necessary to understand antecedents to pronouns, etc.; but do not listen to the subsequent response.
2. Dollard and Auld	For both P and T: "the sentence," the smallest portion of speech that can be fully understood by itself. A minimum free utterance. The single free utterance.	Coder needs to consider preceding and subsequent verbalizations. Coders should know whatever T knows up to the time of the hour being scored, but he should know nothing more than this. Can go to end of typescript page, however, and a little further, if necessary.
3. Leary and Gill	For P, T, and clinical evaluators: "the statement," the shortest verbalization which can be understood to be a combination of subject (whether a person or impersonal) and some characteristic or aspect of that subject.	Statements are coded in 10-minute segments, and apparently are coded in participant-context and sequentially within a particular 10-minute segment.

System	Scoring Unit	Contextual Unit
4. Lennard and Bernstein	For both P and T, three primary units: (1) proposition, a verbalization containing a subject and predicate whether expressed or implied; (2) statement, an uninterrupted sequence of propositions from either P or T; (3) interaction or exchange, a T statement followed by a P statement, or vice versa.	Not explicitly defined. Apparently coders score seriatum, so that in rating a particular P or T proposition the judge is aware of the preceding statements in the interview to that particular point.
5. Matarazzo	For both P and T, "the utterance": separated at either end by two silence periods, one silence following the other participant's last comment and preceding the listener's next comment.	Not explicitly defined. Judges score the inter-action seriatum within a particular interview. Context clearly less crucial when scoring noncontent variables such as those of Matarazzo.
6. Murray	For P, "the statement or meaning phrase": usually takes the form of a sentence. In its purest form it contains a subject and predicate. For T, the unit is everything a T says in between patient statements.	Apparently the same judges score both P and T categories and the sequence is unspecified. Apparently a judge, for a particular scoring unit has available to him all the preceding and subsequent P and T statements to help him in his scoring task.

7. Snyder	For P and T "the idea": a clearly indicated change in the subject matter or attitude of P or T's thinking. (Grammatically varies from a phrase, through a sentence, to groups of sentences).	Coding of typescript done sequentially. Apparently the contextual unit includes all previous interaction for a particular interview.
8. Howe and Pope	Authors not explicit about the exact scoring unit, other than saying that T statements are rated. Apparently the unit involved is the T in the P-T-P sequence.	Not explicitly defined. Apparently includes all typescript interaction for a particular interview. Participant-context present or absent does not affect the ratings.
9. Harway et al.	Single T responses, the T in the P-T-P-T sequence.	The most frequently used contextual unit consists of 3 consecutive P-T exchanges ending with a T remark (P-T-P-T-P-T). Only the final response is scored, the preceding section serves to provide context. In other cases ten consecutive P-T exchanges are used.
10. Siegman and Pope	The "statement": that portion of therapist speech occurring between two patient responses.	Ratings are made from typescripts with the P's responses intact. Judges rate each T unit sequentially as they progress through a particular protocol, after which they rate another total interview protocol.

System	*Scoring Unit*	*Contextual Unit*
11. Strupp	The "therapist communication": the therapist communication occurring between two patient statements.	Judges are aware of the entire transaction as it has developed to the point of a particular T communication, but not beyond that point.
12. Truax	Typically, a 4- or 5-minute tape-recorded segment, randomly extracted from a particular interview.	The contexual unit is identical to the scoring unit. The rater makes his decision only from the contents of the particular 4- or 5-minute segment.
13. Bordin	Apparently the scoring unit is the total 30-minute experimental interview session.	Raters are instructed to listen to at least 10-minutes of the tape, 4 at the beginning and end, and 2 in the middle, while following along with the typescript. They are encouraged to listen more when in doubt, or to sense more fully some significant passage.
14. Gottschalk and Gleser	The "clause": whether independent or dependent. Instances where either the subject or predicate is omitted but is understood are considered as scorable clauses.	Frequently a wider context than the clause to be scored must be considered. May be necessary to take into account the clause immediately preceding and the one immediately following. At times the entire verbal sample (usually 2- or 5-minute segments)

		needs to be considered or relevant material will be omitted in the scoring.
15. Hall and Van De Castle	Apparently the total dream report of the subject, recorded on a 5x8 inch index card.	Apparently the coder considers the entire dream report in making each category judgment. "We generally prefer to score a unit of 50 dreams on each scale" before going to the next scale.
16. Klein et al.	Typically 4- or 5-minute tape-recorded segments, randomly sampled from particular interviews.	The contextual unit is identical to the scoring unit. The rater makes his decision from only the comments present on the particular 4- or 5-minute segment.
17. Truax	Same as 12 above.	Same as 12 above.

Table 2.3

Comparison of the data forms used by the seventeen major process systems

System	*Data Form Used*
1. Butler, Rice and Wagstaff; Rice	Tape recordings only.
2. Dollard and Auld	Predominantly typescripts; only three categories require tape-recordings for scoring ("weeping," "laughing," and "sighing").
3. Leary and Gill	Typescripts only (both of therapy interviews and of clinician evaluations of the interviews).
4. Lennard and Bernstein	Typescripts only.
5. Matarazzo	Originally live interviews observed through a one-way vision mirror. More recently from tape recordings only (although can be scored also from typescripts).
6. Murray	Typescripts only.
7. Snyder	Typescripts only.
8. Howe and Pope	Typescripts only.
9. Harway et al.	Typically typescripts. One study showed tape recordings do equally well.
10. Siegman and Pope	Apparently typescripts only.
11. Strupp	Has used all media: typescripts, sound recordings, movies, videotapes. Undetermined whether they do equally well.
12. Truax	Predominantly tape recordings. Only minimally with typescripts "with only a slight loss of reliability."
13. Bordin	Typescripts *and* tape recordings simultaneously.
14. Gottschalk and Gleser	Predominantly typescripts. One study suggests that tape recordings plus typescripts do equally well, but no better.
15. Hall and Van De Castle	Typescript of the subject's written dream report, types on a 5x8 inch card.
16. Klein et al.	Predominantly tape recordings.
17. Truax	Same as 12 above.

Table 2.4
Comparison of the level of sophistication required of judges by the seventeen major process systems

System	*Level of Sophistication of Judges*	*Training Manual Available*
1. Butler, Rice and Wagstaff; Rice	Typically, minimally experienced graduate students, presumably in clinical or counseling psychology graduate training program.	No.
2. Dollard and Auld	Considerable clinical sophistication required. Needs a knowledge of psychoanalysis, must be free from severe neurotic conflicts. Personal analysis would be helpful.	Yes. (Dollard and Auld, 1959)
3. Leary and Gill	For the clinical evaluations experienced clinicians are needed. Authors feel that naive judges suffice for coding either the clinical evaluations or the patient and therapist verbalizations.	No.
4. Lennard and Bernstein	Judges are not explicitly identified, nor is their level of sophistication discussed.	No.

System	Level of Sophistication of Judges	Training Manual Available
5. Matarazzo	Issue is not explicitly discussed. Apparently naive judges could be used for scoring.	Yes. (Matarazzo and Wiens, 1972)
6. Murray	Not clear. Seems to suggest that some clinical experience as well as grounding in psychoanalytic and learning theory is necessary. On the other hand, implies that naive judges can do as well.	No.
7. Snyder	Undetermined. Snyder has been the single sophisticated judge in most of the studies to date.	No.
8. Howe and Pope	Have predominantly used professional psychotherapists as judges, but one study showed that naive judges could do as well.	No.
9. Harway et al.	Predominantly sophisticated clinicians. Authors emphasize the necessity of clinical experience for valid ratings.	No.*
10. Siegman and Pope	Predominantly professional psychotherapists of various but unspecified levels of clinical experience. Unclear whether naive judges would do as well.	No.

11. Strupp	Judge needs to be sophisticated "trained observer" who is sensitized to issues in the field, knowledgeable about psychodynamics, must have received thorough training, fully cognizant of psychotherapy theory, and preferably have undergone personal analysis.	Part of a manual is available (Strupp, 1966). However, no standardized training instructions or procedures are included.
12. Truax	Typically uses groups of undergraduate students as judges "in an effort to obtain 'objective' ratings uncontaminated by the theoretical bias of the rater."	No.
13. Bordin	To date judges have been advanced graduate students in clinical psychology "all of whom have had diagnostic and psychotherapeutic experience."	No.
14. Gottschalk and Gleser	Clinically unsophisticated judges can perform the rating tasks. Judges, however, should have adequate eduacation, intelligence, and motivation to understand and use the assumptions and instructions.	Yes. (Gottschalk and Gleser, 1969; Gottschalk, Winget, and Gleser, 1969)

System	*Level of Sophistication of Judges*	*Training Manual Available*
15. Hall and Van De Castle	Not explicitly discussed. Apparently the system can be applied by either clinically naive or sophisticated judges.	Yes. (Hall and Van De Castle, 1966)
16. Klein et al.	Typically groups of undergraduate students used as judges, primarily from liberal arts diciplines. One study demonstrated that clinically sophisticated judges rate equivalently in all respects to the usual undergraduate judges.	Yes. (Klein, Mathieu, Gendlin, and Kiesler, 1970)
17. Truax	Same as 12.	No.

*Absence of a manual, however, is consistent with Harway et al.'s desire to develop measures that can be applied by sophisticated clinicians, with little training required.

TABLE 3.1

*Rice's classification system for therapist and client behaviors**

Therapist Classification System

Aspect A: *Freshness of words and combinations.* Some kinds of language are clearly far more connotative than others, in the sense of arousing in the listener more trains of association, a greater wealth of inner experience. Two kinds of language use were distinguished.

1. *Fresh, connative language.* The total response may have a metaphorical quality with high imagery, auditory and kinesthetic as well as visual, or there may be only a few fresh, stimulating words or combinations.
2. *Ordinary language.* Responses are made up of commonplace words and phrases.

Aspect B: *Voice quality.* An attempt was made to locate a limited number of voice patterns that varied among therapists, showed considerable variation over sessions and within sessions, and seemed to differentiate meaningfully among sessions that had previously been characterized clinically as to quality. Once such patterns had been isolated, they were described as closely as possible in terms of pace, hesitations, pitch range, patterns of emphasis, etc.

1. *Expressive.* The voice is characterized by high energy used in a controlled but not constricted way. Color and range are present in the voice, but not to the extent of emotional overflow. The pitch range is wide, and although there is considerable emphasis, it is irregular and appropriate to the structure.
2. *Usual.* A moderate amount of energy is present, and the pitch range is limited. Inflection is moderate and natural, although not usually conversational.
3. *Distorted.* Energy may be high or relatively low. Pitch variation is marked. The most distinguished feature is the regular emphasis, seemingly for effect rather than for spontaneous meaning. There is subtle cadenced or sing-song quality, in which emphasis is shifted from its natural location.

Aspect C: *Functional level.* It seems probable that the stance which the client takes toward his own experience may be much influenced by the expressive stance that the therapist takes in responding to his message. Three such stances or functional levels were defined, with a fourth subclass for responses so far outside the client's frame of reference as to make them unscorable on this aspect.

1. *Inner exploring.* Here the focus is on exploration of the client's immediate inner experience. The emphasis is on the idiosyncratic quality of the experience rather than on finding a label for it.
2. *Observing.* The therapist joins the client in observing and analyzing the self as an object.
3. *Outside focus.* The therapist's responses are within the client's frame of reference but refer to and focus on something outside the client.
4. *Unscorable.*

Client Classification System

Aspect A: *Voice quality.* In line with the decision to classify style of participation rather than specific content, no attempt was made to distinguish particular emotional states. The strategy used was to locate a limited number of voice patterns that varied among clients, showed variation over sessions, and seemed to differentiate meaningfully among sessions that have previously been characterized by therapists as good or poor hours. The patterns thus located were then described in terms of energy, pitch range, tempo, stress patterns, etc. . . . The four subclasses include qualitatively different kinds of voice patterns and are not intended to form a scale.

1. *Emotional.* Responses placed in this first subclass may take a number of different forms, but in general there is energy overflow rather than control. The voice breaks, trembles, or chokes. The general impression is one of disruption of the usual voice patterns with varying degrees of effort at control.
2. *Focused.* These responses are characterized by a good deal of energy, but not by a wide pitch fluctuation. There are irregularities in the stress of syllables, and stresses are not usually accompanied by much pitch rise. There are marked irregularities of tempo. Impressionistically, the total effect is one of pondering, of energy turned inward in an exploring fashion.
3. *Externalizing.* These responses are characterized by comparatively high energy and by a wide pitch range in the sense defined by Trager (1958). There is an unusually regular stress pattern, with the heavy stresses accompanied by a rise in pitch. This stress pattern, together with the presence of terminal contours that rise or fall in unexpected places, gives an effect of cadence or preformed pattern. The total effect is one of energy turned outward, a "talking at" quality.
4. *Limited.* Responses placed here are characterized by low energy, a narrow pitch range, and an even tempo. The stress pattern is typical for English, but the stresses themselves are relatively weak. The voice is thinned from below. The general impression one gets is that of limited involvement, or distance from what is being expressed.

Aspect B: *Expressive stance.* The second main class, the lexical, has been designated expressive stance because it focuses on the stance that the client takes in relation to whatever he is discussing. Here again the four subclasses are not intended to represent a scale.

1. *Objective analysis and description.* The client may be discussing himself or things outside himself but in either case it is as if he steps outside and views himself and the world as objects to be described, categorized, or analyzed. Example: "Whenever I get into difficult situations, I'm likely to make a mess of them."
2. *Subjective reaction.* The client is focusing on the subjectivity of his own reaction to things impinging on him. He is dealing not with generalities, but with an immediate subjective response to a specific stimulus. Example: "When he did that, I felt cheated, like I was being used."
3. *Static feeling description.* The client is discussing feelings, but in a static, objectified manner, as things to be reported, labeled, or explained. Although feelings are subjective by definition, they are dealt with here in a generalized or analytical fashion that is similar to the form of the first subclass. Example: "This feeling of anger is one I have had since childhood."
4. *Differentiated exploration.* Here the client explores an inner experience in an immediate and differentiated fashion without subjecting it to cognitive operations. He focuses on the idiosyncratic qualities of his experience, often in highly sensory and expressive language. Example: "I felt utterly flat, emptied out."

*The contents of this table are slightly abridged versions of those presented in Rice (1965, pp. 156-57) and in Rice and Wagstaff (1967, pp. 558-59).

TABLE 3.2
*Dollard and Auld's motivational system for scoring patient and therapist behavior in psychotherapy**

Categories for patient

A. Refers to anxiety and/or fear. "A refers to an internal stimulus which might be called apprehension, distress, tension or fear. Anxiety is the sequel or residual of painful experience. If the outward stimulus is known and believed adequate to cause a reaction (e.g., mad dog) we speak of fear; if it is vague or unknown we speak of anxiety. In either case the appropriate score is A. A should be scored when: (1) a patient reports manifest anxiety, (2) the patient reports being under tension, (3) the patient describes a situation where anyone would be bound to be afraid, (4) the patient reports making an avoidant response which could be motivated by anxiety, (5) the patient reports guilt, (6) the patient reports embarassment. The use of A as a single sign is the exception rather than the rule. It is far more frequently seen in combination with other signs. . . . Both A and any combined sign may be either conscious or unconscious."

Conf. Refers to confirmation of a therapist's statement. "Conf is the score used for a particular response by the patient to an interpretation by the therapist. To be called Conf the response must have two characteristics: (1) the patient must show that he understands the interpretation, even if only in a minimal way, (2) the patient must react in such a way as to confirm the interpretation. Confirmation could consist either of bringing forward new information (new in the sense that it had not been previously available to the therapist) or of displaying a pertinent emotional reaction." Conf is not combined with any other sign.

Dep. Refers to dependency needs. "It has to do with one person's relying on another for support, maintenance, or help when helping is one-sided rather than reciprocal. Behavior is dependent when one person makes claims on another, or waits for another person to act instead of acting himself; when one tries to coerce another by expecting things of him; when one of a pair fails to initiate necessary planning (at the mental level) but instead relies on the other to do it; when a patient expresses helplessness, self-pity, yearning, or nostalgia. Failing to make decisions and to act while awaiting signals from others as to what to do is dependent. Passivity, helplessness, and loneliness are all related to Dep." Dep can be combined with other category scores.

Dream. "The text of a dream when it is first told. If details which are part of the dream are added later, they are also scored Dream. When dream elements are taken as starting points for association, the association is scored not as Dream but according to content. Resistant material, such as deprecating the importance of a dream, whether appearing before or after the dream is scored Res. The sign Dream is never combined with any other."

H. Refers to a hostile act or motive. "H is social, defined by the culture in which it occurs. A hostile *action* is one which would tend to injure another person. A physical assault would, of course, be hostile but so also would behavior which tends to put another person in his place, lower his self-esteem, or cut him down to size. Criticism and gossip are hostile. Hostile *motives* are those which give rise to actions which would injure others. Anger, enmity, envy, jealousy, spite are hostile motives. If allowed free rein they would excite actions which would be dangerous to other people. . . . H can be combined with other signs, and it appears especially frequently in combination with anxiety (A)."

H/self. Refers to hostility toward self. It is "scored when the patient makes critical remarks about himself, expresses negative thoughts concerning himself, or describes punishing himself."

L. Refers to love. "L is an undescribable but delightful emotion. When shown toward persons, it takes the form of actions and sentiments such as liking, approaching, taking care of, highly evaluating, sparing, pitying, cherishing, valuing, affiliating, appreciating them. L can also be felt and shown toward things, places, or activities, such as sports or hobbies. . . . In our system L is not used to describe sexual motives or action, though it can be a derivative of sex rewards. . . . We are tempted to say that L should not be combined with any other sign. Being a sublimated activity, L should not have inner opposition. In general it seems best to let L stand alone."

Lf. Refers to laughter. "Our position is that laughter is detectable by intelligent people with their ordinary social training. Thus we rely on those who transcribe our records to be able to tell a laugh when they hear one. . . . In studying the laughter behavior in our records, we discovered that two kinds of laughter can be distinguished: (1) a kind of laughter which we call 'relaxed' expressing mirth and gaiety (Lf+); (2) anxious or embarrassed laughter, which expresses tension rather than tension-release (Lf-)."

Mob. Refers to social mobility. It is "used in the sense defined by Warner and Lunt (1941, p. 82) and refers to a change of social position on the system of social classes, and to all activities and habits related to such a change. Indeed we have extended the term beyond Warner's use of it to include any response to stable status as well as to change in status." Mob can be combined with other signs, most often with A.

N. Refers to negation. "Any negation not expanded and not considered resistant is scored N. . . . It may indicate a disagreement with the therapist, a refusal to act as requested, or a different understanding of fact. A large N count would certainly indicate that the patient has the firmness to oppose the therapist. . . . This score is never combined with any other."

Obs. Refers to obsessional. "Any sentence describing an obsessional thought or act is scored Obs. The obsessional event is mysterious; it is not related to the on-going current of mental events. It is intrusive. It is strongly motivated, but the source of the motivation is unknown. Ambivalent behavior, that which shows rapidly alternating feelings of love and hate, is scored as obsessional. This sign is never combined with any other."

PSS. Refers to psychosomatic symptom. "The idea is that some emotional factor produces a physical symptom. One is most likely to score a physical symptom PSS when medical examination has failed to reveal a physical cause, when the symptom seems to appear and disappear in response to mental or social cues, and when a psychosomatic mechanism for particular symptom is known and has been demonstrated in other cases. . . . PSS is combined with one other sign only, namely r. Thus PSS:r would indicate the sudden termination of psychosomatic symptom, which is accompanied by marked reduction in stress."

r. Refers to reward or reduction in drive. "The reward sign is added as a kind of postscript to the sign for the drive that has been reduced; for example A:r is used for reduction of anxiety, S:r for reduction of sex drive. Any sentence of the patient describing his own experience of drive reduction, relaxation, pleasure or comfort should be scored with the subscript r attached to the symbol for motive. It can be used alone in one case only: for the state of affairs described by the sentence 'I feel happy,' provided that the speaker gives no further evidence as to why he feels happy. Thus an unanalyzed feeling of well-being would be scored r."

Reas. Refers to reasoning and "is our 'insight' sign. The process of Reas has to do with the manipulation of sentences, imageal responses, and emotions so that a mental solution of a problem is achieved. Reas covers the unbidden, impulsive emergence of a solution, as well as the achievement of it by laborious formal reasoning. It is not combined with any other sign."

Res. Refers to resistance. i.e. "any response of the patient that operates against the therapeutic process (Knight, 1952). Resistance prevents the uncovering and dissolution of the neurotic conflict. We score as Res any such response for which there are identifying cues in the patient's speech or behavior. In addition, we score as Res 5 any silence of five seconds in length. . . . Res is not combined with any other sign."

S. Refers to sex. "S is scored when the patient describes erotic feelings or motives in himself. Definite genital feeling or reactions are the clearest sign of S. S is also scored when the situation described is one in which erotic reactions are expected to occur, or when we know the patient has had erotic feelings in similar situations. Libidinous fantasies are, of course, scored as S. When behavior is reported which can be understood only by positing an unconscious sexual motive, S can be scored. Planning for sexual satisfaction is scored as S. Courtship and dating frequently contains erotic elements which deserve the scoring S. Homosexual and masturbatory behavior are scored as S; similarly for 'heavy' kissing and petting, and for various categories of perverse behavior. We have used the one sign S for all types of sexual arousal. . . . " S is combined with other scoring categories.

Sigh. "We assume that the recognition of a sigh is a capacity common to intelligent people in our culture. Since the persons transcribing therapy protocols are assumed to be intelligent, it will be understood they can identify and record the behavior of sighing. If sighs are inaudible they will of course be missed. . . . Each sigh is counted as a separate unit. If a sigh occurs in the midst of a sentence it is counted as a unit apart from the sentence itself."

W. Refers to weeping. "[We] say that weeping is what the transcribing typist can identify and report as weeping; of course the typist has not only the sounds which she hears but also the context to guide her. Obviously this is a common-sense definition of weeping, a definition which depends on the general social training of intelligent people. It must be granted that some barely audible elements of weeping may be missed in a case record. The typist does not have the facial gestures to guide her in identifying weeping. We argue, nevertheless, that where weeping is important in a case it will come through strongly enough so that the transcribing person will identify it and report it. Each instance of weeping, no matter how short, is to be designated as one unit; if it lasts for more than seven seconds it is to be counted as more than one unit, the number of units being the number of 5-second intervals occupied by the behavior to the nearest five seconds. Weeping is to be scored as behavior even when it occurs simultaneously with speech. . . . Weeping indicates such responses as sobbing, sniffling, and talking through tears."

Y. Refers to an affirmation not expanded. "If the affirmative statement is expanded, it is scored by its content (such as H, S, Mob) rather than as Y. Any agreement to perform some act is scored Y, unless it should be scored Unsc. (as having to do with pleasantries at the beginning and end of the hour, with the administrative arrangements, etc.)."

Unsc. Refers to unscorable. "A category to which are assigned any units which cannot be alloted to any other of our categories. . . . Unsc is by no means entirely a wastebasket category. There are certain indications for its use. Thus we assign to Unsc unintelligible materials, as well as sentences for which no category can be found and which do not seem important enough to warrant the creation of a new category. Also in Unsc are the trivia of conversation before and after the session begins and ends, and legitimate questions put to the therapist by the patient. . . . Unsc is not combined with any other signs."

Categories for Therapist

D. Refers to drive or demand. "Any therapist unit which is thought to raise motivation in the patient is labeled D. Thus a question would likely be scored D, as would a comment raising anxiety."

Interp. Refers to interpretation. "interp is the sign used for naming an unconscious motive, for connecting motives or ideas not previously thought to be connected, for discriminating meanings falsely believed to be connected. We have sometimes lumped naming, connecting, and discriminating under the single term 'labeling.' The therapist's utterances leading up to an Interp are sometimes also scored Interp. Interps deal with unconscious motives and conflicts, but they are not judged from the standpoint of tension. Interps may raise or lower tension and this feature is not isolated by a score."

M. Refers to mm-hmm. "Many therapists have a sound such as 'mm-hmm' which signifies that they are listening to what the patient is saying. It is a mildly reinforcing utterance. It certainly indicates that the therapist is not objecting to what the patient is saying, even if it also indicates that he is not 'heavily' accepting what the patient is saying. . . . Therapists may say 'yes' or 'no' when these words do not have the sense of affirmation or negation but only signify the therapist is listening; in this case 'yes' or 'yeah' would be scored M. Thus M means mild agreement, mild assent, social facilitation, the mooing and cooing of social interaction. . . . 'No' could be scored M if it is an answer to a question like, 'Do you mind if I smoke?'–where the question itself is a mere form of politeness and the questioner has no doubt that the answer will be affirmative. What is important is that the verbal response be a token of mild social affirmation."

Pretni. Refers to a serious error by the therapist (it is Interp spelled backwards). "Thus marked countertransference reactions, egregious failure to understand what the patient is saying and therefore failure to interpret at the right time, notably incorrect interpretations would all be scored Pretni. We use Pretni grudgingly; if there is any plausible way in which the therapist's utterances can be favorably interpreted, any reasonable point of view by which what he does can be defended, we do not use Pretni. . . . It should immediately be granted that Pretni would be defined differently according to different theories of how therapy occurs and of how the therapist's intervention brings it about. . . . We have invented the Pretni sign because we conceive that to locate such points as they would be viewed by different theorists could lead to a detailed, objective discussion of theoretical differences."

R. Refers to tension reduction. "It is used for a therapist's utterance which causes relaxation and reduction of motivation in the patient. . . . In the case of this sign, drive reduction is presumed to have its usual effect in reinforcing what the patient has just done, said, or felt."

Unsc. "Used for unscorable utterances of the therapist. There are three subcategories of Unsc. The first might be called 'unintelligible.' Because of garbled transcriptions or deleted words, the utterance cannot be deciphered. A second variety might be called 'not evaluatable.' Some things the therapist says are enigmatic; the patient might respond to them in any erratic way. Thus the scorer cannot evaluate therapist's statement. A third kind might be called 'slush'—the introductory and terminal greetings, talk about arrangements or about change in arrangements, when these do not seem to have dynamic value, and other casual speaking before and after. . . . In point of fact, we use Unsc quite sparingly. The scorer must be in real conflict to have recourse to it. The usual thing is for the scorer to struggle to assign the therapist's utterances to one of the other categories; if the struggle proves in vain, the 'out' is Unsc."

*This table is an abbreviated version of the scoring categories presented in detail with many illustrative examples in Dollard and Auld's 1959 manual. (pp. 30-218) The reader is referred there for greater detail. Many of the patient categories or signs presented above can be scored as conscious or unconscious. In all situations where a sign is deemed to be unconsciously present, the sign is listed in lower case, rather than in capital letters. The authors also define, exemplify, and distinguish the many possible combinations of patient scores (e.g., S-A, S-a, s-A, A:r). Each of the therapist categories is always used singly, and never in combination with any other.

TABLE 3.3

Leary and Gill's system for analysis of the content of clinical evaluations and patient-therapist verbalizations

The Five Clinical Categories Derived from the Psychological-Psychotherapeutic Model

number	*category*	*example*
5	Constituent (ideational or non-ideational)	The patient is hostile.
4	Discharge	The patient inhibits her hostility.
3	Admission into awareness	The patient is unaware of her hostility.
2	Admission into speech	The patient admits her feelings of hostility to the therapist.
1	Intellectual insight-oriented intervention	The therapist interprets her hostility.

Variables in the Clinical Categories

first category	*second category*	*third category*	*fourth category*	*fifth category*		
insight oriented interventions	processes of admission, denial or alteration of ideas in verbalization	processes of awareness, repression or alteration of ideas in consciousness	processes of expression, inhibition or alteration of impulses	action, speech, motive, affect and idea		
				bodily motive, action, idea	derived motive, action, idea*	affects
structure therapy +, 0, –	admit +, +–, –	aware +, +–, –	express +, +–, –	*Sexual*	A : dominate	calm
question +, 0, –	(The remaining variables are the same for 2nd and 3rd categories)		attenuate	sex (unspecified)	B : enhance self	excited
focus +, 0, –			alter	orgasm	C : compete	depressed
summarize +, 0, –	attenuate		reverse	impotence	D : punish	elated
relate +, 0, –	alter		substitute	frigidity	E : attack	anxious
interpret +, 0, –	reverse		self-substitute	suck	F : complain	secure
			other-substitute	retain	G : distrust	
					H : derogate self	

	substitute		penetrate	I : submit
	self-substitute		incorporate	J : admire
	other-substitute		castrate	K : depend
	project		impregnate	L : cooperate
	subject project		show	M : approve
	object repress		look	N : support
	produce +, +–, –		manipulate	O : nurture
	think +, +–, –		kiss	P : teach
	internalize +, +–, –		*Aggressive*	★ : therapeutic neutrality
	emotionalize +, +–, –		beat (unspecified)	
	deepen +, +–, –		bite	
	clarify +, +–, –		expel	
	process +, +–, –		rape	
	structure +, +–, –		kill	

Source: From the Kaiser Foundation Interpersonal System of personality diagnosis.

The codes, "+, 0, –, and +–," modify the variables. The code "+" indicates the presence of the variable; "0" means the absence of the variable; "–" indicates the presence of the opposite of the variable or the inappropriate use of the variable; and "+–" indicates a less than direct presence of the variable (i.e., "indirectly, subtly, partially, almost," etc.).

Categories for Classifying Subjects of a Statement

code	*initial*	*name*	*example*
A	PT	The patient's behavior in therapy	The patient during the hour
	T	The therapist	
	PO	The patient outside of the therapy hour	
	PKP	People personally known to the speaker	Specify, e.g., the patient's father
	NKP	Persons not personally mnown to the speaker	Specify, e.g., the President
	AN	Animals	Specify, e.g., the patient's dog
B		Psychological subjects i.e., abstractions	Schizophrenia, aggression, Jungian therapy
C		Somatic subjects	The central nervous system
D		Sociological subjects	The role of a housewife
E		Inanimate subjects	The patient's car

Categories for Classifying the Inanimate, Social, and Biological Characteristics of Persons or Impersonal Subjects

number	*letter code*	*name*	*example*
11*		Inanimate (physico-chemical) characteristics	The lamp is lined with cork.
	M**	Miscellaneous behavior	The patient walked to the store.
	G	Geographic-temporal	The patient is a New Yorker
	I	Intellectual-educational	The patient is a German major.
10	P	Philosophic-religious	The patient went to church.
	S	Sociological-political	The patient is a Democrat.
	A	Aesthetic	The patient is a good painter.
	R	Recreational	The patient is a Giant fan.
	O	Occupational-financial	The patient makes a good salary.
9		Biological-somatic	The patient has a headache.

*Characteristics of this category are rarely attributed to persons.

**If at all possible, an action is scored in terms of its motive. If the patient "walked to the store" because she wanted the exercise the score would be 10 Recreational; if she had done so to express her anger at her husband the score would be in Fifth category "E" on the interpersonal circle. Ten Miscellaneous is used for an action where motive is unknown, or for an action in a social role which does not fit into one of the other social categories.

The Special Clinical Categories

number	*name of category*	*example*
8	Vocal-Kinesic	The patient speaks in a low voice.
7	Psychotherapeutic	The therapist is a Freudian.
6	Psychological symptomatic	The patient is phobic.

Areas of Content Defined by Subject and Characteristic Continua

<table>
<tr><td colspan="3"></td><td colspan="9">categories of subjects</td></tr>
<tr><td colspan="3"></td><td>PT</td><td>T</td><td>PO</td><td>PKP</td><td>NKP</td><td>B</td><td>C</td><td>D</td><td>E</td></tr>
<tr><td rowspan="2">categories of characteristics</td><td>Physico-chemical
Miscellaneous
Geographic-temporal
Intellectual-educational
Philosophic-religious
Sociological-political
Aesthetic
Recreational
Occupational-financial
Somatic</td><td>11
10-M
10-G
10-I
10-P
10-S
10-A
10-R
10-O
9</td><td></td><td colspan="4">Non-clinical talk about people
(the talk of ordinary social
conversation.)</td><td colspan="4">Impersonal, objective
talk, either scientific
or informational</td></tr>
<tr><td>Vocal-Motor
Psychotherapy
Psychological symptoms
Constituent
Expression
Admission into Awareness
Admission into Speech
Intellectual insight-oriented</td><td>8
7
6
5
4
3
2
1</td><td colspan="2">Nondynamic clinical talk about patient in therapy and therapist

Dynamic clinical talk about patient in therapy and therapist</td><td colspan="2">Nondynamic clinical talk (gossip or by patients early in therapy)

Dynamic clinical talk about patient outside of therapy and personally known people</td><td>Clinical talk about not known people</td><td>abstract psychological talk</td><td colspan="3">Anthropomorphic,
metaphorical,
autistic talk</td></tr>
</table>

The Modifiers by Which Statements are Qualified

code	*description*	*example*
A. Attitudinal modifiers		
?	Interrogation	Is he angry?
¿	Conditional	If he were angry . . .
!	Imperative	Be angry!
B	Negative value	His anger is a bad thing.
G	Positive value	It is good that he is angry.
W	Wish	He wishes to be angry.
F	Fear	I fear he is angry.
N	Negative	He is not angry.
Dr	Dream qualification	I dreamed he is angry.
Fan	Fantasy qualification	In my fantasy he is angry.
Iv	Involuntary	He couldn't help being angry.
Sig	Significant or important	His anger is important.
B. Dynamic modifiers		
No code	Nonverbal overt action	He behaves angrily.
V	Talk or verbalization	He said he is angry.
C	Conscious ideation	He thinks he is angry.
△	Conscious affect	He feels angry.
O	Unconscious impulse	He is unconsciously angry.
UN	Unconscious ideation	He has the unconscious image of himself as angry.

C. Connective modifiers

(Simple connections, subdivided into four variables)

con	Connection	His anger is conencted with . . .
equ	Equivalence	His anger is the same as . . .
com	Comparison (of two characteristics)	He is more angry than hurt.
cnf	Conflict	His anger makes it impossible for him to feel his . . .

(Causal connections, subdivided into two variables)

S	Stimulate	His anger is an attempt to get . . .
C & E	Cause and effect	His anger causes him . . .

(Change-improvement connections,* subdivided into six variables)

wor	Worse	His anger is worse.
N ch	No change	His anger has not changed.
imp	Improved	His anger is less of a problem.
gro	Growth	He expresses his anger more maturely.
reg	Regression	He expresses his anger more childishly.
<	More than (temporal)	His anger is increased.
>	Less than (temporal)	His anger is less.

*Implicit in all change-improvement connections is variance over time (temporal change); the first five listed are more specific and take scoring precedence over the purely temporal connections.

TABLE 3.4

*Lennard and Bernstein's interaction categories**

Units of Quantity

A. *Proposition*: "a verbalization containing a subject and a predicate either expressed or implied . . . the verbal expression of a single idea."

B. *Statement*: "an uninterrupted sequence of propositions from either the therapist or patient. While therapist statements rarely consist of more than three propositions, patient statements sometimes contain more than 100 propositions."

Quantity of information: the quantity of information contained in a statement "is estimated by counting the number of propositions it contains.

C. *Interaction or exchange*: "defined as a therapist statement followed by a patient statement, or vice versa. It may consist of several propositions, but it represents a complete interaction."

Rate of interaction: "the number of exchanges per hour or per transcribed page . . . provides a measure of the frequency with which a therapist speaks or interacts."

Categories of Therapist Informational Specificity

A set of eight categories "to roughly quantify the amount of structure or information contained in each therapist message. The amount of information contained in any therapist proposition is defined as its 'informational stimulus value'; this corresponds to the extent to which it tends to place limits upon the array of verbal responses from which the patient may choose a reply. . . . A message that reduces the number of possibilities a great deal gives a large amount of information."

A. "The therapist indicates that he is listening and passively encourages the patient to continue."
B. "The therapist indicates he is listening and actively encourages the patient to continue."
C. "The therapist limits the patient to a single subject matter area."
D. "The therapist refers to a specific proposition which has already been introduced in either of the two immediately antecedent interactions."
E. "The therapist introduces a new proposition."
F. "The therapist introduces a sequence of new propositions."
G. "The therapist introduces a specific proposition with the intention of soliciting a particular item of information."
H. "The therapist excludes a specific topic or proposition as a subject for communication."

Grammatical Form of Propositions

Each therapist or patient proposition is judged as either:

A. Declarative
B. Imperative
C. Interrogatory

Affective Content of Propositions

The content of each proposition of either a patient or a therapist is coded as either:

A. Affective, expresses or refers to feeling
B. Nonaffective, clearly did not express or refer to feeling
C. Affective content indeterminable

"Therapist propositions were categorized as affective when they were directed toward eliciting patient affect."

Interaction Process Categories

Six of Bales' twelve categories were condensed into three. "Our method tries to classify . . . what we might call the 'process significance' of the single 'interaction'; that is, the pragmatic significance of each act in relation to prior acts and acts expected to come."

A. *Descriptive propositions*: "ask for or convey information. They give or ask for orientation, repetition, or clarification."
B. *Evaluative propositions*: "ask for or convey appraisal or statements of value. They give or ask for opinions, expression of feeling, or analysis."
C. *Prescriptive propositions*: "express or ask for directives. They give or ask for suggestions."

Role System Reference Categories

"We are now concerned in a limited sense with what the proposition refers to, with what it is about. . . . We are particularly concerned here with identifying propositions in which the therapist or the patient discusses their roles and expectations with regard to therapy. . . . The subject matter of each proposition was therefore classified in terms of the following frames of references":

A. *Primary system*: "patient or therapist propositions that refer to their roles during treatment and the process of therapy, and to the purposes, goals, and accomplishments of therapy."
B. *Secondary system*: "propositions in which the manifest content refers to therapist and patient in other than their primary roles as patient and therapist" (e.g., transference phenomena)
C. *Tertiary systems*:
   1. *The Family*: "propositions that refer directly to the patient's status in the family system."
   2. *Other Social Systems*: "propositions that refer to specific social systems other than the family."
D. *The self*: "references to life experiences past and present that do not refer directly to other reference systems."

*This is an annotated version of Lennard and Bernstein's system. The more detailed version, with examples of each category, can be found in their 1960 volume, pp. 37-57.

TABLE 3.5

Matarazzo's three speech interaction categories for scoring interviewee and interviewer verbalizations

1. *Interviewee* Mean Speech Duration.*

This variable includes the total amount of time (in seconds) the interviewee speaks divided by his total number of speech units. A speech unit, as defined by these investigators, is an utterance separated at either end by two silence periods—one silence following the other participant's last comment (i.e., the speaker's latency), and the second silence following the speaker's own comment and prededing the listener's next comment (i.e., the listener's latency). Pauses for breathing, for choosing words, for reflection, etc., are included in the speech unit when the *context* clearly suggests that the speaker has not yet completed that utterance. An example of *one* utterance or unit is: "Yes, I can tell you about . . . (pause) . . . my father. He was a . . . (pause) . . . how can I say it . . . (pause) . . . a man of many talents. You would . . . (pause) . . . have . . . (pause) . . . liked him.") However, pauses (again determined by context) which precede the introduction of new ideas or thoughts by the same individual, *without an intervening comment by the other interview participant,* signal the onset of a new speech unit. For example: "It's true that I've . . . (pause) . . . enjoyed hunting for most of my life." . . . (pause three to four seconds) . . . "Speaking of hunting, I'm reminded of a favorite dog I had several years ago." The context clearly suggested that one unit ended with "life" and a *second,* or new unit, began with "Speaking." The reader is also referred to Rogers (1942, pp. 265-437) and Wolberg (1954, pp. 688-780) for numerous other examples of typical single interview units as scored by the authors. Matarazzo and Wiens (1972) also recently published a whole verbatim interview to clarify what they mean by a speech unit.

2. *Interviewee Mean Speech Latency.*

This variable includes the total latency time divided by the number of units of interviewee latency. A latency is that period of silence separating two *different* speech units. Latencies occur either between exchanges of the interview participants (i.e., at the time one terminates and the other begins an utterance) or between two consecutive but clearly separate and different speech units spoken by one individual.1 This variable, too, is nothing more than what is observed in ordinary conversation and readily recognized by layman and expert alike.

3. *Interviewee Percentage Interuption.*

This is merely the total number of times (frequency) the interviewee spoke divided into the number (frequency) of these same speech units which were interruptions of his partner.

*For a definition of these speech variables for the *Interviewer,* merely substitute his name for the Interviewee in the above definitions.

Table 3.6

*Murray's content analysis method for studying psychotherapy**

Scoring Patient Content

A. Drive Categories

1. *Sex approval.* Includes all statements referring to the positive or approach component of the sexual drive; direct expression of sexual needs and wishes, description of sexual attraction and arousal, sexual activity not mixed with fear or guilt, planning for sexual satisfaction, courtship and dating among unmarried people where the erotic element is present but institutionalized, description of homosexual feelings and other perversions, descriptions of masturbation, discussion of normal sex education.

2. *Sex anxiety.* Includes expressions of fear, anxiety, or guilt about sex; nervousness, irrational fears, phobias, compulsions, depression, hopelessness, confusion, helplessness, conflict, tension, blocking; avoidance behavior, denial of a sex drive, negative attitude toward sex, rationalizing one's behavior, deprecating self; feelings of inadequacy, somatic symptoms, impotence, frigidity.

3. *Sex frustration.* Includes hate, anger, resentment, criticism, or complaint about the frustration of the sex drive; description of behavior designed to, or expression of desire, to, destroy, hurt, attack verbally or physically, disparage, humiliate, domineer, or deprecate in any way; frustrating another person, withholding the symbols of affection, making someone uncomfortable.

4. *Affection approval.* Includes direct expression of needs for love and affectionate behavior; needs for and appreciation of affection, friendship, acceptance, understanding; feeling of loving, giving affection, etc., or having entered into an affectionate relationship; doing something positive for or with a person; holding someone in high regard, respecting, appreciating, etc.
5. *Affection anxiety.* As in sexual anxiety but related to affection.

6. *Affection frustration.* As in sex frustration but related to affection.

7. *Dependence approval.* Includes expressions of needs to depend on someone, let someone else take the initiative, to be told what to do, to be helped, to be cured by an outside agent; description of dependent behavior or nurturant actions by others to self; being appreciative of being taken care of by another; making personal security contingent on another.

8. *Dependence anxiety. As in sex aniety but related to dependence.*

9. *Dependence frustration.* As in sex frustration but related to dependence.

10. *Independence and self-assertion approval.* Includes expression of needs to be independent, adult, mature, assertive, ambitious, competitive; standing up for one's rights, defending against attack, saying "no" when one has to, expressing an opinion or warrented criticism; descriptions of behavior or plans to be independent, etc.

11. *Independence anxiety.* As in sex anxiety but related to independence.

12. *Independence frustration.* As in sex frustration but related to independence.

13. *Unspecified anxiety.* As in sex anxiety but related to no apparent drive. To be distinguished from generalized anxiety by the fact that it is related to some specific person or thing.

14. *Unspecified frustration.* As in sex frustration but related to no apparent drive.

B. Special Categories

1. *Disturbances of free association.* Asking questions, seeking directions, entering into bilateral discussion with therapist; not following the rule of free association, enlisting therapist in this; expressing difficulty in talking or thinking of things to say.

2. *Agreement with therapist remarks.* "Mm-hmm," "yes" "surely," etc.; "I agree," "I think so," etc.; "No," if the therapist's remarks require "no" for agreement; etc.

3. *Disagreement with therapist remarks.* "No. I disagree," "I don't think so," etc.; "Yes, but . . . " "I agree, but . . ." "that's so, but . . . " etc.; "Yes," if the therapist's remarks required "No" for agreement; Alarm or startled reactions; "I don't know," "I'm not sure," etc.

4. *Intellectual Discussion.* Includes discussion of abstract psychological theory, philosophy, art, literature, science, politics, etc. (except where the activity is a professional one).

5. *Generalized Anxiety.* Includes all psychological and object; general "free-floating" anxiety and guilt.

Scoring Therapist Content

1. *Instruction to Free-Associate.* Whenever the therapist explains the rule of free association, the need for it, the benefits to be gained from following it, or directly insists on it. Whenever the therapist asks the patient to tell him what he was thinking about during a pause.

2. *Labels.* Wherever the therapist tells the patient what it was he was feeling or doing. Wherever the therapist points to the patient's own feelings or behavior in a situation where the patient has only talked about the other person. Most causal statements are labels.

3. *Discrimination.* Wherever the therapist points out a difference between two situations, feelings, or behavior patterns. The main instances are where he points out the difference between past and present conditions, and the difference between what the patient expects from people and what they are like.

4. *Similarities.* Wherever the therapist points out two situations, feelings, etc., which are similar or have a common element. It may be done in the form of a question or leading statement.

5. *Strong Approvals.* Any form of strong approval for the way the patient has just been speaking or for an outside action that the patient has described. Strong agreement, encouragement, reassurance, and explicit permissiveness.

6. *Disapprovals.* Some indication that the therapist doesn't want the patient to continue talking about what he has been talking about, or the way in which he was talking about it. Any indication that the therapist does not feel the topic is important, interesting, or acceptable. Any surprise, alarm, anxiety, or disturbance on the part of the therapist. Any of the typical social punishments such as belittling the patient or his statements; holding up an example in contrast to what the patient says; replacing a patient's interpretation with the therapist's own and different one in such a way as to reject what the patient has said. Giving a negative evaluation to something the patient says.

7. *Demands.* An attempt to elicit verbalization about a topic that hasn't immediately preceded the demand. That is, a unit is scored as a demand only if it is an attempt to bring up a new topic or one which has been dropped by the patient. In order to qualify as "new" a topic must not have been mentioned by the patient in the ten patient statements just previous to the therapist's remark.

8. *Directions.* Wherever the therapist tells the patient what to do (other than to free-associate). Also any statements of opinion about general questions.

9. *Mild Probes.* This category is for instances where the therapist is encouraging what the patient is talking about but where he asks the patient to continue talking about the topic, asks for elaboration of one point, or asks for information directly related to what the patient is talking about. It will also include confession of ignorance or lack of understanding on the part of the therapist. The typical "tell me more" remark.

10. *Mild Approvals.* This category is for instances when the therapist shows a minimum response which is generally positive: "Yes," "Oh, I see," "I understand," etc.

11. *Mm.* This category is for instances when the therapist grunts or verbally nods. It includes "Mm" and "Mm-hmm" but includes no words.

12. *Irrelevant.* All general opening and closing remarks; discussion of technical details in therapy such as "O.K. Tuesday at 10"; other irrelevant remarks. In addition, any response on the part of the therapist which cannot be put in other categories. Any unscorable self-phrases or mumbling.

* The scale presented here is an abbreviated version of Murray's scale. Further details and examples of each category can be bound in the total scale presented in Murray (1956).

TABLE 3.7
Snyder's 1945 and 1963 versions of his nondirective classification system for therapist and patient responses

1945 Version

Definitions of counselor categories

A. *Lead-taking categories* (those which seem to determine the direction of the interview; which indicate what the client should be talking about).

XCS– *Structuring*. Remarks that define the counseling situation. Remarks indicating the purposes the interview may be expected to accomplish, or the responsibilities of both individuals, i.e., telling "what we can do here." Also includes remarks setting the time and limits of the interview; would include "You can have just and hour," but wouldn't include "I see you've come to the end of the hour."

XFT– *Forcing client to choose and develop topic*. Includes all efforts of the counselor to reject responsibility for the direction of the interview. For example: "What shall we talk about today?" or "Well, how do *you* feel about it?"

XDC– *Directive questions; specific types of questions*. Asking outright question which requires the giving of a factual answer. It does not include interrogative statements which are merely intended to redefine, clarify, or redescribe a feeling. It would include "What do you think of that?" "How old are you?" "Do they resent the fact that you are not agressively going out after jobs?" It would not include "And you aren't too happy about it?" or "It's rather unpleasant for you, is that right?", particularly when such questions follow somewhat similar statements.

XND– *Nondirective leads and questions*. Statements that encourage the client to state the problem further. This excludes leads that would greatly limit the client in what he could bring out about the problem or his feelings about it. It would include "Tell me more about it," or "Would you like to tell me how you feel about it?" or "How are you today?" (asked in a general sense). In general this type of lead is one that encourages a statement without limiting the nature of the response except in a very general way, as in "Tell me more about it."

B. *Nondirective response-to-feeling categories* (those which seem to attempt to restate a feeling that the client has expressed, but not to interpret or to offer advice, criticism, or suggestions).

XSA– *Simple acceptance*. "Yes," "Mm-hmm," "I see," "That's right" (if not answering question) or similar responses. Must not imply approval or criticism.

XRC– *Restatement of content or problem*. A simple repeating of what the client has said without any effort to organize, clarify, or interpret it, or any effort to show that the counselor is appreciating the feeling of the client's statement by understanding it. The wording need not be identical with that of the client.

XCF– *Clarification or recognition of feeling*. A statement by the counselor that puts the client's feeling or affective tone in somewhat clearer or more recognizable form. "It makes you feel very much annoyed," "You love your mother but you resent her telling you what to do," "I think sometimes you wish you'd never been born."

C. *Semidirective response-to-feeling category* (Those responses that are interpretive in character).

XIT– *Interpretation*. Responses in which the counselor points out patterns and relationship in the material presented. This category is always used when causation is implied or indicated. "You do this because . . . " If the counselor attempts even vaguely to say "why" the client does or feels something, it is considered interpretation. "Perhaps you are revealing feelings of inferiority." "When people feel frustrated they often act the way you do." "There's your problem."

D. *Directive Counseling Categories* (categories of responses that imply a relationship in which the counselor attempts to change the immediate ideas of the client or to influence his attitude toward them).

XAE—*Approval and encouragement*. "That's fine." "You've covered a lot of ground today." "You bet!" Any statement which lends emotional support or approval to the client's insecurity.

XIX—*Giving information or explanation*. Answers to any questions about the nature of psychology or any other informational material; anything which is recognized as a generally established fact; any personal information about the counselor.

XCA—*Proposing client activity*. Any statement that imply that the client should take any sort of action.

XPS—*Persuasion*. Attempts to convince the client that he should accept the counselor's point of view. "Don't you think it would be better that way, now?"

XDC—*Disapproval and criticism*. "You need to get hold of yourself."

E. *Minor categories* (those responses that do not seem to be related to the principal problem of the client).

XEC—*Ending of the contact*. Any responses dealing with the bringing to a close of the contact, or with the setting of a time for a future contact.

XES—*Ending of the series*. Responses relating to the bringing to a close of the series of interviews, or to the beginning of the client's feeling that he does not need further contact.

XFD—*Friendly discussion*. Material unrelated to the client's problem, and serving only the purpose of establishing good rapport between client and counselor.

XUN—*Unclassifiable*. Any response which cannot be classified in one of the above categories.

Definitions of client content categories

A. *Problem category* (the category that includes the client's definition of description of his problems).

YSP—*Any statements of the problem* or the symptoms. This includes accounts of incidents which illustrate the problem in the client's opinion. "I would term it a blocking which has manifestations in several fields."

B. *Simple response categories* (responses which are not statements of a problem understanding or insight, or specific minor types of statements).

YAI—*Asking for advice or information*. Any attempts to obtain advice or information, or to place the responsibilities for solution of the problem on the counselor.

YAQ—*Answer to a question*. Any simple answer to a direct question (XDQ) which gives information but does not indicate feeling on the part of the client. This category does not include acceptance of a counselor's interpretation.

YAC—*Simple acceptance* or acquiescence to a clarification of feeling. "Yes," "Mm-hmm," "You bet," "That's right!"

YRS—*Rejection of a clarification or interpretation*. "No, not exactly," "Well, I don't think it's like that," "I'm not sure."

C. *Understanding or action-taking categories* (those that show insight into the courses or remedies of the problem; those that discuss plans that may be followed).

YUI– *Understanding or insight.* Under this category fall any expressions indicating that the client has been able to see patterns and relationships in the material he has presented in the interview. Statements about the "why" of his behavior that indicate a logical and reasoned explanation rather than a rationalization. "Maybe that thing of being so important went to my head." "Maybe having everybody waiting on me that way made me so spoiled that I haven't been able to get along since without that attention."

YDP– *Discussion of plans*, decision, possible outcomes of plans. This category is used in referring to plans and decisions which may have resulted from the counseling. Discussion of past plans are not included. Future goals are included, when they appear to have resulted from the counseling. "I'm gonna go home and lay this thing out before her, and from now on I'm gonna stop hidin' those little things I don't want people to know about for fear they won't have a good opinion of me." "I could get a job, I think."

D. *Minor categories* (those responses that do not seem to be related to the principal problem of the client).

YEC– *Ending of the contact.* Any response dealing with the bringing to a close of the contact, or with the setting of a time for a future contact.

YES– *Ending of the series.* Responses relating to the bringing to a close of the series of interviews or to the beginning of the client's feeling that he does not need further counseling.

YNR– *Not related to the problem.* Any material which does not seem to be a basic part of the problem and yet is not considered friendly discussion or any other type of material listed above. Expressions of facts of an unemotional character. This includes statements about self or others, so long as no feelings or emotions seem to be expressed. "Of course, some work's awful monotonous—but the higher up you go, the more interesting it becomes." "I like flowers; I wouldn't mind making a garden next spring."

YFD– *Friendly discussion.* Material unrelated to the client's problem and serving only the purpose of establishing friendly relationships between client and counselor.

YUN– *Unclassifiable.* Any response that cannot be classified in one of the above categories.

Definitions of client feeling categories

A. *Positive attitudes*

PAS– Positive attitude toward the self; favorable or defensive.
PAC– Positive attitude toward the counselor or counseling situation.
PAO– Positive attitude toward other persons or situations.

B. *Negative attitudes*

NAS– Negative attitude toward the self; unfavorable or critical.
NAC– Negative attitude toward the counselor or counseling situation.
NAO– Negative attitude toward other persons or situations.

C. *Ambivalent attitudes*

AMS– Ambivalent attitude toward the self.
AMC– Ambivalent attitude toward the counselor or counseling situation.
AMO– Ambivalent attitude toward other persons or situations.

1963 Version

Coding symbols and categories for therapist responses

Lead-Taking Responses
- XST Structuring
- XND Non-directive lead
- XDL Directive lead
- XDQ Question

Reflective or Reeducative Responses
- XRC Restatement
- XCF Clarification
- XIT Interpretation
- XAT Attenuation
- XAV Advice
- XEI Information

Relationship Response
- XRL Relationship

Supportive Responses
- XRS Reassurance
- XOH Offer of help
- XAP Approval

Redirecting Responses
- XCA Calling attention
- XCH Challenging
- XWH Withholding support
- XPS Persuasion
- XDC Disapproval

Coding symbols and categories for different types of therapist interpretations

XIT_4 Therapist connects two aspects of the contents of previous client statements.

XIT_5 Therapist reformulates the behavior of the client during the interview in a way not explicitly recognized previously by the client.

XIT_6 Therapist comments on the client's bodily or facial expressions as manifestations of the client's feelings.

XIT_7 Therapist uses a preceding client statement to exemplify a process that has been building up during the interview and of which the client is seemingly unaware.

XIT_8 Therapist speculates as to the possible childhood situation that may relate to current client feelings.

XIT_9 Therapist deals with inferences about material completely removed from the client's awareness.

Coding symbols and categories for client need-responses

symbol	*category*	*symbol*	*category*
Anx	Anxiety	Dom n	Dominance need
Hos n	Hostility need	Dom p	Dominance pressure
Hos p	Hostility pressure	Aff n	Affiliation need
Dep	Dependency need	Aff p	Affliation pressure
Ego	Ego need	Voc	Vocational concern
Nur	Nurturance need	Mob	Mobility concern
Sex n	Sex need	Phy	Physical concern
Sex p	Sex pressure		

Coding symbols and categories for client's begavior in therapy

symbol	category
Ins	Shows insight
Plans	Makes plans
Res	Shows resistance
Conf	Confirms an interpretation
Rel	Deals with the relationship
Ques	Asks a question
Drm	Reports a dream
Unc	Reveals unconscious material

Coding symbols and categories of major and minor sources (or objects) of client affect

Major categories		*Minor categories*	
symbol	*category*	*symbol*	*category*
self	the client	Masc	client's masculinity
par	client's parents	enur	client's enuresis
fa	father	phys	adequacy or physique
auth	authority figure (other)	prof	professional adequacy
mo	mother	rival	admirer of spouse
sib	sister or brother	matur	client's maturity
wife	client's wife	intel	client's intelligence
peers	associates	child	client's child
ther	the therapist	nur. peo.	nurturant people in general
het	heterosexual love object	anim	animals of the client
homo	homosexual love object	relig	client's religion

TABLE 4.1

Harway et al's depth of interpretation scale

1	2	3		4		5	6	7
Therapist merely repeats the material of which the patient is fully aware (1.1)	Restatement of material of which the patient is aware (1.8)	Implied focusing with regard to material of which the patient is aware (2.3)	Therapist connects for the patient two aspects of the content of the previous patient statement (3.4)	Reformulation of the behavior of the patient during the interview in a way not explicitly recognized previously by patient (3.9)	Therapist comments on patient's bodily and facial expressions as manifestations of patient's feelings (4.4)	Use of preceding patient statement to exempligy a process that has been building up during an interview and of which the patient is seemingly unaware (4.9)	Therapist speculates as to a possible childhood situation that might relate to current patient feeling (5.9)	Therapist response deals with inferences about material completely removed from the patient's awareness (6.9)

Source: Harway et al. (1954) and Speisman (1959)

TABLE 4.2

Howe and Pope's parallel therapist verbal activity level scales A and B, and mean activity level of each paired item

Scale A		*Scale B*	
mean AL	*descriptive responses*	*mean AL*	*descriptive responses*
1.7	Therapist uses a single word or syllable to give the patient an invitation to continue.	1.6	Therapist says "Mm-hmm" to convey acceptance and understanding of the patient.
3.3	Therapist repeats exactly what the patient said except for random changing of one or two words.	3.7	Therapist makes a verbal response of two or three words, given as simple acceptance and understanding of what the patient says.
4.3	Therapist states a question or incomplete sentence which contains a key word or phrase from the patient's previous response.	4.4	Therapist asks the patient to tell him more, to elaborate a little, on a topic already mentioned.
5.8	Therapist asks for "an example" of what the patient has just reported.	5.7	Therapist parries a question put to him by the patient by directing it back to the patient.
6.2	Therapist focuses upon an objective, factual aspect of patient's life (age, job, salary).	6.3	Therapist inquires how long patient's symptoms have been present.
6.7	Therapist restates things the patient has said in a different way, to make the import clearer.	6.7	Therapist asks when some event (described by the patient) actually happened.
7.4	Therapist asks patient how he feels about something or some event which the patient has just talked about.	7.5	Therapist question focuses upon patient's transient thoughts within the interview situation, at a particular instant.
7.8	Therapist confronts the patient with a reformulation of things the patient has said, and asks if that is what he means.	7.8	Therapist reflects a feeling or need clearly implied in the patient response, but not actually verbalized by the patient.
8.5	Therapist conveys his impression that there is something missing from the patient's story.	8.7	Therapist summarizes a number of different responses made by the patient, which are essentially concerned with the same feeling, of which the patient is aware, and therapist labels the feeling.
9.1	Therapist suggests that what the patient has just said is inconsistent with certain other things said earlier by the patient.	9.3	Therapist points out some reality condition that is inconsistent or incompatible with the patient's wishes or expectations.

Source: Howe and Pope (1961a).

TABLE 4.3

Siegman and Pope's therapist specificity scale

Category of Therapist Statement	*Scale Value*
1. Th uses a single word or syllable to indicate that he is listening and accepting.	1.7
2. Th makes a brief remark to encourage pt to proceed.	3.0
3. Th repeats a key word or phrase from the pt's previous response as an invitation to pt to continue.	3.6
4. Th asks pt to speak about a broad, as yet unexplored area, i.e. "your troubles."	4.1
5. Th asks pt to speak about a more limited subject area.	6.3
6. Th labels or specifies the feeling implicit in the preceding pt remark, or makes some other limited inference regarding it.	6.9
7. Th asks pt to explain or elaborate on a specific proposition, phrase or word included in his preceeding response.	7.6
8. Th makes an interpretation that is more than a limited inference.	8.6
9. Th responds to a pt remark, either by discouraging the pt from any further talk in the topical area concerned, or by raising challenging questions about the remark.	9.0
10. Th asks for specific factual information.	10.9

Source: Siegman and Pope (1962).

TABLE 4.4

Strupp's multidimensional scales for measuring therapist activity

Type of Therapeutic Activity

00. *facilitating communication* (minimal activity)
- 01. Silence
- 02. Passive acceptance, acknowledgment
- 03. General invitations to talk or to proceed (nondirective leads)

10. *exploratory operations*
- 11. Simple questioning: asking for further information, clarification, examples, elaborations; simple probes, case history questions; accenting by repeating one or more words.
- 12. Focal probes (with hypothesis), questions to stimulate the patient's curiosity, encouraging self-exploration.

20. *clarification* (minimal interpretation)
- 21. Reflection of feeling, restatements for purposes of clarification (may include "?")
- 22. Summaries (essentially noninterpretive)

30. *interpretive operations*
- 31. Interpretations, analysis of defenses, establishing connections, definitions of the patient's problem (interpretive)
- 32. "Reality Model": any operation by which the therapist's communication asserts the patient's rights, needs, etc., and represents a reasonable model of reality (usually interpretive)
- 33. Summaries (essentially interpretive)

40. *Structuring*
- 41. Structuring the therapeutic situation, describing the functions and tasks of therapy in general terms
- 42. Discussions about theory (relatively abstract)
- 43. External arrangements, time, place, fees, etc.

50. *direct guidance*
- 51. Direct suggestions for activity within the therapeutic framework
- 52. Direct suggestions for activity outside the therapeutic framework
- 53. "The therapist as an expert": Giving information, stating an opinion, answering direct questions, speaking as an authority. Such communications may seem primarily objective, but they may also convey reassurance (warmth) or rejection (coldness). Approbation, reassurance, support, criticism, sarcasm, cynicism, etc., are included.

60. *Activity Not Clearly Relevant to the Task of Therapy*
- 61. Greetings, "small talk," endings, etc.
- 62. Unwitting emotional reactions (countertransference)

70. *Unclassifiable*

Depth-Directedness

non-inferential	mildly inferential	moderately inferential		highly inferential
		<--------------degrees of interpretation--------------->		
	<------------------------- intensification of therapeutic activity------------------------->			
Silence Passive acceptance Facilitating communication	Simple questioning: requests for further information, clarification, examples, elaboration Simple probes Case history questions Accenting ("epitomizing") Nondirective leads Mild statements and opinions	Restatements of feelings (reflections) Focal probes (with hypothesis) Definitions of the therapeutic relationship Stimulating P's curiosity about himself; encouraging self-exploration	Interpretations Analysis of defenses Establishing connections (pointing out inconsistencies) Hypothesis testing Definitions of the problem (interpretive)	Deep interpretations Direct confrontation (without preparation)

Dynamic Focus

Sector A	*Sector B*
Therapist accepts the patient's formulation (minimal interference) without introducing a new frame of reference: Passive acceptance, facilitating communication, repeating word or phrase Reflections of manifest feeling	Therapist directs the patient's communication into a different channel and/or introduces a new frame of reference: B-1 Indications that additional information, clarification, examples, elaboration, etc. is needed to further the therapeutic operation B-2 Focus on *dynamic* events in the *past* B-3 Focus on *dynamic* events in the *present* B-4T Focus on the dynamics of the *therapist-patient relationship* (analysis of the transference) B-4 Focus on the *therapist-patient interaction* (therapist emerging as a person, authority, or expert)

Initiative

absence of initiative	*mild* forms of initiative	*moderate* initiative	*strong* initiative
<- - - - The therapist is "anonymous" - - - ->		The therapist is more active, assumes the role of an "expert"	The therapist assumes the role of an authority
Silence*	Simple questioning Simple probes Accenting Nondirective leads	Focal probes Definitions of the therapeutic relationship Interpretations - - - - - - - - - - -> Analysis of defenses - - - - - - - - -> Hypothesis testing - - - - - - - - - -> Changing the subject - - - - - - - - ->	Authoritative statements and formulations
	Reflections of feeling (↑)		

*Certain forms of silence are scored higher on the scale; see text.

Therapeutic Climate

Coldness		Neutrality		Warmth
<- - - - - - - - - - Withholding - - - - - - - - - -			- - - - - - - - - - Giving - - - - - - - - - ->	
Rejection Sarcasm Cynicism Derision Hostility Criticism Brutality	Milder degrees of -2	Objectivity Task-orientation	Milder degrees of +2	Acceptance Understanding Tolerance Empathy Respect

TABLE 4.5

Truax's three therapist conditions scales for accurate empathy, nonpossissive warmth (positive regard), and genuineness (self congruence)

A Tentative Scale for the Measurement of Accurate Empathy

Stage 1.

Therapist seems completely unaware of even the most conspicuous of the client's feelings; his responses are not appropriate to the mood and content of the client's statements. There is no determinable quality or empathy, and hence no accuracy whatsoever. The therapist may be bored and disinterested or actively offering advice, but he is not communicating an awareness of the client's current feelings.

Stage 2.

Therapist shows an almost negligible degree of accuracy in his responses, and that only toward the client's most obvious feelings. Any emotions which are not clearly defined he tends to ignore altogether. He may be correctly sensitive to obvious feelings and yet misunderstand much of what the client is really trying to say. By his response he may block off or may misdirect the patient. Stage 2 is distinguishable from Stage 3 in that the therapist ignores feelings rather than displaying an inability to understand them.

Stage 3.

Therapist often responds accurately to client's more exposed feelings. He also displays concern for the deeper, more hidden feelings, which he seems to sense must be present, though he does not understand their nature or sense their meaning to the patient.

Stage 4.

Therapist usually responds accurately to the client's more obvious feelings and occasionally recognizes some that are less apparent. In the process of this tentative probing, however, he may misinterpret some present feelings and anticipate some which are not current. Sensitivity and awareness do exist in the therapist, but he is not entirely "with" the patient in the *current* situation or experience. The desire and effort to understand are both present, but his accuracy is low. This stage is distinguishable from Stage 3 in that the therapist does occasionally recognize less apparent feelings. He also may seem to have a theory about the patient and may even know how or why the patient feels a particular way, but he is definitely not "with" the patient. In short, the therapist may be diagnostically accurate, but not emphatically accurate in his sensitivity to the patient's current feelings.

Stage 5.

Therapist accurately responds to all of the client's more readily discernible feelings. He also shows awareness of many less evident feelings and experiences, but he tends to be somewhat inaccurate in his understanding of these. However, when he does not understand completely, this lack of complete understanding is communicated without an anticipatory or jarring note. His misunderstandings are not disruptive by their tentative nature. Sometimes in Stage 5 the therapist simply communicates his awareness of the problem of understanding another person's inner world. This stage is the midpoint of the continuum of accurate empathy.

Stage 6.

Therapist recognizes most of the client's present feelings, including those which are not readily apparent. Although he understands their content, he sometimes tends to misjudge the intensity of these veiled feelings, so that his responses are not always accurately suited to the exact mood of the client. The therapist does deal directly with feelings the patient is currently experiencing although he may misjudge the intensity of those less apparent. Althought sensing the feelings, he often is unable to communicate meaning to them. In contrast to Stage 7, the therapist's statements contain an almost static quality in the sense that he handles those feelings that the patient offers but does not bring new elements to life. He is "with" the client but doesn't encourage exploration. His manner of communicating his understanding is such that he makes of it a finished thing.

Stage 7.

Therapist responds accurately to most of the client's present feelings and shows awareness of the precise intensity of most of the underlying emotions. However, his responses move only slightly beyond the client's own awareness, so that feelings may be present which neither the client nor therapist recognizes. The therapist initiates moves toward more emotionally laden material, and may communicate simply that he and the patient are moving towards more emotionally significant material. Stage 7 is distinguishable from Stage 6 in that often the therapist's response is a kind of precise pointing of the finger toward emotionally significant material.

Stage 8.

Therapist accurately interprets all the client's present, acknowledged feelings. He also uncovers the most deeply shrouded of the client's feelings, voicing meanings in the client's experience of which the client is scarcely aware. Since the therapist must necessarily utilize a method of trial and error in the new uncharted areas, there are minor flaws in the accuracy of his understanding, but these inaccuracies are held tentatively. With sensitivity and accuracy he moves into feelings and experiences that the client has only hinted at. The therapist offers specific explanations or additions to the patient's understanding so that underlying emotions are both pointed out and specifically talked about. The content that comes to life may be new but it is not alien.

Although the therapist in Stage 8 makes mistakes, these mistakes are not jarring, because they are covered by the tentative character of the response. Also, this therapist is sensitive to his mistakes and quickly changes his response in midstream, indicating that he has recognized what is being talked about and what the patient is seeking in his own explorations. The therapist reflects a togetherness with the patient in tentative trial and error exploration. His voice tone reflects the seriousness and depth of his empathic grasp.

Stage 9.

The therapist in this stage unerringly responds to the client's full range of feelings in their exact intensity. Without hesitation, he recognizes each emotional nuance and communicates an understanding of every deepest feeling. He is completely attuned to the client's shifting emotional content; he senses each of the client's feelings and reflects them in his words and *voice*. With sensitive accuracy, he expands the client's hints into a full-scale (though tentative) elaboration of feeling or experience. He shows precision both in understanding and in communication of this understanding, and expresses and experiences them without hesitancy.

A Tentative Scale for the Measurement of Nonpossessive Warmth

---

Stage 1.

The therapist is actively offering advice or giving clear negative regard. He may be telling the patient what would be "best for him," or in other ways actively approving or disapproving of his behavior. The therapist's actions make himself the locus of evaluation; he sees himself as *responsible for* the patient.

Stage 2.

The therapist responds mechanically to the client, indicating little positive regard and hence little nonpossessive warmth. He may ignore the patient or his feelings or display a lack of concern or interest. The therapist ignores the client at times when a nonpossessively warm response would be expected; he shows a complete passivity that communicates almost unconditional lack of regard.

Stage 3.

The therapist indicates a positive caring for the patient or client, but it is a *semipossessive* caring in the sense that he communicates to the client that his behavior matters to him. That is, the therapist communicates such things as "It is not all right if you act immorally," "I want you to get along at work," or "It's important to me that you get along with the ward staff." The therapist sees himself as *responsible for* the client.

Stage 4.

The therapist clearly communicates a very deep interest and concern for the welfare of the patient, showing a nonevaluative and unconditional warmth in almost all areas of his functioning. Although there remains some conditionality in the more personal and private areas, the patient is given freedom to be himself and to be liked as himself. There is little evaluation of thoughts and behaviors. In deeply personal areas, however, the therapist may be conditional and communicate the idea that the client may act in any way he wishes—*except* that it is important to the therapist that he be more mature or not regress in therapy or accept and like the therapist. In all other areas, however, nonpossessive warmth is communicated. The therapist sees himself as *responsible to* the client.

Stage 5.

At Stage 5, the therapist communicates warmth without restriction. There is a deep respect for the patient's worth as a person and his rights as a free individual. At this level the patient is free to be himself even if this means that he is regressing, being defensive, or even disliking or rejecting the therapist himself. At this stage the therapist cares deeply for the patient as a person, but it does not matter to him how the patient chooses to behave. He genuinely cares for and deeply prizes the patient for his human potentials, apart from evaluations of his behavior or his thoughts. He is willing to share equally the patient's joys and aspirations or depressions and failures. The only channeling by the therapist may be the demand that the patient communicate personally relevant material.

A Tentative Scale for the Measurement of Therapist Genuiness or Self-Congruence

Stage 1.

The therapist is clearly defensive in the interaction, and there is explicit evidence of a very considerable discrepancy between what he says and what he experiences. There may be striking contradictions in the therapist's statements, the content of his verbalization may contradict the voice qualities or nonverbal cues (i.e., the upset therapist stating in a strained voice that he is "not bothered at all" by the patient's anger).

Stage 2.

The therapist responds appropriately but in a professional rather than a personal manner, giving the impression that his responses are said because they sound good from a distance but do not express what he really feels or means. There is a somewhat contrived or rehearsed quality or air of professionalism present.

Stage 3.

The therapist is implicitly either defensive or professional, although there is no explicit evidence. (Two patients are present in the sample given.)

Stage 4.

There is neither implicit nor explicit evidence of defensiveness or the presence of a fàcade. The therapist shows no self-incongruence.

Stage 5.

The therapist is freely and deeply himself in the relationship. He is open to experiences and feelings of all types—both pleasant and hurtful—without traces of defensiveness or retreat into professionalism. Although there may be contradictory feelings, these are accepted or recognized. The therapist is clearly being himself in all of his responses, whether they are personally meaningful or trite. At Stage 5 the therapist need not express personal feelings, but whether he is giving advice, reflecting, interpreting, or sharing experiences, it is clear that he is being very much himself, so that his verbalizations match his inner experiences.

Source: Abridged from Truax and Carkhuff (1967, pp. 47-57, 60-68, 69-72).

TABLE 5.1

Bordin's scales of free-association, including the original overall scale, and the subsequent three subscales

6-Point Scale: Free Association

1. Severely Blocked . . . many, many pauses. Long silences perhaps with remarks about nothing coming to mind, or complaints or questions about the task. Often, but not necessarily, obviously upset by/about the task. Silences or intellectual argument, and/or query about task predominates.

2. Uninvolved Listing . . . primarily describing, with minimal overt affective involvement (though much tension and strained inhibition may be evident), the room or physical details related to it—or leafing through a series, be it of events, places, people, etc., which are fairly clearly dealt with as class/category of objects, this with minimal overt affective involvement. Emphasis here is ordinarily *less* on meaningful interpersonal or experiential "categories," and the impression is mainly one of listing, of marking time in an avoidant fashion. Cool, often somewhat stiff.

3. Selected Little-Involved, Light Conversation . . . emphasis here on conversational quality. Coherent, spoken in customary everyday fashion, with no notable spontaniety. Sentences, fairly standard pacing, deliberate. Note: wider range, *more* involvement and less obvious "categories"-if any-than 2, but still on impersonal side, could be casual talk with acquaintence.

4. Relaxed, Animated Conversation . . . spontaneous, only moderately censored, dealing with emotionally significant matters with at least medium involvement. Little concern with connected, related-topic, organized narrative. But selection and editing still easily evident, and still slight relaxation of ordinary secondary processes, with no or only occasional breakthrough of sudden, tangential transitions and ruptured sentence structure.

5. Mixed Conversation-Associate . . . spontaneous, unprepared, little-selected, strongly involved and meaningful, primarily conversational in nature, but permitting significant fragmentation of sentences and overtly "incoherent," unusual transitions.

6. Loose Free Association . . . irregularly paced, spontaneous, highly involved and meaningful, fragmented nonconversational form with "illogical" transitions, unprepared and not studied or deliberate.

INVOLVEMENT: to be evaluated in terms of the subject's attitude toward the material spoken, how much he *cares* about material spoken, as well as how much overt affective expression there is. Affect here refers to the full scope of feeling-fondness, anger, hurt, exasperation, joy, sorrow, etc.-but specifically *excludes* anxiety, tension. Amount they "care" is to be judged on the face, the surface of the material, deeper inferences *not* to be made (e.g., rater must not say "It's cool, neutral, and half-hearted, but he spends a lot of time telling about it, so he must really care greatly about it . . . ").

Note: Affective expression about or care about the task itself, e.g., angry rejection or overwrought perplexity about why such a task, etc., is *not* to be evaluated on this scale (C. Ego vs. Task-Orientation Scale). Where there is such strong task rejection or such strong blocking that there is little material remaining/emerging on which to base an "Involvement" rating, simply rate *XI*.

(1) Minimal: virtually no concern or feeling visible, generally cold, flat, impersonal, half-hearted indifference (tension may or may not be visible).
(2) Not totally gutless and icy, but generally neutral, cool, with only occasional evidence of significant feeling and concern.
(3) Moderate: Affect and personal import often visible, though always well-modulated and balanced by cooler material.
(4) Frequently strong concern and affect, clearly visible but not passionately so.
(5) Intense: reaching sharp peaks of affect, literal outbursts of emotion, and deeply felt concern almost always visible.

FREEDOM–INHIBITION: to be evaluated in terms of degree of blocking, caution and circumlocution, censorship, and stiffness/constriction . . . Note: as a given period of silence approaches 30 seconds, the presumption of inhibition is great. With silences less than 30 seconds, inference is required as to its nature which may or may not be "inhibitor ." Many of the briefer silences, often amidst relatively freely flowing material, *may* simply represent genuine fallow moments as subject awaits next thought.

(1) Strongly inhibited: rarely or never loose, free, unchecked, but loose enough so can still talk, even if haltingly. Often with a few quite long, or many, many short periods of silence; much constraint, reserve.
(2) Moderately inhibited: notably restrained, relatively stiff, at least everyday censoring. Few significant periods of silence, no marked halting quality, fairly smooth flow.
(3) Moderately informal, only somewhat less than ordinary-everyday censoring, checking, restraint. Restraints noticeable but not predominant feature.
(4) Distinct departure from normal conversational quality-visibly pushing beyond ordinary constraint, cautions, hesitancies or delicacies, but not severely so.
(5) Notably unguarded, rarely blocking or stiffening control for any length of time: little checked, or qualified but *not* necessarily to any degree approaching anarchy.

PLANNED–SPONTANEOUS: to be evaluated in terms of degree to which prepared, deliberate, formally structured and ordered, polished. If severe blocking, etc., permits so little material that a meaningful rating cannot be made, rate "XO."

(1) Highly formal well-ordered, well-connected, and even integrated, polished. Perhaps even lecture-like. Virtually no peripheral irrelevancy admitted, almost no unrelated bits or splotches.
(2) Relatively formally ordered, connected, balanced presentation. Occasional drifting off, disconnected material, and less delayed/unembedded pieces of expression, but these still playing quite a minor role. Notably deliberate.
(3) Ordinary conversational quality, mixture of moderately organized and related material, with relatively relaxed, little-structured, unembroidered talk.
(4) Quite irregular, brief comments not formally presented much tangential relating of material, minimal polishing. Some manifest structuring efforts still visible, but much overshadowed.
(5) Almost "chaotic" from ordinary rational view. Scrampled, seemingly unrelated, scattered quality, highly irregular in form, unforseen and unexplained switches, bits and fragments of expression.

Source: Taken from the mimeographed form of Bordin's scale, available from him.

TABLE 5.2
Gottschalk and Gleser's scales

*Schedule 1: Anxiety Scale**

1. Death anxiety—references to death, dying, threat of death, or anxiety about death experienced by or occurring to:
   a. self (3).
   b. animate other (2).
   c. Inanimate objects destroyed (1).
   d. denial of death anxiety (1).
2. Mutilation (castration) anxiety—references to injury, tissue, or physical damage, or anxiety about injury or threat of such experienced by or occurring to:
   a. self (3).
   b. animate others (2).
   c. inanimate objects (1).
   d. denial (1).
3. Separation anxiety—references to desertion, abandonment, loneliness, ostracism, loss of support, falling, loss of love or love object, or threat of such experienced by or occurring to:
   a. self (3).
   b. animate others (2).
   c. inanimate objects (1).
   d. denial (1).
4. Guilt anxiety—references to adverse criticism, abuse, condemnation, moral disapproval, guilt, or threat of such experienced by:
   a. self (3).
   b. animate others (2).
   d. denial (1).
5. Shame anxiety—references to ridicule, inadequacy, shame, embarrassment, humilation, overexposure of deficiencies or private details. or threat of such experienced by:
   a. self (3).
   b. animate others (2).
   d. denial (1).
6. Diffuse or nonspecific anxiety—references by word or in phrases to anxiety and/or fear without distinguishing type or source of anxiety:
   a. self (3).
   b. animate others (2).
   d. denial (1).

*Numbers in parentheses are the weights.

Schedule 2: Hostility Directed Outward Scale—Destructive, Injurious, Critical Thoughts and Actions Directed to Others

I Hostility outward – overt thematic categories	*II Hostility outward – covert thematic categories*
a 3* Self-killing, fighting, injuring other individuals or threatening to do so.	a 3 Others (human) killing, fighting, injuring other individuals or threatening to do so.

I Hostility outward – overt thematic categories	*II Hostility outward – covert thematic categories*
b 3 Self-robbing or abandoning other individuals, causing suffering or anguish to others, or threatening to do so.	b 3 Others (human) robbing abandoning, causing suffering or anguish to other individuals, or threatening to do so.
c 3 Self-criticizing adversely, depreciating, blaming, expressing anger, dislike of other human beings.	c 3 Others criticizing adversely, depreciating, blaming, expressing anger dislike of other human beings.
a 2 Self-killing, injuring, or destroying domestic animals, pets, or threatening to do so.	a 2 Others (human) killing, injuring, or destroying domestic animals, pets, or threatening to do so.
b 2 Self-abandoning, robbing, domestic animals, pets, or threatening to do so.	b 2 Others (human) abandoning, robbing, domestic animals, pets, or threatening to do so.
c 2 Self criticizing or depreciating others in a vague or mild manner.	c 2 Others (human) criticizing or depreciating other individuals in a vague or mild manner.
d 2 Self-depriving or disappointing other human beings.	d 2 Others (human) depriving or disappointing other human beings.
	e 2 Others (human or domestic animals) dying or killed violently in death-dealing situation or threatened with such.
	f 2 Bodies (human or domestic animals) mutilated, depreciated defiled.
a 1 Self-killing, injuring, destroying, robbing wild life, flors, inanimate objects or threatening to do so.	a 1 Wild life, flora, inanimate objects, injured, broken, robbed, destroyed, or threatened with such (with or without mention of agent).
b 1 Self-criticizing adversely, depreciating, blaming, expressing anger or dislike of subhumans, inanimate objects, places, situations.	b 1 Others (human) criticizing adversely, depreciating, expressing anger or dislike of subhumans, inanimate objects, places, situations.
c 1 Self using hostile words, cursing, mention of anger or rage without referent.	c 1 Others angry, cursing without reference to cause or direction of anger. Also instruments of destruction not used threateningly.
	d 1 Others (human, domestic animals) injured, robbed, dead, abandoned or threatened with such from any source including subhuman and inanimate objects, situations (storms, floods, etc).
	f 1 Denial of anger, dislike, hatred, cruelty, and intent to harm.

*The number serves to give the weight as well as to identify the category. The letter also helps identify the category.

Schedule 3: Hostility Directed Inward Scale—Self-Destructive, Self-Critical Thoughts and Actions

I Hostility inward

thematic categories

a 4* References to self (speaker) attempting to threatening to kill self, with or without conscious intent.

b 4 References to self wanting to die, needing or deserving to die.

a 3† References to self-injuring, mutilating, disfiguring self or threats to do so, with or without conscious intent.

b 3 Self-blaming, expressing anger or hatred of self, considering self worthless or of no value, causing oneself grief or trouble, or threatening to do so.

c 3 References to feelings of discouragement, giving up hope, despairing, feeling grieved or depressed, having no purpose in life.

a 2 References to self needing or deserving punishment, paying for one's sins, needing to atone or do penance.

b 2 Self-criticizing adversely, depreciating self; references to regretting, being sorry or ashamed for what one says or does; references to self mistaken or in error.

c 2 References to feeling of deprivation, disappointment, lonesomeness.

a 1 References to feeling disappointed in self; unable to meet expectations of self or others.

b 1 Denial of anger, dislike, hatred, blame, destructive impulses from self to self.

c 1 References to feeling painfully driven or obliged to meet one's own expectations and standards.

*The number serves to give the weight as well as to identify the category. The letter also helps to identify the category.

†This code is reduced to a weight of 2 if the injury is slight. It is then written Ia.

Schedule 4: Ambivalent Hostility Scale—Destructive, Injurious Critical Thoughts and Actions of Others to Self

II Ambivalent hostility

thematic categories

a 3 Others (human) killing or threatening to kill self.

b 3 Others (human) physically injuring, mutilating, disfiguring self or threatening to do so.

c 3 Others (human) adversely criticizing, blaming, expressing anger or dislike toward self or threatening to do so.

d 3 Others (human) abandoning, robbing self, causing suffering, anguish, or threatened to do so.

a 2 Others (human) deriving, disappointing, misunderstanding self or threatening to do so.

b 2 Self threatened with death from subhuman or inanimate object, or death-dealing situation.

a 1 Others (subhuman, inanimate, or situation), injuring, abandoning, robbing self, causing suffering, anguish.

b 1 Denial of blame.

*Schedule 5: Social Alienation and Personal Disorganization (Schizophrenic) Scale**

weights	*content categories and scoring symbols*
	I. Interpersonal references (including fauna and flora)
	A. To thoughts, feelings, or reported actions of leaving, deserting, spurning, not understanding of others.
0	1. Self avoiding others
+1	2. Others avoiding self.
	B. To unfriendly, hostile, destructive thoughts, feelings, or actions.
+1	1. Self unfriendly to others.
+1/3	2. Others unfriendly to self.
	C. To congenial and constructive.
−2	1. Others helping, being friendly toward others.
−2	2. Self helping, being friendly toward others.
−2	3. Others helping, being friendly toward self.
	D. To others.
0	1. Being bad, dangerous, strange, ill, malfunctioning, having low value or worth.
−1	2. Being intact, satisfied, healthy, well.
	II. Intrapersonal references
+2	A. To disorientation—references indicating disorientation for time, place, person, or other distortion of reality—past, present, or future (do not score more than one item per clause under this category).
	B. To self
0	1a. Physical illness, malfunctioning (references to illness or symptoms due primarily to cellular or tissue damage).
+1	1b. Psychological malfunctioning (references to illness or symptoms due primarily to emotions or psychological reactions *not secondary* to cellular or tissue damage).
0	1c. Malfunctioning of indeterminate origin (references to illness or symptoms not definitely attributable either to emotions or cellular damage).
−2	2. Getting better.
−1	3a. Intact, satisfied, healthy, well; definite positive affect or valence indicated.
−1	3b. Intact, satisfied, healthy, well; flat, factual or neutral altdudes expressed.
+1/2	4. Not being prepared or able to produce, perform, act, not knowing, not sure.
+1/2	5. To being controlled, feeling controlled, wanting control, asking for control or permission, being obliged or having to do, think, or experience something.
+3	C. Denial of feelings, attitudes, or mental state of the self.
	D. To food.
0	1. Bad, dangerous, unpleasant, or otherwise negative; interferences or delays in eating; too much and wish to have less; too little and wish to have more.
0	2. Good or neutral.

weights	*content categories and scoring symbols*
	E. To weather.
−1	1. Bad, dangerous, unpleasant, or otherwise negative (not sunny, not clear, uncomfortable, etc.)
−1	2. Good, pleasant, neutral
	F. To sleep.
0	1. Bad, dangerous, unpleasant, or otherwise negative, too much, too little.
0	2. Good, pleasant, or neutral.
	III. Disorganization and repetition
	A. Signs of disorganization.
+1	1. Remarks or words that are not understandable or inaudible.
0	2. Incomplete sentences, clauses, phrases; blocking.
+2	3. Obviously erroneous or fallacious remarks or conclusions; illogical or bizarre statements.
	B. Repetition of ideas in sequence
0	1. Words separated only by a word (excluding instances due to grammatical and syntactical convention, where words are repeated, e.g., "as far as," "by and by"; also excluding instances where such words as "I" and "the" are separated by a word).
+1	2. Phrases or clauses (separated only by a phrase or clause).
	IV. References to the interviewer
+1	A. Questions directed to the interviewer.
+1/2	B. Other references to the interviewer.
+1	*V. Religious and biblical references.*

*The weights given in this table are those we now use. The original weights used for this scale are described in our 1958 publication (see also Gottschalk and Gleser, 1969). It was thought that these original weights might be more sensitive in logitudinal studies. It should be noted that in this earlier study, categories signifying evidence of the schizophrenic syndrome were given negative weights, whereas currently, such items are given positive weights.

It is possible that the original (nonzero) weightings might result in more accurate discrimination whenever repetitive measures of severity of the schizophrenic syndrome are to be made. A discussion of these weights may be found in Gottschalk et al., 1961; Gottschalk and Gleser, 1969.

TABLE 5.3
*Hall and Van De Castle's classification system for the content analysis of dreams**

I. *Settings.* "Almost all dreams take place in some form of recognizable setting... It is common for the setting to change during the course of the dream... We eventually collapsed all settings into two broad groupings–indoor and outdoor settings" (p. 36).

- A. locale of dream
  1. indoor settings
  2. outdoor settings
- B. degree of familiarity of setting
  1. familiar
  2. distorted
  3. geographical
  4. unfamiliar
  5. questionable

II. *Objects.* Refers to "the various 'props' that remain on the stage or are introduced as the play proceeds. An object is a thing. It has tangibility, palpability, and dimensionality. It also has definite physical boundaries or limits... Persons and animals are not scored as objects because they are handled separately under the classification of characters" (p. 43).

- A. architecture
- B. household
- C. food
- D. implements
- E. travel
- F. streets
- G. regions
- H. nature
- I. body parts
- J. clothing
- K. communication
- L. money

III. *Social Interactions.* "Lines will be spoken, characters will move about the stage, and the plot will develop" (p. 68).

- A. aggressive interactions
  1. an aggressive act which results in the death of a character
  2. which involves an attempt to physically harm a character
  3. which involves a character being chased, captured, confined, or physically coerced into performing some act
  4. which involves the theft or destruction of possessions belonging to a character
  5. in which a serious accusation or verbal threat of harm is made against a character
  6. all situations where there is an attempt by one character to reject, exploit, control, or verbally coerce another character
  7. aggression displayed through verbal or expressive activity
  8. covert feeling of hostility or anger without any overt expression of aggression

B. friendly interactions
   1. friendliness expressed through a desire for a long-term close relationship with a character
   2. expressed through socially acceptable forms of physical contact
   3. expressed by taking the initiative in requesting a character to share in a pleasant social activity
   4. expressed through extending assistance to a character or offering to do so
   5. expressed by offering a gift or loaning a possession to a character
   6. a wide variety of expressions of friendliness that may be conveyed through either verbal or gestural means
   7. friendliness is felt toward a character but it is not expressed overtly

C. sexual interaction
   1. a character has or attempts to have sexual intercourse with another character
   2. the various types of foreplay activities generally preceding intercourse
   3. necking and 'nonplatonic kissing
   4. a character makes sexual overtures to or "propositions" another character
   J.5. a character has sexual thoughts or fantasies about another character

V. *Activities.* "... a system of classifying what characters do in dreams ... indicates activities that may be done by a character acting alone or in conjunction with other characters, as well as interactions between characters" (p. 87).
   A. physical
   B. movement
   C. location change
   D. verbal
   E. expressive communication
   F. visual
   G. auditory
   H. thinking

VI. *Achievement Outcomes.* "Does a character succeed or fail in carrying activities through to some desired outcome?" (p. 96).
   A. success
   B. failure
   C. consequences of success
   D. consequences of failure

VII. *Environmental Press.* "... an impersonal, 'fatalistic,' event ... fate, in a sense, has stepped in and produced certain results over which no character has any control ... (in Murray's system) an environmental force which affects a character" (p. 102).
   A. misfortune
   B. good fortune
   C. consequences of misfortune
   D. consequences of good fortune

VIII. *Emotions.* These are limited to five in number, and indicate which characters experience these emotions.
   A. anger
   B. apprehension
   C. happiness
   D. sadness
   E. confusion

IX. *Descriptive Elements.* "The dreamer may describe some attributes and qualities of objects, people, actions, and emotional states . . . may note the passage of time . . . may describe things, people, and happenings, not in terms of what they were but in terms of what they were not" (p. 115).

A. modifiers (any adjective, adverb or phrase that is used for descriptive elaboration)

B. temporal scale (references may occur to various time intervals or to particular points in time)

C. negative scale (stylistic differences in dreamers' language and expressions—comments by the dreamer on his dream)

X. *Theoretical Scales.*

A. castration anxiety, castration wish, and penis envy.

1. castration anxiety
   a. injury or threat to the dreamer's body
   b. actual or threatened injury, loss, defect, disease, or damage occurring to an animal or object belonging to the dreamer or that is in his possession in the dream
   c. the dreamer reports inability or difficulty in using a gun, airplane, automobile, piece of machinery, or other symbolic phallic objects that are in his possession; difficulty in using a penis; or difficulty in placing an object in a receptacle
   d. a male dreamer reports that he is a woman or changes into a woman during the dream, or that he has acquired female secondary sexual characteristics, or that he is wearing women's clothes or accessories
2. castration wish (only one subclass: same as for castration anxiety, except they do not occur to the dreamer but to another specified person in the dream)
3. penis envy
   a. acquisition within the dream by the dreamer, or by a group of which the dreamer is a member, or an object that has phallic characteristics
   b. the dreamer envies or admires a man's physical characteristics, his prowess, or his possessions that have phallic characteristics
   c. a female dreamer reports that she is a man, or changes into a man during the dream, or that she has acquired male secondary sex characteristics, or that she is wearing men's clothes or accessories.

B. oral activities and oral references

1. the oral incorporation scale (consists of the consummatory activities of eating and drinking, and of preparatory activities that precede and lead up to these consummatory activities)
   a. a character is reported as actually eating, drinking, nursing, swallowing, etc.
   b. a character is actually in an eating place such as a restaurant, bar, dining room, picnic grounds, or cafeteria; or an eating place is referred to in the dream report
   c. a character is preparing food, cooking it, or seeing or using utensils associated with food, or these activities or objects are mentioned in the dream report
   d. a character secures food by buying it, picking it, or some other means, or a character is in a food store, or these are mentioned in the dream report
   e. food is seen or mentioned in the dream report, but not in connection with any of the foregoing activities i.e. it is not being eaten, served, prepared or bought.

2. the oral emphasis scale (deals with oral activities other than eating or drinking, and with references to the oral zone or cavity. It does not include any verbal activities)
   a. a character engages in an activity involving the mouth such as smoking, kissing, playing an instrument requiring the use of the mouth or lips, grinning, blowing up a balloon, smiling, whistling, chewing gum, biting, laughing, singing
   b. reference is made to the oral zone or parts of the oral zone such as the mouth, lips, teeth, and tongue.

C. regression
1. the dreamer dreams of being in a setting or locale in which he has not been for a year
2. the dreamer dreams of being younger by at least a year
3. dreams of someone he has not seen or heard from within a year
4. dreams of doing something he has not done for at least a year
5. dreams of someone who has been dead for at least a year
6. dreams of another person as being younger, by at least a year, than he currently is
7. dreams of an object which he has not had for at least a year

The form of the scale presented is annotated. For detailed descriptions of the scoring categories, examples for each category, and rules for scoring, consult Chapters 4 to 12, pp. 36–143 of the authors' book.

TABLE 5.4
*Klein, Mathieu, Gendlin, and Kiesler's experiencing scale**

Stage One

The chief characteristic of this stage is that the content or manner of expression is impersonal. In some cases the content is intrinsically impersonal, being a very abstract, general, superficial, or journalistic account of events or ideas with no personal referrent established. In other cases, despite the personal nature of the content, the speaker's involvement is impersonal, so that he reveals nothing important about himself, and his remarks could as well be about a stranger or an object.

Stage Two

The association between the speaker and the content is explicit. Either the speaker is the central character in the narrative or his interest is clear. The speaker's involvement, however, does not go beyond the specific situation or content. All comments, associations, reactions, and remarks serve to get the story or idea across but do not refer to or define the speaker's feelings.

Stage Three

The content is a narrative or a description of the speaker in external or behavioral terms with added comments on his feelings or private experiences. These remarks are limited to the events or situation described, giving the narrative a personal touch without describing the speaker more generally. Self-descriptions restricted to a specific situation or role are also at stage three.

Stage Four

The content is a clear presentation of the speaker's feelings, giving his personal, internal perspective or feelings about himself. Feelings or the experience of events, rather than the events themselves, are the subject of the discourse. By attending to and presenting this experiencing, the speaker communicates what it is like to be him. These interior views are presented, listed, or described, but are not interrelated or used as the basis for systematic self-examination or formulation.

Stage Five

The content is a purposeful exploration of the speaker's feelings and experiencing. There are two necessary components. First, the speaker must pose or define a problem or proposition about himself explicitly in terms of feelings. The problem or proposition may involve the origin, sequence, or implications of feelings or relate feelings to other private processes. Second, he must explore or work with the problem in a personal way. The exploration or elaboration must be clearly related to the initial proposition and must contain inner references so that it functions to expand the speaker's awareness of his experiencing. *Both* components, the problem and the elaboration, must be present.

Stage Six

The content is a synthesis of readily accessible, newly recognized, or more fully realized feelings and experiences to produce personally meaningful structures or to resolve issues. The speaker's immediate feelings are integral to his conclusions about his inner workings. He communicates a new or enriched self-experiencing and the experiential impact of the changes in his attitudes or feelings about himself. The subject matter concerns the speaker's present and emergent experience. His manner may reflect changes or insights at the moment of their occurence. These are verbally elaborated in detail. Apart from the specific content, the speaker conveys a sense of active, immediate involvement in an experientially anchored issue with evidence of its resolution or acceptance.

Stage Seven

The content reveals the speaker's expanding awareness of his immediately present feelings and internal processes. He demonstrates clearly that he can move from one inner reference to another, altering and modifying his conceptions of himself, his feelings, his private reactions to his thoughts or actions in terms of their immediately felt nuances as they occur in the present experiential moment, so that each new level of self-awareness functions as a spring board for further exploration.

*The EXP Scale presented here is in an abridged form. For more detailed descriptions for each of the scale stages, as well as for examples of each stage, consult the long form of the scale in the Research and Training Manual (pp. 56-63).

TABLE 5.5
Truax's tentative scale for the measurement of depth of self-exploration

Stage 0.

No *personally relevant* material and no opportunity for it to be discussed. Personally relevant material refers to emotionally tinged experiences or feelings, to feelings or experiences of significance to the self. This would include self-descriptions that are intended to reveal the self to the therapist, and communications of personal values, perceptions of one's relationship to others, one's personal role and self-worth in life, as well as communications indicating upsetness, emotional turmoil, or expressions or more specific feelings of anger, affection, etc..

Stage 1.

The patient actively evades personally relevant material (by changing the subject, for instance, refusing to respond at all, etc.). Thus, personally relevant material is not discussed. The patient does not respond to personally relevant material *even* when the therapist speaks of it.

Stage 2.

The patient does not volunteer personally relevant material but he does not actually evade responding to it when the therapist introduces it to the interpersonal situation.

Stage 3.

The patient does not himself volunteer to share personally relevant material with the therapist, but he responds to personally relevant material introduced by the therapist. He may agree or disagree with the therapist's remarks and may freely make brief remarks, but he does not add significant new material.

Stage 4.

Personally relevant material is discussed (volunteered in part or in whole). Such volunteer discussion is done (1) *in a mechanical manner* (noticeably lacking in spontaneity or as a "reporter" or "observer"); and (2) *without demonstration of emotional feeling.* In addition, there is simply discussion without movement by the patient toward further exploring the significance of meaning of the material or feeling in an effort to uncover related feelings or material. Both the emotional remoteness and the mechanical manner of the patient make his discussion often sound rehearsed.

Stage 5.

This stage is similar to Stage 4 except that the material is discussed either *with feeling* indicating emotional proximity or *with spontaneity,* but not both. (Voice quality is the main cue.)

Stage 6.

In Stage 6 the level of Stage 4 is achieved again, with the additional fact that the personally relevant material is discussed with both *spontaneity and feeling.* There is clear indication that the patient is speaking with feeling, and his communication is laden with emotion.

Stage 7.

Tentative probing toward intrapersonal exploration. There is an inward probing to discover feelings or experiences anew. The patient is searching for discovery of new feelings which he struggles to reach and hold on to. The individual may speak with many private distinctions or with "personal" meanings to common words. He may recognize the value of this self-exploration but it must be clear that he is trying to explore himself and his world actively even though at the moment he does so perhaps fearfully and tentatively.

Stage 8.

Active intrapersonal exploration. The patient is following a "connected" chain of thoughts in focusing upon himself and actively exploring himself. He may be discovering new feelings, new aspects of himself. He is actively exploring his feelings, his values, his perception of others, his relationships, his fears, his turmoil, and his life-choices.

Stage 9.

Stage 9 is an extension of the scale to be used in those rare moments when the patient is deeply exploring and being himself, or in those rare moments when he acieves a significant new perceptual base for his view of himself or the world. A rating at this stage is to be used at the judge's discretion.

Source: Abridged from Truax and Carkhuff (1967, pp. 195-208).

TABLE 6.1

*A summary of minor Univariate process systems for measuring therapist and patient behaviors in psychotherapy interviews**

Measures of Therapist Interview Behaviors

1. *Acceptance* (Regard)
   Carkhuff, Berenson, and Southworth (1964b)
   Halkides (1958)
   Miller (1949)
   Streitfeld (1959)

2. *Ambiguity*
   Bordin (1955)
   Dibner (1953, 1958)
   Heller (1968)
   Osburn (1951)
   Rigler (1957)
   Townsend (1956)

3. *Competence*
   Rank (1966)

4. *Concreteness*
   Truax and Carkhuff (1964)

5. *Congruence*
   Carkhuff, Berenson, and Southworth (1964c)
   Halkides (1958)
   Kiesler (1967)

6. *Countertransference*
   Cutler (1958)
   Fiedler (1951)
   Rigler (1957)
   Russell and Snyder (1963)
   Yulis and Kiesler (1968)

7. *Egosyntonic-Egodystonic Responses*
   Sklansky, Isaacs, and Haggard (1960)

8. *Empathy*
   Carkhuff, Berenson, and Southworth (1964a)
   Halkides (1958)

9. *Experiencing*
   Klein and Mathieu (1970)

10. *Flexibility*
    Carnes (1959)

11. *Interpretation*
    Collier (1953)
    Dittmann (1952)
    Fisher (1956)
    Somer, Mazo, and Lehner (1955)

12. *Lead* (Participation)
    Danskin and Robinson (1954)
    Dittmann (1952)

13. *Liking for Client*
    Abeles (1967)
    Caracena (1965)
    Garfield and Affleck (1961)
    Gottschalk, Mayerson, and Gottlieb (1967)
    Lowinger and Dobie (1966)
    Redlich, Hollingshead, and Bellis (1955)
    Stoler (1963)
    Strupp et al. (1963)
    Tomlinson and Stoler (1967)

14. *Role Assumption*
    Campbell (1962)
    Danskin (1955)
    Hoffman (1959)

15. *Silence* (Pauses)
    Bandura, Lipsher, and Miller (1960)
    Goldman-Eisler (1952)
    Heller, Davis, and Myers (1966)
    Tindall and Robinson (1947)

16. *Style*
    Dipboye (1954)

17. *Warmth*
    Halkides (1958)
    Raush and Bordin (1957)

Measures of Patient Interview Behaviors

1. *Anxiety* (Frustration, Tension)
   Aronson and Weintraub (1967)
   Boomer and Goodrich (1961)
   Dibner (1956)
   Dimascio, Boyd, and Greenblatt (1957)
   Dollard and Mowrer (1947)
   Goldman-Eisler (1955)
   Krause (1961)
   Krause and Pilisuk (1961)
   Mahl (1956)
   Pope, Blass, Siegman, and Raher (1970)
   Raskin (1962)
   Thetford (1952)
   White (1947)

2. *Dependency*
   Ashby et al. (1957)
   Heller (1959)
   Rottschafer and Renzaglia (1962)
   Winder, Ahmad, Bandura, and Rau (1962)

3. *Expectational Discrepancy*
   Block (1964)

4. *Free Association*
   Colby (1960)
   Fitzgerald (1966)
   Meerloo (1959)
   Temerlin (1956)

5. *Insight*
   Curran (1945)
   Reid and Finesinger (1952)
   Rogers (1944)
   Tolor and Reznikoff (1960)

6. *Relating* (Relatability)
   Gendlin (1967)
   Isaacs (1956)
   Isaacs and Haggard (1966)

7. *Resistance* (Defensiveness, Transference)
   Ashby et al. (1957)
   Crisp (1964a, 1964b)
   Daulton (1947)

9. *Self* (Affirmation-negation, self-awareness, real-ideal discrepancy, locus-of-evaluation, respect for self, self-attitudes)
   Aidman (1951)
   Bowman (1959)
   Bugental (1952)
   Raskin (1952)
   Rosenman (1955)
   Sheerer (1949)
   Stock (1949)
   Vargas (1954)
   Zavalloni (1954)

10. *Self-Disclosure* Self-reference, revealingness, self-exploration
    Ashby et al. (1957)
    Braaten (1961)
    Bugental (1952)
    Doster (1968)
    Fitzgerald (1966)
    Gendlin et al. (1968)
    Pope and Siegman (1962)
    Raimy (1948)
    Suchman (1965)
    Todd and Ewing (1961)
    Tomlinson (1967)
    Van der veen and Tomlinson (1967)
    Walker, Rablen and Rogers (1960)

11. *Speech and Silence*
    Carnes and Robinson (1948)
    Cook (1964)
    Dittes (1957)
    Goldenberg and Auld (1964)
    Jarrett (1966)
    Kanfer (1960)
    Mahl (1956)
    Tindall and Robinson (1947)
    Toman (1953)
    White, Fichtenbaum, and Dollard (1964)

12. *Values*
    Ehrlich and Wiener (1961)
    Parloff, Goldstein, and Inflund (1957)
    Sommer and Killian (1954)
    White (1947, 1951)

Dittes (1957)
Gillespie (1953)
Goldenberg and Auld (1964)
Haigh (1949)
Hogan (1952)
Mick (19566)
Rawn (1958)
Speisman (1956)

8. *Responsibility* (Maturity)
Elton (1950)
Hoffman (1949)
Rosenman (1955)

13. *Vocabulary (Content) Diversity*
Blau (1953)
Jaffe (1958)
Page (1953)
Roshal (1953)

14. *Word Choice*
Berg (1958)
Boder (1940)

*For a complete up-to-date summary of all process systems, the reader should consult, in addition to this table and the preceding section of this chapter, both Table 2.1 and Chapter 7.

Included in this Table are some analogue studies which defined a particular variable either in terms of experimental manipulations or as a dependent variable measure.

Name Index

Subject Index